Portrait of Elg

Edward Elgar in 1904

Portrait of Elgar

MICHAEL KENNEDY

LONDON
OXFORD UNIVERSITY PRESS
NEW YORK TORONTO

Oxford University Press, Ely House, London W. 1

GLASGOW NEW YORK TORONTO MELBOURNE WELLINGTON
CAPE TOWN IBADAN NAIROBI DAR ES SALAAM LUSAKA ADDIS ABABA
DELHI BOMBAY CALCUTTA MADRAS KARACHI LAHORE DACCA
KUALA LUMPUR SINGAPORE HONG KONG TOKYO

Limp edition ISBN 0 19 315432 3
Cased edition ISBN 0 19 315414 5

Oxford University Press 1968

First published 1968
Reprinted 1968 and 1973

*Printed in Great Britain by
Butler & Tanner Ltd, Frome and London*

For Neville, John, and Martin

Preface

Since this book was published five years ago the renewal of interest in Elgar has intensified, the issue of recordings has multiplied, and all sorts of hitherto unlikely people now declare themselves Elgarians. I hasten to add that I do not pretend this is cause and effect, but it is very encouraging to see this widespread championship of our great composer. Of particular interest has been the publication of Rosa Burley's memories of the youthful Elgar (*Edward Elgar: the record of a friendship*, London, 1972). These reinforce the points I made, unpalatable to some, about Elgar's very human inadequacies of character. Miss Burley described him at their first meeting in 1891 as 'obviously repressed' and later as 'a musical fanatic whose energy was constantly frustrated by the frightful respectability of the provincial milieu into which he happened to be projected'. She discloses, with apparent authority, that part of Elgar's sense of inferiority was attributable to the disadvantage of being a Roman Catholic and the rest to 'a humiliation [connected with his social class] so cruel and so crushing that he could not bear ever to speak of it'. It is profoundly sad that the eventual fame and honours he won through his music were no compensation to him for this early suffering. Yet he was fortunate compared with some other artists. Even the decline in his music's appeal for some years before and after his death was not so steep as to make performances at all infrequent. And today! It is all around us.

I have written this book from thirty years of close acquaintance with the music. I have not written analyses or programme-notes of the works. This has been done in other books, from Ernest Newman to Diana McVeagh, as well as it could possibly be done. Anyone who buys a recording of an Elgar work receives also an analysis of the music, usually very comprehensive. I have assumed that readers of this book will know the major works well, and I have therefore preferred to discuss them within the context of the composer's life.

My thanks are due to Elgar's daughter, the late Mrs. Carice Elgar Blake, for reading the book in typescript and for her help, and to Mr. Alan Webb, former curator of the Elgar Birthplace, for his kindness in dealing with my enquiries. I had help from Sir Adrian Boult, the late Sir John Barbirolli, and Dr. Percy Young who generously allowed me to draw on the fruits of his scholarship in assembling the

Elgar–Jaeger correspondence. I am grateful to the Trustees of the Elgar Will for permission to reproduce extracts from Elgar's letters and writings; to Messrs. Novello and Breitkopf and Härtel for permission to use extracts from his scores; to Sir Osbert Sitwell and Macmillan & Co. for permission to reprint an extract from *Laughter in the Next Room*; to the Society of Authors and the Public Trustee for the use of extracts from letters written by Bernard Shaw; to Longmans Green & Co. for permission to quote from Bernard Shore's *Sixteen Symphonies* and from Sir Arnold Bax's *Farewell, My Youth*, and to J. M. Dent & Sons for permission to reprint an extract from W. H. Reed's *Elgar*. My thanks, too, to the Editors of *The Times*, *The Daily Telegraph*, *The Guardian*, and *Sunday Times* for allowing me to quote from articles which appeared in their newspapers, and to all those people who have helped me by answering my queries. The quotations from Lady Elgar's diaries are by special permission of Mrs. Elgar Blake. I would also like to thank Miss Pamela Willetts, Assistant Keeper of Manuscripts, British Museum, for her help. Incidentally, I have been careful to preserve all the oddities of spelling and punctuation in Elgar's letters: they have their own special flavour.

Manchester, 1973

Contents

Illustrations

PART I

ASCENT
1857–1898

1 Prelude

On 13 December 1921 Elgar confided to his friend Sir Sidney Colvin: 'I am still at heart the dreamy child who used to be found in the reeds by Severn side with a sheet of paper trying to fix the sounds and longing for something very great. I am still looking for this . . . but as a child and as a young man and as a mature man no single person was ever kind to me.'

Elgar was sixty-four when he wrote this letter. He was acknowledged to be the foremost English composer of his time; nearly every kind of official honour had come his way; self-taught, he had risen from provincial obscurity to international fame; he had achieved in his music the 'something very great'. Yet he still regarded himself as an 'outsider' and looked back on his early struggles not with self-satisfaction but with bitterness. What did he mean when he said that no one was 'kind' to him? Biographical facts prove that he was offered many a helping hand. Nevertheless he spoke and wrote often of the discouragement he received from his friends and of their slighting attitude to his music. 'One's own friends are the people to be most in dread of,' he wrote shortly before *Froissart* was performed, 'I have always been wrong hitherto'. And after *The Dream of Gerontius*: 'All my best friends only made one remark: "Now a popular song or two will make up for this." ' His musical self-portrait, the last of the *Enigma Variations*, has a defiant ring because it was a retort to friends who were 'dubious and generally discouraging' about his future as a composer. It was this that rankled: he told Colvin in the same letter how much he admired Bernard Shaw for his friendly encouragement of young people.

From his youth onwards Elgar knew that he possessed special gifts, and he resented the circumstances which made him work as a 'local musician' until he was nearly forty. He is often described as a 'late developer'. He himself knew better. He could have written *Caractacus* (1898) ten years earlier, he said, if he had not been compelled to earn his living by teaching, by the chores of music, by helping behind the counter in his father's music-shop in Worcester even after he had had a work produced at the Three Choirs Festival. He encountered snobbery, both social and artistic, and it wounded him and produced an outsize chip on his shoulder.

But ambition spurred him, as it did many nineteenth-century youths of poor birth who were determined to 'get on'. The story has often been told of an occasion when he was asked his name at school. 'Edward Elgar.' 'Say sir.' 'Sir Edward Elgar.' This sounds apocryphal. Elgar's eyes were on a much loftier target than the mere acquisition of a title —something he did not want when it was offered and which he only accepted out of a sense of gratitude to his wife, to whom these outward signs of esteem meant a great deal. Compton Mackenzie[1] gives us the truth: 'Elgar once told me that when he was a young man he had declared to his mother that he should not be content until a postcard from abroad addressed "Edward Elgar, England" should find him.'

[1] In *The Gramophone* (June 1957).

2 Wand of Youth

Edward William Elgar was born in the village of Broadheath, just outside Worcester, on 2 June 1857. He was the fourth child of William and Anne Elgar. They had married in 1848, and she had become a convert to Roman Catholicism in 1852, her husband following her at a later date. William Elgar, a Dover man born in 1822, settled in Worcester in 1841. He had served a musical apprenticeship with Coventry and Hollier of Dean Street, Soho. This firm was approached by the Comptroller of the Household of the Queen Dowager, Adelaide (widow of William IV), to provide a piano-tuner for the instruments at Witley Court, Worcestershire, where Adelaide took up residence in 1844. They immediately selected their former apprentice, who had established a music business in Worcester, then a city of 27,000 people. Thus he naturally received similar piano-tuning commissions from the other 'county families' and was drawn into various local musical activities as pianist and violinist. Though he was a Protestant he was appointed organist of St. George's Roman Catholic Church in 1846 at a salary of £40 a year.[1] The picture could no doubt be multiplied from towns throughout England—lower-middle-class tradesman with musical gifts, able to display a royal warrant on his business stationery, on call to the homes of the gentry. William Elgar was fortunate in his wife, sister of the Mr. Greening with whom and his wife he lodged when he first went to Worcester. Anne Elgar was a remarkable woman. Her natural bent was towards the arts. She read widely and remembered what she read. She sewed, collected wild flowers, sketched, and wrote verse. Her strength of character was such that bringing up seven children did not, as would usually be the case, stifle her pursuit of learning and artistic matters. Few husbands of the Elgars' social class in the 1850s would have expected to receive, as William Elgar did, a sonnet from his wife on the birth of their first daughter. Altogether, life was good to William and Anne Elgar. They had not much money—William was not very interested in the book-keeping side of his business, though he showed a marked sense of showman-salesmanship

---

[1] His piety may be doubted. It was said of him that he handed round his snuff-box before Mass, 'damned' the organ-blower and, during the sermon, slipped out for a drink at Hop Market—an endearing and convincing picture.

by riding to his piano-tuning engagements on a thoroughbred horse—
but both were able to indulge the artistic side of their nature, and they
had a certain standing in Worcester's provincial but not entirely sterile
musical life. William was engaged to play in the Three Choirs Festival
orchestra when it was Worcester's triennial turn and he was sufficiently
influential for his advice to be sought and taken on programme planning—he suggested the inclusion of Masses by Cherubini and Hummel.
For the first eight years of their marriage they lived in the College
Precincts and there Harry (1850), Lucy (1852), and Susannah, known as
Pollie (1855) were born. In 1856 they moved to a cottage three miles
north-west of Worcester at the village of Broadheath. There, within
sight of the Malvern Hills, Edward William was born. But in 1859 or
1860 the Elgars moved back into Worcester, to 1 Edgar Street, and
William was joined in his business by his twenty-seven-year-old
brother Henry, who had worked for Kirkman's of London and for
Hime and Addison in Manchester where he had tuned pianos for
Charles Hallé. A final move in 1866 was to accommodation above
Elgar Bros. at 10 High Street. Three other children, Joe, Frank, and
Helen Agnes, known as Dot (who became a nun), were born in
Worcester. Edward was the only child to be born at Broadheath.

Although Edward was one of seven children (of whom two brothers,
Harry and Joe, died young, in 1864 and 1866) it seems that he was
always of a solitary, introspective disposition, lonely by nature. He was
particularly responsive, as was to be shown by his music, to topo-
graphy, to landscape, and to the countryside in all its moods; and as he
had a remarkable memory, these early impressions made an indelible
mark on his personality. He explored the historic nooks and crannies of
Worcester, and when he returned to Broadheath to stay on a farm he
came to know intimately rural Worcestershire: country sayings, cus-
toms, and personalities. He was encouraged by his mother to read
everything he could lay hands on. He was one of those people—
Vaughan Williams was another—with a lifelong habit of early rising,
so that hours before the rest of the household were awake Edward was
reading Voltaire or Holinshed, Drayton and Sidney, anything historical or translated from the classics. Mrs. Elgar was a devotee of
Longfellow and her son followed her taste. He came to know by heart
The Saga of King Olaf and *Hyperion*. I possess a copy of *Hyperion* which
belonged to Elgar. He knew it so well that he has noted in the margin
all textual divergences from an earlier edition.

In a household which derived its living from musical instruments,
obviously all the children received some kind of instruction. Edward

was not given any special attention—indeed his brother, Joe, who died aged seven in 1866, was regarded by the family as the musical prodigy. William Elgar's admirable intention was merely that his children should become useful musicians of his own calibre. When Edward was seven, in 1864, he went to a 'dame school' run by a Miss Walsh in Britannia Square, Worcester, and had pianoforte lessons from a Miss Tyler. At the same time, his father sent him to Frederick Spray, a violinist who led the Worcester Glee Club orchestra, for lessons on the fiddle; and, like many another organist's child, Edward sat in the organ-loft at St. George's to watch his father at work. It was about this time that Edward was found sitting on the river bank with a pencil and music paper. He said he was 'trying to write down what the reeds were saying'.

Years later, W. H. Reed recalls in his *Elgar As I Knew Him*, when Sir Edward Elgar was rehearsing the London Symphony Orchestra in the Trio of the second movement of the First Symphony, he told them 'Play it like . . . like something you hear down by the river.'

For a brief spell, young Edward attended a Roman Catholic school at Spetchley. This was under the patronage of the Lord of the Manor, Robert Berkeley. Many years later Elgar told Ernest Newman[1] that 'as a boy he used to gaze from the school windows in rapt wonder at the great trees swaying in the wind; and he pointed out to me a passage in *Gerontius* in which he had recorded in music his subconscious memories of them'. Although Newman did not enlarge upon this, it is fairly reasonable to suppose that the passage concerned is in Part II, rehearsal cue [68] at 'the summer wind among the lofty pines'. At the age of eleven he went to Littleton House, a school for about thirty boys in Powick Road, run by Francis Reeve. He it was who, as Elgar himself liked to relate, fired the young pupil's imagination, during a scripture lesson on Christ's disciples, with the remark: 'The Apostles were young men and very poor. Perhaps, before the descent of the Holy Ghost, they were no cleverer than some of you here.' This observation brought these men to life as human beings so that they fascinated Elgar, with the results to be heard in *The Apostles*.

Edward had by this time written music, some of it for a play devised with his brothers and sisters and which found its way in due course into the *Wand of Youth* suites, and was becoming proficient on three instruments. The violin was his chief interest. He had had brief tuition from Spray, but it was in 1869, after he had heard 'O thou that tellest' sung in Worcester Cathedral during a performance of *Messiah*, that he

---

[1] *Sunday Times*, 23 October 1955.

returned home determined to master the instrument so that he could play this aria, and this he did by teaching himself. When he left school at the age of fifteen in 1872 he wanted to go to Leipzig to study music, and had been studying German for the purpose. But the family finances could not run to such a venture, and there were no council grants for music at that date. A boy had to make his way, or go under. So Edward was sent to work in the office of a solicitor, William Allen, a member of St. George's congregation. He had been head boy of Littleton House for his last nine months and his lifelong friend, Hubert Leicester, who was at school with him and whose family printing business was near to the Elgars' music shop,[1] described him at this stage of his life as 'a most miserable-looking lad—legs like drumsticks—nothing of a boy about him'. Yet the boy's looks belied his physical prowess, for he would ride the Malvern Hills bareback, saving himself from death on one occasion when his horse bolted. Allen thought his new employee a 'bright lad', but the drudgery of a lawyer's office, even though it taught Elgar some methodical ways, was unattractive to a boy of artistic imagination and he left at some time in 1873. During the time of his employment by Allen, two important events occurred in Edward's musical life. On 14 July 1872, according to his sister Lucy's diary, 'Ted played the organ at church for Mass for first time'; and in January 1873 he made his first public appearance as a violinist at a concert at the Union Workhouse when, with others including his father and uncle and Frederick Spray, he played in works by Rossini, Weber, and Hullah. No doubt these events stood him in good stead when he told his parents that he had no use for the law, nor, which he contemplated at one time, for a career in chemistry. He considered that he could be of use to his father's business, perhaps helping to straighten the erratic book-keeping. But we can be sure that, while he had been in the dead end of Allen's office, he had pondered ways of achieving the enormous ambitions he cherished and had decided that by helping his father he could also help himself.

So it proved. In his father's shop he had unrestricted access to the scores of Mozart's masses and Beethoven's sonatas and his symphonies in pianoforte-duet arrangements. There, too, he found text-books: Cherubini's *Counterpoint*, Catel's *Treatise on Harmony*, translated by Mary Cowden Clarke, Stainer's *Composition* and *Harmony*, and Sabilla Novello's translation of *Succinct Thorough Bass*, then thought to be by Mozart and which, so Shaw wrote in his Preface to *Music in London*

---

[1] Elgar spent much time in the printing-shop and it was from these days that the critical and knowledgeable interest he took in the printing and engraving of his scores came.

(1935), Elgar said was 'the only document in existence of the smallest use to a student composer'. From the organ tutors of Rink and Best he learned so that he could relieve his father of some of his St. George's duties. He played the pianoforte works of C. P. E. Bach, Schobert, and Kotzeluch. He wrote a church anthem. He went to the Anglican cathedral, where William Done, a staunch conservative who abhorred Schumann as 'a modern', was in the midst of his long reign in the organ-loft (1844–95). There he heard Byrd, Tallis, Gibbons, and Purcell, music which it is probable his temperament even then rejected as being too austere, for he said in later years that, with a few exceptions in Purcell, English music of the sixteenth and seventeenth centuries interested him only as museum-pieces. If, as is practically certain, Elgar attended the concerts of the Worcester Festival Choral Society, of which Done was conductor, he made close acquaintance with the music of Corelli, Haydn, and Handel. But he was a performer more often than a passive listener and his most active musical education was at the concerts of the Worcester Glee Club, of which his father had long been a member. This club met at the Crown Hotel in Broad Street and its members drank and smoked at candlelit tables while music was performed. Mozart, Handel, Bellini, Auber, Rossini, and Balfe were the composers favoured by the Glee Club. Young Edward Elgar accompanied the singers at these functions, but he soon became violinist, composer, arranger, and, in 1879, conductor. It was the eighteenth-century musician's life and in its diversity, despite its parochialism, it stood Elgar in good stead. Worcester was indeed well served for music, by standards then applicable, and it was visited on occasions by the Haig-Dyer Opera Company. Elgar had first heard them before he was ten, and so came to know *Il Trovatore*, *La Traviata*, *Don Giovanni*, and *Norma*. In his father's workshop, too, he extended his literary knowledge in company with Ned Spiers, an odd-job-man, who had been a Shakespearean actor. They recited the great speeches together, and Edward went to the theatre to see Mrs. Macready.

Throughout the 1870s Edward Elgar learned his craft. With his father in 1875 he was among the second violins for the Worcester Philharmonic's *Messiah*. Four years later he was the leader. In 1876 he arranged Wagner's overture to *The Flying Dutchman* for a Glee Club concert. In 1877 there was formed the 'Worcester Instrumental Society for the Cultivation of Instrumental Music', and Elgar was appointed its director. He was also by now giving violin lessons to help bring him in some money. His aim again was to go to Leipzig for instruction, but he could not afford it. So instead he went to London for twelve days for violin lessons from Adolphe Pollitzer, aged forty-five and leader of the New Philharmonic. Teacher and pupil got on well together, but Elgar's resources would not run to a full course. His visit cost him £7. 15s. 9d., of which £3. 12s. 6d. accounted for the rail fare and Pollitzer's five lessons. He was 'living on two bags of nuts a day', he said later. Pollitzer discerned exceptional musicianship in Elgar and pleaded with him to return for a full course of tuition, because he felt sure he had the makings of a fine soloist. Elgar did return intermittently but later, after hearing Wilhelmj play, he decided he had not a full enough tone to justify cherishing ambitions of an outstanding career and gave up the idea and the lessons.

Home in Worcester he continued his private life of composing and his growing activities in public as a talented local musician. He arranged Christy Minstrel songs for 1s. 6d. apiece, and on 12 June 1878, ten days after his twenty-first birthday, at a concert by the 1st Worcestershire Artillery Volunteers' Amateur Christy Minstrels, his *Introductory Overture*, 'written expressly for this occasion', was performed. That year the Three Choirs Festival met in Worcester and Elgar was among the second violins; three years later he was in the firsts. (Elgar's father was also in the violin section and his sister Pollie was among the sopranos.) By this time, too, he was a member of a wind quintet, playing the bassoon (and later the cello) with his brother Frank (oboe), Hubert Leicester (flute), William Leicester (clarinet), and Frank Exton (flute). Elgar arranged and wrote music for them and, by the light of a carriage lamp, they serenaded their girl friends with 'Sweet and Low'. Also in 1877 he was among the players in the band of the County of Worcester Lunatic Asylum at Powick, where the superintendent was an early believer in the therapeutic effect of music on the inmates. The band comprised piccolo, flute, clarinet, two cornets, euphonium, about eight violins, and viola, cello, double bass, and pianoforte. Quadrilles were much in demand as well as arrangements of the classics and when, in 1879, Elgar was appointed conductor, he not only arranged music for this unusual assembly but included some pieces of his own.

The years 1877–82 were crucial to Elgar's career. Whether he resented the denial of an academic career, it is certain that his genius as an orchestrator, his absolute certainty of effect, so that he could later boast to Jaeger 'I never have to alter anything', were due to the lessons learned in the multitude of activities which he undertook as a local jack-of-all-trades musician in his early twenties.

He knew by this time the standard oratorios of Handel, Mendelssohn, Haydn, Spohr; he was soaked in Beethoven and Mozart, and in

the lighter overtures (Balfe, Gounod, Rossini, Auber, Weber, etc.); he
knew the keyboard works of C. P. E. Bach and Chopin; at St. George's
he studied and played motets and organ music by Pergolesi, Haydn,
Hummel, Beethoven, and others. All this spurred his busy creative
mind. For the wind quintet he gave himself the exercise of arranging
the last movement of Beethoven's op. 23 violin sonata, a Corelli concerto, and various other works. For St. George's he arranged the Allegro
from Mozart's violin sonata in F (K.547) as a Gloria. He took themes
from Beethoven's Fifth, Seventh, and Ninth Symphonies and, under
the pseudonym Bernhard Pappenheim, arranged them as a Credo. For
the orchestras in which he played he arranged Handel's *Ariodante* overture and *Adeste Fideles*. For friends he arranged a *Fantasia on Irish Airs*
for violin and pianoforte. There is also the famous exercise which he set
himself in 1878—the Symphony in G minor, after Mozart: 'I once
ruled a score for the same instruments and with the same number of
bars as Mozart's G minor symphony, and in that framework I wrote a
symphony, following as far as possible the same outlines for his themes
and the same modulations. I did this on my own initiative as I was
groping in the dark after light, but looking back after 30 years I don't
know any discipline from which I learned so much.'[1]

This brings us to the original compositions of those years. In 1878,
for St. George's he wrote a *Salve Regina*, a *Tantum Ergo*, an Easter
anthem 'Brother, For Thee He died', two Hymn Tunes, one in G major
and the other in F major. The latter was later published in the *Westminster Hymnal* as No. 151. It is quoted in the Aubade of the *Nursery
Suite* of 1931. In 1879 there was a Credo in E minor, a *Domine Salvam
fac*, and in 1882 a bass solo O *Salutaris Hostia*. An earlier setting is dated
1880 and was published by Cary in 1888. For orchestra there exists a
menuetto (scherzo), dated 1 October 1878, which may have been part
of a symphony. Under this heading come the compositions for Powick
Asylum: five Quadrilles called *La Brunette*, five called *Die Junge Kokette*,
dated 19 May 1879 and dedicated to Miss Holloway, the asylum's staff
pianist and organist, five called *L'Assommoir* (11 September 1879), five
called *Paris*, also dedicated to Miss Holloway (17 October 1880), *The
Valentine*—5 Lancers (2–15 February 1880), and polkas dated 1880, 1881,
1882, 1883, and 1884. A *Minuet grazioso* was played at a concert of the
Worcester Early Closing Association on 22 January 1879. At another
Worcester concert on 14 March 1882, were played his *Air de Ballet* and
March—Pas Redoublé. Another *Air de Ballet* was played on 16 August
1882, at a soireé held by the British Medical Association, meeting in

[1] *Strand Magazine* (May 1904).

Worcester. But it was in the field of chamber music that he was most copious, in music for himself to play at recitals or for his friends of the wind quintet and other combinations. There were, for violin and pianoforte, an incomplete *Fantasia* of 1878, two unfinished *Polonaises* (1879), a *Fugue in F sharp minor* (1881, incorporated over 50 years later into sketches for the opera *The Spanish Lady*), and, for violin, a *Study for Strengthening the Third Finger* (1877, re-copied in 1920 and dedicated to Jascha Heifetz). From 1878 date two incomplete string quartets, a string trio and a pianoforte trio, and the wind quintet pieces known as *Promenades* (including the titles 'Madame Tussaud's' and 'Hell and Tommy'). *Harmony Music* (1879 and 1881) has seven sections for the quintet, and also from 1879 are five *Intermezzi* which, when he looked at them again in later life, Elgar called 'mine own children', as indeed they are. An Allegretto, a Gavotte, a Sarabande (also re-copied for *The Spanish Lady*), a Gigue, an Andante con Variazioni (sub-titled 'Evesham Andante' and dedicated to Hubert Leicester), and an Adagio Cantabile are also all 1879 wind quintet products. An Allegro for oboe, violin, viola, and cello of late 1878 was unfinished, and a Fugue in D minor for oboe and violin, written in May 1883 'for Frank Elgar and Karl Bammert,' displays contrapuntal skill.

Obviously 1879 was an important year for the development of Edward Elgar's gifts. Though the works written at that time have no merit in themselves, there are indications, not solely discernible by hindsight, that the Elgarian style already existed. There are not many composers whose music written at the age of twenty-two betrays its authorship so strongly. The *Romance* for violin and pianoforte published in 1885 by Schott was written in 1878 or 1879. There is a breath of 'Nimrod' in the 1882 O *Salutaris Hostia*. The *Sérénade Mauresque*, which in 1883 was the first work to bring him a relatively wider fame, was composed in 1879. The *Cantique* for orchestra of 1912 is a revision of the 1879 'Adagio Solenne' from the *Intermezzi*. Similarly, *Rosemary* (1915) was written at Settle, Yorkshire, on 4 September 1882. Parts of the 1930 *Severn Suite* originate in wind quintet music of 1879. Bits of *King Olaf* (1896) were developed from 1879 sketches. So was the opening of *The Black Knight* (1893). As for the *Wand of Youth* suites, some of the material for these is known to have been written for the Elgar children's plays. The overture of the first suite exists as sketches dated 1879, and 'Fairies and Giants' Elgar himself dated 1867. The Minuet existed in 1881, and 'Sun Dance' was an 1879 waltz. Of the second suite, 'Wild Bears' was a Powick quadrille and 'Moths and Butterflies' was sketched in 1879. But the origins of these pieces can safely be dated 1867. And in 1901 when Edward VII congratulated Elgar on the tune of the Trio of the first *Pomp and Circumstance* march, the composer replied 'I've been carrying that around in my pocket for 20 years'—which dates 'Land of Hope and Glory' at about 1880. What is more, as W. H. Reed pointed out, the Quadrilles for Powick contain striking examples of sudden 'crashes' in the middle of a bar, such as can be found in the Second Symphony finale, in the finale of the Cello Concerto and elsewhere. The style was the man.

3 Apprentice

The 'Paris' quadrilles of 1880 were a souvenir of Elgar's first visit abroad, when he went to the French capital with Charlie Pipe, who was to marry Lucy Elgar the following year. They heard Saint-Saëns play the organ at the Madeleine and saw Molière's *Le Malade Imaginaire*. Edward evidently had another brief preoccupation for in 1933, when Elgar visited Delius in France, after he left Grez-sur-Loing the scent of the countryside 'recalled a romance of 1880. . . . I decided to go to Barbizon, but when I passed the cross-roads the longing had passed away. That belonged to the romance of 1880, now dead.'[1] He returned to Worcester, to his teaching and his work at the asylum; he took the Royal Academy of Music's local examination in violin and 'general musical knowledge', passing with honours in company with the blind musician William Wolstenholme, then aged fifteen; and he was promoted to the first violins at the Worcester Festival. This led in the following year to his engagement to play in the first violins of W. C. Stockley's orchestra in Birmingham. Stockley's Popular Concerts were a well-established Midlands event and he was also chorusmaster for the Birmingham Festival, held triennially.

At the very end of 1882 Elgar achieved his ambition, after hard saving, to visit Leipzig not, as he had once hoped, to study, but to hear concerts by the Gewandhaus Orchestra conducted by Carl Reinecke, and to go to the opera. Schumann's *Overture, Scherzo and Finale* seems to have made a deep impression on him—'my ideal!' he called Schumann in a letter to Dr. Charles Buck of Giggleswick, Yorkshire, who attended the B.M.A.'s 1882 Worcester conference and became one of Elgar's firmest friends, the first, in fact, of the Elgar 'circle', and one with whom he enjoyed playing chamber music. 'I heard no end of stuff,' he wrote on 13 May 1883. 'Schumann principally and Wagner no end. They have a good opera . . . & we went many times.' 'We' comprised Elgar and a seventeen-year-old English girl who later became Mrs. Edith Wood-Somers, of Blewbury, Berkshire, and sometimes a German girl who was attached to Elgar enough to visit him in Worcester the following summer, as he explained to Dr. Buck on 1 July 1883: 'The vacation at Leipzig begins shortly; my "Braut"

¹ *The Daily Telegraph*, 1 July 1933.

arrives here on Thursday next remaining till the first week of September; of course I shall remain in Worcester till her departure. After that 'twould be a charity if you could find a brokenhearted fiddler much trio-playing for a day or two.' By this time, as the same letter indicates, Stockley had agreed to include Elgar's *Intermezzo: Sérénade Mauresque* in one of his concerts, and it was duly played at Birmingham, with the composer playing in the orchestra, on 13 December 1883. 'Melodious, graceful and pleasing' was one critic's description, 'and the scoring, more particularly for the strings . . . is tasteful and musicianly.' This was some encouragement, and he sent the parts to Pollitzer in London who had offered to try to interest August Manns in it for a Crystal Palace concert.

Elgar's eyes were on a fame wider than that so poignantly conveyed by the phrase 'talented local composer'. Already he had experienced something of the harsh side of musical life when he had offered to re-score a church musician's anthem, after the original effort had failed disastrously, and had not received even a word of thanks when the revision was a success. He wrote to Buck in explanation of an adverse criticism of the *Intermezzo*: 'The man who wrote the slighting article is a Mus. Bac. who had sent in two pieces and they were advertised and withdrawn because the orchestration wanted so much revision as to be unplayable. And in the same letter: 'My father was ill just before Xmas . . . the younger generation at the Catholic Ch: have taken an objection to him and have got him turned out of the organist's place; this he had held for 37 years!!' Here, in these early letters, we see the Elgar so many came to know—ebullient one minute, downcast the next. 'My prospects are about as hopeless as ever,' he wrote to Buck in April 1884. 'I am not wanting in energy I think; so, sometimes, I conclude that 'tis want of ability and get in a mouldy desponding state which is really horrible.' And about the same time: 'I have no *money*— not a cent. And I am sorry to say I have no prospects of getting any.'

As he taught the young ladies of Malvern the violin and used up his earnings on journeys to London to hear a Manns concert or to try to sell his work to a publisher, he must have known only too well what kind of struggle lay ahead of him. In an unpublished article which he wrote in the last years of his life, he described his day trips to London in his twenties: 'I lived 120 miles from London. I rose at six, walked a mile to the railway station, the train left at seven; arrived at Paddington about 11, underground to Victoria, on to the [Crystal] Palace arriving in time for the last three-quarters of an hour of the rehearsal; if fortune smiled, this piece of rehearsal included the work desired to be heard·

but fortune rarely smiled and more often than not the principal item was over. Lunch. Concert at three. At five a rush to Victoria; then to Paddington, on to Worcester arriving at 10-30. A strenuous day indeed; but the new work had been heard and another treasure added to a life's experience.' One of his own compositions was played in Worcester on 1 May 1884, when the organist Dr. Done—he who disliked Schumann—conducted *Sevillana* at a Worcester Philharmonic Society concert. *Sevillana*, dedicated gratefully to Stockley, also went to Pollitzer and thence to Manns, who included it in a Crystal Palace concert on 12 May 1884, the first music by Elgar to be heard in London.

Some emotional crisis, whether over a woman or because of the collapse of a plan to settle in London is not known, eradicated the effect of this first success outside the area of Worcester, and Elgar went for a holiday to Scotland. 'I got in a very desponding state . . . (you ken what happened),' he explained to Buck, 'and it behoved me to do something out of the common to raise my spirits. . . . Came home "well". I have been working away ever since.' It is not far-fetched to deduce that this 'desponding state' was connected with the lady from Leipzig. She had, after all, spent eight weeks in Worcester with Elgar, not a common kind of holiday in those days, and he was twenty-six, not an impressionable boy of nineteen. As was always to happen, a change of scenery stimulated his creative faculty and in 1885 he had begun a 'Lakes' overture, souvenir of a previous Windermere holiday with Buck, and a 'Scottish' overture. In later life Buck recalled the 'extraordinary' effect on Elgar of his first sight of Lake Windermere. 'Not a word could be got out of him, and then suddenly he began to write furiously. . . . He said he had never known quite the same sensation before and that he was simply obliged to write.' Both these overtures were abandoned. Elgar described them as 'of no account but they serve to divert me somewhat and hide a broken heart'. He showed the Scottish overture later in 1885 to 'old Stockley' who was 'afraid of it. He says candidly he cannot read the score and would like to hear it first—I am sorely disappointed.' He returned to the subject in another letter to Buck six weeks later, this time adding that Stockley had found it 'disconnected'. 'So I have retired into my shell and live in hopes of writing a polka some day—failing that a single chant is probably my fate.'

There is plenty of the jocular, facetious, and whimsical Elgar in these letters to Buck, a hearty yet curiously ill-at-ease strain which intensified as he grew older and is particularly prevalent in letters to Jaeger,

Dora Powell, and Troyte Griffith. He carried writing material wherever he went so that he could use time spent in waiting for trains in keeping his correspondence up to date—'I am busy now [1884], and have to "fake" considerably to get lessons in—not that I am full up really, but it takes so much time getting from one place to another.' His gift for friendship is always evident in his letters, with their conversational style and detail. Buck and his wife gave Elgar a dog, Scap, in 1885, and accounts of Scap's adventures punctuate the musical news in the letters sent from Worcester to Settle.

'I took him up the road for a run before turning in. This morning I had him out at 7.30 into the river and he had his first fight with a Newfoundland brute which began it—; no harm done. . . . The Bath Road presents a perfect paradise of new smells all of which he has duly examined and *"reported"* on. . . .' 'I took him over to Stoke [Stoke Prior] for the weekend & had a vagabond day on the common after rabbits etc. . . . He has developed into a much more affectionate animal than I anticipated & loves me. . . . I shut him up at the shop this morn: while I went to give a lesson, he whined so his grandmother [Elgar's mother] let him out, he darted down the stairs, caught his leg in twenty concertinas that are piled on the staircase & rolled over with all the lot into the middle of the shop! There were some ladies there & my old father enjoyed it awfully. We live in an atmosphere of Scap. . . .' '. . . got an 'orrid cold, shouting in the rain election night. Scap & I were out 'till 12.30!! & owing to our exertion we have got a Conservative in—for this Radical hole. Scap wore his colours like a man. . . .' 'Scap is getting fat & is very well now; no news in particular of him; he stole ½ a fried sole up here & a beef steak at mother's & has caused the cat to kitten prematurely by his antics. . . .'

There is nothing in either the *Intermezzo* or *Sevillana* to suggest that Elgar was the possessor of anything but a picturesque and melodious talent for salon music. He himself knew his own possibilities better, and few events can have had a greater effect on his future development than the Three Choirs Festival at Worcester in September 1884, marking the cathedral's 800th anniversary, when Dvořák, who had visited England for the first time the previous March, conducted his *Stabat Mater* and his nowadays too rarely heard D major symphony (op. 60, formerly known as No. 1 and now as No. 6). Elgar again played in the first violins, played this gay and melodious symphony dedicated to Dr. Hans Richter, and wrote of it to Buck: 'I wish you could hear Dvořák's music. It is simply ravishing, so tuneful & clever & the orchestration is wonderful; no matter how few

instruments he uses it never sounds thin. I cannot describe it; it must
be heard.'

Much is said of the influence of Brahms and Wagner on Elgar's
music, but in neither case is their influence as strong as has sometimes
been made out. For a much more powerful influence, both instru-
mentally and aesthetically, it is profitable to look at the works of
Schumann and Dvořák, two composers whose combination of romantic lyricism and strong rhythmical contrast finds similar expression in
the music of Elgar. That he learnt much from a study of their scores is
obvious whenever we hear the transition passage from scherzo to
finale of Schumann's D minor symphony, the overture and the introduction to Act III of *Manfred*, the first climax of the first movement of
Dvořák's D minor symphony, op. 70, and a passage towards the end of
the finale of the G major symphony, op. 88: they might have been
scored by Elgar. Most remarkable of all is the slow movement of
Dvořák's early D minor symphony, op. 13 (now known as No. 4 in
D minor), which might almost be by Elgar and contains an extraordinary anticipation of the 'New Faith' theme in *The Kingdom*.
Both Elgar's concertos effectively 'borrow' Dvořák's scheme in his
Cello Concerto of nostalgically recalling earlier themes towards the
end of the finale. In Elgar's own B minor concerto, for violin not cello,
his theme from the slow movement:

Ex. 1

is strongly reminiscent of this, from the slow movement of Dvořák's
Violin Concerto:

Ex. 2

Tovey found a similar relationship between Elgar's Violin Concerto
and Saint-Saëns's Third Violin Concerto, also in B minor. This points to
another, less obvious continental influence but one which is nearer in

some ways to Elgar's musical character than are either Wagner or
Brahms. At any rate, the 1884 experience of Dvořák, repeated two
years later, on 21 October 1886, when Dvořák again conducted the D
major symphony at Birmingham with Stockley's orchestra, seems to
have spurred Elgar to further efforts on his own behalf. As soon as the
Worcester Festival was over he went to London to try to interest the
Covent Garden Promenade Concerts in his work, without any luck,
and he told Buck he had 'a big work in tow'—no one has discovered
what that may have been: perhaps a violin concerto which he eventually destroyed in 1890, or a string quartet. He was by now conductor
of the Worcester Amateur Instrumental Society and he repeated his
Sevillana on 9 April 1885. Charles Buck's brother-in-law, John Beare,
a London musical instrument dealer and publisher, with whom Elgar
sometimes stayed, helped him, as did Pollitzer, to get his music into
print for the first time. *Une Idylle* (op. 4, No. 1) written in 1883 and
dedicated to Miss E. E. of Inverness, another 'long-forgotten romance'
of a Scottish holiday in 1883, was published by Beare—'John was good
enough to encourage me by taking the little piece for violin', Elgar
wrote to Buck on 8 March 1885, still, incidentally, addressing him as
'My dear doctor' and signing himself 'Edward Elgar', nothing less
formal— and Schott brought out the op. 1, a *Romance* for violin and
pianoforte which was written in 1878 and played in Worcester at a
concert in the Deanery on 20 October 1885. Elgar's friendly loyalties
are displayed in the dedications of these early pieces—the *Romance* to
the grocer Oswin Grainger, who played in local bands with Elgar; a
violin *Gavotte*, published by Schott, to Dr. Buck 'in memory of the
old days'; *Virelai*, op. 4, No. 3, to Frank Webb, a Worcester furniture
dealer and member of the W.A.I.S. (who evidently wrote to its new
conductor urging more adventurous programmes and received the
reply: 'The average taste in music, as you must have seen, is extremely
low. . . . I fear 'tis useless asking them to devote their energies to something higher and consequently more difficult.'); the *Allegretto* for
violin and pianoforte on a theme of five notes G E D G E, dedicated
to the Gedge sisters of Malvern Wells to whom Elgar was tutor, and
published by Schott. In November 1885 he became organist of St.
George's, and it must have seemed as though this put the final seal on his
rôle for life: local musician, available for all occasions, sacred or secular.

*   *   *

This period of Elgar's life coincides with what is known as the English
Musical Renaissance. But the more steadily one looks at those years,

the less apparent does the renaissance become. It was, unquestionably, a renaissance of *atmosphere*. Music began to be taken much more seriously and to be seen as an integral part of human life rather than as mere titillation of the ear. It became entwined with romantic literature and philosophy, not always to its advantage. The opening of the Royal College of Music, the foundation of the Oxford University Musical Club, the Bach revival, the Crystal Palace concerts under Manns, the Handel festivals, visits to London of great musicians, such as Wagner and Hans Richter, and of great instrumentalists and singers—all these educational and expository happenings betoken a genuine revival of musical life which was not wholly confined to the capital. Hallé in Manchester, Stockley in Birmingham, and, later, Godfrey in Bournemouth made their contributions. The Leeds, Birmingham, and Three Choirs Festivals were regarded as the goals to which all composers should aspire—and since the public's appetite for oratorios appeared to be insatiable, they catered for this taste in a manner which now seems almost indecently callous.

Out of all this activity how much living, creative music has come down to us after nearly a hundred years? Parry's *Scenes from 'Prometheus Unbound'*, in 1880 at Gloucester, is often used as the first milestone on the road to revival. But milestones soon become covered with weeds and obscured from view. Stanford's *Veiled Prophet*, Mackenzie's *La Belle Dame Sans Merci*, Cowen's *The Water Lily*—who now knows a note of these 'milestones', and who outside a very select few knew a note of them seventy years ago? Stanford and Parry were remarkable men, as teachers, administrators, and publicists. As composers they were overshadowed, even in their own day, not only by their European counterparts, but by Arthur Sullivan—and Stainer's *Crucifixion*. Sullivan was the genuine, creative, thoroughly musical talent of English Victorian music, the creator of a *genre*, the Savoy operas— Offenbach in gaiters—which by its tunefulness and resource looks like staying the course for a long time still to come. An obituarist of Frederic Cowen wrote in 1935 that Cowen had offered his listeners and performers 'a great deal of refined enjoyment'. Compared with Cowen's kind of refinement, Sullivan seems almost crude. Yet there is no need to analyse the reasons for Sullivan's pre-eminence. Quality tells. His tunes were better, his scoring was better, his sense of rhythm was better than those of his contemporaries. Eduard Hanslick, revisiting London in 1886 after twenty-four years, remarked that Sullivan's music was 'stylistically consistent' and that the composer 'has accom-

plished something, if in a secondary genre, which no Englishman has
ever accomplished before: to be melodious and amusing for an entire
evening'. He spoke from experience, for after enduring Mackenzie's
opera *The Troubadour*—'one of the dullest and most disagreeable
affairs I have ever encountered in the form of music in costume'—he
concluded that opera 'requires melodic invention, strong sensuality
and a fresh, consistent style—all characteristics with which the English
are not notably endowed'. Strong sensuality is hardly to be found in
the Savoy operas, but the melody and style are proof against change.
Yet Sullivan was out of favour with the musical intelligentsia because
of this lighter side of his art—the same disfavour which was eventually
to be transferred to Elgar by the same people. And Sullivan allowed
himself to be deluded into adding to the deluge of moribund cantatas
and oratorios, though he could not prevent his superior talent from
making *The Golden Legend* the most passable and attractive of a bad
bunch.

Parry and Stanford laboured in a different vineyard from Sullivan—
Stanford's lighter side, his genuinely beautiful Irish rhapsodies and
songs, suggests that he might have enjoyed similar success had luck
run his way—and no doubt they felt his artistic and financial success
as an injustice. 'The English public is curious,' Parry said in 1918 to
Thomas F. Dunhill. 'It can only recognise one composer at a time.
Once it was Sullivan. Now it is Elgar.' Later it was Vaughan Williams,
then Britten. All the four composers named, to use another of Parry's
phrases which he originally applied to Elgar, 'reached the hearts of the
people' without debasing their ideals and without stooping to vulgarity.
The big men will always win acclaim; the smaller men make their contribution to the age which produces the big man. These contributions
may be of great value and one does not make Elgar's achievement any
greater, rather the reverse, by belittling his contemporaries. But facts
remain; and if we really wish to set a *realistic* date to the renaissance of
English musical composition, or, at any rate, to its coming-of-age, then
it is 19 June 1899, when Hans Richter conducted the first performance
of the *Enigma Variations*.

*   *   *

The four years from 1886 occupy hardly any space in books about
Elgar, yet in them his frustration must have been greater than at any
other time. He was approaching thirty. It seemed as if London was
closed against performance of his salon pieces; even his local reputation
had no lasting effect. Yet he did not lose heart. His organ-playing led

c

to renewed church compositions: an *Ave Verum* in January 1887, four Litanies in 1888 and *Ecce sacerdos magnus*, dedicated to Hubert Leicester and first performed at St. George's on 9 October 1888, when the Roman Catholic Bishop of Birmingham visited the church. 'Some special things had to be sung for which we had no music,' he told Buck, 'thus I had to set to work & compose it all & copy out the parts! Had to get it in anyhow & broke my neck doing it. Anyway the leading paper says the new composition was "exquisite" so I suppose 'twas good enough.' He was determined, he told Buck, 'to do everything I can lay my hands on'. He gave violin recitals—his fee was two guineas —violin lessons, and played in orchestras throughout the Midlands— an experience at a Hanley Festival in the then new Victoria Hall was typical: 'The arrangements for our accommodation were "frightful" & we all struck & eventually the committee telegraphed to all the neighbouring towns to get hotels for us. I was travelling all night after & sitting up & incessant playing has made my eye very queer.' That is the first mention of a chronic complaint which was to plague him all his life. He frequently mentioned his ailments to Buck; for example: 'I have been ill for a long time off and on; got a severe cold which has, as usual, played the plague with my b—ls. . . . I have lost ever so much work.' He needed all the money he could get so that he was no burden on the married sister with whom he lived. In 1886 he added to his other tasks a teaching post at Worcester College for the Blind where he again came into contact with William Wolstenholme, accompany-ing him as amanuensis in the following year when he went for three days to Oxford to sit for his Mus. Bac. degree, a typical act of gener-osity. Elgar read out the questions to him and, according to F. Bonavia,[1] noticed a mistake in one of them with the result that the authorities agreed it must not be attempted.

His only major encouragement, in a relative sense, in these years was the performance at Birmingham on 1 March 1888 by Stockley's orchestra of the *Suite in D*, originally of four movements including the *March-Pas Redoublé* (first played separately at Worcester on 14 March 1882) and incorporating the *Sérénade Mauresque*. When this was revised for publication as op. 10 ten years later the March was dropped. The suite, obviously, was not a particularly 'new' work. He had told Buck in November 1883 that it was finished 'in my head if I could but get time to write it down'. He had hoped for an earlier performance (letter to Buck 12 December 1887, 'My Suite is still silent & postponed at Birmingham: fate!'). He conducted the work and

[1] In 'Elgar', *The Music Masters* (ed. A. L. Bacharach), iii, p. 138.

attributed some unfavourable notices to this fact: 'The critics, save two, are nettled. I am the only local man who has been asked to conduct his own work—& what's a greater offence, I *did it*—and *well* too; for this I must needs suffer.' One critic recommended 'judicious operations with the pruning knife' and the *Musical Times* correspondent, writing of the composer as 'Mr. Algar', noted 'fancy as well as tunefulness' and also a lack of 'cohesion and artistic development'—a fair example of fence-sitting. The revised suite contains, in the finale 'Contrasts: the Gavotte A.D. 1700 and 1900',[1] one of Elgar's most delightful lighter pieces, a thoroughly charming example of pastiche, ingeniously handled. This movement derives from an incident during the Leipzig visit of 1883: 'I saw two dancers once in Leipzig who came down the stage in antique dress dancing a gavotte: when they reached the foot-lights they suddenly turned round & appeared to be two very young & modern people & danced a gay & lively measure: they had come down the stage *backwards* & danced away with their (modern) faces to-wards us—when they reached the back of the stage they suddenly turned round & the old, decrepit couple danced gingerly to the old tune.'[2]

On 7 May 1888 Elgar conducted the Worcester Amateur Instru-mental Society in his Three Pieces for String Orchestra. The manuscript of this work is lost, but there seems every reason to suppose that, in a revised form, it became the well-known *Serenade for Strings*, op. 20. The titles of the original suite are in themselves a strong clue: I Spring Song (Allegro), II Elegy (Adagio), III Finale (Presto). '*I like 'em* (the first thing I ever did),' he told Buck in July; and in later life he often referred to the *Serenade* as his favourite work. The same letter to Buck adds jubilantly, 'Also there's a terrific (!!!) song in this month's Maga. of Music'. This song, 'The Wind at Dawn', won Elgar £5 in a com-petition organized by Joseph Williams, the publishers. Its words were by Caroline Alice Roberts.

Miss Roberts had become one of Elgar's Malvern pianoforte pupils on 6 October 1886. He was then twenty-nine. She was thirty-seven (born 9 October 1848), an age, at that period of history, at which spinsterhood seemed confirmed. She was the daughter of Major-General Sir Henry Gee Roberts, a stalwart of the Indian Army in the Mutiny and the Sikh Wars, and his wife Julia Raikes, granddaughter of Robert Raikes, founder of Sunday Schools. The General died in 1860 when Caroline Alice, youngest of his four children was twelve.

[1] The original order of movements was: Mazurka, Intermezzo, Fantasia gavotte, March.
[2] Letter to A. J. Jaeger, 4 February 1899.

The other three children were boys: one died young, and the other two were educated at Cheltenham and joined the Indian Army, one of them dying in 1882. Alice, therefore, like many a Victorian daughter, was left to look after her mother in the Georgian house at Redmarley d'Abitot in Worcestershire. She had an artistic nature. She studied geology, she translated Hoffmann's *Ritter Glück*, and she wrote and had published a two-volume novel and some poetry. She also took part in Shakespeare readings and in village concerts. She sang in a choir which was often accompanied by a string orchestra in which Elgar played. It is not known exactly when they first met, but from 1886 onwards her friends noticed a marked increase in her musical activities, especially in her piano-playing. In 1887 Lady Roberts died and Alice, who inherited a small private income, left Redmarley and took a furnished room at Malvern Link. On 22 September 1888 she announced her engagement to Elgar, to the horror of her cousins and aunts. Here was Alice, nearly forty, throwing herself away on a tradesman's son, a music teacher with no prospects. Not only that but worse—he was a Roman Catholic.[1] One of her aunts cut her out of her will. Another stipulated that certain family money allowed to Alice should not pass to any children of the marriage. When Alice Elgar died in 1920, Elgar wrote to Frank Schuster (17 April 1920): 'I am plunged in the midst of ancient hate and prejudice—poor dear A's settlements & her *awful aunts* who cd. allow nothing to descend to any offspring of *mine*—I had forgotten all the petty bitterness but I feel just now rather evil that . . . my Carice [his daughter] should be penalised by a wretched lot of old incompetents simply because I was—well—I.'

But Alice Roberts knew what he was, and all credit to her for it. She knew, to use a metaphor some of her family might have understood, that the colt she had picked was a Derby winner. Never in all the years that followed did she waver in her faith and belief, born of some deep instinct, that Edward Elgar was a creative genius of the highest order. She must have persuaded him during their engagement to abandon his teaching and his choir practices, his organ-playing and Stockley's orchestra, his amateur instrumentalists and his chamber music in Malvern villas, and to move to London, the centre of music-making, and to try his fortune with publishers. On 8 May 1889 they were married at Brompton Oratory. Elgar was within a month of his thirty-second birthday; Alice was forty. Father Knight of St. George's Church, Worcester, gave as a wedding present

[1] Alice Elgar was converted to the Roman Catholic faith in 1893.

to his departing organist John Henry Newman's poem *The Dream of Gerontius*, into which he had copied underlinings and markings made by General Gordon in the copy sent to him at Khartoum five years earlier.

4 Retreat from London

The years 1889 to 1899 are the most important in Elgar's life. In this decade he went from obscurity to fame, by way of cruel discouragement. These are the years which explain why the composer of *Salut d'Amour* turned into the composer of the *Enigma Variations*. He did not, as has often been asserted, become a great composer overnight in one work. No artist in any art in the history of mankind has done that. The seeds and roots of greatness grow obscurely sometimes, but their progress is traceable and recognizable, and human experience plays its part.

After a honeymoon in the Isle of Wight, the Elgars settled first in West Kensington, then in Upper Norwood and finally returned to Kensington to live at 51 Avonmore Road. 'This is a time of deep peace & happiness to me after the vain imaginings of so many years & the pessimistic views so often unfolded to you on the Settle highways have vanished! God wot!' So Elgar wrote from Ventnor to Charles Buck. He entered fully into all the possibilities of hearing music which living in London presented. Their home was near the Crystal Palace and they took season tickets for Manns' concerts. There were Wagner and Verdi at Covent Garden; the Richter concerts; celebrity recitals. They went frequently to the London Library to read. Alice entertained on a scale rather beyond what they could probably afford (one day she sold her pearls). Visitors from Worcestershire, relatives (the Dowager Lady Thompson), Army-family friends: she was determined they should all know her Edward. When they went for a Malvern holiday for festivities with the Fitton family, they called on the Hon. Mrs. Roper-Curzon —and Edward wrote in his diary, as well he might, 'Gosh!' The true business of life, in London, was on a less exalted level. Elgar, overcoming a natural shyness, swallowed his pride and visited publisher after publisher with his short pieces, not without success. Orsborn and Tuckwood accepted pieces for violin and pianoforte and eleven organ voluntaries ('E . . . *drew cheque*', Alice noted in her diary about these), and a setting of Tennyson, 'Queen Mary's Song'; Novello's took the unaccompanied part-song 'My Love Dwelt in a Northern Land', to words by Andrew Lang. To Schott's he sold, for either two guineas or £5 but not more, a short pianoforte piece he had written while staying with Dr. Buck at Settle. This was *Liebesgruss*, better known as *Salut d'Amour.* In September 1889 he received proofs of it and wrote to Buck (by now 'My dear Charles') on 6 October: 'I sent you the *score* which may amuse you: they (Schott's) do it for p.f. solo—v. & p.f.—orch. parts & score!!! four editions!! gusto!!! I forget whether the ending of your 'cello arrngt is the same as at present.' At first few copies of *Liebesgruss* were sold. Schott's then switched to the title *Salut d'Amour* and printed the composer's name as Ed. Elgar, leaving his nationality vague. He explained in a letter to Frank Webb dated 29 November: 'About "Salut d'Amour", the arrangement for *Strings* I did not think satisfactory so it was not proceeded with; but the arrangement for small orchestra is now done. . . . About giving French titles to things: it is only done so that they may sell abroad: if you put an English title only, you confine yourself to the English market while a French title secures its circulation in France (if it's of *any good*), Italy, Russia, anywhere in fact. I *don't like* doing it as my own name is so "peremptorily" English . . . but I can't afford to wait 'till the English is the universal language & *don't intend to* if I could. . . . By the way there are several things with *Latin* names, but people never grumble at these. I would try Greek if it would sell! . . .' Sell it did, making its publisher a fortune and its composer nothing beyond the purchase fee, enough to pay a bill or buy more music paper. Much superior scorn has been poured on *Salut d'Amour.* Café music, yes; but not lacking in charm, melodic distinction and period flavour. Possibly in the mid-twentieth century, when we are exposed daily to a ceaseless torrent of banality, *Salut d'Amour* seems less offensive to squeamish tastes than it did fifty years ago. It is a pretty trifle, especially in its original orchestration, marked by taste and restraint.

But selling songs and salon pieces to publishers was not Elgar's principal reason for moving to London. He hoped to have his music played and sent his *Suite*, his string pieces, and a revised *Sevillana* to various conductors. The directors of the Covent Garden Promenade Concerts were sufficiently impressed to invite him to rehearse them one morning. He went along, and it was explained to him that some songs had to be rehearsed first. While they were in progress, Sir Arthur Sullivan arrived unexpectedly wanting to run through a selection from one of his operas. He used up all the rehearsal time. Elgar went despondently home. Two similar occurrences befell him at the Crystal Palace; on one occasion the conductor had received a Royal command to give up some rehearsal time to a composition by Ethel Smyth. Not every cloud was black, however. August Manns conducted *Salut d'Amour* on 11 November 1889, and the *Suite* on 22 November the latter being repeated on

24 February 1890. Of another occasion Alice's diary records that at a rehearsal 'string pieces played through roughly'. Frederic Cowen, then the conductor of the Philharmonic Society and perhaps the most illustrious executive English musician of the day, also took an interest in the unknown young man from Worcestershire and, probably by introductions to publishers, gave a 'helping hand' which was publicly acknowledged by Elgar many years later in a speech at a banquet in honour of Cowen in 1925.

The conclusion is inescapable that, bitterly as he looked back on this first London venture, Elgar had very little at that time to offer the metropolitan concert-goer. Much no doubt was 'in his head', but he had again had no time to write it down, and the eye and throat trouble which throughout his life recurred at intervals—usually when the creative flame was low—afflicted him in the first year of marriage. His first big chance was to come not from London but from his native West Country. Six days after their first anniversary, when Alice was six months pregnant,[1] she wrote in her diary 'E. commenced a tale'. The previous month, in April, he had been delighted to receive, at last, an invitation from the Worcester Festival committee to write a short orchestral work for the secular concert during the 1890 Three Choirs meeting. This was to be the overture *Froissart*, composed between April and July of 1890. On 29 July he wrote to Frank Webb with revealing candour about his misgivings regarding Worcester: 'My overture is finished & I do not think will be liked but that must take its chance: I find in my limited experience that one's own friends are the people to be most in dread of: I could fill a not unentertaining book with the criticisms passed on my former efforts: when I have written anything slow they say it ought to have been quick—when loud, it shd. have been quiet—when fanciful—solemn; in a word I have always been wrong hitherto—at home.' Having offered the score in June and July to Novello's and to Goodwin & Tabb, he heard on 8 August that Novello's had accepted it, and the string parts were printed in time for the first performance in the Public Hall on 9 September 1890. Elgar conducted.

Froissart, said the critic of the *Musical Times*, was much applauded although in his view it lacked coherence of ideas and conciseness of utterance and betrayed the marks of youth and inexperience. The *Manchester Guardian* spoke of 'spirited themes' but also of 'excessive elaboration and a tendency to monotony'. Despite the poor acoustics

---

[1] A daughter was born on 14 August 1890. She was christened Carice Irene, the first name being derived from her mother's Caroline Alice. Elgar sometimes referred to Alice as Carice, and dedicated *Salut d'Amour* to her under that name.

of the Public Hall, in which Elgar's orchestration must have sounded
to its disadvantage, Elgar was pleased by the way the work was
received. He wrote on 28 September to Frank Webb, 'I have had very
good notices in nearly all the papers especially in those most to be feared
& the overture was much liked by the *musicians* present'. *Froissart* had
its origin in a passage from Scott's *Old Mortality* in which John Graham
of Claverhouse speaks of his enthusiasm for Froissart's historical romances
with their loyalty to kingship, pure faith towards religion, hardihood
to the enemy, and fidelity to woman. On the score Elgar inscribed a
line from Keats, 'When chivalry lifted up her lance on high'. It would
be unreasonable to expect the critics of the day to have remarked upon
what now first strikes the listener guided of course by hindsight—the
flashes of mature Elgar. But they ought to have noticed the polish of
the scoring. This overture and what I feel sure I am correct in regarding
as its predecessor, the *Serenade for Strings*, show that Elgar was already
a master of the orchestra rare in English music, that he lived in and
breathed the orchestra as naturally as the air around him, and that,
given the spur of the chance of performance in a suitable setting, this
kind of music was already within his power. All Elgar's characteristics
are in *Froissart* and the *Serenade*; the love of sequences, the upward
sweeps, the detailed use of expression marks. Anticipations of *Gerontius*,
the symphonies, and the *Enigma Variations* abound. What could be
more typical of Elgar than these two themes from *Froissart*:

Ex. 3 Andante

and

Ex. 4 Allegro (poco meno mosso)

or this from the *Serenade*?—

Ex. 5 Larghetto

Already in *Froissart* is the profusion of themes that is found in the symphonies and the Violin Concerto. The orchestration is clear and assured.
W. H. Reed[1] points out that at the second bar the woodwind and brass
are combined against the holding-note of all the strings except the
double basses, 'showing that even at this period Elgar had discovered
the inherent weakness of the bass of the orchestral wind and so used
his double basses to reinforce the bassoon and the bass trombone instead
of wasting them to double the strings.' It is a work quite obviously
conceived in terms of the orchestra: it is not a piano piece orchestrated.
What is especially remarkable is the restrained use of instrumental
groups: the overture is less brassy and blaring than might be expected.
On the other hand, the two critics quoted above were by no means
unperceptive. The work does tend to monotony because the tunes are
never developed, merely repeated or inflated. Having invented a beautiful slow melody, Elgar did not seem to know what to do with it. The
overture sounds to contemporary ears like a mixture of Dvořák with
short but vivid bursts of the real Elgar. It is striking as an example both
of how much Elgar already knew and how much he had to learn.

Alice Elgar had been unable to attend the first performance because
of Carice's birth, but Stockley's orchestra played it at Birmingham on
5 February 1891, where she was proud to see Edward called on the
platform to acknowledge cordial applause. 'I think it is too long,' he
told Frank Webb, and nine years later he was to write to Jaeger: 'It's
old & not quite what I'd write now but it's good healthy stuff.' The
critics this time were more favourable, though none grasped the significance of the work: that Elgar had lifted up his lance on high in his
first real assault on the citadel held securely in 1890 by Cowen, Sullivan,
Parry, Stanford, and Mackenzie. But one overture does not make a
reputation, and back in London after the Worcester performance there
was no sign that any citadel was under siege. No conductor rushed to
put *Froissart* into his programmes, though Elgar took the parts to
Manns at Crystal Palace. He wrote another song. He started, or re-
started, a violin concerto, felt it was of no quality, and destroyed it.
He had more eye trouble and a septic tooth. Alice had the baby to tend,
but each day she ruled the bar lines on his manuscript paper to save him
time. An advertisement for pupils was unanswered, so he resumed
weekly visits to Malvern and Worcester. A German had taken over his
'practice' in the area, and to help build it up again Elgar wrote on New
Year's Eve, 1890, to Manns, to the tenor Edward Lloyd, whom he had
met, to William Wolstenholme seeking permission to give their names

[1] *Elgar* (London, 1939), p. 50.

as references. The previous night Alice wrote in her diary: 'A. thought this the coldest day she ever felt (I cried with the cold)'. Their brave venture had failed and in that bleak winter they acknowledged it and prepared to retreat. 'The winter has been truly awful,' he wrote to Frank Webb, 'the fogs here are terrifying & make me very ill: yesterday [7 February 1891] all day & today until two o'clock we have been in a sort of yellow darkness. I groped my way to church this morning & returned in an hour's time a weird & blackened thing with a great & giddy headache.' The weather always seems colder when the world is indifferent to one's work, and Elgar was not the first nor the last man from the provinces to experience the chilling frost of London's complacent unconcern. So in January 1891 he sent out notices in Worcester about his teaching, and soon had such a response there and in Malvern that the Kensington house was vacated and in June 1891 they settled at Malvern in a house called 'Forli', named after Melozzo da Forli.

He resumed his old activities as if the intervening two years had never been: teaching; leading the orchestra for the Hereford Philharmonic and various choral societies; giving violin recitals; forming a ladies' orchestral class. It is probably from this period that an amusing story comes which Elgar many years later told to Vaughan Williams. He was sometimes driven from one teaching engagement to another in a countryman's pony and trap. On their journeys Elgar would tell his companion stories and anecdotes. One day, feeling jaded, he said: 'Now, Joe, I'm always telling you things. You tell me something for a change today.' A heavy and prolonged silence prevailed while Joe thought. Then at length inspiration came. 'Charlie Peace,' he intoned, ''e feared the rope.' Elgar's composition reverted to salon music and violin solos such as *La Capricieuse*. The London years had undermined his health, and the inevitable reaction set in: quinsy, influenza, headaches, from April until the following spring. 'Edward very mouldy' was Alice's frequent description of him at this time. This extremely sensitive and thin-skinned man felt deeply that he had failed. The composer of *Froissart* was back teaching the fiddle to genteel young ladies. 'I am not writing much now, but hope to sometimes,' was the best he could manage even to Charles Buck at Christmas.

But 1892 was to hold brighter prospects. The urge to compose returned. He began revising his Three Pieces for strings, calling the result a *Serenade*. Chanot published his *Very Easy Exercises* and his *Etudes caractéristiques*, both for violin. Novello's took his part-song 'Spanish Serenade' with light orchestral accompaniment. In May he began sketches for what, significantly, he called not a cantata but a 'symphony for chorus and orchestra': a setting of *The Black Knight*, Longfellow's translation of Uhland's ballad *Der Schwarze Ritter*, which is to be found in *Hyperion*. Here Elgar was turning to words he had known and liked from youth but one wonders, too, if Alice's advice is discernible. No English composer at that date had made a reputation from orchestral music. The ballad was a way to make one's name with the public, but not at the kind of level at which Elgar aimed. If Edward was to succeed, so perhaps she argued, then the festival choral work was the only thing. No one *made* his name at the Crystal Palace, Philharmonic, St. James's Hall, or Hallé concerts: it was there that established reputations were maintained or advanced. To attract attention, to gain a hearing from all the critics, with most of the leading lights of English musical life in the audience, it was necessary to have a work performed at one of the Leeds, Birmingham, Sheffield, or Three Choirs Festivals. If Parry, Stanford, and others could go from festival to festival collecting critical encomia, if not general acclaim, why could not Edward? Nothing is more futile than bemoaning the past, wishing things had been otherwise than they are. But this advice, if advice it was, or even if it was Elgar's own reasoning, was only partially successful. He certainly gained the hearing; he probably gained some experience; but it was nevertheless a waste of several years of an orchestral genius's life for him to set these rubbishy lines of Longfellow. The orchestra is plainly his chief interest and the chorus comes off second best: no wonder that when Novello's were reprinting the score in 1897 Jaeger asked for the words to be altered at a point where a chorus he had recently heard 'could not get the words in edgeways'. The music is vital, occasionally characteristic, but generally uneven: it is at its best when light and fanciful, at its worst in strenuous moments. There is no reason to suppose, however, that Elgar was in any way halfhearted in his approach to *The Black Knight*. It was not in his nature to write anything in which he did not fully believe, and he was certainly trying to get away from the usual deadly 'festival cantata' of the time, in many of which he had played, by giving his example the character of a choral symphony. 'I intended the work to be a sort of symphony in four divisions founded on the poem,' he wrote to Jaeger on 1 March 1898, 'different to anything, in structure, ever done before, where "the picture" is fixable for a little time the words are repeated—in dramatic parts the words "go on": it's not a proper cantata as the orch: is too important.' It was a stage through which he had to go.

Working on a big undertaking chased Elgar's 'mouldiness' away, at any rate temporarily. Friends helped Alice to cheer him up, notably the

Fittons and the Bakers of Hasfield Court, near Gloucester—William Meath Baker and his sister Mary Frances. Miss Baker had been one of Alice's fellow-students of geology and she proved her friendship now by arranging to take the Elgars for a much-needed summer holiday in Germany. They went to stay at Hasfield to discuss it and Elgar took his manuscript-paper with him. Mrs. Dora M. Powell—'Dorabella' of the *Enigma Variations*—has given[1] a charming picture of Elgar that hot summer at Hasfield: 'He used to bring in hedgehogs from the woods and feed them in the house. He sat in the strawberry bed and wished that someone would bring him champagne in a bedroom jug.' They must have left for their holiday in high spirits, because on 11 June Mr. Hugh Blair, who had been acting organist at the cathedral since 1889 and with whom Elgar already had a happy musical relationship, called at 'Forli' while Elgar was working and picked up a few sheets of *The Black Knight*. 'If you will finish it, I will produce it at Worcester,' he told Elgar. Abroad, the Elgars visited Beethoven's birthplace in Bonn, heard *Parsifal* twice, *Tristan* and *Meistersinger* in Bayreuth, and spent some time in the Bavarian countryside. They came home through Nuremberg, where they saw *Cavalleria Rusticana*, then only two years old, and Heidelberg, where Elgar, to bring him luck, asked Miss Baker to stamp and post some of *The Black Knight* which he was sending to Novello's to test their opinion. On his return he wrote more songs, including 'Like to the Damask Rose', and by the end of September he had completed the sketch of *The Black Knight*. For the next six weeks, while he resumed his round of lessons and recitals, he awaited a verdict from Novello's. This arrived, favourable, on 11 November and he began to score the work on New Year's Eve. Blair redeemed his promise on 18 April 1893, when he conducted the first performance with the Worcester Festival Choral Society. Eleven days previously the Larghetto of the *Serenade for Strings* had been played at Hereford. The press notices of *The Black Knight* were respectable, but no more. Encouraged, though, Elgar journeyed to London and on 4 May left the score for Manns to see. But no performance followed. That August there was another holiday in Germany, this time to Munich, where they heard all *The Ring*, *Tannhäuser*, *Meistersinger*, *Tristan*, and even *Die Feen*. They had to be home by early September when Elgar was engaged to play in the Worcester Festival. Was it, I wonder, Parry's *Job* which caused a momentary return of depression as Elgar contrasted his lot with that of others and wrote on his festival programme: 'I played 1st violin for the sake of the fee as I cd. obtain no recognition as a composer'?

[1] *Edward Elgar: Memories of a Variation* (Second Edition, London, 1947), p.2.

5 Recognition

Recognition, of a kind, was not far away. Novello's accepted another part-song, 'O Happy Eyes', to Mrs. Elgar's words, early in 1894, and Elgar composed a ceremonial anthem for brass, organ, and strings, *Sursum Corda*, for the Duke of York's visit to Worcester in April. Holidays in Sussex and, for seven weeks, at Garmisch in the Bavarian Highlands, are a sign of more relaxed nerves. But the greatest tonic is success, a sign that one's work is wanted, and the interest shown in Elgar by Hugh Blair, rewarded by the dedication of *The Black Knight* and by orchestrating Blair's *Advent Cantata* for him, was enough to stimulate further creative efforts. In July 1894 Elgar turned again to Longfellow and began work on *Scenes from the Saga of King Olaf*. In doing so, he was not only setting a favourite poet of his and his mother's—while in Heidelberg in 1892 he had sent her a letter describing a students' torchlight procession, adding, 'I must send a line from *here* about which we have read & thought so much . . . it did remind me of Hyperion & the beer scandal etc etc'—but he was, if unconsciously, following a fashion for Scandinavian lore which can also be traced in William Morris's Icelandic Sagas, in Delius's *Fennimore and Greda*, and in Schoenberg's setting of Jacobsen's *Gurrelieder*. At the same time, on returning from Garmisch, he worked on a suite of part-songs of Bavarian Dances, to words which Alice had written in imitation of Bavarian folk-songs. She also wrote the words for two other part-songs which still rank among Elgar's finest creations in this medium, 'The Snow' and 'Fly, singing bird', for women's voices with two violins and pianoforte, though a light orchestral accompaniment was added later.

In the winter of 1894 there were two performances of *The Black Knight*, at Hereford and at Walsall. This was what Elgar must have longed for—to attract the attention of the more enterprising conductors of the flourishing choral societies in the Midlands and the North. He knew only too well that audiences, then as ever, had a built-in resistance to new musical experiences, and, from practical experience, he had a perceptive understanding of the conservative nature and limited technique of many choral conductors. He allowed Novello's to describe *The Black Knight* as a cantata because this 'wd. not frighten the mildest conductor that ever misdirected vocal miscreants whereas the bold statement that it's not a cantata at all might lead to trouble';[1] and when they told him that it was not a success commercially he confided to Jaeger: 'I think it is too artistic for the ordinary conductor of choral societies—I find they are an inordinately ignorant lot of cheesemongering idiots. The chorus & orchestra *go* for my things but the *conductors* always, or nearly always, find them too difficult—to conduct.'[2] At Hereford and Walsall, and again at Wolverhampton in February 1895, the idiots were absent and Alice Elgar recorded in her uninhibited diary that at Wolverhampton there was 'such a reception of E. Mr. Adams introduced him saying the B.K. was the work of a genius. Tremendous enthusiasm . . . Wonderful evening.' And no doubt it was, for it can be readily imagined that to choral singers inured to over-familiar classics or to the turgid church cantatas of the 1880s Elgar's exciting new idiom came as a breath of fresh air. We should not find it so today, because we know the later and greater Elgar, and we do not have to make do with the lesser; but to a choir five years before *The Dream of Gerontius* was written, there was enough challenge and adventure in Elgar's early choral works to compensate for the deficiencies of the libretto, provided adequate rehearsal-time was allotted to them. A performance of *The Black Knight* in Birmingham in 1895 nearly came to grief because the work had not been sufficiently prepared.

Now Elgar was in full spate creatively—and it should be remembered that at this time he was still having to write his music in the evenings and far into the night, perhaps after expending his energies on a long day's teaching (which he disliked) or a choir practice or orchestral rehearsal. He wrote his Organ Sonata in June 1895, continued work on *King Olaf*, accepted an invitation to write an oratorio for the 1896 Worcester Festival, and put the finishing touches to *Scenes from the Bavarian Highlands* which was performed for the first time on 21 April 1896, at Worcester. The oratorio, *Lux Christi*, to a libretto by the Rev. Edward Capel-Cure, was produced at Worcester on 10 September 1896, having been written in the first six months of the year. Its dedication, to Dr. Charles Swinnerton Heap, is of some significance. Heap, who had studied in Leipzig, was forty-nine and the leading choral conductor in the Midlands. He had founded the North Staffordshire Festival at Hanley and persuaded Elgar to conduct the first performance of *King Olaf* at Hanley on 30 October 1896. With two first performances of big works within eight weeks, Elgar's reputation took a rapid leap forward, though the tone of the critics' notices was still faintly patronizing in its encouragement of the 'Malvern composer'. *Lux*

[1] Letter to Jaeger, 9 March 1898.   [2] Letter to Jaeger, 28 May 1899.

Christi did not attract a large audience. 'It is now clear that Mr. Elgar has endowments sufficient for important results,' the *Musical Times* said. 'He is no wayside musician whom we can afford to pass and forget.' *The Times* found *King Olaf* 'a work of high importance . . . which should turn expectant eyes upon its composer'. These are cautious judgements. A reporter in the *Staffordshire Sentinel* quoted an anonymous critic as saying that Elgar was the first contemporary English composer to show 'distinct genius'. True to his usual custom, Elgar at once took the score of *King Olaf* to Manns at Crystal Palace. This time he was rewarded, and the work had its first London performance on Saturday, 3 April 1897. It was favourably received. One critic pointed out that the choir was not at full strength because of the rival attractions that afternoon provided by the Boat Race and an international football match at Sydenham. In the same year the *Bavarian Scenes* were also performed at Sydenham—to the pleasure of Sir George Grove, then seventy-seven, who preferred them to *King Olaf*—but it was still outside London that Elgar's music was most eagerly seized upon. Nicholas Kilburn, of Bishop Auckland, an enthusiastic amateur who became a close friend of Elgar, conducted *King Olaf* in April 1897. Hanley heard it again, so did Worcester. Cowen conducted it in Liverpool and Bradford in 1897 and in Manchester at a Hallé Concert in December 1898. This last performance was the occasion for a notice in the *Manchester Guardian* by Arthur Johnstone, its music critic since 1896, and at thirty-seven the most gifted of the new generation of critics. He found *King Olaf* 'fragmentary and incoherent', mainly because 'he throws away the resources of his remarkable art upon a text that is in places unfit for any kind of musical treatment', but prophesied that something of lasting value would follow when Elgar found the right subject. It is to Johnstone's credit that he was one of the few to recognize 'something of value' when it arrived and to proclaim it as a masterpiece.

It was not *King Olaf* that made Elgar's name in London. Queen Victoria celebrated her Diamond Jubilee in 1897, an occasion for national rejoicing in which Elgar, a monarchist and a Conservative (though with certain radical leanings), wholeheartedly joined. In preparation for the event he had written an *Imperial March* and sent it to Novello's early in 1897. At the same time he revised a short choral work *The Banner of St. George*, which had been sung in St. Martin's Hall, Trafalgar Square, in March 1895. It was these two works, especially the March, which caught the Londoners' imagination in 1897 and made Elgar's name well known. But Elgar's letter of 9 January 1897, accompanying the score of the March, shows how insecure his position still was. He hoped it might be of 'material good' if permission were sought to dedicate it to the Queen; he knew Sir Walter Parratt, Master of the Queen's Musick (having met him the previous autumn during London rehearsals of Lux Christi) and would ask him, 'unless there is a recognised way unknown to me'. The letter ends: 'I shall be glad to hear your views as to the above points & as to terms: I should not have mentioned the last item, but that the Term will shortly recommence & it will depend entirely upon this matter whether I return to teaching or continue to compose—or try to?' This was still the rub. If it had not been for Alice's small private income things might have been even harder for Elgar, and his natural pride made him ashamed of relying on her money. They lived economically but spent money on whatever they thought might further Edward's career. He belonged to a London club, for instance, and travelled fairly often to London to attend Covent Garden or Richter and Lamoureux concerts: to hear great music well performed was as essential to him as food and drink. If one looks at the growing number of Elgar performances in 1896–8, one might think that success in a material sense had come to him at last as he entered his forties, but there was little to be made from cantata performances and it still rankled that London had heard so few of his larger works. In 1897 he wrote to the secretary of the Philharmonic Society at whose concerts he was 'naturally anxious to obtain a hearing . . . and should be glad to introduce an orchestral work, not necessarily a long one, during your post-Xmas season'.[1] On being told that any work submitted would receive careful attention, Elgar replied that he did not intend to submit any work of his to a board of directors. At the same time he wrote to Charles Villiers Stanford, whom he had met with Swinnerton Heap in 1896, asking for the chance of a performance by the Bach Choir. Stanford replied that the moment was financially inopportune and added, 'You need not worry over the slowness of societies in London to take up your works. You're better off in the way of performance than many others. . . . Composers' names to attract entrepreneurs must now end in "vitch" or "offski" '—a complaint stemming from the growing interest in London in Russian music, particularly Tchaikovsky's.

If London remained impervious to all except patriotic works, the Three Choirs had asked for another work, for the 1897 meeting at Hereford, and Elgar had written a Te Deum and Benedictus dedicated to Dr. George R. Sinclair, organist of Hereford. Of more significance than the composition itself is that it was this work which first brought

---

[1] Robert Elkin, Royal Philharmonic (London, 1947), p. 93.

Elgar into personal contact with August Johannes Jaeger, nearly three years his junior, who had come to England from Düsseldorf in 1878 and joined Novello's in 1890 as a music reader, when the firm was in Berners Street and controlled by Alfred Henry and Augustus James Littleton. With his continental and cosmopolitan background, Jaeger found himself out of sympathy with the music of Parry and especially with those other composers of songs, anthems, and church cantatas on whose sales among organists and drawing-room ballad singers Novello's largely relied. Consequently for much of the time he was out of sympathy with his employers. At the time of his first contact with Elgar he was publishing office manager and responsible for all the detailed work of putting a general publishing programme into effect. He was never the firm's official adviser on music though in the course of time the soundness of his judgement came to be respected. The advent of Elgar was a revelation, and he recognized his stature at once. 'I am forever pushing, and have pushed since I played through your *fine Black Knight*, Mr. Elgar's claim to attention . . . I am conceited enough to think that I can appreciate a good thing and see genius in musicians that are *not* yet dead, or even not yet well known, or Cathedral organists, or Directors of music in colleges for boys . . . Our Editor and other good folk keep on saying very clever, *very* clever etc etc and I say hang your cleverness, *that* won't make *any* music great and "alive".'[1]

This was a strain which found a ready, perhaps too ready, response in Elgar's nature. To Jaeger he confided his secret hopes and his suppressed anger. When Jaeger first wrote to Elgar on 3 August 1897 about the *Te Deum*, which Novello's had accepted at the end of June— 'Mr. Jaeger quite as enthusiastic as he should be over E's music for Hereford', Alice characteristically wrote in her diary—Elgar's reply was revealing. 'You praise my new work too much—but you understand it;—when it is performed will anyone say *anything* different from what they wd. say over a commercial brutality like the "Flag of England" [a setting of Kipling by Sir Frederick Bridge] for instance: naturally no one will & the thing dies and so do I.' Jaeger's reply 'put new heart' in Elgar who answered: 'Please do not think I am a disappointed person either commercially or artistically. What I feel is the utter want of *sympathy*; they i.e. principally the critics lump me with people I abhor—mechanics.' It is sometimes said that 'in later life' Elgar developed the pose that he was no longer interested in music. In fact it was an attitude he adopted all his life, perhaps as some form of

[1] All extracts are from the Jaeger–Elgar correspondence in the Elgar archives at Worcester and published in *Letters to Nimrod* (London, 1965), ed. Percy Young.

defence mechanism. In early letters to Jaeger in 1897 and 1898, for instance, occur: 'I have no intention of bothering myself with music' and 'I'm really giving up *all music* & am refusing everything—I cannot afford to waste my precious few years of remaining out door life—so I fish etc. Much better than your damned old blasted music.' And this, more seriously (19 October 1897): 'Look here! in two years I have written Lux Xti, King Olaf, Impl. March, S. George, Organ Sonata (big), Te Deum. Recd £86 15. Debtor £100—after paying my own expenses at two festivals. I feel a d—d fool! . . . for thinking of music at all. No amount of "kind encouragement" can blot out these simple figures.'

These first letters also throw light on Elgar's views, at this time, of his contemporaries and of English musical life. He was no intriguer. In 1893 when a 'plot' was contemplated for removing a local Worcester conductor Elgar wrote to one of the plotters, 'Much as I should love to be at the head of something which might lean to the artistic . . . I feel that the existing order cannot be done away . . . I am too law-abiding (& lazy?) to lead a revolution.' Similarly after London rehearsals of *Caractacus* in September 1898, he wrote to Jaeger: 'I am not really bitter and my heart warms to anything like naturalness and geniality . . . but I detest humbug and sham and can't talk it well. Q's Hall seemed reeking with it. . . .' Again, 'A 3-choir festival always upsets me—the twaddle of it and mutual admiration'. But, provoked by Jaeger's barbs, the resentment he felt against other composers burst out time and again. Jaeger wrote occasional criticism for the *Musical Times* and resented having had to tone down adverse comments on Parry's *Magnificat* (because both the magazine and Parry's music were published by Novello's) although he rightly acknowledged that 'Parry of all men in England is the one who would not take offence at one's opinion if sincerely stated.' 'Parry's Variations are very good,' he wrote to Elgar in 1898, 'but as usual badly scored.' 'I cannot stand Parry's orchestra,' Elgar answered. 'It's dead and is never more than an *organ part arranged*.' (He had not then heard the *Symphonic Variations* and evidently changed his opinion by 1922 for, mistaking Vaughan Williams's comment 'I suppose this ought to be considered bad orchestration' for a criticism of Parry, Elgar turned on him 'almost fiercely' at the Three Choirs Festival that year and said, 'Of course it's not bad orchestration, this music could be scored in no other way.')[1] 'You are wrong in thinking I don't like some "forms" of music,' he told Jaeger in 1898. 'Anything "genuine" and natural pleases me—the stuff I hate and which I know is

[1] A 'Musical Autobiography', *National Music and Other Essays* (London, 1963), p. 182.

ruining any chance for good music in England is stuff like Stanford's which is neither fish, flesh, fowl nor good red-herring.' Jaeger often sent him the scores of works by other composers published by Novello. Early in 1898 he sent him some of the music of the American composer Horatio W. Parker (1863–1919). This brought on the following: 'I want to see S. *Christopher* soon but I must work and weep over my own tunes for a little. *Hora Novissima* contains more "music" than any of your other Englishmen have as yet managed to knock out including Parry Stanford Mackenzie—these great men seem to be busily employed in performing one another's works.'[1] He was ready to help young and struggling composers and recommended Coleridge-Taylor's name to the Gloucester Festival: 'I should *dearly* like to see a clever man get on and upset the little coterie of "3-choir hacks".' He knew what went on in these affairs—'the disgusting thing is that if two men at the top of the scaffold (I mean *tree* but in their case it shd be gallows) said the word they shd. say, the thing wd be done—but Somervell is the only person they are not afraid of! in the way of honest rivalry.' But Coleridge-Taylor was asked for a work and Elgar hoped he would not write anything 'too startling'—'of course he will want to show the critics what's in him but the easy going agriculturists who support these things also want a tiny bit of consideration'. He was under no illusions about the public. When Jaeger suggested that he should set the Jabberwocky poem from *Alice Through the Looking Glass*, he replied, 'The English never take to anything of that sort—treated mock-heroically—the whole book of "Alice" is now on the stage done by children—go & see it & weep—I know my twaddly grown up countrymen & women & am sick of 'em.' He was always on edge during rehearsals of a new work and perhaps his fiercest outburst came after preliminary Leeds rehearsals of *Caractacus* in August 1898, when Alan Gray was also rehearsing a work, *Song of Redemption*, for the Festival. 'It makes me, an artist, sick to see that fool Gray allowed as long to rehearse his blasted rot as I am who produce with all its many faults an attempt at something like a "work".' Nor can he have endeared himself to his 'rivals' by his reply, reported in the press in July 1899, to a light-hearted question by the 'Tonic Sol-fa Herald' about the best way for a professional musician to enjoy his summer holiday: 'The ordinary professor might study music, if not too violent a change.'

[1] Dr. Percy Young, in *Letters to Nimrod*, pp. 8–9, has interpreted this mention of *Hora Novissima* as the first reference in any extant document to *The Dream of Gerontius*, on the grounds presumably of Gerontius's 'Novissima hora est'. But Elgar is clearly referring to Parker's oratorio *Hora Novissima*, written in 1893, as he has just referred also to Parker's *Legend of St. Christopher. Hora Novissima* was performed at the Worcester Festival in 1899.

If these strictures seem mean-spirited and ungenerous, they are also the measure of Elgar's frustration. He knew that his own music was better than that written by most of his English contemporaries and he saw composers, whom as yet he hardly knew, as mediocrities in professional and university posts, influential in all musical affairs. Most of the critics reviewing *King Olaf* had again drawn attention to Elgar's brilliant use of the orchestra, yet *Froissart* had hardly been played and the *Serenade for Strings* had not yet been heard complete in Britain despite its success at Antwerp in 1896 and 1898. And the years of 1898 and 1899 were years in which the *Enigma Variations* and *The Dream of Gerontius* took shape in his mind. Moreover he was now in his forties. The tone of the complaints denotes an inferiority complex, perhaps, the need to assert by denigration, but no one should underestimate the depth of the wound inflicted on Elgar by the attitude of his wife's relatives to their marriage and by the failure of his attempt to settle in London. Nor, as will be seen, should it be forgotten that with perhaps one exception he bore no grudges. He could be, and was, magnanimous. But in Jaeger he found a sympathetic outlet for repressed frustrations, and this tempted him very often, I suspect, to dramatize himself in his letters, a tendency that can be noted in some of the earlier letters to Charles Buck. It is a tendency that is sometimes reflected in the music.

At any rate one recognition came his way in December 1897, which should have consoled him: he was invited to write a choral work for the 1898 triennial Leeds Festival, then, with the Birmingham Festival, perhaps the English composer's premier platform. He had suggested another type of work, probably a symphony, but Leeds wanted a cantata, and Elgar had a subject in mind which appealed to him. The idea came from his mother, who described it in a letter to Elgar's sister Pollie. She had been staying in the Malverns and 'I said oh! Ed. look at the lovely old hill, can't we write some *tale* about it. . . . "Do it yourself, Mother," he held my hand with a firm grip. "Do" he said. "No, I can't my day is gone by if I ever could," and so we parted. And in less than a month he told me *Caractacus* was all cut and dried and he had begun to work at it.' So the work was inspired first by Elgar's passionate love of the countryside round Birchwood which he could see from his study window and by his sense of its history,[1] and partly by the wave of jubilee patriotism. The story of

[1] He told Jaeger, in August 1898: 'You will see our "woodlands" someday. I made old Caractacus stop as if broken down on p. 168 & choke & say "woodlands" again because I am so madly devoted to my woods.' Birchwood, incidentally, is in Herefordshire.

Caractacus, King of Britain, being driven towards Wales by the Romans, seeking advice from druids, being betrayed, defeated and finally pardoned in Rome by Claudius might have made a good libretto in the right hands, but unfortunately Elgar turned again to H. A. Acworth who had made some additions to Longfellow for *King Olaf*. In this case he had the field to himself and, at Elgar's prompting, let himself go at the end in what Sir Arnold Bax called 'a regrettable chorus' for the Romans who see 'glorious ages coming' when the Roman Empire crumbles and is replaced by the British. But it was what Elgar wanted and he wrote most of the music in the spring of 1898, having now rented a cottage, Birchwood Lodge, near Malvern, where he could go for weekends or for weeks at a time in the summer to have complete and undisturbed quiet. His terms from Leeds were £100 but he had to provide the chorus and orchestral parts. He felt he was writing well—'Caractacus frightens me in places,' he told Jaeger on 1 March 1898—but as usual he was on edge and seven weeks later he was hoping that Sir Frederick Bridge, who was to rehearse the chorus, would not see early proofs: 'If he didn't like it, his remarks, *altho' not unkind*, might prejudice me—for instance if he said (in Aug. or Sept.) that it wd not do for the Albert Hall everybody would hear of that and there would be ructions.' He sent it scene by scene as completed to Novello's and thanked Jaeger 'for not saying *one word* about the work, either for or against, and *please don't yet* or I shall surely die being on edge.' When the first sketch was finished and Elgar began to orchestrate it, Jaeger had plenty to say, and his first target was Acworth's libretto, the final chorus in particular. Elgar's replies are interesting: 'By all means will I ask Acworth to eliminate the "truculent note" in the lines! Any nation but ours is allowed to war-whoop as much as they like but I feel we are too strong to need it—I *did* suggest that we should dabble in patriotism in the Finale, when lo! the *worder* (that's good!) instead of merely paddling his feet goes and gets naked and wallows in it: *now* I don't think he meant by "menial &c" Germany &c, more probably hill tribes and suchlike—jealous evidently, refers to anybody you like.' Three weeks later: 'I knew you wd. laugh at my librettist's patriotism (& mine) never mind: England for the English is all I say—hands off! there's nothing apologetic about me.'[1] It was about this time that he wrote to Joseph Bennett: 'I hope some day to do a great work—a sort

[1] He wrote to Jaeger on 5 November 1899: 'It's no good trying any patriotic caper on in England: we applaud the "sentiment" in other nations but repress it sternly in ourselves: anything like "show" is repugnant to the *real* English—whom you don't know or understand yet nor ever will.'

of national thing that my fellow Englishmen might take to themselves
and love.'

The first choir rehearsals of *Caractacus* were at Leeds on 9 July 1898.
Elgar did not look forward to them: 'a day of dread for me,' he wrote
to Jaeger. 'I can face any orchestra under the sun, the players always
enjoy new effects, but a chorus looks so disgusted if they haven't a
shouting four-pt yell from beginning to end.' In view of what was to
happen at Birmingham with *Gerontius*, this attitude to choruses, the
result of practical experience, is important. Proof-correcting went on
throughout July—Elgar, who loved puns, referring to it as 'correct-a-
cuss'. In one letter he says: 'As to waiting till after the performance
before duplicating the wind, I don't know—I never *have* had to alter
anything but I am very dubious about myself when you suggest waiting'; which, besides being a handsome compliment, is a magnificent
expression of self-confidence in the certainty of his orchestral effects.
More rehearsals at Leeds followed in August, when Elgar met Sullivan,
chief conductor of the festival and by now a sick man, and was able
to tell him of the 1884 incident when Sullivan took up Elgar's rehearsal-
time at Covent Garden. Now the older man made up for that occasion,
of which, of course, he had been unaware, by refusing to rest while
Elgar went through *Caractacus*. Instead he made notes of points which
struck him and was generally helpful. Having heard the work again
Elgar could write to Jaeger (29 August 1898): 'I will alter no more of
C. short of burning the whole thing.'

The first performance was on 5 October. This time the Queen had
accepted the dedication. Most of the celebrities of British music were
present, and Elgar met Parry for the first time. Cowen was there and,
from France, Gabriel Fauré. So too was a cross-section of Elgar's Worcestershire friends, from Lady Mary Lygon, sister of Earl Beauchamp,
of Madresfield Court and a pioneer of the musical festival movement,
to Dr. Sinclair, the Hereford organist, and some Malvern pupils.
Nicholas Kilburn came from Bishop Auckland. The soloists were
Medora Henson, Edward Lloyd, Andrew Black, and John Browning.
All was set for a triumph, but this did not happen. The performance
was not as good as it might have been. Miss Rosa Burley, a Malvern
school teacher, who was present, wrote that the kind of chorus which
Elgar had in mind 'did not then exist. . . . The [Leeds] chorus revelled
in the straightforward Handelian choruses & were inclined to resent
Elgar's music which they found finicking and fidgety. They could not
let themselves go, full blast, as they had always done.' The critics were
polite. But at least Edward A. Baughan, in the *Musical Standard*,

devoted two pages to it. He wrote much of the cantata's 'failures', but about its 'excellent workmanship' he had this to say: 'The elaborate and appropriate use of representative themes has never been approached by any living, native composer; the symphonic accompaniment is varied and elastic; the harmony . . . has always the merit of sounding natural and unforced . . .; and the whole texture of the music flows on from note to note with an easy mastery which proclaims Elgar a composer of decided gifts. You may say of him with truth that he writes *music*. . . .'

This delighted Elgar who sent it to his friend the Malvern architect Arthur Troyte Griffith with the comment that it was 'the first to give me the place I've fought for'. *The Times* remarked that the cantata suffered from 'an excess of detail, not from any absence of interest or individuality', and the *Musical Times* detected 'signs of haste in the vocal writing' but found that the score contained 'sufficient material to set up half-a-dozen average composers for life'. Arthur Johnstone, in the *Manchester Guardian*, expressed a hope that Elgar would one day write a genuine music drama, and a few weeks later, when he heard *King Olaf* in Manchester, he declared *Caractacus* to be 'obviously a finer work in every way' than its predecessor. These are hardly bad notices, even if they are not ecstatic, but on his return to Malvern Elgar relapsed, as he usually did after a big work, into his mood of depression and dislike of music, even though he found awaiting him a letter asking for a work for the 1899 Norwich Festival. 'No—I'm not happy at all,' he wrote to Jaeger on 20 October, 'in fact never was more miserable in my life: I don't see that I've done any good at all: if I write a tune you all say it's commonplace—if I don't, you all say it's rot—well I've written *Caractacus*, earning thro' it *15/- a week* doing it, and that's all —*now* if I will write any *easy*, small choral-society work for Birmingham, using the fest. as an advt.—your firm will be "disposed to consider it"—but my own natural bent I must choke off. No thank you.' In the same letter he mentions his idea of a symphony about General Gordon (possibly the work he originally wanted to write for Leeds), a project which Jaeger did everything to encourage. ' "Gordon" sym. I like the idea but my *dear* man *why* should I try?? I can't see—I have to earn money somehow & it's *no good* trying this sort of thing even for a "living wage"! and your firm wouldn't give £5 for it—I tell you I am sick of it all! Why can't I be encouraged to do decent stuff & not hounded into triviality.'

Four days after getting this petulant but accurate grumble off his chest, he was reporting to Jaeger that he had been sketching 'a set of

Variations on an original theme'. Truly the ways of genius are unaccountable.

At least Elgar's growing fame had given him an even higher standing in Worcester. As far back as October 1897 he had thrown himself heart and soul into the formation with Miss Martina Hyde, a solicitor's daughter and pupil of Elgar, of a new musical society in Worcester, the Worcestershire Philharmonic, with himself as conductor. He saw in it a chance, as he told Jaeger in October 1897, 'to do something novel— in fact if they are not disposed to let young England whoop I shall not take it on'. As the society's motto he chose 'Wach auf'—'Wake up'. The first concert was on 7 May 1898, with the first English performance of a work by Humperdinck. Winifred Norbury was joint honorary secretary and Lady Mary Lygon a member. Ivor Atkins, Blair's successor as Worcester organist, was a founder member. The society, for which Elgar wrote the programme-notes, played plenty of English works: Cowen's *Idyllic Symphony*, Parry's *The Lotos-Eaters*, Mackenzie's *Dream of Jubal*, Bantock's *Russian Suite*, Stanford's *Last Post*, and music by Percy Pitt, Sullivan, and Walford Davies. There was, for that date, a high proportion of French music: Delibes, Massenet and Chabrier, as well as Gounod and Berlioz (*The Childhood of Christ*, 'a work of real atmosphere & charm', said Elgar). There was some, but not much, Elgar. 'We *must* do things properly whatever the cost' was his approach, and the performances reflected it. He retained the post of conductor until 1904, when he handed over to Granville Bantock.

Several of the Elgars' circle of friends have by now entered this narrative—the Norbury sisters Winifred and Florence, Rosa Burley, Dora Penny, the Bakers, Troyte Griffith, Lady Mary Lygon, the Fittons. Others saw him often: Matthew Arnold's son, Richard, and his wife; Father Bellasis of Birmingham Oratory, Hew Steuart-Powell and Basil Nevinson, who joined Elgar for chamber music performances in their homes. Most of them saw a different Elgar from the man revealed in letters to Jaeger—perhaps only Alice saw his other side ('a woman's not worth a damn who won't put up with everything except ineptitude and crime', he confided to Jaeger). His high spirits with friends were infectious. He loved his 'japes', as he referred to any 'larks'. He played golf, went cycling, beagling, and hunting. He had a passion for flying kites. Among other hobbies was the intricate and skilled one, requiring great patience, of poker-work. At Birchwood he killed snakes in the garden and enjoyed working outside; as he told Jaeger 'I've been cutting a long path thro' the woods like primitive man only with more clothes'. What, one wonders, did the earnest, sickly little

German at Novello's in Berners Street make of some of the information casually included in letters from his great English composer—'Fox hunting yesterday. No proof-correcting done.' 'There aren't any badgers now—they've gone and deserted the "earth" near us. Never mind, I'll track 'em further away. I *should* like to send one in a sack to Berners Street.' 'I'm fishing & have ruminated over your letter.' 'I am . . . sitting in my shirt with my feet in a bucket of water (it's hot) drivelling.' 'I'm just off to the Beagles & shall be away all day—no music like the baying of hounds after all.' 'I had friends coming & my brain (?) has been a fog of Horse talk, Hound jaw, Fox gossip and Game chatter.' 'You live too well for a composer, you lucky fellow', Jaeger retorted.

To his county friends, even the musical ones, Elgar seemed the very reverse of the usual idea of a composer. He was so normal and healthy, and he didn't even *look* like a composer as W. H. Reed, the violinist and intimate friend and biographer of Elgar, discovered as a young man when, in 1898, he played in the orchestral rehearsals in London of *Caractacus* and later left this unforgettable picture:[1] 'A very distinguished-looking English country gentleman, tall, with a large and somewhat aggressive moustache, a prominent but shapely nose and rather deep-set but piercing eyes. It was his eyes perhaps that gave the clue to his real personality: they sparkled with humour, or became grave or gay, bright or misty as each mood in the music revealed itself. His hands, too, gave another clue: they were never still even when he was not conducting; they moved restlessly, turning up the corners of the pages of the score or giving some indication by a gesture of what he wanted . . . but they were always eloquent, always saying something and giving an inkling of the extreme sensitiveness of his mind and character. He looked upstanding, had an almost military bearing . . . The orchestra, it is almost needless to say, adored him . . . He was practical to a degree, he wasted no time . . . He obtained all he wanted from his executants by the movements of his delicate and well-shaped hands, by his eyes, which expressed the whole gamut of emotions, and by his whole facial expression, which lit up in an amazing manner when he got the response he desired and when his music throbbed and seethed as he intended that it should.'

That was Elgar in his forty-second year. Suppose he had died then what would his reputation have been? I think he would have now had a position akin to that of George Butterworth, leaving behind in *Froissart* and the *Serenade* two works of accomplishment and even more promise. The cantatas might be heard as curiosities, as they are now;

[1] *Elgar*, pp. 50–51.

the trifles would have survived, too, as evidence of a delicious melodic charm which never reached maturity. Just to look at the list of his works as completed by 1898 brings back the flavour and taste of a distant epoch—*The Language of Flowers, The Wind at Dawn, Like to the Damask Rose, Love Alone will Stay, Sérénade Lyrique, Salut d'Amour, Chanson de Nuit, A Soldier's Song, Sursum Corda, O Happy Eyes, King Olaf, Imperial March* . . . Elgar dead at forty-two would not rank so high as Vaughan Williams supposing V. W to have been killed at exactly the same age when he enlisted in 1914. Vaughan Williams would have left the *Songs of Travel, Toward the Unknown Region, On Wenlock Edge*, the *Five Mystical Songs*, the *Tallis Fantasia*, and the *Sea* and *London* symphonies as much richer hostages to fortune. Nevertheless it is profitable to look more closely at those early Elgar cantatas for they did, after all, make his name known as a man of individuality who was 'always himself'—the phrase occurs several times in the reviews of those days. Into everything he wrote he poured himself with uninhibited zest and self-confidence. 'I hold nothing back,' he said. 'It's jolly good, it *is* a damned fine piece of work,' he told Jaeger about *Caractacus*, and '*King Olaf is* a mighty work. Wot ye this? . . . Him wot rote it.' He knew the virtues of the *Serenade*: 'really stringy in effect'. Of *Froissart* he said 'What jolly *healthy* stuff it is—quite shameless in its rude young health.' When he heard the Sheffield chorus in *King Olaf*: 'Never complain of my choral effects again—they're grand and mighty when properly sung.' 'Anybody with any *real* feeling (emotion) was quite stricken and overcome by "Lux Xti"—Albani was quite tearful over the expression of it, so was I. It is naïve but there is nothing else like it—most of the critics don't think that a good thing but the audience don't care—they love it.' This is not conceit, for it shows how complete an extension of Elgar's personality his music was. In one of his first letters to Jaeger, in 1897, he put the point memorably: 'My music, such as it is, is alive—you say it has heart. I always say to my wife (over any piece or passage of my work that pleases me): "If you cut that it would bleed!" *You* seem to see that but who else does?'[1]

What is lacking in *King Olaf, Caractacus*, and *Lux Christi* is a sense of discrimination, part of the price to be paid for self-education and a non-academic training, although exuberance is a fault on the right side. Music came easily to him: he thought music all day long, and he was sometimes too willing to accept what came to him as heaven-sent inspiration. He confessed that he regarded himself as a medium for

---

[1] This phrase about music 'bleeding' was evidently a favourite with him. It occurs in the Birmingham lectures.

music, and he did not mind whether the expression of it was lowly (*Salut d'Amour*) or lofty (*Froissart*) as long as it was done with a professional touch, a well-turned-out article. He never wrote a shoddy or untidy note. But a drawback in this willingness to provide music for all sorts and conditions of men and occasions was that he was not always able to sustain the initial enthusiasm: the early works are all uneven and betray their origins as commissions or offerings to festivals. The libretti, for choice of which the composer must bear responsibility, hardly made his task any easier: their material is not such as to set a composer's imagination alight and keep the flame burning. So these works are significant only for isolated episodes: the Gounod-esque Meditation (prelude) to *Lux Christi* and the tenor solo in that work in which the blind man gives thanks for the restoration of his sight; the attractive opening scene of *The Black Knight*. Best as an entity is still *King Olaf*, with its swaggering opening 'Challenge of Thor', vividly orchestrated, the superbly written and easy-flowing narrative of King Olaf's Return, and the theme representing Astrid. The choral writing is imaginative and vigorous, requiring a big virtuoso Northern choir, and if only the libretto was not so fatuously disconnected and scrappy, the whole work would be worth more than occasional revival. As it is, it is worth hearing for its cornucopia of the future Elgar. In the early 1920s Sir Henry Wood visited Elgar who played *King Olaf* through on the piano and exclaimed 'By Jove, Henry, what jolly fine tunes! I couldn't write them today!'[1] In April 1924, Elgar wrote to Troyte Griffith: 'If I had to set K.O. again I shd. do it just in the same way— the atmosphere is "right" & the technique—I have never done anything like "Dead rides" etc. but you have never heard it with a big Yorks. chorus.'

There are plenty of anticipations, too, in *Caractacus*, but its libretto is even worse and it epitomizes all the faults of the dramatic cantata— neither drama nor cantata. The wish has sometimes been expressed that it could have been an opera (it was performed in costume in Liverpool in February 1928) but putting these cardboard characters into fancy costume, even into woad, will not give them the life they lack in evening dress. Jaeger, in a letter to Elgar in December 1901, made this shrewd plea: 'Don't cook up *Caractacus* for Covent Garden. It will never do. Write a real opera, & wait a year or two . . . You can't alter a cantata into an opera, no one can . . . I cannot imagine Englishmen or Englishwomen, however operatically fashionable & blasé, enjoying Britons being shown on the stage under the conqueror's yoke . . . I

[1] Henry J. Wood, *My Life of Music* (London, 1938), p. 357.

have studied *Caractacus* again & cannot see anything operatically effective in it, except the Love Duet & the March with Britons tied captive
to the conqueror's "wheels". DON'T!!!' The *Sword Song*, the description of morning by the Severn, the British Camp at night, the exquisite
love music, the *Triumphal March*: all these are colourful and picturesque,
and would have made an excellent suite. But the work as a whole, ambitious in concept, falls short of its aim. It is difficult to escape the conclusion that in many respects these cantatas are not really much better
than some of those about which Elgar and Jaeger felt so scornful.
Their chief merit, apart from being by a man of genius, is that they
are never enervating. Their faults are big, just as their virtues are. If
Elgar had, at any time of his life, been a selective and 'refined' composer
he would have been untrue to his real nature and would certainly have
been that much less great and individual a music-maker. These early
works reflect the emancipation of provincial musical life from the
sacred cantatas of the 1880s to the adventures of the 1900s. Something
has already been said about Elgar's musical ancestry, favouring
Schumann and Dvořák rather than Brahms and Wagner. Nor should
the French composers be forgotten, in particular Massenet, whose
harmonies often recall Elgar, or vice versa, and the delicacy of Delibes.
One has only to listen to the orchestral version of the *Bavarian Dances*,
especially the famous 'Lullaby', to appreciate the clarity of the scoring
and that Elgar, long before Thomas Beecham, had perceived the
essential grace and style of the best French light music. Listen to
Massenet's *Last Sleep of the Blessed Virgin*, for strings, and you might
almost be listening to an extra slow movement from Elgar's *Serenade*.
This probably also explains the curious resemblances between Elgar's
music and that of Fauré, his nearest French contemporary. Elgar
admitted that a particularly Wagnerian moment in *Cockaigne* was
suggested by a passage in Delibes' *Sylvia* ballet. He shared with
Vaughan Williams and Stanford a genuine and unfashionable admiration for the music of Meyerbeer which he knew well. Some of the
ceremonial strain in Elgar owes a debt to Meyerbeer. Wagner of course
was an inescapable influence on every composer of the rising generation
in the last twenty years of the nineteenth century. Elgar spent his
savings on seeing Wagner operas abroad; Vaughan Williams took his
wife on honeymoon to Berlin in 1897 so that he could hear *The Ring*
without cuts; Cecil Sharp and Gustav Holst were Wagner addicts, and
so were many more. That a *Parsifal* atmosphere can be breathed in
Gerontius is hardly to be denied, but Gounod and Massenet are there
too. Wagner's influence on Elgar was attributed from *King Olaf*

onwards to Elgar's use of the system of leitmotives, or leading (representative) themes, which dominates *The Ring*. But in the *Musical Times* of October 1900 he disposed of this theory: 'I became acquainted with the representative-theme long before I had ever heard a note of Wagner, or seen one of his scores. My first acquaintance with the *leitmotiv* was derived (in my boyhood) from Mendelssohn's *Elijah* and the system elaborated from that.' He made a neat point to Jaeger who, at the beginning of their correspondence in 1897, was evidently talking in Wagnerian similes. 'It is nice to be told I am a sheep,' Elgar wrote, 'but after all a bell-wether *is* something.'

So, in 1898, Elgar had at last the national fame that was his due. He was 'in demand' as a festival composer. Norwich wanted a work, and so did Birmingham. Yet instead of feeling on the crest of the wave, he was utterly discouraged by the lack of appreciation of his work by A. H. Littleton of Novello's. He unburdened himself, just before Christmas, to Jaeger's ready ear: 'For the last six weeks (about) I have been very sick at heart over music—the whole future seems so hopeless. I wrote to Mr. L.—because I had talked to him of it previously— about the Bir. Fest. work & he does not reply: also I have asked him how my egregious debt to the firm (K.O. &c) stands and they tell me nothing. Now I have worked steadily and honestly till I am offered all the festivals & then the firm seem to have had enough of me. I can quite understand that my big works don't pay ... but I shd. have hoped that on artistic grounds the very small remuneration I ask shd. be forthcoming for things which at least interest the better portion of the musical public. No! the only suggestion made is that the Henry VIII dances are the thing—now I can't write that sort of thing & my own heartfelt ideas are not wanted: why K. Olaf should be worthless when it's done often is a mystery to me when things by, say Mackenzie, which are never touched, shd. be good properties. You see I want so little: £300 a year I must make, & that's all. Last year I subsisted on £200. It seems strange that a man who might do good work shd. be absolutely stopped—that's what it means.'

Jaeger evidently sorted out the trouble at Novello's and replied: 'A day's attack of the blues ... will not drive away your desire, your necessity, which is to exercise those creative faculties which a kind providence has given you. Your time of universal recognition will come. You have virtually achieved more towards that in one year than others of the English composers in a decade.'

Wise, loyal Jaeger. But even he could not yet appreciate the significance of that October evening when Elgar was extemporizing at the piano for his wife. She liked a new theme and asked what it was. 'Nothing,' he replied, 'but something might be made of it. Powell would have done this.' He played another snatch and asked 'Who is that like?' 'I cannot quite say,' Alice replied, 'but it is exactly the way W. M. B. goes out of the room.' She added, with a percipience which was more than just adoring loyalty, 'Surely you are doing something that has never been done before?'

PART II

SUMMIT

1899–1913

'. . . Go, song of mine,
To break the hardness of the heart of man.'

E

6 'Variations', and the 'Friends pictured within'

In approaching the zenith of Elgar's creative life and the apogee of his national fame, it will be necessary to abandon strict chronological biographical methods and to follow his progress by means of the personal associations and early histories of some of the works, and by a closer study of his relationships with a growing circle of friends and acquaintances—and enemies. Despite his grumbling to Jaeger and his almost neurotic preoccupation with wider public and material recognition—though, as has been seen, he had in some respects a poor opinion of public taste—Elgar was fully aware that it was only in Worcestershire that he was able to work in the concentrated quiet that he needed. The peace and beauty of the countryside were as necessary a creative stimulant to him as they were to Beethoven, and he found them in full measure at the cottage, Birchwood, among the woods and within walking distance of the British Camp and all the other associations with Caractacus. When he wrote to Jaeger during the summer of 1898, he would put 'Birchwood (once more!)' or 'Birchwood (in peace)' or 'at Forli but just leaving for Birchwood Deo Gratias!' at the head of his letters. But it was from 'Forli', when the woods were 'decidedly damp and rheumaticky—unromantic just now', that on 24 October 1898 he wrote to him: 'Since I've been back [from a visit to London] I have sketched a set of Variations (orkestra) on an original theme: the Variations have amused me because I've labelled 'em with the nicknames of my particular friends—*you* are Nimrod. That is to say I've written the variations each one to represent the mood of the "party"—I've liked to imagine the "party" writing the var: him (or her) self and have written what I think they wd. have written— if they were asses enough to compose—it's a quaint idea & the result is amusing to those behind the scenes & won't affect the hearer who "nose nuffin". What think you?'

Alice was right. Nothing like this had been done before, except perhaps by Schumann in *Carnaval*, and it is tempting to wonder whence the idea came. Fritz Kreisler, according to his biographer Louis P. Lochner,[1] said that Elgar had told him that the idea for the *Variations* came from listening to Kreisler's transcriptions for violin: a

---

[1] *Fritz Kreisler* (London, 1951), p. 107.

statement, if true, which merely deepens the Enigma. Nearly three weeks after that first letter, Elgar on 11 November told Jaeger that the *Variations* 'go on slowly but I shall finish 'em some day'. He said he was possessed by the idea of the Gordon Symphony which Jaeger had suggested but 'I can't write it down yet'. Worcester—'poor old Worcester'—had asked him for a Festival symphony; he had agreed 'to do the PRINCIPAL novelty for Birmingham' (1900 Festival) and Norwich wanted something new, 'of course', for its festival—'You see,' the usual complaint followed, 'none of this will pay me a cent! So I am doing hack work—orchestrating a comic opera for another chap! for which I shall be paid. Such is life.' In fact the *Variations* were progressing well. Mrs. Powell (Dorabella) tells us in her book[1] that she first heard the pianoforte version of 'sketches, and in some cases, completed numbers' on 1 November 1898. She mentions C. A. E., R. B. T., W. M. B., Troyte, Nimrod, and her own Dorabella. 'I say—those variations I *like* 'em,' he wrote to Jaeger on 5 January 1899. The complete work was orchestrated, according to a note on the manuscript score, between 5 and 19 February 1899. Elgar wrote to Dorabella on 22 February, 'The Variations are finished & yours is the most cheerful . . . I *have* orchestrated you well.' Meanwhile Elgar, on his own initiative, had been in touch with Nathaniel Vert, agent and manager for Dr. Hans Richter, whose fame and reputation as a conductor were at their peak. Friend and interpreter of Wagner, Brahms, and Bruckner, Richter had conducted annually in Britain since 1877. Since 1885 he had been conductor of the Birmingham Festival and at this date, February 1899, he was in the final stages of long and complicated negotiations to leave the Vienna Opera and take up the post of conductor of the Hallé Orchestra in Manchester which had been offered to him immediately after Sir Charles Hallé had died in October 1895.[2] Elgar sent a score of the *Variations* to Richter in Vienna, through Vert, on 21 February, having taken Jaeger into his confidence two days earlier: 'You will see my letter to the firm about the Variations I expect; *only* for mercy's sake don't tell *anyone* I pray you about Richter becos' he may refuse. Vert is keen about it & it wd. be just too lovely for anything if R. did an English piece by a man who hasn't appeared yet . . . but I fear R. has been "got at".[3] I have begged for a very early reply from Vienna.'

[1] Pp. 12–13.

[2] For a full account of these negotiations see M. Kennedy, *The Hallé Tradition* (Manchester, 1960), pp. 97–126.

[3] Elgar evidently feared or suspected some 'plot' against his work being performed in London. He wrote about this time to Dorabella, 'Richter . . . is to see 'em in Vienna very

'A man who hasn't appeared yet.' Elgar still regarded his reputation as regional rather than metropolitan. Novello's were dubious about the *Variations* and it can be deduced from the letters to Jaeger quoted in the previous chapter that Alfred Littleton had in effect rejected them and also the idea of *The Dream of Gerontius* as the Birmingham Festival novelty. This, after all, was the period of discouragement to which the self-portraying 14th Variation (E. D. U.) was an answer—'written at a time when friends were dubious and generally discouraging as to the composer's musical future', Elgar stated. He spent the anxious weeks while Richter studied the score in moving to a new house in Malvern and in revising for publication the score of his *Three Characteristic Pieces* (the 1888 *Suite*), now dedicated to Lady Mary Lygon. Like most husbands, Elgar hated the business of moving house. 'I am awfully worried with this moving & do anything to escape,' he told Jaeger, 'I *flew* out yesterday straight across country to think out my thoughts & to avoid every one.' The house he called Craeg Lea (an anagram of C(arice), E(dward), and A(lice) Elgar) and when he got there he loved it—'my study is a dream! & the view', he told Jaeger. The view was across the Severn Valley to Gloucestershire, with the Herefordshire Beacon as background. They moved in on 21 March and almost simultaneously good news came from Richter. Elgar wrote on 26 March to Dorabella: 'Well: Richter has telegraphed that he will produce the Variations & I think "Dorabella" is to be published *separately* as well (of course) as in the set.'

The *Variations* were rehearsed for the first time under Henry Wood on 3 June 1899. Richter was to conduct the first performance in St. James's Hall on 19 June. He went through the score with Elgar on 16 June, rehearsed the work the next day and again on the morning of the 19th. The first performance was an almost unreserved success. Not only was the music fully appreciated, but the additional interest of the dedication, 'To my friends pictured within', whetted public curiosity. Only the music critic of *The Times* seemed a little peeved by being left out of the secret and wrote that 'it is evidently impossible for the uninitiated to discuss the meaning of the work'. He was guarded in his assessment but conceded that 'on the surface' the music was 'exceedingly clever, often charming and always original, and excellently worked out'. Others were less inhibited. The *Athenaeum* regretted the dedication—'the *Variations* stand in no need of a programme; as

soon and—if he is not prevented by certain London—(mystery!) will play you all in the Spring.'

abstract music they fully satisfy'—but added that the performance was 'perfect' and was 'no mere *succès d'estime*; the *Variations* will, we feel sure, be often heard, and as often admired'. It is, however, to the *Musical Times* (July 1899) that we must turn—naturally!—for the truest appreciation (the writer was Jaeger): 'Here is an English musician who has something to say and knows how to say it in his own individual and beautiful way . . . He writes as he feels, there is no affectation or make-believe. Effortless originality—the only true originality—combined with thorough *savoir-faire* and, most important of all, beauty of theme, warmth and feeling are his credentials, and they should open to him the hearts of all who have faith in the future of our English art and appreciate beautiful music wherever it is met.'

Attention was concentrated on only one of the work's two mysteries: the identities of the dedicatees. These are no longer a mystery, and more ink has since been spent on the name 'Enigma' with which Elgar headed his original theme. In the programme-note for the first performance he said: 'The enigma I will not explain—its "dark saying" must be left unguessed, and I warn you that the apparent connection between the Variations and the Theme is often of the slightest texture; further, through and over the whole set another and larger theme "goes", but is not played . . . So the principal Theme never appears, even as in some late dramas—e.g., Maeterlinck's "L'Intruse" and "Les Sept Princesses"—the chief character is never on the stage.'

This is vague enough, though it shows that there are *two* enigmas: the original theme and the unheard theme. Later, Elgar elucidated it by admitting that the 'larger theme'—strange phrase—was a tune to which the Original Theme was a counterpoint. Many friends tried to guess its identity, including Arthur Troyte Griffith ('Troyte'). He asked Elgar if it was *God Save the King* and received the reply 'No, of course not; but it is so well known that it is extraordinary that no one has spotted it'. Elgar told Dorabella he was surprised that 'you of all people' had not guessed it. She adds 'Elgar made it perfectly clear to us when the work was being written that the Enigma was concerned with a tune'. *Auld Lang Syne* has had its adherents. However, because Elgar used the word 'theme', not 'tune', a school of thought has developed which believes that the 'larger theme' is an idea, such as 'Friendship'. Still more feel that the first Enigma is Elgar himself. Arthur Johnstone, writing in the *Manchester Guardian* on 9 February 1900, remarked that 'however much the composer may call his theme an enigma . . . one can scarcely escape the impression that it represents the temperament of the artist, through which he sees his subjects; for that, and nothing else, is what forms the connecting link between any series of portraits by the same hand'. This theory is actually confirmed by Elgar in a letter to Dorabella which she prints on p. 38 of her book and the significance of which she and everyone else seem to have overlooked. Writing on 25 October 1901, and chaffing her because she has not been to see him lately, he says: 'I forget if you really are nice or if somebody only imagined you to be. So you must come and tell us whether you are as nice as', and here he quotes two bars of the Dorabella Variation, 'or only as unideal as', and then quotes the opening four notes of the Original Theme. In this context can there be any doubt that he is referring to himself as 'unideal' and therefore identifying himself with that phrase, to which the name Edward Elgar 'goes' in almost natural speech-rhythm? Further confirmation can be found in the score of *The Music Makers*, where the Enigma theme is quoted to illustrate the loneliness of the creative artist, Elgar, 'sitting by desolate streams'. Jaeger, according to W. H. Reed, called the whole thing 'a bit of Elgar's humour'. He, Lady Elgar, and the composer were probably the only people who knew the identity of the 'larger theme'. It really hardly matters any more, since no solution can assuredly be said to be correct. Other mysteries which surround the work and its first performances are more easily solved.

One of these concerns the legend that the manuscript score of the *Variations* was sent to Hubert Parry, who was greatly excited by it and, although the night was cold and wet (some versions say foggy), tucked it under his arm and took it to Richter, or to Vert, and insisted that it should be performed soon. This story has been sedulously propagated by Parry's disciples, notably Plunket Greene, Parry's son-in-law, in his life of Stanford[1] and Thomas F. Dunhill in his book on Elgar.[2] It was believed by Vaughan Williams, and Frank Howes[3] states dogmatically that the score was sent by Parry to Richter 'with his enthusiastic commendation'. There is no documentary evidence for this attractive story. It is not mentioned in the official biography of Parry; and there is no reference to it in correspondence between Elgar and Jaeger as assuredly there would have been, for whatever their views of Parry's music both admired and respected the man. In any case the facts undo it. Elgar himself sent the full score in manuscript to Vert who sent it to Richter in Vienna. Jaeger received only a pianoforte score which Elgar despatched from 'Forli' on 13 March 1899, having written three

---

[1] *Charles Villiers Stanford* (London, 1935), p. 157.
[2] *Sir Edward Elgar* (London, 1938), p. 11.
[3] *The English Musical Renaissance* (London, 1966), pp. 178–9.

days earlier, 'Shall I send the P.F. arrgt of the variations—now complete—for inspection or wait for the return of the full score?' Their references to this piano score thereafter concern its correcting for publication, which was on 9 June 1899. The first time Parry's name is mentioned is in a letter to Jaeger dated 27 June 1899, eight days after the first performance, when in a P.S. Elgar says 'I have had a nice rapturous letter from C. H. H. P. Most kind of him.'[1] This is further confirmed by Elgar's letter to Parry on 25 January 1900, which begins 'When Richter produced my Variations you sent me a very kind letter; this, naturally, you will have forgotten—but I have not & never shall—& I also remember that I said I should like to send you a score when printed.'[2] If Parry had played any part at all in bringing about the performance of the *Variations*, it is unthinkable that Elgar would not have acknowledged it in some way or mentioned it in correspondence.

A second performance of the *Variations* was due to be given a month after the first, arranged by Granville Bantock who since 1897 had been director of music at the Tower, New Brighton, a rival to Blackpool. His engagement was to provide ballroom dancing, but aided by one music-loving member of the Tower management committee Bantock promoted concerts of works by Wagner, Dvořák, and other composers. He admired Elgar's music and had chosen an all-Elgar programme for a concert on 16 July, including the *Variations* and the *Three Characteristic Pieces*. Jaeger had written soon after the first performance suggesting amendments to the finale. Elgar (writing on 27 June) was more concerned with other points which show that the Richter performance was not as 'perfect' as the *Athenaeum*'s critic believed: 'I waited until I had thought it out and now decide that the end is good enough for me . . . I always said those celli were—bar one or two—the worst in the world—and a whole heap of passages they have did not come out—including that passage (unheard) on p. 26 (I had forgotten that they actually have it with the bassoon and we never heard it). Again on p. 27 the celli got *no* tone out of those 7ths—

---

[1] Basil Maine in Volume I of *Elgar, His Life and Works* (London, 1933), p. 174, records that Parry said to Landon Ronald on the day after the first performance: 'Yesterday I heard Richter perform the *Enigma Variations* by Mr. Elgar, the finest work I have listened to for years. Look out for this man's music; he has something new to say and knows how to say it.'
[2] There is a reminder in this episode of Elgar's precarious financial position. 'A poor man may not do anything gracefully' he wrote to Parry, saying that he hesitated to 'inflict another' score if Parry already had one. He had previously inquired from Jaeger 'Tell me what you charge *me* for the full score . . . I'm afraid I can't afford it but I shd. like to give one away.' And at this same time he told Jaeger: 'I'm *awfully* hard up just now for a space, but I want to give you a score—can't you take one and put it down to me . . . I've *not* sent a score to Richter . . . I really haven't a brass farden to spare.'

I will assist 'em. You won't frighten me into writing a logically developed movement where I don't want one by quoting other people!' He then suggests waiting till after the New Brighton performance before the score is engraved, so that he can 'touch it up'.

But Jaeger persisted about the finale, saying that Richter had criticized it. Elgar, suspicious as ever of other people's motives, wrote again three days later (30 June): 'As to that finale it's most good of you to be interested & I like to have your opinion—I have my doubts as to some of the rest 'cos it's generally *suggested* to them. Now look here, the movement was designed to be concise—here's the difficulty of lengthening it—I *could* go on with those themes for ½ a day but the *Key* G is exhausted—the principal motive (Enigma) comes in grandioso . . . in the tonic and it *won't do* to bring it in again . . . In deference to you I made a sketch yesterday—but the thing sounds Schubertian in its sticking to one key. I should really like to know *how* you heard that Richter was disappointed—he criticised some of it but not the end—the actual final flourish was spoilt in performance by the insts. going wild. You see there's far too much of this sort of thing said: somebody wants to find fault . . . This sort of thing is of no value to me . . . If I find, after New B., that the end does not satisfy me, I may recast the whole of the last movement but it's not possible to *lengthen* it with any satisfaction I fear.'

By 7 July he was relenting a bit. He wrote 'I am hoping to send you a sketch of a proposed extended finale', and a day or two later, from Birchwood, he wrote 'Aha! I'm here & *at work* in my woodlands. Now: hither comes pp. 1 to 144 end of the Score and *all* the wind &c revised to 76 at this point the Jaerodnimgeresque coda cometh on—I am scoring this prestissimo. Look here—shall I put in *organ* ad lib: just at the end?' Then, on 12 July, 'You're a trump! I'm heartily glad you like the TAIL. *I do* now it's done.' The *Variations* were played at New Brighton in the original version—'Bantock *is* a brick and *really* understands things'—and the final revision of the coda was sent to Jaeger on 20 July. Dorabella was at Malvern when proofs of the new ending arrived: Elgar played it and roared with laughter adding, 'The old Moss was right' ('Old Mosshead' was one of Elgar's nicknames for Jaeger). But it is beyond doubt that wise and experienced Richter had realized the weakness of the original ending and suggested that such a fine work needed to be more convincingly clinched.[1] Elgar acknow-

[1] According to Arthur Troyte Griffith, Elgar intended the original ending to mean 'Well, we have had a very pleasant evening. I am glad to hear what you all think about it. Good night.' It can be studied in the original (June 1899) piano score.

ledged this in a letter to Richter on 5 October 1899, saying: 'Following
the advice of my friends, and I think your own view, I have added to
the Finale making a more symphonic movement of it. It only adds
between 2 and 3 minutes to the length—not more—in place of the
original abrupt ending . . . I hope you may approve of the additional
music which I feel is an improvement in form.'

The third performance, the first with the new ending, was given in
Worcester during the Three Choirs Festival in September 1899,
Elgar conducting, and Richter repeated it in London on 23 October—
'the 1st time anything by an Englishman has been done twice!!' he
jubilantly told Troyte. 'I thought it went well on Monday night,' he
wrote to Jaeger on 25 October (from Worcestershire Golf Club),
'but I wanted the finale quicker—the martial pt. anyhow. I hope you
liked it all.' Then musical politics intervene: 'I fear the "party" are very
sick at its being done again.' The work was soon in frequent demand,
but its first performance had nearly been the cause of a complete rift
with Novello's during August 1899. As has been seen, it was unusual
and fortunate, in those days, in having received three rehearsals before
the first performance—one run-through under Wood and two under
Richter. Alfred Littleton had asked Richter's agent, Vert, for thirty
shillings for hire of the orchestral parts. When this reached Elgar's ears
he went to London on 21 August, saw Littleton, had a fierce argument
with him, broke his connection with the firm and placed his next work
—*Sea Pictures*—with Boosey's. On 1 September he explained the situation to Jaeger:

I have had to write to the firm on one or two matters & have gone on just as
of old & they reply: I think we have only one 'thing' between us & that is
A. H. L.'s objection to my expression of disgust—this is very real & I can't
withdraw it—Vert has lost heaps over the old gang's orchl. attempts & did the
work as a favour—an *extra rehearsal* cost him £40—the letter to the firm containing this information was *not before* A. H. L.—my note to Vert was in reference to the fact that he had *paid* £40 as well as taken the risk of producing an
English piece & the publishers 'try it on' to get 30/- more out of him—this
certainly aroused my disgust. I would have withdrawn the expression &, if need
be, apologised as far as A. H. L. was concerned, *but—this annoyed me more than
anything—he* said V. ought to have got the extra rehearsal out of his men for
nothing!! I was shocked at the sheer brutality of the idea but he repeated it: I
confess the prospect of a rich man seriously considering the fleecing of those
poor underpaid, overworked devils in the orchestra *quite* prevented me from
feeling Xtian. If that is 'business'—well damn your business—I loathe it. Now,
my dear man, do not worry about me in the least: I have told you over & over
again that the state of music in England is simply farcical & depressing & I am

well out of the vortex of jealousy, chicanery, fraud & falsehood. I have to thank
music for your friendship & for this I am grateful.

This letter, disclosing Elgar's fellow-feeling for professional musicians,
also discloses the sheer wonder that an Englishman's music should be
given such preparation for a first performance under a great conductor. (It also discloses something of the publisher's difficulties in
being able only to charge thirty shillings for hire of parts, though in
this case the obstinate Littleton should have had the sense and tact to
forget about it.) The episode proves how strongly Richter believed in
the work, for Vert must have acted under his orders. Elgar's gratitude
to Richter never faded. In 1910, at the height of his fame, he wrote to
him: 'The man you befriended long ago (Variations), be assured this
man will never forget your kindness, your nobility, and the grandeur
of your life and personality.'

The *Variations* are, as every critic has pointed out since the first
performance, completely self-sufficient as absolute music. But something is added by knowing their biographical origins, and credit
should be given Elgar for a brilliant feat of 'absolute programme-
music' and for the skill with which he assembled his portrait-gallery
from friendships with musical associations or possibilities. The design
of the work is particularly fine: the slow, simple and dignified theme
and first variation (C. A. E.), followed by eight short thumbnail
sketches; the central 'slow movement' of Nimrod, the emotional
pivot of the work; the ballet-like intermezzo of Dorabella; a scherzo
in G. R. S., then building to a climax, three successive miniature tone-
poems, the superb cello variation (B. G. N.), the mysterious and
evocative Romanza, and the self-portraying Finale, rumbustious,
assertive, and recalling C. A. E. and Nimrod before the final 'grand
slam'. It is all carefully balanced. In some notes for pianola rolls of the
Variations issued by the Aeolian Company,[1] Elgar wrote the authorita-
tive account of each variation, carefully and often significantly phrased.

No. I, 'C. A. E.' is Alice Elgar, 'a prolongation of the theme with
what I wished to be romantic and delicate additions'. II, 'H. D. S.-P.'
is Hew David Steuart-Powell, one of Elgar's chamber music cronies.
'His characteristic diatonic run over the keys before beginning to play
is here humorously travestied in the semiquaver passages; these should
suggest a Toccata, but chromatic beyond H. D. S.-P.'s liking.' III,
'R. B. T.', Richard Baxter Townshend, is a caricature. The Variation
'has a reference to R. B. T.'s presentation of an old man in some

---

[1] Reprinted by Novello's as *My Friends Pictured Within*.

amateur theatricals—the low voice flying off occasionally into "soprano" timbre'. Dorabella expands this by dating the incident about 1895 at W. M. Baker's home, Hasfield Court. Townshend had never acted before and did so against his will. She describes him as an amiable eccentric, riding about Oxford on a tricycle with a permanently ringing bell so that people could hear him coming because, being slightly deaf, he could not hear them. 'Elgar has got him with his funny voice and manner—*and* the tricycle! It is all there and is just a huge joke to anyone who knew him well.' But if you did not know him, as Arthur Johnstone of the *Manchester Guardian* did not, you might have agreed with Johnstone's description of this Variation (9 February 1900) as 'a very unsympathetic personality, garrulous, querulous, trivial, meanly egotistic and rather ape-like'—which says rather more for Elgar's powers of musical portraiture even than Dorabella says.

IV, 'W. M. B.' is Baker of Hasfield Court, 'a country squire, gentleman and scholar. In the days of horses and carriages it was more difficult than in these days of petrol to arrange the carriages for the day to suit a large number of guests. This Variation was written after the host had, with a slip of paper in his hand, forcibly read out the arrangements for the day and hurriedly left the music-room with an inadvertent bang of the door. In bars 15–24 are some suggestions of the teasing attitude of the guests.' He was a devoted Wagnerian.

V, 'R. P. A.' is Matthew Arnold's son Richard, 'a great lover of music which he played (on the pianoforte) in a self-taught manner, evading difficulties but suggesting in a mysterious way the real feeling. His serious conversation was continually broken up by whimsical and witty remarks'—and it is these which are portrayed by the wind instruments, though Dorabella heard his 'funny little nervous laugh' in the same passages. VI, 'Ysobel' is Isabel Fitton, a member of the Malvern music-loving family whom the Elgars knew well. She was a viola player and the opening bar 'is an "exercise" for crossing the strings—a difficulty for beginners'. The big intervals, according to Dorabella, depict Miss Fitton's tall stature, and the whole movement— 'pensive and, for a moment, romantic', says Elgar—suggests that the composer was fully aware of the charms of the grave statuesque beauty whose steady gaze meets us from her photograph.

VII, 'Troyte'. This is Arthur Troyte Griffith, the Malvern architect who remained a very close friend of Elgar up to Elgar's death. The Variation is not a portrait. It merely records 'maladroit essays to play the pianoforte; later the strong rhythm suggests the attempts of the instructor (E. E.) to make something like order out of chaos, and the final despairing "slam" records that the effort proved to be vain'. Elgar added that 'the boisterous mood is mere banter'. Troyte was a great sharer in 'japes', as Elgar called the lighter side of life. He was outspoken and brusque in his manner, almost to the point of seeming uncouth. Perhaps this, too, is remembered in the music. In any case, it is hard to know why Dunhill found Elgar's account of this Variation 'impossible to believe'.

VIII, 'W. N.' is 'really suggested by an 18th century house': Sherridge, near Malvern, where the Norbury family lived. Both Winifred and Florence Norbury were music-lovers, and Winifred was part-secretary with Miss Hyde of the Worcestershire Philharmonic Society. 'The gracious personalities of the ladies are sedately shown,' Elgar wrote. 'W. N. was more connected with music than others of the family, and her initials head the movement; to justify this position a little suggestion of a characteristic laugh is given.'

IX, 'Nimrod'. Elgar admits that 'something ardent and mercurial, in addition to the slow movement, would have been needed to portray the character and temperament of A. J. Jaeger'. Then follow these important words: 'The Variation ... is the record of a long summer evening talk, when my friend discoursed eloquently on the slow movements of Beethoven, and said that no one could approach Beethoven at his best in this field, a view with which I cordially concurred. It will be noticed that the opening bars are made to suggest the slow movement of the eighth sonata (Pathétique).'

Thus Elgar firmly pins this emotional Variation to a purely musical link between the two men. In her book on the Variations, Dorabella recounts in detail (pp. 110–11) a conversation she had with Elgar in 1904 in which, she says, he described the background of 'Nimrod' as 'the story of something that happened'. Briefly, Elgar (says Mrs. Powell) was 'down in the dumps'. He wrote to Jaeger and said he was 'sick of music' and was 'going to give it up'. Jaeger wrote a 'screed' in reply, 'all about my ingratitude for my great gifts,' and suggested he should visit Elgar for a talk. They went a long walk and 'he preached me a regular sermon, pointing out that Beethoven, faced with his worries, had written still more beautiful music—"and that is what you must do"'. Either Mrs. Powell's memory played her false, or Elgar's memory telescoped several events into one, for the chronological likelihood of this story is impossible. The phrases of Jaeger about 'great gifts' are in the letter quoted in the previous chapter—'your necessity ... is to exercise those creative faculties which a kind providence has given you'—and were written in reply to Elgar's outburst about his lack of support from Novello's—'the whole future seems hopeless' etc. But Elgar's letter was written on 17 December 1898, and Jaeger's on 31 December 1898—nearly eight weeks *after* Elgar had written to Jaeger (24 October) describing the *Variations* and saying 'You are Nimrod'; and Mrs. Powell heard 'Nimrod' on 1 November. Jaeger was married on 22 December 1898, and paid no visits to Malvern. Elgar went to London and saw the couple's new home in January 1899. Probably the occasion to which Elgar referred was as early as August 1897, when he had written about 'never putting pen to paper' and had received a reply 'which has put new heart into me.' They met at the Three Choirs that September and probably it was then that the conversation about Beethoven's adagios occurred. The great piece of music has become a traditional 'requiem' for commemorating the dead; to this use of it there has been some objection, but, in appropriate cases, what could be better than this intimate record of a real friendship? 'I have omitted your outside manner & have only seen the good lovable honest soul in the middle of you,' Elgar wrote to him in March 1899. 'The music's not good enough: nevertheless it was an attempt of your E. E.'—and, in November 1900, 'What a jolly fine tune your Variation is: I'd forgotten it & have been playing it thro'—it's just like you—you solemn, wholesome, hearty old dear.' To Joseph Bennett, writing in *The Daily Telegraph* after the first performance, 'Nimrod' sounded a 'suave and meditative character ... a cheery personage beaming through gold-rimmed spectacles'. At any rate, Elgar eliminated the cheeriness by conducting it himself at a slower tempo and, in 1903, altering the metronome mark in the score from $\quad = 66$ to $\quad = 52$ and changing the direction *moderato* to *adagio*.

X, 'Dorabella' was Elgar's nickname, from *Così fan tutte*, for Dora Penny, daughter of the Rector of Wolverhampton who, as his second wife, married in 1896 Mary Frances Baker, sister of W. M. B. 'The movement suggests a dancelike lightness,' Elgar wrote; and Dorabella herself noticed many years later that he had parodied her youthful stammer. Her enthusiasm, her gifts as a musician, and her merry chatter made her a frequent and welcome guest of the Elgars at Malvern. As can be inferred from her book, she was responsive to Elgar's rapid changes of mood; and he found her a good and intelligent listener. In XI, 'G. R. S.' (Dr. G. R. Sinclair, organist of Hereford Cathedral) some injustice is done, for as Elgar noted, the Variation has 'nothing to do with organs or cathedrals or, except remotely, with G. R. S. The first few bars were suggested by his great bulldog Dan (a well-known character) falling down the steep bank into the River Wye (bar 1); his paddling up stream to find a landing place (bars 2 and 3); and his rejoicing bark on landing (2nd half of bar 5). G. R. S. said "Set that to music". I did; here it is.' Nothing more needs to be said except that Dan has further claims to immortality. Inscribed by Elgar in Sinclair's visitors' book at Hereford between 1897 and 1903 were several themes representing 'The moods of Dan'. Among them, as will emerge, were themes later to be used in *Gerontius*, *In the South*, and *The Apostles*.[1] XII, 'B. G. N.' is Basil G. Nevinson, an amateur cellist and the third member of the piano trio with Elgar and Steuart-Powell—'a serious and devoted friend. The Variation is a tribute to a very dear friend whose scientific and artistic attainments, and the wholehearted way they were put at the disposal of his friends, particularly endeared him to the writer.' Elgar stayed often at Nevinson's London home. This glorious Variation is as heartfelt as 'Nimrod' and seems to commemorate Nevinson's faith in Elgar in the days of struggle. It is also a cellist's delight.

About XIII, '***' there has been more mystification. 'The asterisks,' Elgar wrote, 'take the place of the name of a lady who was, at the time of the composition, on a sea voyage. The drums suggest the distant throb of the engines of a liner over which the clarinet quotes a phrase from Mendelssohn's "Calm Sea and Prosperous Voyage".'

The lady was Lady Mary Lygon, sister of Earl Beauchamp, of Madresfield Court, near Malvern. In 1895 she had been appointed a Woman of the Bedchamber to the Duchess of Teck (later Queen Mary) and she accompanied her brother to Australia in 1899 when at the age of twenty-seven he was appointed Governor of New South Wales. Elgar knew her through the Madresfield Festivals of Music and she became friends with him and Alice. In 1905 she married the Hon. W. H. Forbes-Trefusis and, as Lady Mary Trefusis, played an important part in the affairs of the English Folk Dance Society, becoming its first president in 1912. (She had met Cecil Sharp while in Australia.) Sketches for this Variation refer to it as 'L' and sketches for the finale show that Elgar contemplated re-introducing 'L. M. L.' Lady Mary was not in fact on a voyage at the time of composition. The *Variations* were completed by February 1899, and on 24 March of that year Elgar, in writing to Jaeger about the dedication of the *Three Characteristic Pieces*, says 'I want to know if you get the *title* done *very* soon as Lady

---

[1] Dan died on 1 July 1903. A letter to Elgar from Sinclair on that date says: 'Poor dear old Dan died an hour ago. He was my best friend.' On 6 July Sinclair wrote: 'He has a quiet little grave under the big apple tree.'

Mary is going away & I should like her to see it first . . . She is a most angelic person & I should like to please her.' Elgar then evidently had second thoughts about putting Lady Mary's initials in the published score of the *Variations* and, as by then she had sailed, he replaced initials by asterisks. Dorabella says that 'in the mind of the composer' the asterisks stood for 'My sweet Mary'.

All of which is fairly conclusive but would not, I suspect, have satisfied Ernest Newman who, writing in the *Sunday Times* on 18 November 1956, stated: 'There is much expression of personal experiences in his music, but the more tremendous these had been for him the more he resorted to either complete concealment of them from the public eye or to a playful mystification with regard to them. The famous thirteenth variation of the "Enigma" is a cardinal case in point. It is time we heard the last of the old legend that the subject of this variation was Lady Mary Lygon . . . A present-day listener to the "Enigma" must surely be devoid of all sensibility if he does not see that, whoever the human subject of the No. 13 may have been, it is a poignant brooding upon some personal experience or other that had made a profound and enduring mark on him: to take one feature of it alone, that moving sound-picture of the throbbing of the engines of a great liner and the sad quotation from Mendelssohn's *Calm Sea and Prosperous Voyage* overture would never have been wrung out of Elgar by the fact that the good lady at Madresfield . . . had chosen to go on a sea trip. A study merely of Elgar's scoring of the variation should make it clear to any person of more than average sensitivity that he was here dwelling in imagination on somebody and something the parting from whom and which had at some time or other torn the very heart out of him.'

Newman then implies that the parting concerned was that with the Leipzig girl. She and Elgar, who referred to her as his Braut, i.e. bride or fiancée, had been deeply attached. But is it putting too great a weight on this delicate miniature tone-poem to suggest that it carries the burden of lost love still longed for? Perhaps Elgar cast a fleeting glance behind him as he thought of separation by sea and land. Perhaps Mary Lygon's journey was merely a pretext, in the only tragic Variation (and the 13th), for using a quotation with Leipzig connections. The music at any rate, is full of dream-like regret.

The throbbing of the liner's engines is one of several imaginative and inventive strokes of instrumentation in Elgar's music. In the score he specifies that the effect should be obtained by using side-drum sticks for the timpani roll, but most timpanists find that they are too

PLATE I

Elgar aged 23

PLATE II

Birchwood, in summer

On the Wells Road, Malvern. Elgar with his daughter Carice, and Troyte heavy to produce the remote poetic sound Elgar had in mind. When the work was first rehearsed Elgar himself was not satisfied with the result of his directions and the famous timpanist, Charles Henderson, had the brilliant idea, since almost universally adopted, of using two half-crowns near the rim of the drum. But unless a second player is employed, Elgar has left no time for the timpanist to change from coins or sticks to ordinary timpani sticks: he must either cut short his roll or omit the first few strokes of the *naturale* which follows—a rare miscalculation.[1] It is amusing to discover from Elgar's letters to Jaeger that he was on the verge of disguising or deleting the Mendelssohn quotation. 'The pretty Lady is on the sea & far away,' he wrote on 2 May 1899, '& I meant this (originally) as a little quotation from Mendelssohn's Meeresstille u. Glückliche Fahrt—but I did not acknowledge it as the critics—if one mentions anything of the kind—talk of nothing else—so I have now cut out the reference. . . . Tell me what else reminds the critics of something else. I might alter it.' He was extremely sensitive about having his attention called to similarities between his music and other men's. Dorabella once pointed out a place in *Gerontius* which reminded her of Chopin's *Polonaise Fantaisie* and was sharply told: 'I know nothing about pianoforte music. I hate the piano as an instrument and I don't care for Chopin and I never heard the piece you mention.'[2]

XIV, 'E. D. U.' is Elgar himself 'bold and vigorous in general style', but only one side of him, and only the expression of one 'I'll show 'em' mood. E. D. U. is a paraphrase of his wife's name for him, 'Edoo', pronounced as (and no doubt derived from) the German Eduard. Dorabella[3] interestingly points out that the woodwind phrase four bars before rehearsal cue No. 73 in the full score, a phrase which also occurs in C. A. E., is a whistle with which Elgar signalled to Alice his return home or used to attract her attention. In this finale it serves to recall C. A. E. 'Nimrod,' too, is recalled in the revised section upon which he was so insistent, and the work ends in a burst of grandiose assertiveness. (The original ending was just after cue No. 76.) Whether the revised finale was an improvement remains a matter of controversy and a question of taste. It is honest in its blatancy. One does sense that the material after [76] is tacked on and that, being the thinnest in the work, it has (probably for that very reason) the thickest orchestral padding. The 'Nimrod' theme does not really suit the magniloquent treatment it is accorded in the peroration, but this insensitivity to the

---

[1] See Percival R. Kirby, *The Kettle-drums* (London, 1930).
[2] Op. cit., p. 52.　　　　　　　　　　[3] Op. cit., p. 116.

F

nature of some of his finest tunes is typical of Elgar who no doubt believed that if a tune was good it was good enough for anything. There are numerous other examples of essentially noble or delicate melodies being inflated after their first appearances to a size where they threaten to burst: the middle tune of *Froissart*, the second subject of the Violin Concerto, the 'Welsh tune' of the *Introduction and Allegro*, and several themes in the symphonies.

Out of such personal characteristics as the whistle, Dorabella's stammer, Dan's bark, W. N.'s laugh, R. B. T.'s voice, and R. P. A.'s wit, Elgar concocted a work of art which is all music, through and through, because no knowledge of the work's 'programme' is required for its full appreciation. It is the apotheosis of the miniaturist Elgar. Those who hold that there is no connection between the Elgar of the salon music and the Elgar of the major works overlook the *Variations*, which are *Salut d'Amour* and *Chanson de Matin* raised to a higher degree. The poetry present in all Elgar's slighter and lighter works pervades every bar of the *Enigma*; and so does his technical skill which in this work amounts to sleight of hand: a perfect canon embedded in W. M. B., subtle and contrasting use of tonality, rhythmical rather than melodic variations of the theme. The theme itself is superb, with the alternation of minor and major emotionally as well as functionally a master-stroke. The variations themselves are notably free, except, designedly, C. A. E. In 'Dorabella' and the 'Romanza' there is only the slightest connection with the theme. Those who find Elgar's symphonic methods too diffuse or short-winded can usually admire the *Variations* because of their epigrammatic nature. Each change of mood, each delineation of character or episode is complete in itself, a polished jewel. The orchestration is a perennial delight. As Tovey wrote,[1] 'There is many an ambitious composer of brilliant and revolutionary reputation who ought to be . . . washed in its crystal-clear scoring until he learns the meaning of artistic economy and mastery.' Here, if anywhere, is the Gallic influence on Elgar: its delicacy, fantasy, poetry, and imaginative freedom owe far more to French music, and even to Russian, than they do to Bayreuth or Vienna.[2] It is a moving and intimate work, yet it is perhaps the least subjective of all Elgar's works except the *Introduction and Allegro*; it has passion as well as humour, but it does not have the intense, secret waywardness, in terms

[1] *Essays in Musical Analysis*, v (London, 1936), p. 150.
[2] Towards the end of his life Elgar told Troyte Griffith that if the *Variations* had been written by a Russian they would have 'long ago' been produced as a ballet. He visualized the setting as a banqueting hall, with a veiled dancer as the Enigma.

of rubato, of the Violin Concerto nor the chromatic splendour of *Gerontius*. It strikes a perfect balance between the classical, the romantic, and the rhapsodic. It is Elgar's orchestral masterpiece and it is, in my opinion, the greatest orchestral work yet written by an Englishman.

For the remainder of 1899 Jaeger and Elgar attended to proofs for the publication of the full score of the *Variations*. Various inquiries about performance of the work were received, among them one from the Scottish Orchestra in Glasgow. This projected performance was abandoned and Elgar wrote (27 December) rather testily, 'When *will* those Vars: (score) be ready? I think my MS must have frightened poor [Max] Bruch at Glasgow—so they have put off the performance &, probably, I shall have to thank your firm for another entire loss of performance.' Yet only a month previously he had written: 'I don't mind altering the scores at all: nothing can make me miserable regarding my music, thank you.' Jaeger, in fact, took endless trouble to see that the score and the work were alike perfect. He had been worried still about the ending and after hearing the new finale played at Worcester and in London under Richter in October he wrote: 'I was a little disappointed that the sudden burst into E flat at [82] did not quite come off as explosively and surprisingly as I had anticipated . . . I put it down to the fact that the first fiddlers have not the short quaver rest that many of the other instruments have. They seemed at the performances to glide up to the B flat instead of sharply plunging, hammering on it as with stroke of Thor's war axe! Would it not give you a stronger B flat and a stronger E flat chord and a greater surprise if *all* instruments had the crotchet rest before [82]? . . . Excuse my impertinence.' Elgar agreed. 'I've done it to please you (grrhh!) & must put it right in the wind pts when the revision comes if it ever does.'

It was for constructive, helpful, and clear-sighted criticism of this kind that Jaeger was valued by Elgar and other composers. But he played no part in Elgar's op. 37, the *Sea Pictures*, which had gone to Boosey's because of the temporary breach with Novello's. This song-cycle was written for and first performed at the 1899 Norwich Festival on 5 October. Elgar conducted and the contralto soloist was Clara Butt, then aged twenty-six. ('She dressed like a mermaid,' he told Troyte Griffith, and to Jaeger he wrote 'She sang *really well*.') The songs were a success with the public and the critics. One of them, No. 2, 'In Haven' to words by Alice Elgar, had been written as early as 30 May 1897, when it was called 'Love Alone will Stay' and had been published as 'Lute Song' in *The Dome* in January 1898. The other four had been written at Birchwood in July 1899. Today these songs have only to appear in a programme for someone to castigate the words of the poems Elgar chose to set. In the cases of No. 3, Elizabeth Barrett Browning's 'Sabbath Morning at Sea' and No. 5, Adam Lindsay Gordon's 'The Swimmer', the criticism is justified, but the remaining three, Roden Noel's 'Sea-Slumber Song', Alice Elgar's 'In Haven', and Richard Garnett's 'Where Corals Lie' are respectable enough and certainly received the best settings. Once again, however, it is the orchestral part which commands attention, notably in 'Sea-Slumber Song' where the swell of the sea is conveyed by octaves in the strings, harp chords, and the gong struck with a sponge-headed stick. One feels, throughout the cycle, that the words evoked *orchestral* images and tunes and then had to be fitted in willy-nilly. The exception is the delightful and seductive 'Where Corals Lie'. And though Elgar makes an impassioned and convincing climax to Mrs. Browning's poem, bringing back the very characteristic violin figure that opened the cycle, he could do little for Gordon's verses except, as Ernest Newman remarked, to preserve faithfully in the musical setting the 'absurdity of rhyme'. The description by the orchestra of a stormy sea is finely done, but the big tune is altogether too rigid for its purpose, and echoes from the first song and from 'Where Corals Lie', while giving the cycle some kind of unity, only throw into relief the poverty of invention in this finale. Whereas Elgar's salon style is sublimated in the *Variations*, this cannot be said of *Sea Pictures*, where three of the songs hover precariously on the edge of drawing-room balladry and are only kept from toppling over by Elgar's orchestral taste and the perform-ance of a sensitive singer. The work as a whole bears signs of being completed in haste to meet a commission, but its best moments have a real kinship with the *Variations* and the scoring throughout is that of a mature master. The songs were performed in London two days after the Norwich performance. On 20 October Ada Crossley sang two of them by Royal command at Balmoral Castle. This was not the first mark of Queen Victoria's favour in that year: on 24 May he had been invited to Windsor by Sir Walter Parratt, Master of the Queen's Musick, to conduct at a concert marking the Queen's eightieth birth-day for which madrigals in praise of the Queen (on the lines of *The Triumphes of Oriana* for Elizabeth I and *A Garland for the Queen* for Elizabeth II) had been written by several English composers. Elgar's contribution was 'To Her Beneath Whose Steadfast Star' and his *Chanson de Matin* and *Chanson de Nuit* were also played. On 18 October, in the private chapel at Windsor, ten of Elgar's compositions were given including the *Sword Song* from *Caractacus*. 'I've all sorts of mouldy japes & things to tell you,' Elgar wrote that day to Troyte.

It was the success of the *Variations*, however, that took Elgar to the forefront. Richter's second London performance was a mark of special favour, and he lost no time in including it in his first season as Hallé conductor in Manchester where, on 8 February 1900, as Arthur Johnstone of the *Manchester Guardian* put it the next day, 'the audience seemed rather astonished that a work by a British composer should have had other than a petrifying effect upon them'. Apart from Bantock, Elgar, and Stanford, the first British conductor to take it up was Henry Wood, who put it in a Queen's Hall programme in April 1901. It is a comment on the commercial dictates of the time that a professional British conductor waited so long to perform a British work that had been generally welcomed. As Jaeger said in letters to Dorabella: 'He [Wood] has just written to me "How beautiful the Variations are!" *At last!* . . . I can assure you Wood makes these things hum. I have never heard anything more daringly devilishly brilliant & boisterous than Troyte or G. R. S. . . .' Henceforward the work was never to suffer neglect; its popularity has increased from year to year. In 1902 it was played in London by the Meiningen Orchestra under Fritz Steinbach, whose comments are illuminating. 'Here', he said,[1] 'is an unexpected genius and pathbreaker in the field of orchestration. Nowadays nearly every composer is content merely to adapt Wagner's innovations, but Elgar, as this work shows, is a real pioneer with a new technique in orchestration, combining entirely original effects with almost unique virtuosity.' Alexander Siloti conducted the first performance in Russia in St. Petersburg in 1904 and wrote to Elgar telling him of a 'very great success both with the public & with the "musical world" . . . Mr. N. Rimsky-Korsakov & Mr. A. Glazunov were particularly pleased with them'. A Moscow performance followed.

In a sense the *Enigma Variations* are symbolic: they sum up the world Elgar was leaving for the world into which they took him. In the pages of this score he remembered the scenes and friends of his days of struggle when his world seemed bounded by the Malvern Hills: friendly chamber music, amateur theatricals, local gentry, the cathedral organist, the encouraging friend in the publishing house. In 1899, when the 'friends pictured within' heard themselves in music, new friends' names occur in correspondence and Alice's diary: Frank Schuster, music-loving financier; Alberto Randegger, conductor; Hans Richter; Alfred E. Rodewald, a wealthy Liverpool amateur

[1] Edward Speyer, *My Life and Friends* (London, 1937).

musician of German descent; Alfred Kalisch, music critic and trans-
lator of Richard Strauss opera libretti; Henry Ettling, wine merchant
from Mainz and friend of Richter; Adolph Brodsky, violinist, friend of
Brahms and Tchaikovsky and since 1895 Principal of the Royal
Manchester College of Music.

Of these the closest friends were Schuster and Rodewald. More will
be said about Rodewald in a later chapter. Leo Francis Schuster was to
be a generous friend to Elgar for nearly thirty years. He devoted his
wealth to music; his beautiful Thames-side house, 'The Hut', by
Monkey Island and three miles from Maidenhead, was a meeting-
place for musicians, writers, and painters, as was his London home at
22 Old Queen Street. He was a friend of Gabriel Fauré, who wrote
many of his songs while staying at 'The Hut', and for Elgar he had a
special and close affection. He had early appreciated Elgar's talent.
Writing in August 1903 to Elgar about a concert he had attended in
order to hear a work by another contemporary composer he said:
'Don't you seriously think it good of me to go? I do it out of a Consci-
entious Curiosity, and I may add that but for this C.C. I might never
have discovered a certain E. E. perhaps a *little bit* before the ruck!'
After he had stayed with the Elgars for the Three Choirs Festival of
1903 he wrote: 'How I enjoyed those walks and talks with you,
Edward, and if my speech must have appeared only stupider than my
silence, you must make allowances for the fact that I am always, so to
speak, paralysed in the presence of genius: in the matter of friendship
we are, and I thank God for it, on terms of equality, but try as I may I
can never forget that *you* have written a "Gerontius" and I have only
listened to it!—the gap *awes* me.'

William McNaught, Charles Stanford, Percy Pitt, Hubert Parry,
Alexander Mackenzie, and Edgar Jacques were among the English
musicians whom Elgar met from time to time. Although—and this
must be remembered—he was still teaching in Malvern, he visited
London more often to go to concerts and operas, to see art exhibitions,
to lunch at Pagani's or his club. He even turned up at the first annual
general meeting of the Folk-Song Society. He had previously taken
Lucy Broadwood out to dinner and his interest had perhaps been
awakened momentarily by Kalisch and Jacques or even by Parry. He
moved the adoption of the committee's report and with that gesture
both opened and closed his connection with the folk-song revival. As
late as 1929 he was saying in public that inclusion of a folk-song in a
piece of music was a sign that the composer was shirking his job, and
to Troyte he once said: 'I write the folk songs of this country'.

A new and larger world was opening to him, but perhaps instinctively he recoiled from some of its implications and, as he always did, clung more tightly to past memories. As the nineteenth century ended, he wrote two letters on 29 December from Craeg Lea. One was to Charles Buck, with whom Alice and he had spent a few days after the Sheffield *King Olaf*. 'A patch in the old year which bears thinking of with pleasure'—the year of the *Enigma* and *Sea Pictures* triumphs—'was our little visit to Settle,' he wrote. Perhaps his melancholy mood was induced by his father's illness (William Elgar was 'just hovering 'twixt this world & the next . . . the end cannot be far away', but he recovered to live until 30 April 1906). Whatever the cause, he added a postscript which was to recur frequently: 'Oh! the mad days'. To Jaeger he sent the old lament: 'All is flat, stale & *unprofitable*'. He was in the throes of composing *The Dream of Gerontius*.

7 'Gerontius': Disaster and Triumph

Elgar was asked in November 1898 for a work for the 1900 Birmingham Triennial Festival. He wrote to Littleton of Novello's: 'Now I have to consider the subject, which must be sacred: can you suggest anything? and will your firm want the work? I want to make this my chief work . . .' Littleton did not trouble himself to reply. At first, Elgar considered St. Augustine as a subject. He told Joseph Bennett, the critic of *The Daily Telegraph*, in January 1899 that this idea had been rejected as 'too controversial: this is as I feared'.[1] He was considering 'a purely scriptural thing, but have not fully decided'. There is no clue from Elgar's correspondence for the first nine months of 1899 about progress on the work for Birmingham. But Dorabella says[2] that she heard 'a good deal' of the piano score of *The Dream of Gerontius* while on visits to Craeg Lea and Birchwood in May, June, and July 1899. On her visit on 31 July, she heard the Introduction to Part II and 'Praise to the Holiest' in nearly complete form. When Elgar asked her what she thought of the latter she replied: 'It gives me the impression of great doors opening and shutting.' 'Does it?' Elgar said. 'That's exactly what I mean.' He had been pondering a setting of Cardinal Newman's poem since Father Knight had given it him on his wedding day and they had had several discussions on reducing it to a libretto. What became the 'Prayer' theme, first heard in the Prelude at three bars after [2] was inscribed in Sinclair's visitors' book at Hereford on 19 April 1898 as a mood of the bulldog Dan musing on the order to be muzzled. During the Three Choirs meeting at Worcester in September 1899, Alice noted that 'E. walked with Father Bellasis', of Birmingham Oratory. Bellasis had known Newman. This walk has sometimes been interpreted as the starting-point for work on *Gerontius*, but Dorabella's testimony is undoubtedly accurate. It is more likely that the discussion with Fr. Bellasis was on the mundane subject of permission to use the libretto.

But in November 1899 Elgar sent Jaeger 'Judas & another scrap'. 'Judas' was a theme, later used to introduce the Angel of the Agony in *Gerontius*, which was intended for a work about the Apostles. Possibly at this point he thought still that he might provide Birmingham with

[1] Letters published in *The Daily Telegraph*, 4 September 1937.
[2] Op. cit., pp. 17–19.

'a scriptural thing', for Jaeger in reply does not refer to *Gerontius* but says, 'That "Judas" or "night" theme from your new work is a *discovery*! It makes me *shiver* when I think of the effect of soft low brass (Five Tubas, Eh! You'll get them at Bayreuth, but where else?).' It is clear that between late November 1899 and mid-January 1900, the *Gerontius* project was in the melting-pot. On 18 November Elgar wrote to Jaeger: 'I'm glad you like my idea of Judas. I'll send you another wildly expressive bit, but it's very hard to try & write *one's self* out & find that one's soul is not *simple* enough for the British Choral Society.' His next specific reference is on 10 January 1900: 'Judas is dropped! I may have some news for you concerning my works very shortly—but I am sick of the whole thing and wd. never hear, see, write or think of music in shape, form, substance or wraith again.' A letter from Elgar on 5 February 1900, in which he discusses *Gerontius*, establishes beyond doubt that the sketches he was sending to Jaeger in November 1899 were *not* in their *Gerontius* form: 'I say, that Judas theme will *have* to be used up for death and despair in this work, so don't peach.'

Littleton of Novello's was dubious about *Gerontius* for Birmingham not on theological grounds alone, but because it contained no rôle for the leading oratorio singer of the day, Mme. Albani, whose participation in a new festival work was considered essential to success. This kind of discouragement, combined with his perpetual pleading of poverty, caused Elgar (as he told Jaeger on 5 February 1900) to 'give up' the Birmingham commission, 'as I really could not afford to go on writing'. On New Year's Day 1900 G. H. Johnstone, chairman of the festival committee, and Mrs. Johnstone went to church with the Elgars in Malvern—being a Roman Catholic, Johnstone had no fears that Gerontius might prove as controversial as Augustine—and, in Alice Elgar's words 'arranged for E.'s work Birm. Fest. Deo gratias'. Johnstone offered to relieve Elgar 'of all trouble in the matter rather than lose me' and, the next day, Elgar sent a telegram accepting the terms and 'began again at former libretto'. On 12 January Elgar visited Birmingham Oratory to see Fr. Bellasis again, and set to work revising and orchestrating. To Jaeger he continued in a vein of melancholy— 'I am sick of music and all that's connected with it & long for Birchwood & pigs & cattle. . . . Music is a trade and I am no tradesman'—and he also kept up a mystifying secrecy about *Gerontius*: 'I am working away at my thing for Birmingham . . . but I have nothing to do with the publishing this time & must not talk about it even to you.' Why not, asked Jaeger, understandably, adding: 'So you are "sick of music" eh? Papperlapapp! That's what Wagner said . . . so I take it your "blues" are a good sign.' Elgar then explained the arrangements with Birmingham and that he had heard from 'nice good Mr. Alfred' Littleton on 23 January that Novello's were to publish the work. 'I am setting Newman's "Dream of Gerontius" awfully solemn & mystic. . . . Now I must go on to my Devil's chorus—good!'

On 2 March he sent forty-four pages of the manuscript score to Jaeger, with the typical injunction, 'Deal tenderly with it it's the *only* copy there is—I can't yet afford a copyist—poor divvil.' On 20 March he sent fifty-five more pages, up to the end of Part I. 'The final chos. is godly effective &, I think, not quite cheap . . . As soon as this "Dream" (nightmare) is done—I'll write such a lot of things for Ysaiah—& all the profits—I *should* dearly love to get out some of my chamber music!' This last punning remark was in reply to a suggestion from Jaeger that he should write 'a big fiddle piece' for Ysaÿe.

Proofs of the vocal score began to arrive at Malvern from 3 April.[1] Now also began the remarkable series of criticisms and suggestions about the work made to Jaeger by Elgar. Of few established masterpieces have the birth-pangs been so fully recorded, nor in such racy language. Jaeger had already (25 March) written, 'By Jove! What a task for you. Yet I feel sure you will be equal to it . . . the greater the difficulty the more surely you will rise to it.' On 8 April Elgar copied out the Angel's song 'for your own Angel to sing'—this being Mrs. Jaeger who was expecting a child very shortly. Jaeger found the song 'uncanny, because it has a character unlike anything else in music as far as I know. Simple as it is, its very simplicity is its wonder, for it is a kind of simplicity I have never met with before, so aloof from things mundane, so haunting and strangely fascinating.' He had studied again Part I in proof 'and have been tremendously stirred by it. . . . Since *Parsifal* nothing of this mystic, religious kind of music has appeared to my knowledge that displays the same power and beauty. . . . I am now most curious and anxious to know how you will deal with that part of the poem where the soul goes within the Presence of the Almighty. *There* is a subject for you! Whatever else you may do, don't be *theatrical*.'

To this Elgar replied, 'Please remember that none of the "action" takes place in the *presence* of God: I would not have tried *that* neither did Newman. The Soul says "I go before my God" but *we* don't, we stand outside—I've thrown over all the "machinery" for celestial music,

---

[1] Dorabella, on p. 21 of her book, says that 'Gerontius proofs were arriving in batches every few days' in November 1899, but she has confused these with the final proofs of the *Variations*.

harps etc.' On 29 April a letter to Jaeger contains a hint of anxiety about the need for the chorus at Birmingham to have their parts to learn as soon as possible: 'I want you to push on the printing of what I sent and shall send today or tomorrow. Then if the Birm. people like, they can have copies up to the end of the Demons' chorus. The end of the work requires some consideration & I don't want to send the MS until I've been thro' it (as usual) again—again—again—again & after that once more!'

It will perhaps be easier to follow the course of the discussions henceforward if they are set out in the form of a dramatic dialogue:

ELGAR (7 May): I want you to look very carefully at Pt. II of Gerontius as it comes from the printer and tell me if you think those conversations between the Angel and the Soul are wearisome. . . . I know the poem too well and you (as an outsider as it were) might see if you would further curtail it. Between ourselves this is the only part of the work that I fear or even think twice about. If the words are sufficiently interesting the music will do. . . . I wanted the Angel's song & two or three other in tempo portions to stand out.

JAEGER (22 May): Oh! I am half undone and I tremble after the tremendous exaltation I have gone through. . . . I have not seen or heard anything since *Parsifal* that has stirred me and spoken to me with the trumpet tongue of genius as has this part of your latest, and *by far* greatest work. . . . Your wonderful music is inexpressibly and most wonderfully elevating, 'aloof', mystic and heart-moving, as by the force of a great compassion. . . . That solo of the 'Angel of the Agony' is overpowering. . . . Those poignant melodies, those heart-piercing *beautiful* harmonies! I recognise the chief theme as having belonged to 'Judas'. Nobody could dream that it was not originally *inspired* by *these very words of Newman's.* You must not, *cannot,* expect this work of yours to be appreciated by the ordinary amateur (*or critic!*) after one hearing. You will have to rest content, as other great men had to before you, if a few friends and enthusiasts hail it as a work of genius. . . . Goodnight, my friend, and go on with your magnum opus to the joy and benefit of us poor ordinary mortals and ad majorem dei gloriam! Much love!

Alice Elgar's diary records on 21, 22, and 23 May: 'E. writing hard'. On 25 May 'E. very engrossed last chorus Gerontius'. On 29 May 'Very hard at last chorus', 30th 'Nearly finished great chorus'.

ELGAR (31 May): By this post comes the great Blaze [Praise to the Holiest]. . . . There's still some more MS to come but not much. I can't tell you how much good your letter has done me: I *do* dearly like to be *understood.*

On 6 June, four days after Elgar's forty-third birthday, Alice entered these words: 'E. finished the Dream of Gerontius. Deo gratias. Rather poorly.'

ELGAR (7 June): God bless you, Minrod.[1] Here's the end.
JAEGER (8 June): The more I study the work the more I marvel. It is wonderful. Come & discuss some little points with me.

In a letter to Dorabella on 9 June Jaeger said, 'E. E. has sent the completion of his blessed Gerontius. The work undoes me utterly if I am in the mood. [That reservation is important.] . . . The Chorus Parts will not be in the hands of the B'ham singers for another 3 weeks or more; so your honoured aunt must possess her soul in patience. . . . The majority of the B'ham audience will not be able to appreciate Gerontius first time; too subtle & original & too mystic & beautiful. . . .'

Already it was becoming clear that the chorus, of whom Dorabella's aunt, Mrs. Hodgson, was a member, and indeed the soloists, would have their work cut out to learn the work in time for the first performance on 3 October:

ELGAR (14 June): Plunket Greene [who was to sing the Priest and the Angel of the Agony] leaves middle of July & wd. like to squint at his part previous. Will the rough 8vo. copies be ready by the end of this month? . . .
JAEGER (14 June): There is a lot of *Joseph* and *Mary* about the work: very proper for a Roman Catholic lying at death's door to sing about, but likely to frighten *some* d—d fools of Protestants. I had a long talk to the Secretary of one of the big Glasgow Societies yesterday and showed him proofs. . . . He *at once*, on reading the words, spoke of the 'Roman Catholic element' being so prominent!! 'Tommy rot' you say: *ditto*, says I, who am rather an Agnostic than anything else. But alas! one must deal with people as one finds them, and if, without bowdlerising a superb poem, one can remove Mary and Joseph to a more distant background, it may not be a bad thing.
ELGAR (15 June): . . . Of course it will frighten the Low Church party but the poem must on no account be touched! . . . Them as don't like it can be damned in their own way—not ours. It's awfully curious the attitude (towards sacred things) of the narrow English mind: it puts me in memory of the man who said, when he saw another crossing himself 'Oh, this *devilish crossing*'. There's a nice confused idea for you.
JAEGER (16 June): *I* have often said 'Oh this *devilish crossing*' and yet I am not bigoted. There is one outside our shop . . . where I have often been all but killed! Otherwise I agree with you. . . . My wife's Irish (Roman Catholic) nurse nearly had a fit when she saw in my wife's bedroom a picture of *Martin Luther*! 'Religion' (*Dogma*) is a damnable thing at times and responsible for more misery and cruelty and general badness than any other thing the devil ever invented.
(15 June): There is one page [159 of vocal score, containing the Soul's 'Take me away'] I can make nothing of, i.e. nothing adequate to Newman's words

[1] Not, as usually quoted, Nimrod. Elgar liked to vary his nicknames.

or the situation, though I have played and sung it over and over again. . . .
But all the rest is *most beautiful, exquisite, ethereal*. That lovely contrapuntal
movement beginning at [rehearsal cue number] [126] [the *Andante tranquillo*
orchestral theme, leading into the Angel's Farewell] has gone straight to my
heart and burned itself into my brain. I fancy I have not seen any such lovely
writing of a quiet soothing character since *Die Meistersinger*! . . . It almost
seems a dream *to me*, for with all my appreciation of English music I did not
expect such a work to come out of this tight little island, and I felt quite sure
it would not—much as I admired him—come out of E. E.! All the greater
seems the marvel and all the intenser my *delight*!!

(16 June): . . . Page 159 I have tried and tried and tried, but it seems to me the
weakest page in the work! Do re-write it! Surely you want something more
dramatic *here*!! It seems mere weak whining to me and not at all impressive.
As I have said, *all* the rest of the finale is wonderful. Yes, even page 161, with
a return (for a while) to the music of page 159 is beautiful! . . . That passage
'I ever had believed' (page 63) I *cannot* take, too. I fancy that against that most
solemn Judgment theme, the voice in *monotone* would sound *much more*
impressive. Here we require no 'tune' in the voice, surely. At any rate, that
rise to E on 'had', and the accent on 'on the moment' grate on me, also the
voice moving in thirds with the theme at 'forthwith it fell' I *can't abide*.
Again, what about 'that now thou dost *not* fear'? (page 64) Think of something more important to pierce one's brain and *stick there*!

ELGAR (19 June): I was awfully glad to get your letter about the end. I'm so
sick of the whole thing: 'cos why? 'Cos every ass I meet says 'I suppose' or 'I
hope' you're going to keep to the old A. & M. tune 'Praise to the Holiest'!!!!
Blast the B.P. [British Public]—they have no souls, hearts or minds worth a
thought. . . .

(20 June): . . . I've been through all your suggestions for which a heap of
thanks: I'm truly glad you like the thing cos I've written it out of my insidest
inside. Some of your remarks are just & I've endeavoured to meet them: Some
I can't see the force of & will be pigheaded & sit tight. . . . P. 64 I enclose
revised: the accent on 'had' must be for sense; the rest is mere talking. . . .
A tenor's monotone is never effective I feel—contraltos & baritones can do
it, but sops. & tenors squeak & hum. . . . P. 159. You must read the poem; I
cannot rewrite this: the Soul is shrivelled up & voiceless & I only want on
this page a musing murmur & I've got it—it wakes up later—but I can't
do this better if I try for fifty years. . . . I don't think you appreciate the
situation—the soul has for an instant seen its God—it is from that momentary
glance shrivelled, parched and effete, powerless & finished, & it is condemned
to Purgatory for punishment or purging—he sighs &, if you prefer it, whines.
I've given him some of his aspiratory tunes in the middle but the situation is
as sad as can be—deepest dejection & sorrow . . . therefore my final cadence,
which is good, then comes the Angel, peaceful & soothing. . . . I can't see
how you can ask for the Soul to have a dramatic song here: he is in the most

dejected condition & sighs 'Take me away anywhere out of sight'. No, I can't alter that.

JAEGER (27 June): Don't think you have convinced me. . . . I had read the poem well, and appreciated the situation at the end (Soul after seeing God) well. But, surely, the first sensations the Soul would experience would be an awful, overwhelming agitation; a whirlwind of sensations of the acutest kind . . . a bewilderment of fear, excitation, crushing, overmastering hopelessness etc. etc. . . . *Your* treatment shirks all that . . . *your* view, as expressed in the music, suggests to me nothing so much as an 'Oh lor, is that all. What a poor show, take me away, it gives me the *miserables*'. Yes, a whine I called it. . . . Wagner would have made this the *climax* of *expression* in the work, especially in the orchestra. . . . I *don't* want your 'Soul' to sing a dramatic *'Song'*. Heavens! But what is your gorgeous orchestra for? and why should you be dull and sentimental at such a *supremest* moment? . . . Here is your *greatest* chance of proving yourself *poet*, seer, and do-er of *impossible* things and you shirk it. Bah! . . . Did I not hold your splendid powers in such reverence and admiration, and were the rest of the work less superb, I should hold my peace and be *content* with a 'mere English cantata'! But you 'can't alter that passage', and so I will merely sing to *myself* 'my sad perpetual strain'.

ELGAR (27 June): . . . I've kept back p. 159 for consideration but all the time know I'm right & that you're wrong. However I'll see—one thing does annoy me. You say I've 'shirked' it—now I've shirked nothing—I've only set the thing as I feel & see it, which is not shirking at all, at all.

JAEGER (30 June): So that poem of N's has beaten you after all at its supremest climax! and you are *no* Wagner! . . . Anyhow, you have improved the whine summat and that's summat to your credit. But sure-*ly*, that alteration at just before 126 is *no* improvement . . . . No, please don't alter it as per the MS you have sent. It takes away the *surprise*, and the dramatically appropriate 'gliding in' of the new, *lovely* peaceful theme. *Please* don't alter that if you can't alter it any better way than as per your MS. . . . I know *you* dont' like the new way better than the old, do you? . . . I wanted you to suggest, in a *few* gloriously great and effulgent orchestral chords, given out by the whole force of the orchestra in its most glorious key, the momentary *vision* of the Almighty. A few chords! . . . and then for a few bars the Soul's overwhelming agitation with a quasi-choked, suppressed 'Take me away', *molto agitato*, and *then* as miserable a whine as you like. . . . No, it need not have been done 'theatrically' at all, at all! And to suggest the *glory* of the momentary vision need not have been blasphemous either. But, I grant you, it wanted a Wagner or R. Strauss to do that, nobody else would dare attempt it. No! as I know now, not even E. E.

ELGAR (1 July): Very well; here's what I thought of at *first*—I've copied it out

& sent it—of course it's biggity-big. . . . The following alterations will have to be made: viz: the *souls* chorus[1] will *follow* the 'Take me away' That is to say: I enclose p. 157—the top of it is all right & I've attached the Judgment theme, (I can't get it in the rushing string passages!) at end of second p. (of my M.S. enclosed) the Solo 'Take me away' comes in, as it stands in typo. Now enclosed I send the *end* of the solo which *must join* on to the *Souls* chorus. It is in type. And again the Souls Chorus joins on to the end (last) movement—this 'join' I also enclose. . . . I hope you'll like the emendation.

So those commentators who have assumed that Elgar's 'I can't alter that' was his last word have not taken into account this letter of 1 July. From the evidence above, we can deduce that the Souls in Purgatory chorus of 'Lord Thou hast been our refuge' was placed immediately before the Soul of Gerontius's 'Take me away': hence Elgar's reference in his 20 June letter to wanting only 'a musing murmur—it wakes up later' on this page (159) of the score. When he removed this chorus to its present position at cue no. 125 he replaced it with the marvellous orchestral passage which now stands at cue nos. 118–19, presumably in response to Jaeger's suggestion of 'a few chords'. A later passage in the letter shows that the final cadence of the Soul's 'Take me away' (now p. 163 of V.S. rehearsal cues nos. 124–5) was immediately followed by the Angel's Farewell beginning at 126. The Souls in Purgatory's interjections during the Angel's solo at 129 (p. 167 V.S.) are apparently the other 'join' to which Elgar refers. Elgar refers to this matter—which he again stresses was his original intention—in a letter of 11 July when he returned the last proofs:

'You are as usual a brute to me—will those bars do? You don't say. I can tell you one thing, old Mosshead, you might ask—, or—, or—, to turn you out a few bars like that in vain! Never mind. I'm glad I did it after all. I had in my original sketch marked it out so, but I thought it too much for the fat mind of the filistine. We shall see.'

Once again, Elgar feared that the 'stupid' British public might not follow his trend of thought and also that British choral societies and orchestras would not appreciate the poetical subtlety of this work. He was to be proved right. But Jaeger still hankered after something more at 'Take me away'. It is strange that so sensitive an Elgarian failed to appreciate the stroke of genius of that blinding flash on the orchestra as Gerontius sees his God. On 17 July Elgar wrote to him: 'I *won't* alter p. 159 & be darned to you ... —at 120 for *one semi-quaver* value fffffffzzzz is the one glimpse into the Unexpressible—then it (the Music) dies down into the sort of blissful Heaven theme which of course

[1] Chorus (Souls in Purgatory) 'Lord, Thou hast been our refuge', p. 163 V.S.

fades away into nothing.' That really was the last word. Jaeger let the
matter drop except for pointing out that Edward Lloyd would run out
of breath on 'Take'.

Throughout the July and August of the glorious summer of 1900
Elgar worked at Birchwood on correcting proofs of the chorus parts
and on copying out the full score. As usual the effort of composition
had left him physically weak—he had stopped work in April for a
fortnight because of a cold—and now he relaxed with country pursuits.
He learned to ride a bicycle, took to felling and sawing trees, and
learned about growing potatoes—'What names: "Beauties of Abram",
(they mean Hebron!), Adirondacks etc, etc'. Birchwood always
induced an idyllic mood. On 11 July he headed his letter to Jaeger with
a quotation from the Woodland Interlude in *Caractacus*, adding: 'This
is what I hear all day—the trees are singing my music—or have I sung
theirs? I suppose I have? It's too lovely here.' He loved the view from
his study window—'a lot of young hawks flying about—plovers also—
150 rabbits under the window & the blackbirds eating cherries like
mad'. His letters for those seven weeks are peppered with references
of this sort. 'Felling one tree in view—blasting another & learning to
bicycle & fifty 1000 nice things to do & all the time I have to be writing
new bars to please an old duffer who won't acknowledge 'em.' . . .
'The heat has been really awful & upsetting everyone—I don't like to
say a word about these woods for fear you shd. feel envious but it is
godlike in the shade with the snakes & other cool creatures walking
about as I write my miserable music' . . . 'I was out all yesterday with a
sawmill, sawing timber into joists, planks, posts, rafters, boarding yea!
boarding with feather edge: how little ye townsmen know of real life.
Anyhow I got a chill over my exertions. . . . Now to come down to the
damned music.' He finished the full score on 3 August and he wrote on
it 'Birchwood. In summer'. Knowing that he had created a masterpiece, he also wrote this quotation from John Ruskin's *Sesame and
Lilies*:

> This is the best of me; for the rest, I ate, and drank, and
> slept, loved and hated, like another: my life was as the
> vapour and is not; but *this* I saw and knew; this, if anything
> of mine, is worth your memory.

It had been decided that Jaeger should write an analysis (extended
programme-note) of the new work so that the public could study it
beforehand: few English works had had this helpful attention, although
Joseph Bennett had written one of *King Olaf*. Jaeger sent it to Elgar for

PLATE III

'My dear Nimrod'
Letters between Elgar and Jaeger
(below) about *The Dream of Gerontius*,
1900

PLATE IV   Elgar's early Champions

Augustus Jaeger at Bettws y Coed, 1903

Hans Richter, photographed by Elgar at Bayreuth in 1902

Alfred Rodewald, with 'Sam', at Bettws, 1903

approval and from comments on it written in August 1900 we learn much that is of interest about the composer's attitude to *Gerontius*. Jaeger picked out from the Prelude the various leitmotives, giving them names such as 'Prayer', 'Sleep', 'Judgment', 'Ruin'. Elgar challenged 'Sleep,' then added:

I suppose after all 'Sleep' will be right—I meant 'to be lying down weary & distressed' with your poor head buzzing & weak &—have you ever been really ill? Sleep will do but it's the ghastly troubled sleep of a sick man. Look here: I imagined Gerontius to be a man like us and not a priest or a saint, but a *sinner*, a repentant one of course but still no end of a *worldly man* in his life, & now brought to book. Therefore I've not filled *his* part with Church tunes & rubbish but a good, healthy, full-blooded romantic, remembered worldliness, so to speak. It is, I imagine, much more difficult to tear one's self away from a well-to-do world than from a cloister. Your No. 6 might be Anguish but Despair will do . . . I didn't give this 'prayer' theme to Gerontius too plainly—solidly—as he *wanders*: rather—If he'd been a priest he wd. have sung or said it as a climax but as he represents ME when ill he doesn't—he remembers his little Churchy prayey music in little snatches—see? He's of the world—or was & is going thro' a bad time, even if quite repentant etc. . . . My wife fears you may be inclined to lay too great stress on the *leitmotiven* plan because I really do it without thought —intuitively, I mean. For instance, I did not perceive till long after it was in print that 'In Thine own agony' & the appalling chords I last bar p. 150 II 3rd line, bar 2, p. 154 introducing & dismissing the *Angel of the Agony* were akin but they are, aren't they?

Referring to the theme used in various guises in the orchestra in Part II (where Gerontius sings 'I see not those false spirits', where the Angel tells him 'Thy judgment now is near' and at Gerontius's 'I go before my Judge'), Elgar said he meant to describe 'an indefinable feeling that there's more around you than you know: have you ever been in a pitch dark room & have *felt* the presence of people when you have no proof or knowledge that anyone is there. I *have* & it feels like that. Yah! don't bother me about music. I ride a Bicycle.'

Even after the analysis was published and the work had been performed Elgar asked Jaeger to eliminate the term 'Ruin': 'the idea is quite right—but the word is *heavy*—too direct—the "sense of ruin" is the thing & that's too long a title—but I fear the outsider will scoff inwardly & outwardly at that little theme being supposed to represent RUIN. I intended all this peaceful music (start of Part II) to be "the memory (remembrance) of the soul"—an utter childish (childlike) peace—as described in an unset portion of the poem—the word *flight* wd lead the ASS to think of *rapid* movement—rapid movement *did* (or

G

rather) *was* taking place but the Soul was not conscious of it exactly. Twig?'

Elgar was deeply touched that his friend should devote so much time and labour to the analysis. Jaeger worked on it after office hours and on Sundays, making himself tired and nervy. Novello's offered to pay him five guineas for it, although Elgar had suggested ten guineas to Littleton. Elgar was furious when he heard about it: 'You must stick out for more. ... Your firm is enough to make one disgusted with one's fellow creatures forever. I will not say what I think, but all other publishers are so different and nice and pleasant to do with even if things are not smooth, and all others are reasonable and obliging and considerate. ... Boosey wd. fly rather than ask *me* to arrange about the libretto in order to save himself a possible fee, but your firm is incomprehensibly—.' Elgar made his own gesture of thanks to his analyst. On 27 September he sent him his two 'very first' sketches of *Gerontius*: 'If you don't want 'em throw 'em in w.p.b. I am not getting conceited (don't fear) and think my scrawl worth having—ciel! but somehow I couldn't tear up these two bits and I'm an ass.'

*   *   *

The first performance of *The Dream of Gerontius* on 3 October 1900 (the day before polling day in a general election)[1] is the most famous, or notorious, bad performance in the history of English music. It is well, if contradictorily, documented and it is impossible to blame one man or one factor for that disastrous Wednesday morning in Birmingham. The basic cause was the haphazard condition of English music-making at that date. The performance was heading for trouble from the start. One major contributory cause was the short time the chorus had in which to learn a work which, as they (or some of them) realized as soon as they saw the score, broke new ground. This was not *Judith* or *Job* or *The Dream of Jubal*. Dorabella, in an article in the *Musical Times*,[2] blames Elgar for 'being dilatory in getting the chorus parts corrected and returned to the printers'. Presumably she had not seen Elgar's letters to Jaeger or she would never have committed herself to this opinion. He delivered Part I to Novello's on 2 March and Part II on 20 March. Proofs of Part I arrived at Malvern on 3 April. By mid-May he was getting revisions of his corrections, some of them muddled by the printer. By 20 June he had dealt with all he had received. On 24 June he

---

[1] This week was to prove doubly important in English life. *Gerontius* was performed for the first time and Winston Churchill was returned to Parliament for the first time. Neither event was then appreciated at its full significance.   [2] February 1959, pp. 78–79.

complained 'I've had a proof of the finale for *ten* days and no *read* proof or MS yet! Where the divvle is it? Aren't we wasting time sadly? . . . Thanks for sending Plunket Greene his "songs". Now he'll be happy.' On 5 July he returned another batch of proofs, adding 'I am very anxious to get all the Chorus copies out now, & a voc. sc. as *soon* as possible, 'cos I must consult the Birmingham people early about semi-ch. etc.' On 11 July he returned the last proofs. The alterations he had made caused some delay. '*Your!* confounded alterations have left me with nothing to work with—for instance the new bar on p. 64 (old paging) I've no copy at all & haven't an idea what I put in. Do send me this quick. . . . Now, dear man, do keep the thing going & let's have those chorus parts ready.' He had wanted long bar lines in the vocal parts but expense had precluded it. Copies of the vocal score were available by 21 July and the orchestral parts and full score were corrected during August: running it close, but this was hardly Elgar's fault. He was agitating for them to be ready by September so that he could go through it with Richter, who was to conduct.

The chorus had their parts in August. There is a note for the 24th in Alice's diary: 'Heard chorus were delighted with Dream of Gerontius'. This was to prove an over-optimistic piece of hearsay and probably came from Dorabella's aunt, Mrs. Hodgson, wife of an archdeacon. She was a soprano and a fine sight-reader and said to her niece: 'How lovely this music is! but shall we *ever* learn it in time?' The answer was no, and a chief reason for it—and perhaps the biggest single blow to the performance—was the death in June at the age of fifty-three of Swinnerton Heap, the chorus-master who had so brilliantly trained the North Staffordshire Festival choir for *King Olaf* in 1896. He knew Elgar's secret of writing the kind of music Midlands choirs thoroughly understood. His sudden death before a copy of *Gerontius* had been seen by the chorus might not have sealed the work's fate if the festival committee had been able to call on his equal as a substitute. But at the tenth hour this was impossible and they called Stockley, who was now seventy, out of retirement. He was not in sympathy with the way his former orchestral violinist had developed and, as a nonconformist, he was not in sympathy with the Roman Catholicism of Newman and Elgar. In any case he now no longer had the energy and control needed to instil not only *Gerontius* but other new or unfamiliar works into the chorus in the comparatively short time at his disposal. Besides the Elgar, the festival included Parry's *De Profundis*, a revival of Byrd's five-part Mass, and Coleridge-Taylor's *Hiawatha's Departure* (first produced in London the previous spring). W. T. Edgley, a tenor in the chorus, told Dorabella[1] that, because the chorus were supplied only with single-voice parts, 'one section of the choir had no idea what the others were doing (or not doing)'. Some of the tenors practised *Gerontius* at home and knew their parts well; the basses did not know their parts at all and there was some 'buffoonery' in that section of the chorus. It is not true that Elgar attended only the final rehearsal on Saturday, 29 September, or that Stockley, because of his lack of sympathy, did not invite him before then. Elgar went to a rehearsal at Birmingham on 12 September as is proved not only by Alice's diary entry but by Elgar's letter to Jaeger of 13 September: 'I sent a wire this a.m. on my return from Birmingham'. As late as 20 September Elgar was still correcting the orchestral parts. Jaeger had written on the 18th, 'For God's sake return all *proofs* at once or we shall get landed in a fine quandary.' Elgar went to London on 21 September for an orchestral rehearsal at Queen's Hall and wrote to Jaeger afterwards: 'Somehow, after thinking of the rehearsal, I feel very much ashamed of myself as author of "Gerontius"—a sort of criminal—and wonder if I shall ever get up sufficient courage to go to Birmingham at all'.

At the final joint choral and orchestral rehearsal at Birmingham on the Saturday (29 September), Elgar realized how very far short of his intentions the reality was likely to prove in this performance. The 'best of him', the ideal tapestry of music which he had imagined while he worked amid the sounds of summer at Birchwood, was now presented to him as an unpalatable piece of work by a choir that had very little interest in the vision he had created. As will perhaps have been gathered by now, he was not the man to rise above disappointment with a blithe spirit: he was either up or down, there was no level-headed medium mood. He sat next to Richter, explaining what he wanted and indicating tempi. 'Things got very chaotic,' Edgley says, 'and everyone worked up to a high pitch and unfortunately E. E. more than anyone, naturally. He seemed desperate, with whom I cannot remember, but it was not all "the choir" as most people think.' Be that as it may, Richter invited Elgar to address the choir. Instead of exhorting them to do better, Elgar ticked them off from the front of the orchestra, using the words 'It is no better than a drawing-room ballad.' This was much resented. 'Chorus dull and wretched,' Alice wrote in her diary that evening, echoing Elgar's opinion. That same day, Jaeger wrote to Dorabella: 'Richter likes the work as much as I do.' Richter, too, was horrified by the choir's inability to grasp the implications of the music, and realized that he himself had under-

[1] See Diana McVeagh: *Edward Elgar: His Life and Music* (London, 1955), pp. 30–31.

estimated the novelty and magnitude of the work, that it required far more insight than the *Variations* and a close knitting-together of choir and orchestra. He tried to salvage the situation. He called an extra rehearsal for the Monday and spent the weekend pacing up and down his hotel room with the score propped on the mantelpiece, learning its every nuance so that he could instil his own knowledge and enthusiasm into the choir. He was too late. The six hours' rehearsal on the Monday over-strained the chorus, who thus began the festival on Tuesday tired and stale. Other composers suffered, too. The critic of the *Sunday Times* was 'rudely awakened' in Parry's *De Profundis* 'to the fact that something was wrong'. Bach's *St. Matthew Passion* was given a performance 'worthy of a fourth-rate provincial choral society'. *Gerontius* had the place of honour on the Wednesday morning. Richter went to the chorus's dressing-rooms, and according to one of the sopranos, 'with unforgettable voice and gesture besought us to do our very best for "the work of this English genius".'[1] His words fell on a majority of deaf and resentful ears.

Not only were the conductor and choir ill-equipped to do justice to a masterpiece; the soloists (if the best then available) were inadequate to their task. Edward Lloyd was fifty-five and within two months of retirement. He had had a successful career for the previous thirty years in oratorios and songs, and had sung in several previous Elgar first performances. Gerontius was the last major rôle he undertook. A fine singer of Handel arias and drawing-room ballads was Dorabella's verdict. He sang Gerontius, according to Vaughan Williams who was present, 'like a Stainer anthem, in the correct tenor attitude with one foot slightly withdrawn'.[2] At the end of Part I, in the great 'Go forth' chorus, the choir sang flat and during the interval, Ferruccio Bonavia said, 'Richter, bitterly disappointed, paced the artists' room like a caged tiger. The second part, begun in an atmosphere of apprehension, did nothing to change the fortunes of the day.'[3] Plunket Greene sang the bass rôles. He began the Angel of the Agony's solo in Part II a semitone flat and stuck to it till the bitter end. Only the Wagnerian mezzo-soprano, Marie Brema, as the Angel, appears to have redeemed the affair. Dorabella says that she 'saved the situation in Part II several times' and W. H. Reed speaks of 'complete mastery and understanding'. Vaughan Williams, on the other hand, in stating that Greene had 'lost his voice', added that Miss Brema 'had none to lose'. In a letter to her

---

[1] *Birmingham Post*, 8 March 1934.
[2] M. Kennedy, *The Works of Ralph Vaughan Williams* (London, 1964), p. 389.
[3] Op. cit., p. 144.

dated 24 April 1903 Elgar wrote, 'I have, of course, in memory your fine and intellectual creation of the part; and, although I never thought the "tessitura" suited you well, as the magnificent artist you are, you *made* it go very finely'; a tactful evasion rather than a heart-felt compliment.

Elgar told Arnold Bax in 1901: 'The fact is neither the choir nor Richter knew the score.'[1] Henry Wood in *My Life of Music* writes: 'I shall never believe he [Richter] was to blame for its failure.' Ultimately of course, responsibility must lie with the conductor and Richter's fault lay in his failure, when he first saw the score, to appreciate its subtlety and the need, therefore, for him to supervise every rehearsal from the start. Elgar did not hold it against him, though he conducted most of his own first performances thenceforward. He blamed a higher authority than Richter. Six days after the performance—not in the trough of reaction on the next morning—he poured out his bitterness to Jaeger in perhaps the most astonishing letter he ever wrote:

I have not seen the papers yet except one or two bits which exuberant friends insisted on my reading and I don't know or care what they say or do. As far as I'm concerned music in England is dead—I shall always write what I have in me of course.

I have worked hard for forty years & at the last, Providence denies me a decent hearing of my work: so I submit—I always said God was against art and I still believe it. Anything obscene or trivial is blessed in this world and has a reward—I ask for no reward—only to live & to hear my work. I still hear it in my heart and in my head so I must be content. Still it is curious to be treated by the old fashioned people as a criminal because my thoughts and ways are beyond them. [A hit, presumably, at Stockley.]

I am very well and what is called 'fit'! I had my golf in good style yesterday & am not ill or pessimistic—don't think it, but I have allowed my heart to open once—it is now shut against every religious feeling and every soft, gentle impulse *for ever*.

While at Birmingham the Elgars received news of a financial loss and Alice had a slight operation performed on her throat. In a second letter to Jaeger, on 12 October, Elgar claimed that these were what had upset him. No doubt they aggravated his disappointment but there is no disguising the calculated disillusion which he was expressing so eloquently if incoherently: 'I'm rather pleased with my work—privately— but it is annoying—whatever *you* may think, to know that it's *no good* commercially, and that with *one* exception (your own good self) all my best friends including the highest thinkers only made one remark

---

[1] Sir Arnold Bax, *Farewell, My Youth* (London, 1943), p. 30.

during my "exaltation", "now you must write a few popular songs" instead of a word of appreciation, in its best sense, fifty times, by the men even who had promised to finance my work, during the week, nay on the very moment of performance did they drum it into my poor ears "now a popular song or two will make up for this"—my wife ill, and our money gone. Damn Gerontius: I'd really forgotten it when I wrote to you last.'

But what was the reaction of others to the music and the performance? The wife of W. M. B. of the *Variations* perhaps summed it up in her remark to Dorabella, 'A very poor performance but what a wonderful work!' Mrs. Stanford left the hall with Vaughan Williams and said to him 'Is not that a fine work!' A correspondent of the *Observer* was at the rehearsal on 29 September and reported that one of the musicians present—Parry, Stanford, or Manns—'roundly asserted *Gerontius* to be the finest work yet written by a British musician'. Yet dissentient voices spoke out too, some of them to Jaeger who wrote to Dorabella on 14 October: 'I have been . . . "pitched into" . . . for being enthusiastic over *Gerontius*. I don't mind a bit. It was *lack* of enthusiasm both in the performers & amongst the critics which riled me at B'ham & afterwards, when I read the critiques. Now you Englishers *have* a composer *at last*. You might be excused if you waxed enthusiastic over him for once in a way. But oh dear no! If this were only a wretched new opera or a dull new oratorio by Mascagni or Perosi, the papers would have had *columns* of gossip & gush about those 2 frauds. But it's only an English *musician* (not an actress or a jockey or a Batsman) and he is treated like a very ordinary nobody. Oh you unpatriotic creatures. I won't say a word about the performance but I suffered purgatory!! . . . old Stockley the choir-mess-ter ought to be boiled & served on toast. . . . Dear E. E. sent me quite a depressing letter last week. I told him it was *weak & wicked* to write like that. . . .'

Do the critics deserve the obloquy they have received for their notices of *Gerontius*? Some were disturbed by the subject, one commiserated with Novello's 'whose philanthropy had risked overloading their shelves with more useless copies'. Fuller Maitland in *The Times* could summon up nothing less fence-sitting than 'a remarkable and in some ways a beautiful, work'. He described the tenor rôle as 'seldom either grateful to the singer or very attractive to the average hearer. . . . How to write a long and dramatic soliloquy with no lack of melodic beauty or affecting expression has been shown in Sir Hubert Parry's *Job* and it is only necessary to allude to this in order to point the vast difference that exists between the two composers in this regard. . . . If only he

[Elgar] would more often yield to the instinct for melodic beauty . . the new composition would merit very high rank indeed.'

This was Olympian damning with faint praise, but if one reads through all the other many and lengthy notices of the first performance, one discovers that every critic almost without exception acclaimed the work as one of the most remarkable, beautiful, and impressive ever written by an English composer and castigated Birmingham for the wretched performance. Herbert Thompson, of the *Yorkshire Post*, for instance, called it 'the most powerful and profound utterance of one of the most individual composers'. Charles L. Graves, in the *Spectator*, spoke of its creating 'a deep impression by its beauty, its earnestness, and its distinction' despite the 'imperfections' of the performance. Arthur Johnstone in the *Manchester Guardian* on 4 October drew an unconventional parallel: 'A comparison with Berlioz is simply inevitable—for Edward Elgar's dramatic power admits of comparison with the great masters. . . . Elgar's music, like parts of the poem, fairly merits the epithet "Dantesque". . . .'

Nor, I should have thought, could any composer less thin-skinned than Elgar reasonably have complained of the column-long notice on 4 October in *The Daily Telegraph* whose critic, Joseph Bennett, dealt fairly with the theological aspect: 'I must confess inability to see quite clearly that a subject so awful, and as regards each individual of us so profoundly intimate, belongs to those which should be decked in musical trappings for the delectation of a festival crowd. Such things properly belong to the Church. . . .'

Bennett's opinion of the music, though raising a smile today, was expressed dogmatically but with dignity: 'What he has written he has honestly written, and his critics, who are inclined to condemn, must do so with all respect. . . . I do not complain of a free harmonic method as such, provided its effect be good, but it is not given to me to say why in the present case the ear is almost continuously assailed by chromatic phrases and chords, which none can accuse of being beautiful. . . . But against this must be set precious pages in which the conditions have forced Mr. Elgar to take up other ground and sing the song of that in music which is naturally expressive. . . . [It is] a work possible only to the highest gifts of imagination, feeling and skill. . . . "The Dream of Gerontius" advances its composer's claim to rank amongst the musicians of whom the country should be proudest. It is with sincere regret that I speak of the performance as inadequate to the claims of the work and the importance of the festival. . . . True the music was difficult but there had been time to prepare it. . . . It is not my business to discover why the chorus could not sing six lightly accompanied bars without losing the pitch or why all the concerted music was rendered in a hesitating and pointless fashion.'

The Birmingham fiasco did not, of course, kill *Gerontius* but it might have done. No other choir rushed to do justice to it, for the rumour had gone round that it was formidably difficult. Richter, however, was determined to make amends. In Manchester, where the Hallé Choir had R. H. Wilson as chorus-master, he worked for several years to bring orchestra and choir to a pitch where he could perform *Gerontius* really well. 'All the night,' he told Wilson, 'I have a gimlet that bores into my forehead, and that gimlet is *Gerontius*.' When the soloists and conductor signed Elgar's manuscript score on 3 October 1900, Richter, whose command of English was erratic but forthright, wrote: 'Let drop the Chorus. Let drop everybody! but let N O T drop the wings of your original genius.' He knew what sort of work it was, and if Germany had not forestalled him, there is no doubt that Richter's Manchester performances would have rehabilitated it within five years.

Elgar returned to Malvern deeply anxious about his financial position and proceeded to write one of his most cheerful and humorous works, the overture *Cockaigne: In London Town*—'It's cheerful and Londony: "stout and steaky"' he told Jaeger. It had been requested by the Philharmonic Society, and at the end of his manuscript he wrote, from *Piers Plowman:* 'Meteless and moneless on Malverne Hills'.

The P. won't pay anything [letter to Jaeger, 26 October]. Now look at this:

To copying parts	12. 0. 0.
Rehearsal ex.	3. 0. 0.
Do. & concert	6. 0. 0.
net loss	21. 0. 0.

Now what's the good of it? Nobody else will perform the thing. . . . I really cannot afford it and am at the end of my financial tether. Don't go and tell anyone but I *must* earn money somehow—I *will not* go back to teaching & I think I must try some trade—coal agency or houses— I really wish I were dead over & over again but I dare not, for the sake of my relatives, do the job myself. Well we shall see—I've not read the papers yet re *Gerontius* & never shall now. I'm sorry you've been bothered over it—just like my influence on everything & everybody—always evil!

More self-dramatization? Or was he genuinely haunted by the 'sense of ruin' he had expressed with such vivid truth in his masterpiece?

Ernest Newman met Elgar for the first time in October 1901 in Liver-pool, and recalling the occasion over fifty years later he wrote: 'He gave me even then the impression of an exceptionally nervous, self-divided and secretly unhappy man; in the light of all we came to know of him in later life I can see now that he was at that time rather bewildered and nervous at the half-realisation that his days of spiritual privacy—always so dear to him—were probably coming to an end; while no doubt gratified by his rapidly growing fame he was in his heart of hearts afraid of the future. I remember distinctly a dinner . . . at which Mrs. Elgar tactfully steered the conversation away from the topic of suicide that had suddenly arisen; she whispered to me that Edward was always talking of making an end of himself.'[1]

It is as hard to understand a man's mind as it is to relate art to life—*Cockaigne* after financial loss and the failure of *Gerontius* has the in-congruity of the Beethoven last quartets in the midst of frenzied bickering with relatives. Art is not the product or result of its creator's daily life, but of his inner life; and to that only he holds a key. Elgar for most of the time disguised his unhappiness and his sense of ruin and inferiority, as well as his sense of scorn, beneath the extrovert exterior known to the Malvern locals or beneath the studied jocularity of his letters to Jaeger. To Jaeger alone at this time he revealed himself consciously or sub-consciously—'I do want to see you or somebody as knows suffin—I am bored to death with commonplace ass-music down here—the bucolics are all right when they don't attempt more than eat, drink & sleep but beyond those things they fail'; and: 'It's raining piteously here and all is dull except the heart of E. E. which beats time to most marvellous music—unwritten alas! and ever to be so.' He checked the published score of *Froissart*, and spent what might seem an extravagant amount of time on the pianoforte version of 'Dorabella' until one remembers that Novello's paid him royalties only on the sale of arrangements other than orchestral. (By 1904 he reckoned that the *Enigma Variations* had made him about £8.[2]) He spent the winter months of 1900-1 preparing the *Prelude and Angel's Farewell* from *Gerontius* for separate publication and performance for orchestra alone, with solo voice or in its original form. He took care with it, but he must have been depressed by the prospect of this of all works existing only in the form of concert extracts. The first performance of the two excerpts was given at Bradford in the orchestral version, with Elgar conducting, on 16 February 1901. Four days later Henry Wood conducted them at Queen's Hall with Kirkby Lunn singing the Angel.

[1] *Sunday Times*, 23 October 1955.   [2] Letter to Jaeger, 10 August 1904.

As will be related in a later chapter, other works were brewing at this time—'In haste & joyful (Gosh! man I've got a tune in my head),' he wrote to Jaeger on 12 January—but here we are concerned with the future of *Gerontius*.

Jaeger, to his eternal credit, did all he could speedily to bring about a second performance. On 27 December 1900, he wrote to Dorabella, 'I'm still trying hard to get *Gerontius* performed in London, but it is almost hopeless. I still hope Wood will do it.' But at least Wood conducted the two extracts and Jaeger was delighted. 'It is the highest thing in English art (musical art),' he told Dorabella. '... Wood conducted it with loving care; spent 1½ hours on it & the result was a performance which completely put Richter's in the shade.' With Jaeger at the Birmingham performance were Professor Julius Buths, musical director of the city of Düsseldorf since 1890 and conductor of the Lower Rhine Festivals there since 1893, and Otto Lessman, editor of the *Allgemeine Musik-Zeitung*. They perceived the magnitude of *Gerontius* and that it was in the mainstream of European nineteenth-century music. 'Directly it was over,' Jaeger wrote to Dorabella, 'Buths grasped my hand (coram publico) & blurted out: "A wonderful work; it's the most beautiful work I know" etc. etc.' Lessman's eulogistic review was sent to Elgar by Richter's friend Ettling to whom Elgar replied on 30 October 1900: 'My wife has translated the articles to me and I am—I need not say—intensely gratified at being taken seriously & being understood. I wish my own countrymen could do this—but alas! in England this can never be—& I know it.' What he resented was the English critics' appraisal of *Gerontius* solely within the context of English music, whereas he knew that it merited international assessment. Rimsky-Korsakov had told him the *Variations* were 'the best since Brahms' and Richter thought the crescendo in 'Nimrod' better than Wagner's in the *Die Meistersinger* overture. But the English, excepting Johnstone, compared him only with Parry and Stanford or accused him of subservience to Wagner's methods. It was Jaeger who had suggested to Novello's in the summer of 1900 that Buths, 'one of the ultra-moderns of Germany, great propagandist for Richard Strauss', should be invited to Birmingham to hear some English music. The invitation went, it is said, on the strength of *Hiawatha's Departure*. But Jaeger followed it up with a score of the *Variations*. In acknowledging them Buths wrote of their 'aristocratic character ... sensitive, thoughtful and full of feeling. ... "Hats off" to such artistry.' Buths, who was forty-nine, took the score of *Gerontius* back to Düsseldorf and at once began to translate the poem into German. In the meantime he conducted the *Variations*, their first performance in Germany, on 7 February 1901. 'A great and genuine success,' he told Jaeger. During April Elgar was anxiously inquiring about progress with the German translation as he had heard that other towns there might undertake a performance. Though he was working, the failure of *Gerontius* was still at the front of his mind: 'I know nothing of *any* festivals,' he wrote to Jaeger, '& fully conclude my countrymen do not want me any more—they want something which they can do without having to see the score & they can't read mine!' Alice wrote to him too: 'When are we going to hear those wonderful sounds again, the sooner you can tell us so the better for my dear Dr!'s spirits & consequently for his work.'[1]

In fact the wonderful sounds were next heard in Elgar's own Worcester, on 9 May, in an abbreviated performance by the Philharmonic Society, whose gesture of confidence in their conductor and his music is too often overlooked.[2] William Green sang Gerontius, Hélène Valma the Angel, and F. Lightowler, of Worcester, the bass rôles. Evidently Elgar had been as edgy with the chorus during rehearsals as he had been at Birmingham for, after the performance, he wrote a congratulatory note combined with an apology: 'I was, a month or two ago, very much hurt at what I felt (erroneously, it seems) to be a want of interest in the practices. I know now that this was a mistake on my part.' The *Prelude and Angel's Farewell* were included in the Gloucester Festival programme in September, when *The Times*, in approving this 'effective selection', ominously added the rider 'Even if we cannot hope for frequent revivals of the whole oratorio'. But by then, early in July, Elgar had received news of the date of Buths's performance at Düsseldorf. 'I note with joy & tears Dec. 19th,' he wrote to Jaeger, 'my devotion to Buths.'

Two incidents of the summer of 1901 illustrate Elgar's generosity and kindness to his friends. Although he was busy at this period with several new works in various stages of gestation,[3] he offered to help in the orchestration of the cantata *Emmaus*, which Dr. Herbert Brewer, who had succeeded Lee Williams as organist of Gloucester in 1897, had composed for the Three Choirs meeting there in September. Work had been delayed by illness and Brewer offered to withdraw. Elgar told

[1] Elgar had received the honorary doctorate of music at Cambridge University on 22 November 1900.
[2] The omissions were pp. 68–94, 113–55, and 163–4 of the vocal score. This is authenticated from the records of G. S. Chignell, assistant conductor and accompanist to the Society. (See letter from his son, W. R. Chignell, published in *Musical Times*, March 1956, pp. 146–7.)   [3] For details see Chapter 12.

Jaeger on 26 June that he was arranging to assist Brewer '& hope it will relieve his mind & perhaps his wife's—oh, these wives of musicians—what they go through—& *suffer*—my heart bleeds for them sometimes, we MEN can buck up & fight, but the others—. . . Brewer always says how can he "*re*pay me" & you said "pay me"—I don't want any pay or return—I only want *them* to sleep a little in peace instead of lying awake o' nights.' He had not forgotten his own struggles. Then, when the Elgars moved to Birchwood in July ('in the intense quiet & solitude which I love') they lent Craeg Lea to the Jaegers, who could otherwise not afford a holiday, and to Buths and his daughter. Elgar already had his fears about Düsseldorf: 'I *hope* it will be a success for your sake and Buths' but it (being English) cannot be & will only be another mill-stone round the neck of me—for which I shall be expected to write polki or something to pay for the blasted expense.' (He had arranged some of the *Gerontius* choruses for S.A.T.B. and had then been asked by Novello's 'for more Ladies' trios'.) Nine days later he was telling Jaeger: 'Remember (Private) that your countrymen never approach an English work with even a semblance of interest or respect—it is only something "pour rire" after all & I cannot hope that my work will fare better than Sullivan's etc.'

The Elgars went to Düsseldorf, arriving there on 16 December. Their departure had been delayed by Alice's cold and by more eye trouble of Elgar's—'the doctor wants me to give up as much music writing as possible!' he told Jaeger. 'So do the publishers & the critix—and the public—and the other composers & so does Ed: Elgar.' There are two vivid accounts of the performance of *Gerontius* on 19 December, one by Elgar in a letter to Littleton of Novello's and the other by Jaeger in a letter to Dorabella. The Gerontius was Ludwig Wüllner—'splendid', said Elgar, 'not in voice but intelligence *genius*—he carried everyone away and made Gerontius a real personage—we never had a singer in England with so much brain—even here he is exceptional'. The Angel was sung by Antonie Beel, who failed, and the bass—'fine', said Elgar—was Willy Metzmacher. The chorus, the Städtische Musikverein, was, again according to Elgar, 'very fine and had only commenced work on 11 November. This disproves the idea fostered at Birmingham that my work is *too difficult*. The personnel of the chorus here is largely amateur, and in no way, except in intelligence and the fact that they have a capable conductor, can they (or it) be considered superior to any good English choral society. . . . Professor Buths was unsurpassable as conductor and took *infinite* pains to make everything "go". . . .'

Jaeger fills in the details of the rehearsals. The orchestra numbered over eighty, 'not like Wood's 110 for reading powers or tone, but they answered every purpose. . . . Buths . . . is not a great "interpreter"—I mean *co-creator* and there were many passages of which more might have been made. . . . But directly Wüllner opened his mouth to sing "Jesus, Maria, meine Stunde Kam" we said that man has *Brains*. . . . Next morning there was another orchestral rehearsal when E. interfered more frequently to secure readings more in accordance with his conceptions. Then in the evening, *the* Event. The Hall was crammed full though it was a beastly night. . . . We (E., Mrs. E., A. Johnstone of the *Manchester Guardian*, & yours truly) sat in the third row of the balcony right facing the orchestra and we heard marvellously well. . . . The Chorus was perfect, there is no other word for it. . . . That masterful piece (Demons' Chorus) which was so completely ruined at B'ham, was given with perfect ease & yet with strenuous dramatic force. . . . Wüllner did not seem in very good voice & he made one serious blunder. . . . In Part 2 Wüllner was *great*, especially in the "Take me away". The big chorus "Praise to the Holiest", which astonished the German musicians by its monumental architecture, was a masterly performance & the Finale, that wonderful Finale, was another revelation to those who heard it only at B'ham. Unfortunately the Angel was anything but angelically perfect . . . the audience could not have realised, thanks to Buths' alertness, how dangerously near collapse the performance came once or twice through this d— Angel's shortcomings. . . . Well, at the end E. was enthusiastically called, & though he had to fight his way through thronging crowds of people down the stairs & to the front, the applause & shouts were kept up until . . . he reached the podium. . . . I rushed out . . . & wired 400 words to *The Times* . . . another wire which I sent to the Central News was much mutilated by that agency & only a few papers thought the event of sufficient importance to give the 8 or nine lines to it. . . . If this had been Dan Leno's first appearance in Germany there would have been *columns* in all the English papers. Ye Gods! You have a lot to do yet to be considered a musical nation.'

Elgar was fêted and honoured, dined and wined by Düsseldorf musicians and painters—this, it should be remembered, at a time of fierce anglophobia in Germany. He visited Franz Wüllner, director of the Cologne Conservatoire, and father of Ludwig, who said he might include *Gerontius* in his next season. He returned to London on 1 January 1902, to lunch at Pagani's with the Henry Woods and to attend part of a Queen's Hall concert. Awaiting him were the words of a hymn—'O mightiest of the mighty'—which he was to set for Edward

VII's Coronation. The contrast was too much: 'the horrible musical atmosphere I plunged into at once in this benighted country nearly suffocated me—I *wish* it had completely,' he wrote to Jaeger from Malvern on 3 January. Six days later he was asking if any money was due to him ('Mazurka, Violin arrangement for instance. I should be glad to have it as it is an awkward time of year financially'). He had influenza by mid-January, but his chronic pessimism, rather than influenzal depression, accounts for the by now familiar lament in a letter written on 13 January in reply to Jaeger's good news that Buths was to repeat *Gerontius* at the Lower Rhine Festival at Düsseldorf in May: 'I am glad to hear about *Gerontius* at the Fest—more for your sake than my own. I am dead to these wonders . . . . My things are successful among musicians but the public don't buy them . . . . My music does not arrange well for the piano & consequently is of no commercial value. If I had a free mind I shd like to write my chamber music, & symphony etc etc, on all of which forms of art providence has laid the curse of poverty. Bless it! . . . Providence, as I've often told you, is against all art so there's a satisfactory end.'

The second Düsseldorf performance was on 19 May. Wüllner again sang Gerontius, Johannes Messchaert was the bass, and the Angel's music was for the first time sung to true and beautiful effect by the English contralto Muriel Foster. The Lower Rhine Music Festivals had been a triennial Whitsuntide event, held since early in the nineteenth century successively in Düsseldorf, Aachen, and Cologne. Mendelssohn had conducted them, and some of his successors had been Joachim, Anton Rubinstein, Brahms, Richter, Richard Strauss, and Steinbach. Buths had been responsible for the Düsseldorf event since 1893, and his services to English music included not only his Elgar performances but also performances of works by Delius, notably *A Mass of Life*. Again, Elgar's eye trouble delayed his departure for the festival, but he and Alice arrived there on 16 May and listened to rehearsals in company with Rodewald from Liverpool, Johnstone of the *Manchester Guardian*, Henry Wood, and Alfred Kalisch. Wood writes[1] of the chorus having been rehearsed 'for nearly two years', which is patently nonsense. Elgar, he said, 'was recalled 20 times after the end of the first part. I have never seen an audience so excited nor a composer so spontaneously acclaimed; certainly not an Englishman—unless, perhaps, Sullivan after the first performance of *The Golden Legend*.' Johnstone's report in the *Manchester Guardian* states that 'full justice was done to the instrumental part of the work by the magnificent Festival orchestra of 127

[1] *My Life of Music* (London, 1938), pp. 324-5.

performers . . . . The part of the Angel was given by Miss Muriel Foster with the wonderfully beautiful and genuine voice that has long been recognised as her most remarkable gift, and with considerably greater and more expressive eloquence than any previous experience might have led one to expect from her. . . . The semi-chorus, seated in a line before the orchestra, acquitted themselves almost to perfection in the delicate task that they have to perform throughout the death-bed scene.' Next day, at a dinner in honour of Elgar, Richard Strauss proposed the toast 'to the welfare and success of the first English progressivist, Meister Edward Elgar, and of the young progressive school of English composers'. Elgar commented on this speech in a letter to Jaeger on 11 June 1902: 'What a fuss about Strauss's speech! too ridiculous & nobody seems in the least to know what he said or meant. I always said British musicians were several kinds of fool & ignoramus—but this is worse than usual from them.' He was referring here to Strauss's survey of British composers in which he said that Arne was somewhat less than Handel, Sterndale Bennett than Mendelssohn, and some Englishmen of later day 'not quite so great as Brahms'. Elgar pointed out in one of his Birmingham lectures a few years later that these words were 'purposely misunderstood' in some quarters.

It is, perhaps, an over-dramatic simplification to say that this Düsseldorf triumph secured the future of *Gerontius*, though no doubt it encouraged choirs to tackle it. In Berlin, six months after Düsseldorf, the *Prelude and Angel's Farewell* were included in a concert conducted by Busoni and were afterwards described as 'the most barren piece of senseless music-fabrication that has been heard for a long time'. But performances in 1903 of the complete work in Danzig and Darmstadt were successful, and this seems to be an appropriate place in which to give some account of the Elgar 'boom' on the Continent which followed Buths's advocacy.[1] Steinbach's opinion of the *Variations* has already been quoted. Fritz Volbach, musical director at Mainz, conducted *Gerontius* and *The Apostles* in 1903 and 1904. Felix Weingartner became an ardent Elgarian at this period on the strength of the *Variations* and *Cockaigne*. Richter, who once told Ettling he preferred Elgar's music to Brahms's and Tchaikovsky's, wrote to Elgar in 1902 about Wilhelm Backhaus: 'He is a grand player and he plays your March in D, some Gerontius etc. by heart, wonderfully well'. Richter,

[1] It had repercussions for others, too. Parry's *Blest Pair of Sirens* had a great success at the Duisburg Festival in May 1903. Jaeger accompanied him, and Elgar's comment to him in a letter was: 'Duisburg isn't a Lower Rhine Fest. after all—I suppose you'll all try to make out it's a bigger thing.' But on their return Elgar wrote: 'I . . . rejoice that dear old Parry had a good time with his "Sirens".'

Backhaus, and Adolph Brodsky were all working in Manchester simultaneously, and each vied with the other in admiration of Elgar. Ettling introduced *Cockaigne* to Paderewski, about whom Schuster, in a letter to Elgar dated 26 November 1902, told one of the best of all Elgar stories. Paderewski, at a party, was asked where Elgar studied. 'Nowhere'. Then who taught him? 'Le Bon Dieu,' he replied. In June 1904, Ettling wrote of visiting Fritz Kreisler and finding him at the piano 'deep in *The Dream of Gerontius*, he told me full of enthusiasm for you, whether it is true you once wrote a violin concerto & if so, he would feel happy if you would trust it to him'. These were all Continental musicians of a certain type who would immediately recognise the cosmopolitan backbone of Elgar's music, the saturation of its orchestral sound with the influences, to their ears, of Brahms, Wagner, Dvořák, and Schumann. This was meat and drink to them. This was recognized at the time by Johnstone in his perceptive account of the May Düsseldorf performance of *Gerontius* in noting that the festival gave 'only the most typically excellent of newer compositions, and of older compositions only those upon which it is felt that contemporary genius had been more particularly nourished'. The 1902 festival included Liszt's *Faust Symphony;* nor, said Johnstone, 'is it accidental that the preference is given to Strauss among German and Elgar among English composers. For those are the men who really carry the torch, and the Germans are not to be deceived in such matters.' But sixty-five years later we can be warned by the word 'progressivist' in Strauss's toast. If we seek an explanation of the short-lived nature of Continental enthusiasm for Elgar's music it is to be found in the musical personalities of his Continental enthusiasts. He came at the end of an epoch in European music, at the dawn of a renaissance in England. Already, disruptive and revolutionary forces were at work. You will not find in the careers of Richter, Brodsky, Strauss, Kreisler, Steinbach, and Weingartner evidence of special 'progressivist' sympathy with the symphonies of Mahler or the early works of Schoenberg. To Richter, the music of Debussy and Franck was anathema. The 'European mainstream' to which Elgar belonged was, in the first ten years of the twentieth century, to branch out into many stimulating tributaries. Europe, always preoccupied with novelty, thereafter found time, amid new claims on its attention, to interest itself still in Brahms and Wagner; it had no time for Elgar, who stood in their shadows, and who seemed, after first acquaintance with his serious and substantial manner, to be a contradictory English gentleman, slightly pompous, disturbing in his mixture of extroversion and introspection,

H

not quite romantic enough, and not even remotely erotic. So his claim to a place in the company of Berlioz, Liszt, and Brahms—where choral music was concerned—ceased to exercise the European musician's curiosity, especially after the political and national disruptions of the 1914–18 war.

But this was in the future. If Elgar had felt the contrast between German and English musical life after his first Düsseldorf success, he must have been again painfully conscious of the puritanical provincialism of the English attitude to art at the time of his second visit, which he prolonged with trips to Kassel, Eisenach (Bach's birthplace), and Leipzig. *Gerontius* was to be included in the Worcester Three Choirs Festival of 1902, but in April the festival committee had doubts about the 'propriety' of performing such a Roman Catholic work in an Anglican cathedral.[1] The Bishop, Dr. Gore, was a prime mover, but somebody had 'put him up to it'. Elgar wrote to Jaeger on 9 May: 'The whole objection now is manufactured by one man with the express purpose of (as he thinks) ruining the work and me.' Who this was is not at all clear. Can it have been Dr. Davidson, Archbishop of Canterbury, who four years later was to express public disapproval of the new *English Hymnal* on the grounds of its alleged Anglo-Catholic bias? According to Sir Steuart Wilson,[2] Elgar told him that Bishop Gore wrote to Dean Forrest forbidding the performance and that, owing to the Trollopian relations between a bishop and a dean, it became an obligation on the Dean to see that the performance happened. Later Elgar received a handsome retraction from the Bishop. It is interesting that Elgar, so often referred to as a 'devout Catholic', was not in any way offended by suggestions for 'de-Romanizing' the libretto. He wanted the music to be heard, and the composer outweighed the Catholic. He asked Fr. Bellasis if textual alterations would be permitted, and it was proposed to omit the passage in Part I between cues [29] and [32]—the litany of saints—to substitute 'Jesus', 'Lord', or 'Saviour' for 'Mary' and 'Joseph' and to substitute 'prayers' for 'masses' in the Angel's farewell. 'It's a dreadful mix-up,' said Elgar, 'and as usual in these petty things they all seem to hide somewhere and expect me to "play the man!" I am only anxious to do what is sensible.'[3] Elgar conducted the performance, with Marie Brema, William

---

[1] Bigotry was not the sole cause of such stupidities at that time. The Dean and Chapter of St. Paul's Cathedral held out against Parry's *Blest Pair of Sirens* for many years because of the implications of the word 'sirens'.   [2] *Musical Times*, June 1957, p. 304.

[3] *The Daily Telegraph* critic's comment on the suppressions was: 'Surely it is time for the cathedral clergy to recognize that if a work of art cannot be performed in its integrity it should not be produced at all. . . . Great is the mystery of some godliness.'

Green, and Plunket Greene as soloists: a letter inviting Jaeger to come and hear the work suggests that the composer had still not heard the music as he had imagined it—'You must come to Worcester & hear what Gerontius *might* be—the building will do it.' Three weeks later, he conducted it again at the Sheffield Festival, with John Coates, David Ffrangcon-Davies, and Muriel Foster, but again a curse seemed to be on the work, for the choir made their first entry a semitone flat. There were no further performances until March 1903, when two on successive evenings at last established it as performable without mishap.

On 12 March, at a Hallé concert in Manchester, Richter atoned for Birmingham. Johnstone of the *Manchester Guardian*, the English critic who had heard more *Gerontius* performances than anyone else and who thoroughly understood Elgar's music, wrote that it had been 'possible to hope that the Manchester performance of his great oratorio would be a striking success, and perhaps even throw a new light on the merits of the composition; and it can scarcely be questioned that the experience . . . fulfilled those hopes. It was doubtless the most carefully prepared of the performances that have been given thus far in this country. Dr. Richter was, for various reasons, peculiarly anxious that it should go well.' It was 'a rendering that sounded spontaneous and unembarrassed, as though the singers were sure of the notes and could give nearly all their attention to phrasing, expression and dynamic adjustments. In the highest degree remarkable, too, was the orchestral performance . . . . Experience of all the complete performances yet given induces us to think that the difference between thorough success and ordinary half-success with this oratorio depends more on the semi-chorus than on any other point, and this is where the preeminence of last night's rendering, among all yet given in this country, is most unquestionable . . . .'

John Coates, Marie Brema (Johnstone admired her 'nobly expressive style'), and Andrew Black were the soloists. Elgar did not hear this performance. It had been postponed for a week because of Coates's illness and was given the evening before the performance he was himself to conduct at Hanley. Adolph Brodsky wrote to him: 'We [he and his wife, Anna] just came home from the concert. It was an ideal and overwhelming performance. The impression we have from this work: greatness and sincerity; and then only you begin to realise that it is also a great master work from the technical point of view. Only a genius & a pure practical soul could have created such a work.' Rodewald wrote in equally enthusiastic terms. The Hallé Orchestra, who played again in the Hanley performance, arrived for the rehearsal 'absolutely beaming', as Alice described the occasion in a letter to Dorabella. Again, as with *King Olaf*, the North Staffordshire Chorus did full justice to Elgar's music and was selected to sing the first London performance in the uncompleted Westminster Cathedral on 6 June. Novello's had written to Elgar on 12 November 1902, saying that 'we believe that Mr. Allen Gill intends giving a performance of the work in the spring,' but nothing came of this proposal. A great amount of publicity preceded the cathedral performance when at last the English capital heard this great English music several weeks after both Chicago and New York had presented it. But the critics' reception was still cautious: they were badly placed, the acoustics were unsatisfactory and they did not like Wüllner as Gerontius. Muriel Foster and David Ffrangcon-Davies were the other soloists. No further London performance was given until February 1904. Thereafter the work took its rightful place as a classic of the time. It was even performed in Paris in 1906 when Claire Croiza sang the part of the Angel. This performance was brought about by Fauré, who had been given the score by Schuster. Every British provincial choral society took it up; it was given eighteen times at Three Choirs Festivals in the composer's lifetime and has been performed there at every festival since his death; Richter conducted it several more times in Manchester, where Johnstone wrote in the *Manchester Guardian* that 'to hear the Gerontius music is to become acquainted with by far the most remarkable and original personality that has arisen in musical Britain since the days of Purcell.'

So much space has been devoted to the genesis of *The Dream of Gerontius* not only because of the intrinsic interest of a kind of adventure story but because of the work's historical importance in the development of English music. It remains a unique contribution to English choral music because it broke new ground. Even so sensitive a critic as Johnstone loosely called it an oratorio, whereas the whole point of the work is that it cannot be fitted into such a category. It is simply what Elgar called it on the title-page: a setting to music of a poem. Elgar loved a 'tale'. He had hoped to find an English epic in *Caractacus*, but his mature genius was fired to its highest imaginative point by the most personal and mysterious of all stories, the journey of a man's soul from this world to whatever lies hereafter. Jaeger's reference to it as a 'sacred cantata' offended Elgar—'don't perpetuate that dreadful term unless we're obliged,' he wrote.[1] *Gerontius* has retained

---

[1] Elgar gave his approval to the inclusion of *Gerontius* in the oratorio section of Novello's catalogue, adding in a letter to Jaeger on 23 August 1904, 'there's no word invented yet to describe it'.

the mystique with which its early misadventures endowed it. Reputations have been won in the singing of the solo rôles, which have been distinguished by several notable interpreters. Those with long enough memories like to argue the relative merits of Gervase Elwes, John Coates, Heddle Nash, and Steuart Wilson. In later years Richard Lewis and Ronald Dowd have become identified with the work. Elgar himself, according to Basil Maine, rated Wüllner and Coates highest, and also admired Elwes. None of these three had what in purely vocal terms could be called a great tenor voice, yet it is clear from all that one reads that they were great interpreters of this rôle. Gerontius, as Jaeger rightly wrote, requires brains as well as voice; within my own experience I recall Parry Jones as one of the most moving and impressive singers of Gerontius although the voice itself was not of the first order. Among the most distinguished singers of the Angel's music are numbered Muriel Foster, Clara Butt, Astra Desmond, Gladys Ripley, Kathleen Ferrier, and Janet Baker: a royal line of succession. The bass rôles have fared less well, despite the distinctive contributions of Harold Williams, Norman Walker, and Dennis Noble. Elgar's bass parts are written for a richer, deeper bass than England usually produces. Foreign interpreters of the parts of the Priest and the Angel of the Agony sometimes have the vocal equipment but can never master the English vowels and phrase-rhythms. To this day, therefore, the music awaits its ideal trio of singers.

There are some to whom the combination of John Henry Newman's Catholicism and Edward Elgar's chromaticism is so abhorrent on aesthetic grounds that they cannot hear *The Dream of Gerontius* without acute mental, and even physical, discomfort. For them nothing can be done. For the vast majority not afflicted in this way the work is a musical masterpiece of the highest calibre, and a spiritual and artistic experience which repeated hearings do not lessen in power. One reason for its success is the skilful way in which Elgar adapted the poem, some might say improving on Newman in the process, tautening it and rejecting unerringly the parts unsuitable for musical setting. The marvellous opening of the Prelude, *lento mistico*, scored for muted violas, clarinets, and bassoons with the cor anglais entering unforgettably at the fifth bar, takes the responsive listener at once into the world of Elgar's imagination, and vividly into the sick-room. We follow Gerontius's progress from death to the threshold of eternity with the attention that supreme art compels. Never before in English choral music had the orchestra sounded so expressive, so detailed in its illustrative imaginativeness. Point after point in the text is etched into the memory by the scoring. One thinks immediately of the low flute crescendo in the Demons' Chorus for the 'low hideous purring', the compassionate oboe at 'manhood crucified', the extraordinary writing for strings at 'the emptying out of each constituent' and to illustrate the 'strange innermost abandonment', the hollow chord at the word 'terrible' in 'The thought of death and judgment was to me most terrible', the use of the harp as the Angel sings 'Farewell', the sense of timelessness in the strings' rarefied opening to Part II, the pre-echoes in the orchestra of the Angel's first song, and the splendidly brazen brass snarls in the Demons' Chorus. Yet there is a tendency some-times to write of *Gerontius* as if the orchestration, marvellous as it is, was the whole story. This is, after all, a major choral work and the writing for the voices, soloists and choir, is that of a master, and its originality and brilliance should not be overlooked. Two aspects in particular are outstanding. First is Elgar's use of a semi-chorus to represent, in Part I, the Priest's Assistants at Gerontius's death-bed. Their first entry with 'Kyrie eleison', unaccompanied, could only have been written by a man who thoroughly understood choral singing and who had lived among choirs and cathedrals, as Elgar had. 'The build-ing will do it', he told Jaeger; and to hear the voices steal in at this point during a performance in Worcester Cathedral or York Minster is to realize the completeness of Elgar's conception. He had strong views about the semi-chorus which he thought should be limited to eighteen voices (five sopranos, five contraltos, four tenors, and four basses), 'pure and "sweet" without the slightest hardness of tone'. This he wrote to Nicholas Kilburn in October 1902, in reply to a series of questions about the choral effects in *Gerontius*. 'At Düsseldorf,' he wrote, 'they were placed *between* the soloist & the orchestra & I recom-mend this plan in the printed full score.'

The other specially notable feature is the extremely fluent type of recitative, a true melodic speech-rhythm, which characterizes the part of Gerontius. This is very marked in the beginning of Part II, where the Soul of Gerontius sings of the liberation from the body: 'I feel in me an inexpressive lightness . . . . I hear no more the busy beat of time . . . . This silence pours a solitariness into the very essence of my soul . . . . And hark! I hear a singing; yet in sooth I cannot of that music rightly say whether I hear or touch or taste the tones . . . .' These words, and many other examples from Part I, especially the great opening 'Thou art calling me', are set so inevitably and rightly that once heard it is impossible to divorce them from the music: they have become one and indivisible. There are the usual blemishes in Elgar's word-setting,

where the music takes hold and the words must fend for themselves—
'Within his ample palm' is one ugly moment, and there are several in
the Angel's part, 'Softly and gently' being a particularly jarring example—but for the greater part of the work the union of voice and
verse is perfect. It need not be thought that Elgar was unaware of the
rhythmic stresses of his native tongue and disregarded them to suit his
purpose. He had pronounced views, as expressed in a letter to Jaeger
written on 26 April 1908: 'I hold that *short* syllables may be sustained
occasionally for the sake of effect just as an actor does. There is one
dear good man against whom I wd. not *think anything* & that is Parry.
But he almost if not quite annoys me in the way he sets the words
which swarm in our English—two syllables, both short, the first
accented, e.g. petal. Set in an ordinary way a poem sounds like reading
a newspaper paragraph. I remember insisting on doing[1] a poem of
Tennyson (Lotos Eaters!) by P. I liked it & studied it with the chorus
for months & had great difficulty in getting them to *take* to it . . . .
After the concert a very well educated lady . . . said to me "We have
done our best to please & I am sorry you insisted: I shall never read the
poem again with any enjoyment". This of course simply on account
of the *driven* accents . . . . Only the other day one of your best chorus-
masters said I know nothing of writing for the voice *or* choral effect—
asked why, he pointed to a ff on a C for sopranos: this sort of thing is
annoying as it shews what idiots we write for. If the clown had an
ounce of artistic sense he wd. have seen that the note was to help the
contraltos & to lead into a *diminuendo* impossible to obtain in any other
way.'[2]

The massed choral effects in *Gerontius* are nearly all splendid. He
hardly ever excelled the finale of Part I, 'Go forth in the name of
angels and archangels,' for poetry combined with grandiloquence. The
climax of 'Praise to the Holiest' is thrilling to sing and to hear, and its
brilliance drives from the mind some rather less inspired pages a little
earlier. Here again, the first sounds of 'Praise to the Holiest', coming
from afar, are choral writing *par excellence*. The Demons' Chorus has
been the butt of critics taking a lead from Ernest Newman's 1905 book
in which he referred to 'pantomime demons'. But if it is properly

---

[1] At Worcestershire Philharmonic, 10 May 1902.
[2] This occurrence bears a striking resemblance to a story, told by Reed and others and
transposed to the orchestra, that an academic-minded musician asked Elgar why a bass
clarinet passage was marked *pp* against the rest of the orchestra's *ff* when it could not
possibly be heard. Elgar is said to have pointed to a solo passage for the instrument a few
pages later for which the earlier bars were a 'warming up'. Possibly the passage concerned
is nine bars after cue 31, 1st movement, 1st Symphony.

rehearsed and sung incisively it does convey the composer's sardonic and sarcastic intentions. Sir Henry Coward and Sir John Barbirolli found the way to interpret this section correctly, and so perhaps did Richter, for Arthur Johnstone wrote of 'a welter of infernal but most eloquent sound' at the 1903 Hallé performance. Elgar's use of fugue in this chorus is expressive and free, a startling contrast to the fugue in *Lux Christi* which he said he wrote because he felt it was expected of him—and it sounds like it. The Demons' fugue is tremendous stuff, and it wears its academic dress with a rakish indifference to fashion, as do all the finest choral passages in *Gerontius*. 'You know, Billy,' Elgar said to W. H. Reed after a Lincoln performance of the work, 'I believe there is a lot of double counterpoint, or whatever they call it, in that'—so anxious was he to be free from any suggestion of academic methods or techniques, though of course he knew them inside out.

In *Gerontius*, we find the fullest expression of all Elgar's many-sided gifts. It is his finest work. Part I is practically flawless; tension sometimes slackens in Part II but is skilfully built up again at the end for the Angel of the Agony's aria, Gerontius's 'Take me away' and the Angel's final meltingly beautiful Farewell. Anyone can pick out the weaker moments: far more important is the work's impregnable strength as an impassioned human document. Not only did Elgar bring Newman's poem to life and give expression to his religious beliefs at that time; he expressed unforgettably the darker side of his own nature: the 'sense of ruin' pervades the music, and in Gerontius's anguished cries on his bed of pain can be recognized the tormented spirit discernible in Elgar's letters to Jaeger. From his deepest experience, Elgar created the last great artistic monument of the reign of Queen Victoria and the last of the nineteenth century.

8 Friends and Relations

After the second Düsseldorf *Dream of Gerontius*, Alice Elgar wrote an account of the performance and of Strauss's tribute for her mother-in-law, who had barely three months more to live. In her reply, from the music-shop home in Worcester High Street, Anne Elgar said: 'What can I say to him the dear one—I feel that he is some great historic person—I cannot claim a little bit of him now he belongs to the big world.'

In these moving words are an ironic tribute, for though he *was* an historic person belonging to the big world, the dichotomy of his life in the years to follow was the conflict and contrast of Elgar the Historic Person with Elgar of Worcester. The London Elgar and the Country Elgar were very nearly two different people except that the personality at the heart of both was complex, so that parts of one mixed with the other, not always to happy effect. The results show plainly in his music. His creative life is usually divided for convenience into three periods: the early but unsatisfactory works up to 1899, the masterpieces from 1899 to 1919, then the twilight and virtually silent last fourteen years. But this is an over-simplification, because the 1899–1919 period is strongly sub-divisible. The *Variations* and *Gerontius* stand apart as the most artistically and psychologically complete of all his works. The mainly orchestral works produced from 1908 to 1913 are technically and psychologically far more complicated and diffuse. There can be little doubt that these fascinating nuances reflect the composer's personality and outlook to a larger degree than in most composers' works. Though his creations were his private kingdom, Elgar was constitutionally unable to seal them off from other facets of his mind.

To come nearer to understanding these complexities, it is perhaps a help to look at some of his personal relationships at this period of his life. When his mother died in the late summer of 1902 he lost the first moulding influence on his mind, for it was she who had stimulated his love of literature and the world of nature around him. Although, like all children, he had sometimes felt misunderstood by his parents, Elgar had an abiding love and respect for the 'two honest old burghers' as he called them to Troyte Griffith. After his father died in

1906, Elgar sought Troyte's aid (as an architect) in designing a suitable gravestone. 'I do not feel drawn towards the stonemason monumental-artist sort of thing,' he wrote.[1] 'As we bear an old Saxon name wd. it be too fanciful, if practicable, to take some Saxon thing for a model or rather type?' He was immensely proud to show his parents the proofs of his success. The day after the robes of his Cambridge doctorate arrived at his home (on 3 December 1901), he took them to Worcester to show them to William and Anne. When he was knighted his first thought was to go and tell his father; then an old and ailing widower; but perhaps most fitting and moving of all was his gesture, in September 1905, when he walked in procession along High Street, Worcester, on his way to receive the honorary freedom of the city. As he passed Elgar Brothers' shop he bared his head in salute to his father, who watched the scene from an upper window.

In 1902 Edward and Alice Elgar had been married for thirteen years. To say that she was the greatest influence on his life is no exaggeration, for no other interpretation is possible. She was eight years older; and if any amateur psycho-analyst chooses to notice that Elgar's wife and many of his women friends were older than he and to deduce that he preferred a maternal relationship, no one can stop him, though he will get little encouragement from me. It would be much nearer the mark to say that in Alice, Elgar found wife, mother, friend, mentor, and spur. It is possible to look askance at certain aspects of their life together—in which marriage is it not possible?—but any attempt to 'debunk' the legend of their relationship is doomed to failure from the facts of Elgar's words, his reaction to her death, and the disinterested testimony of others who were by no means blind to Alice's faults. He married out of his class. There must have been great stresses in the 1890s for a patrician lady who married a lower-middle-class shop-keeper's son, a man whose social graces were acquired rather than in-herited, and who ran the risk of being suspected of having married 'above him' for the reason that his wife had a small private income. That they shared literary and artistic tastes would merely be counted against them as an even odder cause for matrimony. That Elgar should have felt gratitude to Alice for her courage, is obvious. She, for her part, marrying beneath her at forty, would be suspected of a wish to be 'off the shelf' at any cost. That she had married for love of a man in whom she had rightly perceived the quality of genius would hardly have occurred to some of the gentry of late Victorian Worcestershire. So when her choice was justified, when her talented local composer

[1] 25 October 1907.

became the acknowledged leader of his profession, friend of kings and marquesses, it is understandable that she rubbed it in, although one may feel that a little less zest would have assisted Edward more. For there were no half-measures, as some extracts already quoted from her diary will have shown. She had never doubted Edward's supremacy and never would:

> Parratt quite carried away with enthusiasm for E's great music [*Lux Christi*] . . . Glorious *King Olaf* a magnificent triumph. D.G. . . . Dear Bavarians [*Scenes from the Bavarian Highlands*] first time. Immense enthusiasm. . . . Great success. D.G. [*Variations*] . . . It was said there had never been such a triumph in Mainz [*The Apostles*]. . . . E. lectured most splendidly, held his audience breathless (Birmingham, 1905). . . . Orch. & large part of audience simply rose, people *wept*. E. looked very *apart* and beautiful being recalled again & again [London first performance of A flat symphony]. . . . This is a day to be marked. E. finished his Symphony [No. 2]. It seems one of his very greatest works, vast in design & supremely beautiful. It is really sublime. . . . Wertheim [piano soloist in Saint-Saëns piano concerto which Elgar conducted] agitating as he left out 1/2 bars. Required a genius to keep it right.

She declared war on any discourtesy, such as this at a rehearsal of *The Music Makers*: 'Most annoying . . . people moving & going in & out & H. Wood quite unbearable even shutting door noisily.' One evening she was engaged in conversation about the Nobel Peace Prize and confided to her diary, 'Pray it may be given to E.' Attending a wartime concert at which Stanford's 'common' *Songs of the Sea* preceded a work by Elgar she noted: 'The great music began—E. looked like the High Priest of Art.' It was Alice's faith which was really sublime, however indulgently we may smile and perhaps feel that the Almighty, too, was being congratulated on His good taste. Had these effusions been limited to private entries in a diary—even with one eye on posterity—no harm would have been done. But they were not. Arnold Bax was at the age of seventeen taken to meet Elgar at Birchwood in 1901. 'The composer's wife, a pleasant-looking fair-haired lady, with—it struck me—rather an anxious manner, welcomed us very kindly in her gentle, slightly hesitant voice. Almost at once she began to speak enthusiastically and a little extravagantly about her wonderful husband and his work.'[1] Vaughan Williams, seated next to Alice at a Three Choirs rehearsal of the Second Symphony in 1912, was nudged during the slow movement and persistently asked 'Isn't it lovely?' She was unable to realize that the adoration of the Malvern group of intimate friends was shared at a less intense level elsewhere. Even Jaeger

---

[1] *Farewell, My Youth*, pp. 29–30.

sometimes found it too much. Describing to Dorabella the first Düsseldorf full rehearsal of *Gerontius*, he wrote: 'As for dear Mrs. E., you can imagine her state of seventh-heaven-beatitude, with eyebrow lifting, neck twisting, forget-me-not glances towards the invisible Heavens! Don't think I am making fun of her! I am not; but you know her signs of deep emotion over the Dr.'s music, don't you?'

Indeed she did, for one of the best pictures of the domestic life of Edward and Alice is contained in Dorabella's book, a picture that, though sometimes feline, is both warm-hearted and shrewd. It tells much 'between the lines'. Though Alice's loyalty was never strained, life was not a bed of roses and it would be wrong to draw a portrait of her as a pliant creature, fondly waiting to worship the latest emanation of her husband's genius. She was an inexorable manager, of a type that Elgar needed. Schuster in a letter to Elgar in 1903 referred to her as an 'indefatigable hostess and *marvellous* manager'. Elgar was lazy and uninterested in business matters, but Alice insisted that they were attended to. 'One can so easily understand how the anxiety and worry of it all would get on her nerves,' Dorabella wrote in her book.[1] 'Letters unanswered and promises &c. unfulfilled, and even the possibility that contracts might be broken.' That Elgar realized her value to him in this respect is evident from the letter from a member of the Baker family at Hasfield Court which Dorabella also quotes,[2] in which the writer recalled an occasion when Elgar was leaving the house at Hasfield to play in the garden with the children. The afternoon post had arrived and Alice held out a packet of letters to him. 'But I'm going out now,' he said, and threw them on the floor, where one of the children picked them up. 'Oh, Edward, that *was* naughty,' she said, adding, 'These must be answered *at once*.' 'With a shout of ribald laughter he took them from her and went straight back upstairs, without another word.' Alice knew, too, the hardship of days when he was deep in writing a new work and she would leave a tray of food outside his study, though often it remained there uneaten. Then, if he came to a meal—one such as Dorabella describes when *The Kingdom* was being written—he would sit, tense and silent, looking pale and drawn, and returning at the first possible minute to his study. Perhaps after midnight he would emerge, the battle won, ready, when the others were tired and sleepy, for conversation and to be amused. On other occasions he was the life and soul of the party. 'He kept up a running fire of absurd remarks, comments, chaff and repartee,' says Dorabella.[3] 'I often laughed so much that I could hardly eat and was positively

[1] Op. cit., p. 83.   [2] Op. cit., p. 102.   [3] Op. cit., pp. 25–26.

afraid to drink. Also it did not help matters to have the Lady [Dorabella always referred to Alice in this way] at the bottom of the table—not always completely approving, particularly if Carice was present—putting in remarks to try to check the flow: "Oh, Edward dear, how *can* you?" or "Oh, Edward, *really*!" "Cheer up Chicky" was all she got for her pains.' Sometimes Alice would apologize to visitors for her husband's behaviour: 'Oh *please* don't mind him. Edward dear, how *can* you?'

No one knew better than Alice that this kind of schoolboyish exuberance would be followed by a mood of dispirited, morose boredom when Elgar needed distraction, and she unerringly picked the people who would cheer him up. Life was complicated, too, for the cheerers-up, as Dorabella found: 'It needed a good deal of tact and care to think of the right things to say or the right line to take; particularly when one found that a person who had been lauded to the skies on a former visit was now flung to earth—though seldom by *him*.'[1] He was not the easiest of men with whom to live, as his outbursts of sulky temper at rehearsals must have made clear to other people. He paid dearly for his abuse of the choir at the Birmingham *Gerontius*, and W. H. Reed has recorded similar examples, notably one at the 1902 Worcester *Gerontius* rehearsal, for instance, when the timpanist made a bad mistake in the orchestral climax before 'Take me away' and Elgar 'stopped the rehearsal, his face a picture of horror—he gazed long and intently at the unfortunate drummer, and then said almost with terror in his voice: "Why—why did you do that?" '[2] Nevertheless, Alice's criticisms of his music were accepted in a generous and complimentary spirit. Though not a technical musician, her claim to the title of 'the first Elgarian' is indisputable: she understood his work and he knew she did. Reed recounts Elgar's words to him on this subject: 'I played some of the music I had written that day, and she nodded her head appreciatively, except over one passage, at which she sat up rather grimly, I thought. However, I went to bed leaving it as it was; but I got up as soon as it was light and went down to look over what I had written. I found it as I had left it, except that there was a little piece of paper, pinned over the offending bars, on which was written "All of it is beautiful and just right, except this ending. Don't you think, dear Edward, that this end is just a little . . .?" Well, Billy, I scrapped that end.'

He scrapped other things, too, that did not win the nod of approval. In 1903 he was planning a ballet on the subject of Rabelais and had gone so far as to speak to Henry Higgins, chairman of the Grand Opera

[1] Op. cit., p. 27.   [2] *Elgar*, op. cit., p. 68.

Syndicate which administered Covent Garden. He wrote to Troyte about this on 19 November 1903: 'He is keen to produce "Rabelais" on the lines I suggested! New costumes & everything—"like a shot". We'll have some fun one day.' But people less broadminded than Troyte, Alice among them, were not at all happy that the writer of Coronation odes and of *The Apostles*, should turn to the subject of Rabelais. So he abandoned the sketches, although he got his own back by adapting one of the tunes as the introductory Maestoso section of his *Coronation March* for George V. If it seems extraordinary that such an attitude should have prevailed, one has only to turn to *Falstaff* and to Elgar's depiction of the 'honest gentlewomen'—Doll Tearsheet, Mrs. Quickly, and company—and then to quote another phrase from a letter to Troyte: 'Alice is horrified I fear with my honest gentlewomen —of course they must be in—do you think I have overdone them?' No one could possibly think he had, for their musical representation is genteel and bowdlerized. Bearing this in mind, it would be unwise to spring to arms and cry, with all the emancipated frankness of today, that the Philistine, narrow-minded, patrician ladies of Malvern had deprived the world of a lusty, rumbustious ballet suite in *Rabelais*. The likelihood is that Elgar would have been quite unable to transpose the world of Pantagruel into music, and no doubt he knew it. An artist is not so easily discouraged if he wants to create something. Alice's disapproval of the subject probably had something to do with the abandonment of *Rabelais*; but the real reason, we may be sure, is that Elgar knew it 'would not work'. He was, in any case, toying with several ideas which came to naught at about that date. The incident is valuable, however, in throwing some light on points where these marriage partners, ideally matched in most ways, found themselves reminded of their different backgrounds. It is unlikely that Alice, gently as she remonstrated, could at all share Elgar's noisy, practical-joke type of humour or that she understood the side of him illustrated by this letter to Jaeger in June 1902: 'I *hate* coming to town—shall miss the haymaking I fear. Had 50 miles ride (on a bicycle) yesterday amongst the Avon country—Shakespeare etc. etc. Oh! so lovely but solus 'cos I can't find anybody here foolheaded enough to eat bread & cheese & drink beer—they've all got livers & apparently live in the country 'cos they can't afford to be swells in a town. Oh! Lor!'

But even if she could not share this part of her husband, Alice knew its importance to him. For his part he tolerated her liking for society, her predilection for the nobility and for outward and visible signs of distinction, even if he sometimes found the company of the 'great' more than a little oppressive. A letter to Schuster in July 1910, when he was staying in Cornwall with the 13th of the Variations, Mary Lygon, by now Lady Mary Trefusis, tells much: 'It is heavenly etc. here! but I would like to choose my company as you allow me to do at The Hut. . . . Lady M. is as of old and always very "nice" & dear & rather severe. Of the rest I will tell you . . . Alice is radiantly happy. . . . I wish you and . . .! and . . .!! and . . .!!! were here. . . .' His natural inclination was to refuse honours, but he accepted them because they meant much to Alice and he owed much to her. When she died, he placed his Court Sword in her coffin, and it is buried with her.[1] Not too much should be made of Dorabella's veiled hints[2] about suppressions by Alice: that, apart from one incident, she never heard horse-racing, one of Elgar's interests, mentioned in the household in her fifteen years of close acquaintance with it. His racing interests were strong enough for him to note, on the day of the first performance of *The Apostles*, that Grey Tick had won the Cesarewich at 20 to 1.

One evening in 1914 Alice read aloud to Elgar from one of her own writings. That night, in her diary, she allowed herself some regrets for her abandoned literary ambitions. But she added: 'The care of a genius is enough of a life work for any woman.' It was as simple as that. We may think she was a snob, we may find oppressive her undiluted, blinkered enthusiasm for her husband's music. But were she to return today and see the position Elgar still occupies, the number of broadcast and concert-hall performances and the growing collection of superb recordings, she could say: 'All this you owe to me.' And she would be right.

                 *   *   *

The other profound influence of the crucial years in Elgar's life was August Jaeger. He made his appearance on the scene in 1897 at the very moment when Elgar knew that, given the chance, he could have the world at his feet. His friendship acted like a catalyst on Elgar, releasing in him the scorn and derision he felt for his English contemporaries. Jaeger, who shared these views, played him along and one has the sensation, reading their early correspondence, that each was using the other as an outlet, each administering to the other's 'chip'. Later, as has been seen and will again be seen in later chapters, Elgar came to respect

[1] F. Bonavia has written that 'all' Elgar's honours were buried with Lady Elgar, and Dorabella gives a supposedly authentic list. Mrs. Elgar Blake assures me that only the sword was buried. When her father became Master of the King's Musick he obtained a new one which is now at the Birthplace at Broadheath.

[2] On p. 8 of *Memories of a Variation*.

his German friend's opinions, to take criticism from him in a tolerant spirit, often to accept his advice, and eventually to sustain a deep affection for him. The letters to Jaeger, many of which have been and will be quoted, are an indispensable guide to Elgar the composer. They also illustrate, more vividly than any other of his letters, even those to Troyte, Elgar's quirky humour, his extraordinary love of puns and plays on words, an aspect of him so integral to a full portrait that it cannot be set on one side as mere decoration. Jaeger, whose native tongue was not English, must have been flattered to be the principal target for these shafts of his strange unpredictable friend. Such spellings as 'orkestration' were commonplace. When Elgar dropped the formal 'Dear Mr. Jaeger' for 'My dear Jaeger' he added 'The Mister-y is soluted'. 'I say nuffin', 'those two daze', 'Indeks', 'Direxshuns', 'Him wot rote it', 'a Joon programme'—what pleasure did Elgar himself derive from this kind of thing? Was it a kind of jocular front to cover the inner despair which broke out time and again (and was always expressed in conventional spelling)? It seems the only logical explanation for the more childish examples, as opposed to the pleasure in punning, an acquired taste, and the crossword-puzzle-addict delight in transposing letters, such as the rather charming 'Cueen's Qopy' and his conversational 'Look, bung yirds' to Dorabella whenever he saw young birds. He played a game with the word 'score', making it more and more unrecognizable to Jaeger, from 'skore' to 'skoughre' to 'ssczowoughohr' and even wilder permutations. He once spelt anxious as 'angkschzsuszcs', and he enjoyed variations of the names Jaeger and Nimrod—'Jägerer', 'Jaegerissimo', 'Jaggs', 'Jay', 'Jaerodnimgeresque', 'Jagpot'. Occasionally, in the later years, he was 'Augustus' or 'Nimrod' or 'Mosshead'. This kind of playfulness sometimes became slightly barbed. In August of 1903 Jaeger confessed that a progression in *The Apostles* set his teeth on edge. 'If I found that in a work by a beginner, I should laugh & say "poor chap, how crude".' (The offending passage is in the voice parts at bars 3 and 4, p. 109 of the vocal score.) Elgar took this kind of thing very much to heart. 'Try it ppp & dolce—I fear your heavy thumb & melodious forefinger are rather stiff, old Boy.' He signed this letter, written on 2 August, 'Edward of the *crude* (you old toad) progression'. The next letter, on 5 August, has a similar signature. 'Edward the Crude', with a drawing of himself cocking a snook and saying 'Yah!' was on a letter on 7 August. By 16 August it was 'Yours Crooder than ever', on 20 August 'Your groping old crudity', and by 20 September a P.S. 'You haven't called me crooood lately—I breathe again.' No wonder he hadn't; by then the point was

PLATE V

Alice Elgar

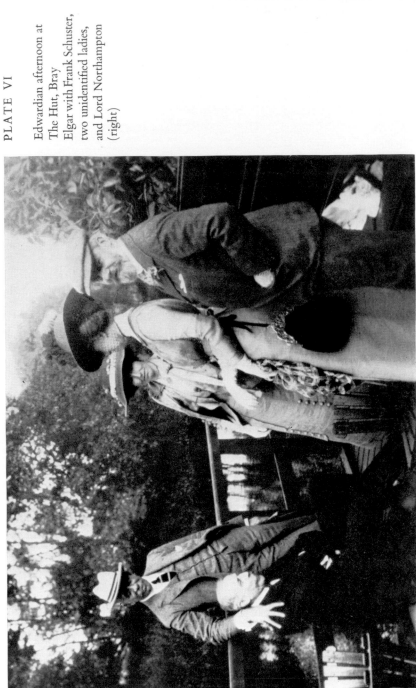

PLATE VI

Edwardian afternoon at
The Hut, Bray
Elgar with Frank Schuster,
two unidentified ladies,
and Lord Northampton
(right)

no doubt well taken. Of course it was all good clean fun, but . . .
Occasionally these verbal fantasies achieved real and penetrating wit,
as for instance in the letter of 14 November 1900, preceding his depar-
ture to Cambridge to receive an honorary degree. This was signed
'Yours gownily' and included the sentence 'I feel Gibbonsy, Croftish,
Byrdlich & foolish all over.' There was also the delightful letter which
Jaeger, as 'Dear Augustus', received at Christmas 1902:

a regular Yule-loggy puddingy, Brandy-saucious letter. . . . I have had Xmas
presents—all Wagner's prose works (translated) 8 vols & & & & & & the
Encyc. Brit & the bookcase!!!! a present (£42). Behold in me a learned prig:
prig mark you—I know the height of Ararat (But don't know how to spell it)
& all sorts of japes. Look 'ere: I'm learned now & no base Nimrodkin (Hebraic
plural) shall look down on me: is not my learning vast in 35 volumes & in a
revolving bookcase—my head too revolves with delight. I can tell you who was
Aaron's mother-in-law's first cousin's bootblack & infinitesimal Calculus etc.
etc. I charge 6d. to enter the study now. I say, I have a lively fine specimen of a
Vanessa—pish! I shd say to one unwise a peacock butterfly who is helping the
Apostles & lives in this study. I feed him—no, drink him on sugar & water & he
lives in a Chrysanthemum—it's all lovely & Japanesy & pastoral—I'm sure the
beast is a familiar spirit—Angel Gabriel or Simon Magus, or Helen of Tyre or
somebody—just fancy sitting in this study surrounded with flowers & a live
butterfly at Xmas—this music's going to be good I can tell you. . . . Your
austere & learned friend (34 vols & a bookcase) Paracelsus Elgar (with a pain
in his stomach) Mince pizon.[1]

To Jaeger the years from 1898 to 1904, when he was midwife to
works he knew to be masterpieces, must have seemed, for all their
trials, a golden age. And when kings and noblemen fêted his protégé
at the Elgar Festival of 1904 he began to fear, for two reasons: selfishly
though understandably that his own day was done, and that the
demands of being a celebrity might harm Elgar as a creative artist. He
wrote a warning note: 'Don't let 'em spoil you, you "dear innocent,
guileless Child" as dear old Hans [Richter] calls you in his fatherly
loving way.' The guileless child of forty-six replied from a Manchester
hotel, beginning the letter formally in a mock-serious vein: 'The
position I now hold—greatly owing to your exertions & friendship—
warrants me in throwing you over. . . . Now, you old Moss, read the

---

[1] A similar letter, signed 'Isaac Newton Elgar', went on the same day to Dorabella (or,
on this occasion, Dorabellissima). She records that the bookcase was soon 'sent away' by
Alice as Elgar 'would turn it round so'.

I

other side.' On the opposite page he wrote: 'Dearie Moss . . . Whenever anything of mine is to be done you beg me not to be conceited & not to forget old friends etc. You are an old PIG & deserve some such letter as the unfinished one on the other side. . . . Don't bother me about conceit again—I haven't any except that I always resent any familiarity from outsiders & I *do* stand up for the *dignity* of our art—not profession.' Nevertheless from 1905 onwards the correspondence diminished. Jaeger was away from Novello's at Davos, hoping to cure his tuberculosis, and so there were fewer musical matters for Elgar to write to him about. Elgar himself was ill about that time and Lady Elgar took over much of his correspondence. In 1907 and 1908 the Elgars spent a good deal of time out of England and by then Jaeger was dying. To Dorabella in 1908 he wrote: 'I say, what *is* Elgar composing now? . . . He never tells me now, the wretch.' A year earlier he had written 'I have worked *terribly* hard for E. E. and ruined my health over it very likely. . . . I have never loved & admired a man more, made myself more a slave for any man out of sheer enthusiasm.' He lived to hear the symphony for which he had hoped since 1898 and to write about its effect on him to 'My dear, great Edward'. But this will be told in a later chapter. The beneficial effects of Jaeger's friendship are obvious. Less salutary was his by no means inadvertent stoking of Elgar's resentment of the academic hierarchy represented by Stanford and Mackenzie. For example, in October 1899, after reading a favourable magazine review of Elgar's music he wrote, 'I should have liked to watch Stanford's face as he read it.' But, in fairness, it did not need a Jaeger to create bad blood between Stanford and Elgar. The characters of the two men made a clash inevitable; and, sure enough, it came, though not from the petty kind of jealousy ascribed by Jaeger (and Elgar) to Stanford of which, indeed, Stanford was incapable.

*   *   *

Charles Villiers Stanford was five years older than Elgar. He was an Irish Protestant, educated in Dublin and at Cambridge University. His academic career was brilliant, and he was also a fine practical musician as conductor and organist. When he was thirty-one he was appointed to the staff of the new Royal College of Music, at thirty-three he was conductor of the London Bach Choir, and at thirty-five he succeeded Macfarren as Professor of Music at Cambridge. When he was twenty-five he had a work performed at the Three Choirs Festival, Richter and Manns conducted his music in London, and he had a Birmingham Festival commission when he was thirty, a year after his first opera had been produced in Hanover. By the 1890s he occupied a commanding position in English musical life as teacher, conductor, and composer. He was warm-hearted, generous, and irascible: his bark was worse than his bite, but not everybody realized it. Some of his pupils (Vaughan Williams was an outstanding example) stood up to him and gave him affectionate respect. Others fled from his tongue to find another teacher. By some critics his achievements were regarded with awe;[1] others led by Bernard Shaw found his music excessively influenced by Brahms, Verdi, and other greater figures. Today his exquisite songs and part-songs, his Irish arrangements, his church music and such excellent choral works as the *Songs of the Sea* keep his name alive. During his lifetime he quarrelled with most people and his relationship with Cambridge was decidedly prickly. It was a law of nature that Stanford the tactless and Elgar the thin-skinned would disagree. Their first meeting in 1896, already recounted, was friendly enough, and it was in that year, as Sir Alexander Mackenzie recalled in his book *A Musician's Narrative*, that Stanford, after hearing *King Olaf*, 'enthusiastically drew my attention to the almost unknown new-comer's splendid gifts.' The next year Elgar asked for Stanford's opinion of, of all things, *The Banner of St. George*, and Stanford, forgetting that he was dealing with a sensitive fellow-artist and not a student's composition exercise, replied that 'it's all very well having fine raiment, but there must be a fine body to put it on'. Coolness lasted for about two years, but on 18 January 1900, Elgar conducted *Sea Pictures* at a Hallé concert the rest of which Stanford conducted. He mentioned to Jaeger ten days later: 'We are quite as before . . . we smoked & supped together.' This rapprochement resulted in Stanford's inclusion of the *Sea Pictures* in a R.C.M. concert on 15 March with Muriel Foster as the soloist, although in the event Parry conducted because Stanford was ill. Elgar made Stanford an honorary member of the Worcestershire Philharmonic Society and performed his *The Last Post* at one of its concerts. Whatever Elgar may have thought of Stanford's music, Stanford genuinely admired Elgar's. His attitude to *Gerontius* was double-edged; the musician in him appreciated it, the Protestant was repelled. He told Herbert Howells that he would have 'given his head' to have written Part I. To T. F. Dunhill he remarked that 'it stinks of incense'. The latter remark got back to Elgar, though when it was

---

[1] Jaeger, writing to Elgar in March 1898, after he had written an unfavourable notice of a Stanford concert for the *Musical Times*, said: 'Really one gets quite disgusted and wants to say something nasty when one sees those critic friends of composers & conductors use only eulogisms to describe whatever the latter do.'

made is not known. Nevertheless Stanford had unqualified admiration for the *Variations*, and it was he who, on the strength of that work, urged Cambridge to make Elgar an honorary Doctor of Music. The letter containing the invitation was received at Malvern on 17 October 1900, exactly a fortnight after the Birmingham *Gerontius* fiasco. Alice was delighted; Elgar's first inclination was to refuse. He said he could not afford the robes, and a deeper-seated reason was his dislike of being in any way associated with the 'academic' musicians he despised. Miss Rosa Burley, in a note quoted by Dr. Percy Young in *Letters to Nimrod*,[1] says that she reminded him that this was a recognition of *Gerontius* and that he could hire the robes. Next day he notified Cambridge of his acceptance and chose St. Cecilia's Day, 22 November 1900, for the ceremony. The story told by Basil Maine[2] that Alice was so anxious for him to accept that she persuaded Rodewald to travel from Liverpool to plead with him is therefore obviously untrue. Cowen was to be similarly 'doctored' and Elgar was sufficiently proud of the honour to write to Jaeger: 'Edwards [F. G. Edwards, then editor of the *Musical Times*] ought to give a list of the people on whom it has been conferred . . . the general public don't know the difference between "it" & the stupid Canterbury commercial transaction.' Stanford was not present at the conference because he had to be in Leeds for talks about the 1901 festival. If he was avoiding anyone that day, as has been suggested, it would have been Cowen, not Elgar, for there was intrigue at that time over the conductorship of the Leeds Festival, in which Cowen was deeply involved. He contributed to a subscription list for Elgar's robes sent round by Bantock. Others who helped provide the necessary £45 were Parry, Jaeger, Wood, Plunket Greene, Pitt, Kilburn, Kalisch, and friends of earlier days. It was Rodewald who travelled to Malvern a year later on 8 November 1901 '& announced to me the great surprise about the Robes—I don't know what to make of you all & am in a fit of the *blues* thinking of the kindness of you all for which I have done nothing to deserve—it's very odd & dreamlike & I don't know who I am. . . .'[3]

Stanford's admiration was practical as well as emotional at this time. He insisted that the *Variations* should be played at the 1901 Leeds Festival, where Elgar conducted them at his invitation. He wrote to Elgar appreciatively of the *Cockaigne* overture and the first two *Pomp and Circumstance* marches—'they both came off like blazes, and are uncommon fine stuff'—and he conducted the *Variations* at the R.C.M. on 13 December 1901—'I liked them better every time'. In a postscript to

[1] Pp. 111–12.   [2] Op. cit., i, p. 118.   [3] Letter to Jaeger, 9 November 1901.

this letter he said: 'Will you do me a great kindness? Give us [the College] the première of an orchestral thing some day. There's cheek. I only ask it because I could give such a thing a dozen rehearsals; and that tells. And I'd like a big thing, a Symphony please. I'll pledge my conscience to make them play it right for you.' And in April 1902 Stanford sought permission to have Elgar nominated for the Athenaeum Club. Again, the thought of the entrance fee of 30 guineas made Elgar doubtful about accepting, but Stanford advised him to write a couple of songs, as he had done, and pay the fee with advance royalties. Elgar was elected under Rule 2 on 8 May 1903, and his sponsors were Parry and Stanford.

For *Gerontius*, too, Stanford was a champion. He had his own troubles with the Leeds Philharmonic Society[1] Committee principally because of their failure or unwillingness to consult him. He had wanted *Gerontius* in the 1901–2 season, but the committee had curtly rejected the idea and the following March he wrote to J. H. Green, secretary of the Society:[2] 'A work which is the first English composition to be given at a Lower Rhine Festival (in consequence of which Sheffield upsets its programme to include it) is not a work to be simply dismissed because A or B don't personally care for it. It is the duty of a great choral society in a great town to let its public form their own judgment on such an important composition which has even reached with success Germany in its most Anglophobic temper. . . . Surely it is for a choral society such as yours to lead and not to follow.' He genuinely hoped for the success of this work in London and was so concerned about the proposal to perform it there for the first time in Westminster Cathedral, of which he had had unhappy experience in regard to his own work, that he went to Malvern in April 1903 to warn Elgar (rightly, as it happened) whose reaction, expressed on 20 April in a letter to Littleton, was typically edgy: '*Stanford* has been here and *deeply* commiserated with me on the cathedral performance: thinks it is a *great pity* for *my* sake etc. etc. all on account of the deadly bad acoustics of the building etc. etc. *Is* there anything in all this? . . . I quite appreciate Stanford's kindness in pointing out that the performance *must* be disastrous—they say that about anything I do or compose. . . . The fact is if anything can be *said* not done to throw cold water on the thing it will be done.'

Stanford also comes well out of the muddle Elgar created over a symphony for the 1904 Leeds Festival. Frederick Spark, the cantankerous

---

[1] Stanford had been conductor of this famous Northern chorus since 1898.
[2] This and other letters are quoted from Plunket Greene's *Charles Villiers Stanford.*

and autocratic secretary of the festival, invited Elgar on 27 October 1902 to compose a work for October 1904. Elgar accepted but gave no indication of the type of work he had in mind. So on 18 December Spark commissioned a symphony for 50 guineas. This figure did not satisfy Elgar, who substituted a choral work. However, three months later, he said he could not produce a choral work and Spark raised the fee for a symphony to £100, to which Elgar agreed. Seven months later Elgar, who was low in health and spirits, withdrew the offer of a symphony because, he said, it would preclude his writing a large choral work for the festival in the future. The real reason he told to Troyte Griffith in a letter written on 26 December 1903: 'The history of the Leeds Symphony is this: I always promised the *dedication* to Richter: early this year (I think) I promised the first performance at Leeds; at the Birmingham Festival time I learnt that R. was counting upon conducting the *first performance*—so I withdrew it from Leeds & gave it to him—*if it's ever ready*. That's all.'

But Leeds knew nothing of this. From their point of view, Elgar was prevaricating; and matters were made worse when, after the work had been withdrawn, they read an announcement of an Elgar Festival at Covent Garden to be held the following March, conducted by Richter, and to include 'a new orchestral work' which, the *Daily News* confidently but erroneously proclaimed, was 'the symphony announced for Leeds'. (It was *In the South*.) The committee decided to omit Elgar from the 1904 festival entirely, after a final attempt to get a short choral work from him. The affair, Stanford told Elgar, was 'evidently a sore subject with them'. He wrote in January 1904 to W. S. Hannam, chairman of the committee, reporting Parry's comment that their decision was 'a fatal mistake' and 'simply impossible'. Stanford continued: 'What earthly harm can it do to play *Cockaigne* at the end of the Wednesday evening programme . . .? Fair play, old chap, and a man's artistic work ought to rank independently of his personality. If it had not been that Hans von Bülow had taken this view of Wagner, the Bayreuth theatre would not be standing now.' Eventually the committee thought better of the matter and included *In the South* in the Festival programme.

So, apart from the squally passage in the late 1890s, Elgar and Stanford maintained reasonably cordial relations up to 1904. But on 27 December 1904, according to Alice's diary, Elgar received 'an odious letter from Stanford'. No one knows what it was about, but as a result they did not speak to each other for nearly twenty years. When, in his Birmingham lectures in 1905, Elgar mocked at some of the English music written since 1880 and at the writers of rhapsodies, Stanford took it as a personal attack. It may have been intended personally; it was certainly tactless. 'Some of us', he said in his first lecture, speaking as one who had played in orchestras in the 1880s, 'felt that something at last was going to be done in the way of composition by the English school. . . . It is saddening to those who hoped for so much from these early days to find that . . . we had inherited an art which has no hold on the affections of our own people and is held in no respect abroad. . . . Many respectable and effective works have been written during the twenty years 1880–1900. To me they represent more or less . . . such a phase of art as in another way was represented by Lord Leighton. There you had a winning personality, a highly educated man, a complete artist, technically complete, but the result was cold and left the world unmoved. The musical works produced in the period named leave me in exactly the same way: I am amazed at the dexterity displayed in the finish of the works, but there is absolutely nothing new. . . . Twenty, twenty-five years ago some of the rhapsodies of Liszt became very popular. I think every Englishman since has called some work a rhapsody. To rhapsodize is one thing Englishmen cannot do. . . . It points a moral showing how the Englishman always prefers to imitate'.

W. H. Reed admitted that Elgar scorned the subterfuges of diplomacy and tact 'and went straight to the point, hitting out right and left when he got worked up by his own eloquence. He had an unhappy knack of doing this at times; even in an ordinary short speech he would let a word or a phrase drop which . . . if he had stopped to consider it, he might have left unsaid.'[1]

Elgar and Stanford avoided each other thenceforward. In July 1910, when Parry, Stanford, Mackenzie, and Elgar were all at Bournemouth, Stanford 'fled when he saw E.', Alice noted in her diary, though they appeared together later in a photograph, seated at extreme ends of the group. But Reed, in a letter to Plunket Greene reprinted in the Stanford biography,[2] recalled how, as Lady Elgar's coffin was being taken from St. Wulstan's Church, Little Malvern, to the graveside after her funeral service on 10 April 1920, he was surprised to see Stanford standing at the back. 'He impulsively caught hold of my arm and said "Tell Elgar I *had* to come. I daren't go to the graveside as the doctor has absolutely forbidden me to stand in the open air without a hat, but tell him how sorry I am and that I just felt I *must* come." He was far from well and I firmly believe that he had toiled all the way from

[1] *Elgar*, p. 89.   [2] Op. cit., p. 158.

Great Malvern contrary to the doctor's orders.' Elgar did not discover that Stanford had been present until after the ceremony. He wrote on 18 April to Schuster: 'I only regard it as a cruel piece of impertinence. For years (?16) he has not spoken to me and has never let me know why. . . . His presence last Saturday was a very clever "trick" to make it appear that after all, he is really a decent fellow etc., and that I am the culprit—that the fault (if any) of our difference (which only exists by his manufacture) is wholly *mine* and not his. As to his wanting to show respect and the like, I do not believe a word of it and never shall do: it was a mere political trick. He is an old friend of yours, older than I am and probably more trusted but that cannot alter my opinion. For the good things he has done in the past I still hold respect.'

During the Gloucester Festival of 1922 a memorial tablet to Parry, who had died in 1918, was unveiled. Afterwards, on the lawn of Herbert Brewer's home, Elgar and Stanford were brought together by Granville Bantock. Stanford, holding out his hand, said: 'Let's forget all about it.' Elgar, taken aback and professing still not to know what had to be forgotten, responded. Another event at the same time tells us much more about these two men. A photograph was taken to mark the Parry occasion. In the group were Elgar and Stanford, Bantock and Hugh Allen, Henry Hadow and Brewer. Before they assembled, the bluff Hugh Allen called out: 'Now then, Elgar, don't have your coat all buttoned up like that.' Elgar's reply was devastating. 'Ah,' he said, 'I always keep *everything* buttoned up when I am in *this* company.'[1] Again the old suspicion of the 'academic' establishment. The remark shows how precariously healed was the wound to Elgar's mind delivered by his years of struggle, alone and unrecognized. It would be easy to explain the differences with Stanford on this score alone, but it would be wrong. Elgar held no grudge against Parry. Quarrels of the depth to which this one went are usually personal and often petty. Elgar's letter to Schuster shows how little he wanted to admit, even to himself, that he had given a fellow-artist cause for complaint by his remarks at Birmingham in 1905. For one so thin-skinned himself as Elgar, it was an extraordinarily insensitive blunder; the whole Birmingham lecture experience was an unpleasant memory to him, and he probably wanted to put it out of his mind as much as possible. The only possible cause of the embittered outburst after Alice's funeral can have lain in whatever was written in the 'odious' letter of 1904. Elgar's last reference to the whole matter was in a slightly disingenuous letter

---

[1] *Elgar As I Knew Him*, p. 94.

he wrote, but did not send, to the *Sunday Times* in July 1933, when the publication of Basil Maine's book provoked comment on the relationship of the two composers. He objected to use of the word 'disagreements' in a letter from the *Yorkshire Post* music critic Herbert Thompson which the paper had published on 2 July 1933. 'There could be no "disagreements" [he wrote]. Stanford (Mr., Dr. and Knight) at various times thought it well to avoid speaking to me for periods varying very considerably in length. It was a matter for comment that such periods of silence invariably began when some work of mine was produced. [This was untrue.] I never refused to "shake hands" after these silences although the reason for them was never disclosed; three men whom Stanford asked to "approach" me with a view to a renewal on his part of ordinary civilities were A. E. Rodewald, Hubert Parry and, last of all, Granville Bantock. On every occasion I hoped that the reason for "cutting" me might be told: Stanford only said "We (!) have been under a cloud". I shook hands without comment but I am still without knowledge of the reason for Stanford's somewhat eccentric silences.'

None of this would be of any account today if it were not that some of Stanford's disciples, who were not such big men as C. V. S. himself, were responsible in the 1920s and 1930s for ensuring a cold climate for Elgar's music in circles where they had influence.

Like attracts like, even if the basic reason for the attraction could not be given by either party. Elgar and Stanford were not alike except in some superficial ways. Stanford's buccaneering and irascible manner may have concealed a warm heart but this did not endear him to Elgar. Yet he was as enthusiastic an advocate of Elgar's music as Parry was, so that this is no explanation of the care which Elgar took not to implicate Parry in his criticisms of Stanford. Elgar went out of his way in his inaugural Birmingham lecture to pay a warm tribute to Parry, 'the head of our art in this country'. One cannot explain Elgar's liking for Parry by saying that Parry was an early enthusiast for the *Variations*: so was Stanford. In fact Stanford, as an able and industrious conductor, did more for Elgar practically than Parry did. Parry was, of course, the more likeable man, outwardly the perfect English gentleman and squire. Yet this is a very superficial picture; and it seems likely that Elgar instinctively recognized the idealist artist inside Parry, the radical free thinker who often found himself, as he said, in a minority of one, who felt ill at ease among the hunting, shooting gentry of his native Gloucestershire, who had bouts of black depression and had had to overcome the prejudice of his family against music as a profession. It is significant that Elgar responded wholeheartedly to the agnostic idealism of Parry's cantata *A Vision of Life*,[1] to the composer's own libretto. 'I say,' he wrote to Jaeger on 8 October 1907, after a Leeds Festival performance, 'that "Vision" of Parry's is *fine stuff* & the poem is literature: you *must* hear it some day.' (How Jaeger must have smiled ruefully.) To Parry, in 1909, he wrote: 'I am so delighted we are to have *Job* in Hereford Cathedral. Your Cardiff "Vision" was, I conclude, too strong for the Church, but I hope we may have it soon. It's really strong bracing stuff, and, like your Odes, some of us love it and love you for giving us these things.'

When, in 1905, the Manchester University Press published selected music criticisms by Arthur Johnstone who had died after an operation at the age of forty-three on 16 December 1904, Elgar, of whose music Johnstone was so percipient a critic, was asked to write a preface. He agreed, but when he found that the book was to include Johnstone's review of J. A. Fuller Maitland's book *English Music in the 19th Century* in which Johnstone strongly contradicted Fuller Maitland's eulogistic view of Parry's music, he withdrew because he did not wish it to be thought that he was lending his name to support of such opinions. And when in 1920, in the first issue of *Music and Letters*, Bernard Shaw, in an equally eulogistic appraisal of Elgar, referred to 'the little clique of devoted musicians with the late Hubert Parry as its centre' and their 'initial incredulity as to his genius'. Elgar wrote a letter, published in the second issue, repudiating Shaw and emphasizing that Parry, far from slighting him had shown him 'ungrudging kindness' and had advised and encouraged him on 'many occasions'. Elgar sent Shaw a copy of the letter, which G. B. S. described (8 March 1920) as 'quite the right thing'. He then had the last word: 'P. was a d—d nice chap; and if he had been a little less nice he would also have been a little less d—d. I hope you didn't take his advice as well as his encouragement.'

With the third of the 'academic' trio, Sir Alexander Mackenzie, Elgar maintained polite but frigid relations. They had little in common. Mackenzie was a notable wit, and Elgar's feelings for him would not have been improved by an occasion when they were dining at adjacent tables at a London club where Elgar was a new and ill-at-ease member. When Elgar was offered the cheese-board, Mackenzie leaned across and said: 'Why don't you try the Port-Salut?' adding quietly 'Salut d'Amour'. Jaeger wrote to Elgar in 1903: 'I'm told that Mackenzie foams at the mouth when you say Apostles to him.' But in later years, when Mackenzie had retired and his music was nearly forgotten,

[1] First performed Cardiff Festival, September 1907.

Elgar sent him boxes of flowers and vegetables from his Worcestershire garden. This was another example of the streak of warm-hearted generosity which characterized Elgar. When Jaeger had eye trouble, Elgar sent him to a specialist and, at a time when he himself was often short of money, paid the bill. In 1903, when Jaeger took up bicycling to get fresh air, Elgar made him a present of his old bicycle, and in 1905 he arranged for Schuster to send a fur coat to Jaeger in which he could lie outdoors in Davos.

No discussion of Elgar's friendships at this period of his life would be adequate without fuller mention of a name that has already occurred several times: Alfred E. Rodewald, 'dear Rodey', of Liverpool, who was perhaps the nearest to Elgar's heart of all his many friends. Rodewald, a textile magnate, born in Liverpool and educated at Charterhouse, lived for music. He was a gifted conductor and played the double bass. He was a friend of Richter and he made the mainly amateur Liverpool Orchestral Society good enough to play the works of Elgar, Strauss, Wagner, and Tchaikovsky. He was a great supporter (and, probably, subsidizer) of Bantock's New Brighton enterprise and it was probably at the Elgar concert there in July 1899 that he first met Elgar. Thereafter, whenever Elgar visited Liverpool for performances of his works he stayed with Rodewald at his home at 66 Huskisson Street or at his cottage at Saughall, near Chester. He gave Rodewald and his players the first performance of the first two *Pomp and Circumstance* marches, on 19 October 1901, four days before the first London performance. No. 1 is dedicated to Rodewald and the Liverpool Orchestral Society. Rodewald's letters to Elgar reveal a delightfully gay and sunny personality and a great warmth of heart. They usually began 'Dear old cocky' and were full of jokes and merriment. He genuinely loved Elgar and his music. 'Ah! my dear boy,' he wrote to him after hearing *Cockaigne*, 'you write from the heart and not from the brain, there's the secret.' It was Rodewald who organized the collection of money to buy Elgar his Cambridge robes and who offered to commission a symphony from him. Like many North-Western businessmen, Rodewald also had a cottage in Wales, at Bettws-y-coed. For most of July 1903, when Elgar had finished *The Apostles*, he stayed there with Rodewald and they were joined for part of the time by Jaeger—'it is quite free and easy here,' Elgar told him, 'you dress as you like & do exactly what you please—no formality or any nonsense.' On 7 November 1903, when Rodewald was forty-three, news of his being mortally ill was received in Malvern. Elgar wrote to Jaeger: 'I am writing now to tell you about our poor dear friend Rodewald: it

came as the most awful shock to me yesterday a.m.—he is quite unconscious & four doctors say he cannot possibly recover—I had a
cheerful card from him on Wedy morning last—& now—it is too
awful & my heart is quite broken. On the card he says I shd meet
you there on the 14th—alas! alas! Yours ever Edwd. He thought he
had influenza & said he was over the fever & hoped to be soon all right.'

Two more letters to Jaeger tell the rest of the story, the first on
9 November from the North Western Hotel, Liverpool: 'Too late. I
stood it as long as I could & rushed up here—our dear, dear, good
friend passed away quietly at 12.30. I am heartbroken & cannot believe
it. God bless him. He was the dearest, kindest, *best* friend I ever had. I
don't know how I write or what I've written—forgive me. I am
utterly broken up.' The second was from Malvern, 11 November:

I could not rest so went up on Monday: did not go to the house but called at a
friend's in the same street[1]—they told me—I broke down & went out—*and it
was night* to me. What I did, God knows. I know I walked for miles in strange
ways—I know I had some coffee somewhere—where I cannot tell. I know I
went & looked at the Exchange where he had taken me—but it was all dark,
dark to me although light enough to the busy folk around. I thought I wd. go
home—but could not—so I stayed at the hotel. Now, had I been less stricken I
shd. not have eaten—but in a dazed way I ordered dinner & wine & I believe
ate all thro' the menu—I know not—it probably saved my life I think—but I
lived on as an automaton—& did everything without thought—then I went to
my room & wept for hours—yesterday I came home without seeing anyone &
am now a wreck & a broken-hearted man. Do not send me any more score [of
The Apostles]—yet. I used to pass him every sheet as I finished it at Bettws &
heard his criticisms & altered passages to please him, God bless him! . . . I can't
say what I feel but I have lost my best & dearest—I thank heaven we all had that
bit of time together in Wales: you know a little of what he was.

He wrote in the same vein to Schuster and to Ernest Newman, whom
he had met at Rodewald's house. To modern eyes there seems to be an
exhibitionist note about the carefully observed 'incoherence' of his
own reactions to deep and genuine personal sorrow. No doubt it was
the safety valve for the strength of his emotions: we shall see other
examples in due course. More important is that a few months later he
made sketches of what seven years thence was to become the great
Larghetto of the Second Symphony, the movement in which Alice
heard a 'lament for dear Rodey and all human feeling'. So Rodewald
was another friend 'pictured within'.

[1] Adrian Mignot, tobacco merchant, of 80 Huskisson Street, President of Liverpool
Orchestral Society at this time.

Two other women besides Alice had a strong influence on Elgar's life: the American Julia Worthington, and Alice Stuart-Wortley, daughter of the painter Sir John Millais and second wife of Charles Stuart-Wortley (later Lord Stuart of Wortley), Conservative M.P. for the Hallam division of Sheffield for many years. Not much is known about the friendship with Mrs. Worthington, since few letters survive. According to Dorabella, quoting Alice Elgar as her authority, hers is the 'soul' enshrined in the Violin Concerto. But despite this categorical statement, for which no other evidence is offered, all documentary evidence points to Alice Stuart-Wortley as the inspiration of this work and of parts of the Second Symphony. In letters to her throughout his life he refers to 'our own concerto' and 'your symphony'. She was a good amateur pianist, devoted to Elgar's music,[1] of a deeply artistic nature, and she shared with Elgar a love of the countryside. He idealized women and the romantic idea of beauty in a Froissart-like way, and Alice Stuart-Wortley evoked a strong response from the 'fey' side of his nature. He called her 'Windflower'. When her husband was created a peer at the end of 1916 Elgar wrote to her: 'The Windflower can never become wholly a "conservatory plant", can it? It will sometimes remember its woods.' While composing the Violin Concerto early in 1910 he wrote to her on 27 April: 'I have been working hard at the windflower themes—but all stands still until you come and approve!' And, the next day: 'The tunes stick and are not windflowerish—at present.' In a letter to Schuster in 1910 Elgar referred to Alice Stuart-Wortley and then added: 'I want to end that concerto but I do not see my way very clearly to the end so you had best invite its stepmother to The Hut too. Do.' He makes it clear again and again how much he wants her to like the work and, before the first performance, referring to a spare ticket, he wrote: 'I wish I could use it and you might conduct—but you *will* be conducting the concerto wherever you are.' It is impossible not to infer from these statements that hers was the 'soul' of the work especially when one discovers, on a sheet of her notepaper, the Spanish quotation which heads the work—'Aquí está encerrada el alma de . . . . . ('Here is enshrined the soul of . . . . .') in Elgar's writing with the date 22 September 1910. The five dots stand for Alice or for her initials A. S. C. S.-W. Their relationship was based on her sensitive response to Elgar's music and its highly personal idiom: he warmed to such appreciation. He often quoted to his friends a line from a poem by Sir John Davies (1569–1626)—'Musicians thinke our

---

[1] She is credited with having suggested the Westminster Cathedral performance of *Gerontius*.

soules are harmonies', an idea similar to the theme of *The Music Makers*. Edward Elgar and Alice Stuart-Wortley were souls in harmony as far as his music was concerned, and this understanding was one of deep affection involving no disloyalty or infidelity to either of the other marriage partners. Indeed, the four people concerned were firm friends (Elgar gave Charles Stuart-Wortley some of the early sketches of the Violin Concerto, and Alice Elgar wrote affectionate letters to 'my dearest namesake'). To a man of Elgar's poetic and sensitive imagination, such a relationship was a strong emotional stimulus, and it is one more example of Alice Elgar's noble character that where lesser women might have harboured groundless jealousies, she interpreted the situation correctly because she understood her husband's nature. She, after all, was his reality.

Elgar met Alice Stuart-Wortley in 1897, when he was forty and she was thirty-five, and their friendship ripened from formality in about 1906. She and her husband lived at 7 Cheyne Walk, Chelsea, where Elgar and his wife frequently visited them. She played through many of his works to him. 'I *love* to hear you play,' he wrote in 1911. 'One reason why so many people cordially dislike me is that I cannot stand their music whether written or performed & I pay no compliments & I never ask anyone to play unless it gives me pleasure. I do not like piano solo players' playing but I love yours—you will understand the difference. I am not going to praise you now because you are quite vain enough! but you *must* play when I ask & I would not think of asking you to play to ordinary people who wd. not understand what poetical playing really is.' She encouraged him to write a piano concerto, and his uncompleted work in that form would probably have been dedicated to her. In February 1917, when he was writing *The Sanguine Fan* ballet music he told her: 'I thought of using *your piano concerto*! (Labour exchange!) but you would not allow that would you?' In the same letter he said: 'Where are you? I wanted to tell you that the theme and *every note* must be approved by you (bless you!) before anything can be done. Oh! why are you so far away and so difficult to get at??' His letters over the years do not conceal his affection for her. Thus, shortly after a rehearsal for the second performance of the Violin Concerto in Queen's Hall in 1910: 'The concerto at 9 a.m. in the dark was divine—all seats empty but a spirit hovering in Block A.' And again in October 1915: 'I missed you at Q's Hall but I thought of you and my eyes wandered to empty Block A.' Even more touching is a letter he wrote on 27 April 1916, after she had been unable to attend an evening of private music-making at Elgar's London home, Severn

House: 'The things sounded lovely & the room is divine for a small orchestra—only the goddess of the feast was not there. . . . It was nice to hear Reed's eager voice asking disappointedly "*Where* is Mrs. W.?" & later Landon "*Where on earth* is Mrs. W. in all this music?" I said *to myself* "Everywhere—and alas! nowhere". But you see they all thought it was nothing without you & so did I.' To her he confided his innermost feelings about his own works. In three of the hundreds of letters he wrote to her we obtain vivid glimpses of the man as few knew him. Two date from 1912, shortly after he had finished *The Music Makers*. On 19 July, he wrote from Hampstead: 'Yesterday was the most *awful* day which inevitably occurs when I have completed a work: it has *always* been so: but this time I promised myself "a day!"—I should be crowned—it wd be lovely weather—I should have open air & sympathy & everything to mark the end of the work—to get away from the *labour* part & dream over it happily. Yes: I was to be crowned for the first time in my life. But—I sent the last page to the printer. Alice & Carice were away for the day & I wandered alone on the heath—it was bitterly cold—I wrapped myself in a thick overcoat & sat for two minutes, tears streaming out of my cold eyes and loathed the world, came back to the house—empty and cold—how I hated having written anything: so I wandered out again & shivered & longed to destroy the work of my hands—all wasted. And this was to have been the one real day in my artistic life—sympathy at the end of work. "World losers & world forsakers for ever & ever." How true it is.'

A few weeks later, on 1 September 1912, when he went to Hereford for the Three Choirs Festival, he went back to Plâs Gwyn, the house he had recently left, 'to see if the swallows are still cared for. Alas! the new tenants are "tidy" people—the loft is repainted . . . and the windows closed tight—so my companions of eight years found no welcome this year & have had to seek new homes—we had seen and known them & I resented their disturbance very much.' At Christmas 1914 he wrote: 'I cannot buy you pearls of untold worth . . . so I send you a little scrap of my old, old lonely life *in which no one shared*; I had my dreams &, I suppose, ambitions & I send you one of the little school-books which lightened my entire loneliness'.

The lonely composer walking on the heath, the poet who felt a companionship with the swallows, the romantic artist who drew 'inspiration' from the friendship of beautiful women: this is the true and secret Elgar, and the best of his music reflects this side of the many-sided man.

9 Nobilmente

In none of Mozart's letters is there any reference to the French Revolution. In none of Elgar's is there any reference to the Boer War, although it was in the period of that episode that his fame as a laureate composer grew. Some of the 'jingoism' and 'imperialism' in the political air at the time has been associated with his· music, usually in a superficial and inaccurate manner. Too much can perhaps be made of a composer's national background.

Like most creative artists, Elgar was a man of swift and ready emotional response rather than a deep thinker. He was romantic, chivalrous, patriotic, and loyal—it was the conventional mood of the time, just as the conventional mood in the 1960s is cynical, pacifist, anti-authoritarian, and permissive. Moreover, he was a great craftsman who thought naturally in musical terms. Like Purcell, Handel, and Bach he turned events of any kind into music without questioning their ethical or political, sociological or humanitarian basis. 'I like to look on the composer's vocation as the old troubadours or bards did. In those days it was no disgrace for a man to be turned on to step in front of an army and inspire them with a song. For my part, I know that there are a lot of people who like to celebrate events with music. To these people I have given tunes. Is that wrong? Why should I write a fugue or something which won't appeal to anyone, when the people yearn for things which can stir them?' [1]

Elgar, of course, well knew that some people were stirred by a fugue, but in this context he was thinking of truly popular music which, he considered, could also be good music. All that he did was to write music for certain national occasions: he did not advocate war, aggression, or oppression. Yet because he chose the superb title *Pomp and Circumstance* for a set of marches and because the tune of one of them was fitted to words glorifying Britain at the zenith of her imperial power, writers and journalists have equated Elgar's name with a political condition of which they disapproved. The Edwardian age, the Elgarian age: both sound alike, both are usually intended as opprobrious phrases. To suggest that Elgar consciously set himself the task of expressing in music the Edwardian age in its most blatant aspects is

[1] *Strand Magazine*, May 1904.

PLATE VII

Gloucester Festival, 1922
Left to right:
Herbert Brewer, Elgar,
Lord Gladstone,
Henry Hadow,
Hugh Allen, Stanford

PLATE VIII

Alice Stuart-Wortley: Windflower, the 'soul' of Elgar's Violin Concerto.
A portrait by her father, Sir John Millais

nonsense. The generalization implied by the term Edwardian is itself open to question. Not everything in those ten years was confident, opulent, and grandiloquent. There was as much wind of change blowing about then as in the years that have followed and Elgar was by no means impervious to it. But, for many people, it was also a good time to be alive, a time of and for greatness, and it was far easier to produce art which had a confident foundation. Elgar as a man responded to the thrill and pageantry of the peacetime military parade or ceremonial function; Elgar as a composer had the knack of writing colourful, tuneful music of a kind that caught the ear of the populace. He was under no illusion that he was producing something lasting: these were occasional pieces, and of all Elgar's laureate music, only two or at the most three tunes have survived the occasions which brought them into being. The *Pomp and Circumstance* marches are quite separate; a purely musical exercise. 'I did not see why the ordinary quick march should not be treated on a large scale, in the way that the waltz, the oldfashioned slow march and even the polka have been treated by the great composers; yet all marches on the symphonic scale are so slow that people can't march to them. I have some of the soldier instinct in me and so I have written two marches of which, so far from being ashamed, I am proud.' [1]

It has been said many times that Elgar's 'ceremonial' manner in some way 'infected' his bigger, more serious works. Of course it did, because it was an essential part of the man. He was not divided into self-sealing units. But the ceremonial manner itself has been only superficially examined. It ought to be clear by now that Elgar was subject to a profound melancholy and that he lacked confidence to an almost pathological degree. He at no time imagined that everything was for the best in the best of all possible worlds. He perceived the emptiness behind the façade; and though he expressed this unforgettably in his larger symphonic works, it is present, whether he himself was fully aware of it, in some of the lesser music in his *nobilmente* manner. It was not to be expected that his contemporaries would penetrate to this side of Elgar's music: the outer surface was the more obvious and this was their only concern. But Elgar the laureate and courtier was never at ease with Elgar the dreamer and the lower-middle-class provincial. He was a conservative, the natural result of his upbringing in a family which had relied on royal and squirearchical patronage. In this respect he was the opposite of Parry, born into the landed gentry, who despised conservatism. Yet Elgar too, had the radical streak: he was an artist, a

[1] *Strand Magazine*, May 1904, when only Nos. 1 and 2 had appeared.

K

'dreamer of dreams' in a materialist society. He wanted his music to be widely appreciated, yet part of him despised the public for its narrow and restricted taste. His natural pride in his achievements clashed with the demands made upon him by the upholding of his position of fame. Before discussing some of the ceremonial music, it is essential to probe more deeply into the circumstances of its composition, the changes that its success involved, and their effect on the man himself.

As already related, Elgar had a success in the diamond jubilee year of Victoria's reign with the *Imperial March* and the *Banner of St. George*. The same mood spilled over into the final chorus of *Caractacus*, dedicated to the queen-empress. Acceptance of the dedication was the first sign of royal favour, greatly prized by a man who always felt that in Britain music was the least acknowledged of the arts. Two concerts at Windsor, not attended by Victoria, in 1899, the year of the queen's eightieth birthday, included music by Elgar, one of them no fewer than ten items. But two of the *Sea Pictures* were sung by Ada Crossley at Balmoral by royal command. Although the march and the *Banner* gave him a national reputation, they did not earn Elgar much money. In 1899 and 1900 he was preoccupied with the *Variations* and *Gerontius*. On 22 January 1901 Queen Victoria died. The only references to this event in Elgar's letters to Jaeger are a cheery 'God save the King' at the end of a piece of mundane business correspondence on 27 January and a wish expressed three days later that the title-page of the full score of *Froissart* 'didn't look so like the newspapers' borders over the death of our beloved Queen.' Edward VII was on the throne at last—'fat vulgar Edward' to the intellectuals, 'good old Teddy' to the people, an enigmatic man still, and one, it appears, of irresistible charm. The twenty-six-year-old Winston Churchill, writing to his mother from Winnipeg in January 1901, summed up Society's views on the new reign:[1] 'I am curious to know about the King. Will it entirely revolutionise his way of life? Will he sell his horses and scatter his Jews or will Reuben Sassoon be enshrined among the crown jewels and other regalia? Will he become desperately serious? . . . Will the Keppel be appointed 1st Lady of the Bedchamber?'

It was through the equivalents of Edward VII's Sassoons that Edward Elgar achieved his rapid rise to social distinction. The Elgars already had a friend at court in Lady Mary Lygon, but it was through the Speyers and the Schusters, wealthy patrons of all the arts, who 'knew everybody', who took up each new prominent 'name', that they moved rapidly into circles where Alice considered herself to be in the

[1] Randolph S. Churchill, *Winston S. Churchill*, i (London, 1966), p. 545.

right element and where Elgar was pleased but apprehensive to be. But whatever may be said of the wealthy upper and upper-middle-class strata of Edward VII's reign, a strong section of them, a minority but an influential minority, was anything but philistine and uncultured, and it was in this milieu that Elgar found friends, patrons, and admirers. Schuster and Edgar Speyer brought Richard Strauss and Elgar into friendship; Schuster introduced Elgar to Herbert Beerbohm Tree and J. S. Sargent. Among the aristocracy, the Elgars came to know the Marquess of Northampton, an amateur musician who was competent enough to be able to play Bach fugues in piano duet with Elgar when he went to stay in Hereford; Lady Maud Warrender, daughter of the Earl of Shaftesbury, who sang the solo part in *The Music Makers* on at least one occasion; the Duke of Norfolk and other prominent Roman Catholics such as Lady Winefride Elwes and her husband Gervase, beginning his career as a singer. Conducting at Sheffield, Elgar was invited to lunch with Lady Alice Fitzwilliam (though apparently he was on one occasion 'not pleased with the company or food & excused himself & went off'). It was she who introduced him to the Stuart-Wortleys. This was a group of people brought together by a love of artistic matters, not by any political affiliation, the kind of civilized gathering that has always existed in English society. There is, in any case, no reason why a great composer should have fashionably or even unfashionably progressive views. As Lionel Trilling has somewhere written, no literary figure of the front rank in the first thirty years of the twentieth century was liberal or radical in his ideas: they left these things to the second rankers and went on with their work. The same applies to Elgar. Schuster himself was a Liberal-Radical and after the crushing 1906 defeat of the Conservatives Elgar wrote to him: 'You are a disappointing *toad* & a Radical. All the same my heart warms to you. . . . Having turned out the respectable Hotel Cecil and having installed the Waiters in place of the gentlemen, you will probably have to drop music & musicians to seem respectable among the artistic governing body.'

Credit should be given to Elgar that he relished this patronage, and the royal favour that followed, not because of self-aggrandisement but because it was an official recognition by the 'ruling class' of the growing importance of music. 'I always stand up for the dignity of our art,' as he had told Jaeger. It annoyed him to see the wealth and position achieved by painters. Speaking in July 1904, about the new Musical Copyright Bill he complained that while the world of fashion as well as the middle classes—the *real* supporters of music—honoured the art at Covent Garden, legislators were heaping indignities on it, whittling down the . . . Bill by inserting clauses which will make it inoperative. Why of all the arts should music be supposed to have no rights? . . . We composers are not *genuine* artists if we as much as hint that the work of our brains is worth something. . . . The whole attitude of the world of England is nothing less than an indignity to our art. Wagner was derided because he wore a silk vest and velvet cap and surrounded himself with such luxuries as he could afford. But our second-rate painters may build themselves magnificent houses and indulge in all sorts of eccentric luxuries and no one has a word to say against them.[1] The public cannot reconcile music with any other human activity.

Bernard Shaw remembered Elgar talking about music at a lunch and Roger Fry remarking: 'After all there is only one art: all the arts are the same.' 'I heard no more,' Shaw wrote. 'My attention was taken by a growl from the other side of the table. It was Elgar, with his fangs bared and all his hackles bristling, in an appalling rage. "Music," he spluttered, "is written on the skies for you to note down. And you compare that to a DAMNED imitation." ' [2]

In an after-dinner speech in Aberdeen in honour of Sanford Terry in 1910, Elgar uttered these prophetic but revolutionary words: 'If we educate young people to be first-class players . . . what is to become of them afterwards? . . . I would like you to think seriously whether the humanising sphere of music could not be enlarged by municipal aid—by assisting choral societies and orchestras from the rates. . . . Düsseldorf is not a very beautiful town, but many people go to reside there on account of the music; the town looks upon that orchestra as a valuable asset, and the municipality takes the responsibility of any loss that may arise. . . . The time is coming when all towns must be able to give the people the good music they want.'

These are not the words and outlook of a complacent and reactionary diehard, lulled by association with the 'establishment' into euphoria. They are common sense. True, the keynote of Elgar's greatest music is a regret for the good things—and people—that are gone, but he lived in hope—sometimes against hope—that there were good things still to come. When he lost that hope he ceased to write music.

*   *   *

[1] He was perhaps remembering that Sir John Millais, at the peak of his career, earned over £25,000 a year.
[2] Letter to Virginia Woolf quoted in *Beginning Again* (London, 1964), p. 126, by Leonard Woolf.

In November 1900 Elgar began to sketch his gayest orchestral work, the overture *Cockaigne* which contains a passage where a military procession passes along the streets of London. So it is not surprising that this was also the period of composition of the first two of a proposed set of six military marches, one of which was intended for a soldier's funeral. Four of the marches appeared between 1901 and 1907, a fifth in 1930. A sixth was left in short score and sketches exist for others. None is funereal. On 10 May 1901, the day after the Worcestershire Philharmonic's *Gerontius*, Elgar called Dorabella into his study and said 'I've got a tune that will knock 'em—knock 'em flat.' He then played the D major *Pomp and Circumstance* march No. 1. He had written to Jaeger on 12 January 1901, 'In haste and joyful (Gosh! man I've got a tune in my head),' and there is little doubt that the tune he meant is the Trio section of this march, better known as 'Land of Hope and Glory'. By August 1901 Nos. 1 and 2 were completed and sent to Boosey's for publication— a result of the coolness with Novello's after the *Variations* and *Gerontius*. Boosey had been given *Cockaigne* as well. (Jaeger wrote to Elgar in October 1901, about a cantata commissioned for the 1905 Norwich Festival of which no trace remains: 'Now, you *will* send that to us won't you? . . . We shall pay you just as well as Boosey's. . . . I have had another long talk about you to Messrs. A. & A. L. & you need fear no worries in future. They have had an eye-opener over the Leeds Festival & I'm sure they'll meet you in every way in future.') After the first Liverpool performance of the two marches, they were performed in London at a Queen's Hall Promenade Concert under Henry Wood on 23 October. Elgar was not present. 'I shall never forget the scene at the close of the first of them—the one in D major,' Wood wrote.[1] 'The people simply rose and yelled. I had to play it again—with the same result; in fact they refused to let me get on with the programme. . . . I went off and fetched Harry Dearth who was to sing *Hiawatha's Vision* but they would not listen. Merely to restore order, I played the march a third time.' Jaeger sent Elgar a postcard that night: 'Your splendid marches were the greatest success I have ever witnessed over a novelty at any concert. The hall was only half full alas! (though the Promenade was pretty crowded) but the people made such a row & kept it up for so long. . . .' Wood, with a sense of showmanship, reversed the order of the marches and played the A minor (No. 2) first and the D major (No. 1) second. So that when Stanford wrote to Elgar that he found himself 'in a minority' at Wood's concert in preferring the first march he was referring to No. 2 in A minor. The critic of *The Daily Telegraph*

---

[1] Op. cit., pp. 203-4.

thought that the marches suggested not the orderliness of the Guards but 'the irregular advance of an army of glittering barbarians'.

Was the success of the D major march the result of a demonstration of nationalist fervour? I doubt it. I think the audience immediately recognized that they had heard one of the great melodies of the world, a tune that is at once memorable, stirring, disturbing, and singable. Even before the success of this music, Elgar had had an approach from Henry Higgins with a commission from the Grand Opera Syndicate for a work to be performed at a State performance at Covent Garden on the eve of Edward VII's Coronation on 26 June 1902. Although he was thinking about a symphony for Richter, he put everything aside, as he explained to Jaeger on 12 November 1901: 'Manchester as you say can & will wait—not so Coving Garden & several 100 other things.' He added that his Cambridge robes had not yet arrived: 'I *want* 'em now to appear at Court.' Probably it was at that meeting with his sovereign that an historic suggestion was made to Elgar, as he stated years later in a letter to Clara Butt (21 November 1927): 'King Edward was the first to suggest that the air from the *Pomp and Circumstance* March should be sung and eventually the song as now known was evolved, via the *Coronation Ode*. . . .' Elgar evidently conveyed the idea to Jaeger, who did not think much of it (6 December 1901): 'I say, you will have to write another tune for the Ode in place of the March in D tune (Trio). I have been trying much to fit words to it. That drop to E & bigger drop afterwards are quite impossible in singing *any* words to them, they sound downright vulgar. Just try it. The effect is fatal. No, you must write a new tune to the words & not fit the words to this tune. Consider this carefully & give no choir a chance of scooping down. It will sound horrible. Try it. . . .'

So Jaeger was the first to make a valid criticism that has been repeated many times since. But Elgar, never one to bother too much about whether the words fitted his tunes if he thought his tunes good enough, ignored him, and four days later he received from the librettist the first draft of 'Land of Hope and Glory'. In any case the Ode was not intended for Novello's. They had to be content with the ceremonial arrangement of 'God Save the King' for soprano, chorus, and orchestra, and Elgar took particular care over the score of this work, wanting the English names for the instruments and being annoyed when the printers altered 'clarionets' to 'clarinets' 'in our ignorance', as they explained. 'I wanted in this particular score everything to be "plain English"'; he wrote to Jaeger on 9 May 1902. '. . . The names of the instruments . . . look *very nice* in English I think & *Kettledrums* is a good Handelian-looking word: see West's query as to *Haut-boys*—I feel that Oboes wd. spoil the whole thing—but I don't want to be faddy or silly, only English—which after all may be both!'

The *Coronation Ode*, with words by A. C. Benson about which poet and composer had corresponded since March 1901, was ready by 1 April 1902. Three days before the Coronation, the King was taken ill and operated on for appendicitis. All festivities were cancelled. Elgar's letter to Jaeger on 24 June may be surprising to those who have accepted only a superficial view of his 'laureate' character: 'Don't for heaven's sake *sympathise* with me—I don't care a tinker's damn! It gives me three blessed sunny days in my own country . . . instead of stewing in town. *My* own interest in the thing ceased as usual when I had finished the MS—since when I have been thinking mighty things! [*The Apostles*.] I was biking out in Herefordsh: yesterday & the news reached me at a little roadside pub. I said "Give me another pint of cider." I'm deadly sorry for the King but that's all.'

It is amusing to compare this reaction of England's great composer of royal music with the scene at the Westminster Abbey Coronation rehearsal as described in Parry's diary: [1] 'The Bishop of London stepped on to the dais . . . and, addressing mainly the performers . . . announced the necessity of the King's undergoing an operation . . . ending with an appeal to all to join in a Litany. . . . The choir joined in with a most superb tone and produced an effect I have never experienced before—so solemn and pathetic. A few kneeling figures on the floor of the Chancel.'

'Land of Hope and Glory' was sung by Clara Butt in London in June 1902. The *Ode* had its first performance at the Sheffield Festival on 2 October, some compensation to the chorus who had been selected for the cancelled Coronation performance. Elgar conducted and Muriel Foster was the contralto soloist. Johnstone wrote in the *Manchester Guardian* next day: 'It is popular music of a kind that has not been made for a long time in this country—scarcely at all since Dibdin's time. At least one may say that of the best parts, such as the bass solo and chorus, "Britain, Ask of Thyself", and the contralto solo and chorus, "Land of Hope and Glory". The former is ringing martial music, the latter a sort of church parade song having the breadth of a national hymn. It is the melody which occurs as second principal theme of the longer Pomp and Circumstance march, which I beg to suggest is as broad as "God Save the King", "Rule Britannia" and "See the Con-

[1] C. L. Graves, *Hubert Parry*, ii (London, 1926), pp. 28-29.

quering Hero", and is perhaps the broadest open-air tune since Beethoven's "Freude Schöner Götterfunken". Moreover, it is distinctively British—at once breezy and beefy. It is astonishing to hear people finding fault with Elgar for using this tune in two different compositions. I find it most natural in a composer, to whom music is a language in which, desiring to say exactly the same thing again, one has no choice but to say it in the same notes. Besides, such tunes are composed less frequently than once in 50 years. How then can one blame Elgar for not composing two in six months? The chorus enjoyed themselves over it and so did the audience.'

This surely is the commonsense view. It is perfectly true, as Ernest Newman said,[1] that the vocal version of the march tune can 'hardly be called a success, either here or in the song-arrangement. . . . It is married to the words much against its own will . . . it really will not bear the attempt to make it look heroic. It is dignified in just the right kind of way in its proper place in the march, but when it is dressed up in the pompous sentiments of the *Coronation Ode* its clothes seem several sizes too large for it.' But it is a great tune which people who care little for the niceties of word-setting like to sing, ignoring the correct accentuations. It swept the country in 1902 and became a second national anthem. Attempts to change the words have met with little success, because only the squeamish worry about them any more. It is a fine community song, along with 'Abide with me' and others; as Johnstone recognized, it has the slight ecclesiastical flavour which endears a tune to the sentimental British crowd; and nothing will kill it now. When audiences saw its composer, military in bearing and often mistaken for the Duke of Connaught, it no doubt reassured them that music was not necessarily written by eccentric and possibly immoral hermits. If they saw him in the Malvern countryside, in tweeds and riding boots, as Arnold Bax did, they too might have 'expected him to sling a gun from his back and drop a brace of pheasants to the ground'.[2] Unlike Bax, they could not see in this 'typical' figure a 'morbidly highly strung artist'. Nor could they hear in the tune of the March in D major the note of recessional, the heroic melancholy, which, rather than self-confident assertiveness, we see as its true character if we strip ourselves of the accumulated extra-musical associations. Elgar revelled in 'the glories of our blood and state', but he knew the next line and it is the shadows, as well as the substantial things, that haunt his music.

The success of the *Coronation Ode* set the seal on Elgar's 'official' status. He received honours such as no previous English musician had

[1] *Elgar* (London, 1905), p. 48.   [2] Op. cit., p. 30.

accumulated in so short a time: Durham and Leeds gave him honorary
degrees in 1904, Oxford (where Parry spoke generously) and Yale in
1905, Aberdeen, Pennsylvania, and Birmingham in 1906 and 1907. He
was knighted in the summer of 1904, a few weeks after what was
perhaps the greatest honour a living English composer had been
accorded, a three-day festival of his works at Covent Garden on 14, 15,
and 16 March. The first two concerts were attended by the King and
Queen and the third by the Queen. It had been planned to give a series
of Elgar concerts in Manchester, but a compromise was reached
whereby Richter and the Hallé Orchestra played at Covent Garden.
The idea originated from Alice, who said at a social function 'Why not
have an Elgar festival?' and Schuster agreed with her. The King, with
whom Elgar had by now wined and dined, held a levée at the Palace on
the 14th to which Elgar was invited. On 5 July Elgar returned to
receive the accolade, the King saying to him afterwards 'Good sport to
your fishing', a reference to Elgar's new home, Plâs Gwyn, on the
outskirts of Hereford and near to the Wye. They had moved in on 1
July. It was large and imposing but they liked it, particularly Alice. It
was a home fit for knighted genius. 'I think *great* music can be written
here, dear Dora, don't you?' she said to Dorabella.

Elgar's life at this point was as *nobilmente* as his music. In the autumn
of 1905 he and Schuster sailed on a month's Mediterranean cruise with
the Royal Navy in H.M.S. *Surprise*. In Athens they were entertained by
Schuster's friend Admiral Lord Charles Beresford, C-in-C Mediterranean since May, an ebullient, extrovert personality, with the Waterford
hunt in full cry tattooed across his back and usually accompanied
everywhere he went, like George Sinclair, by a bulldog. He was a son
of the Marquess of Waterford and was twice returned to Westminster
for English constituencies. An advocate of naval strength he was a
bitter adversary of Admiral Lord Fisher. He had been a companion of
the Prince of Wales's wild youth in the 1860s, but their friendship had
been disrupted by a violent quarrel over personal (and feminine) affairs
in 1891. Also there were Lady Maud Warrender and her husband Sir
George, and Lady Charles Beresford. At a reception given by the
British Ambassador in Turkey Lady Maud sang some of the *Sea
Pictures*; while Elgar dined with Lord Charles aboard his flagship *Bul-
wark* the band played *Salut d'Amour* and the *Sérénade Lyrique*. Following
the Akaba crisis, tension between Britain and Turkey was acute, and
Elgar was able to see at first-hand how Britannia ruled the waves. He
had needed such a holiday (of which the piano piece *In Smyrna* is a
memento) to recover from the strain he imposed upon himself by

ill-advised acceptance of an honour from Birmingham University where Richard Peyton had offered £10,000 for the endowment of a Chair of Music on condition that 'it should in the first instance be offered to and accepted by Sir Edward Elgar, Mus. Doc., LL.D.' After some hesitation, Elgar accepted the post in November 1904, principally because he needed the money but on the understanding that he could resign after three years if it interfered with his composing.

The inaugural lecture was fixed for 16 March 1905, and attracted a large press. As the date approached Elgar became more apprehensive, and his spirits were further damped eight days beforehand by the cool reception given to the first performance of the *Introduction and Allegro for Strings*. The first lecture, which contains much common sense and advanced thinking, provoked a storm of controversy because, as has already been shown, some of the comments on British music of 1880–1900 were tactless, if true. 'I must go and buy some strychnine. This is the end for me,' Elgar said as he left the platform. But worse followed. In succeeding lectures he attacked every sacred British cow in sight. He was dubious about the real feeling for music among the middle classes: 'it exists but fitfully and easily expires.' He wanted 'simplicity, manhood, clearness and melody' from the coming generation of composers; he said that Northern choral singers were trained—'perhaps overtrained'—to a perfection of finish and attack never before attempted 'but often there is something wanting: an understanding of the subject sung about.' He cited German choirs as 'superior in education' and also blamed the Northern choirs for their tendency to sing flat. He blamed solo instrumentalists for 'nervousness and tension'. British orchestral players were 'the finest in the world', but concerning English conductors 'we can in no way indulge in very contented feelings. We have heard of snakes in Ireland and we have heard of English conductors.' (He excluded Wood from his strictures.) He spoke of the conductors of his early youth as 'men who treated an orchestral work like a problem of Euclid and thrashed it out without sympathy, without love and without hate.' 'It is all very well to say "conductors are born not made", but have we ever seriously attempted to make them?' The only drawback to orchestral players from British academic institutions was that 'they lack fire; they have to be whipped to enthusiasm. . . . This is the fault of studying under an uninspiring conductor.' Our solo singers—with named exceptions including Lloyd, Santley, Coates, and Muriel Foster—lacked dramatic instinct because there was 'no drama in England . . . dressed-up dolls and dummies fill the stage at most of our theatres. . . . These people cannot act.' In a lecture on Brahms's Third

Symphony he extolled 'absolute music' at the expense of programme music, in utter and still incomprehensible contradiction of his own practice. When this was pointed out, he said in a later lecture: 'Am I so narrow as to admire my own music because I have written it myself? Certainly not. . . . When I see one of my own works by the side of, say, the Fifth Symphony, I feel like a tinker may do when surveying the Forth Bridge. . . .' Although the lectures contained more praise than blame and looked progressively ahead to subsidized music, a national opera, and called for an end to the patronizing attitude to 'people's concerts', these aspects were ignored in the controversy which followed and which made its provoker ill. 'I have been very unwell but am better now,' he wrote to Jaeger on 3 April. 'It really makes me disgusted with English musical life to see the way everybody (except Kalisch who heard me speak) misquotes me! I set a high ideal for the younger men. . . .' Then, on 6 June, came a by now familiar tone of voice: 'I don't hear anything of music now or rather of *music* I hear much, of musicians, little: they are always quarrelling. . . . I have no news of myself as I have for ever lost interest in that person—he ceased to exist on a certain day when his friends interfered & insisted on his—It is very sad.' Even his first voyage to the United States later that month and the ceremony at Yale failed to rouse his spirits. He was ill again on the voyage home. His letters in 1904 are full of complaints about illness and of 'the cook who can't cook' and other domestic afflictions. He had been ill during a holiday in Italy in January 1904. In spite of the honour of the Elgar Festival two months later, its preparation involved him in the kind of business work he disliked. Stress led to headaches, and three days beforehand, when Schuster gave a magnificent dinner at his Old Queen Street home in his friend's honour—'he had even', Henry Wood says,[1] 'conceived a series of emblematic decorations on the panels of his dining-room referring to various phases of Elgar's work'— Elgar had spent all day in bed. After Schuster had proposed his health ('with his heart in his voice', Alice wrote), Elgar made no response but went on talking to his neighbour. 'I have not been well,' he wrote to Nicholas Kilburn in August 1904, in reply to congratulations, and to Schuster on 3 September: 'I am still very low & see nothing in the future but a black stone wall against which I am longing to dash my head—and that's all: a pitiful end for a "promising" youth.'

There is little doubt that the strain of being a celebrity and of not having the solitude to compose severely affected Elgar in 1904–6, and took their toll of the largest composition of the period, *The Kingdom*.

[1] Op. cit., pp. 235–6.

How he must have sighed for the days at Craeg Lea and Birch-wood. Peace and quiet were a necessity to him. He decided in 1903 to leave Craeg Lea because new building development was spoiling the view and bringing noise and less privacy. He had already given up Birchwood because of 'the difficulty of keeping it aired etc'. But, as he told Jaeger,[1] 'I would like to end my days there—only it's too remote for my wife & Carice is now growing up! & must be in the loathèd world. Alas! Alas!' He inquired if Birchwood was for sale, but it was not. It was a deeper blow to him than he ever admitted to his family. To Jaeger he confided:[2] 'You saw my dear place & I hate having to give it up. My life is one continual giving up of little things which I love, & only great ones, I'm told, come into it, & I loathe them. I do like my *little* toys.' But Arnold Bax, who had first met him there, sensitively perceived what the cottage meant to Elgar. In 1910 Bax was invited to submit a work for a Promenade Concert and Wood told him it was Elgar who had recommended Bax's work—'It seems that he never forgot my visit to Birchwood (I think his days there counted as the happiest in his tormented life, and he kept a special regard for anyone who had seen him in those surroundings).'[3]

For an artist who required solitude the months following the 1904 Festival at Covent Garden must certainly have been a torment for which Rodewald's death and the disputes with the Leeds Festival com-mittee were unhelpful preparation. Knighthood in July 1904, the Three Choirs Festival, the Leeds Festival, worry over accepting the Bir-mingham post; then in 1905, the Oxford doctorate, first performance of a new work, the lectures, visits to Hanley, Leeds, and York for performances of his works, the visit to America, the Worcester Festival and the freedom ceremony, the Mediterranean cruise, straight back to the Norwich Festival, and then in November—no doubt because Plâs Gwyn was a drain on the pocket—he took the London Symphony Orchestra on its first provincial tour, conducting his own and others' works in Birmingham, Manchester, Sheffield, Glasgow, Newcastle upon Tyne, and Bradford. Travelling tired Elgar and gave him headaches. He became 'frightfully sick of the tour'. Also, as he wrote to Schuster, more lectures were due in December—'I am killed with the University'. Alice's diary at the end of 1905 records: 'E. oppressed with the Birmingham Prof. & quite unable to write music', though E. himself wrote to Walford Davies on 31 December to say 'I am working away & some of the themes are not bad'.

How much wiser Elgar would have been to have accepted Brodsky's

<hr>

[1] 29 August 1903.   [2] Letter, 27 August 1903.   [3] Op. cit., pp. 31–32.

offer in April 1904 of a joint professorship of instrumentation and composition at the Royal Manchester College of Music and Manchester University, at a salary of £400 a year and all freedom for his own work—'as little as we would expect Franz Liszt to be a piano teacher,' Brodsky wrote, 'as little we are expecting from you to be a "teacher" in the common sense of the word. It is your great personality we want to secure. Your name would give glory to the institutions . . .' It was Alice, perhaps taking her cue from this former suggestion, who rescued Elgar from his predicament. After illness over the 1906 winter lectures, combined with chronic eye trouble, had caused Elgar to suspend them, she proposed to the dean of the arts faculty that the Professor of Music should merely take the chair at lectures given by others. This was the pattern for 1907. On 30 August 1908, Elgar thankfully resigned and Granville Bantock succeeded him. Bantock had also succeeded him early in 1904 as conductor of the Worcestershire Philharmonic Society. There had been friction in November and December 1902, when Elgar resigned and withdrew from a conducting engagement because 'the chorus . . . is singing so badly, and is so extremely ill-prepared this season. . . . I have incessantly warned the members . . . that I should leave immediately if I thought the members showed lack of interest.' This episode was patched up, but he finally left at the end of 1903 because his engagements would not allow him enough time to devote to the society.

If Elgar gained much *réclame* from his elevation to popular fame— like Parry, he had not wanted a knighthood, but accepted to please Alice—he gave much, too, of the most precious commodity any artist possesses: his time. It is true he was working largely on behalf of his own music, conducting it here, there, and everywhere, and not, as Parry was, devoting time to students and administrative bodies. But the hard fact remains: he needed the money. An author could live on his books in the Edwardian age, but a composer could not live on his music. And, since his music was in demand, he was fulfilling a proper purpose in presenting it in the most favourable manner. It was not yet the age of the British conductor, with the exception of Wood, and Elgar knew that he himself conducted his own music better than anyone, though he might have excepted Richter. What he suffered at others' hands he put in a letter to Jaeger on 1 July 1903: 'When they [his works] go as I like—elastically and mystically—people grumble— when they are conducted squarely and sound like a wooden box these people are pleased to say it's better. It's a curious thing that the performances which I have hated & loathed as being caricatures of my thoughts are the very ones held up as patterns!'

It is not easy to guess at whom these remarks were directed. As early as 1903 Richter, Bantock, Buths, Steinbach, Cowen, Stanford, Wood, and Elgar himself had been the chief conductors of his music.

The effect of Elgar's national prestige upon the compositions of 1903–13 will be considered in the two following chapters. We are concerned here with the over-stressed 'laureate' works. In fact, after the *Coronation Ode*, except for two more of the *Pomp and Circumstance* marches (No. 3 in C minor, 1905, and No. 4 in G, 1907) there is little further in this line in King Edward's reign except for two part-songs, a 'Marching Song' for the Empire Concert in 1908 and a further setting of Newman, 'They are at rest' for the anniversary in 1910 of Queen Victoria's death. The accession of King George V brought a *Coronation March*, a short choral work 'O hearken thou', sung at the Abbey ceremony; and in 1912, to mark the royal visit to India and to pay some of the bills incurred by a move into a Hampstead mansion, Elgar composed an 'Imperial Masque', *The Crown of India*, for Oswald Stoll's London Coliseum. Elgar found some of Henry Hamilton's libretto difficult to stomach—'there is *far too much* of the political business'—and deleted the worst lines. He had a month in which to undertake the commission so he fell back on a theme written in 1903 to illustrate the 'sinful growth' of the bulldog Dan and on other sketches of earlier works which had come to naught, much as he used up some of his Rabelais ideas and some sketches written in Rome, for an Italian processional, in the *Coronation March*. *The Crown of India* was assembled from early notes for a work about Falstaff, abandoned ideas from the 1903–4 sketches for a symphony, left-overs from *The Apostles* and from a contemplated second *Cockaigne* overture. The 1914–18 war brought forth the famous *Carillon* recitation for speaker and orchestra, a potpourri called *Polonia* and dedicated to Paderewski, two further attempts to equal the success of *Carillon*, and the finest of all his laureate works, *The Spirit of England*, a setting for soprano and contralto or tenor, chorus, and orchestra of three poems by Laurence Binyon, which can rank with the earlier choral works in the nobility of its utterance. For a theme of this work he drew on another 'Mood of Dan' inscribed in July 1902 in Sinclair's visitors' book to illustrate 'Dan wistful, outside the cathedral', and he recalls the Demons from *Gerontius* to represent the enemy in 'The Fourth of August'. 'To Women' is an exquisite movement and the final 'For the Fallen' produces music as elegiac as the poem that inspired it—'At the going down of the sun and in the morning, we will remember them'. There is no drum-beating, no vainglory, no pomp. Elgar did not confuse the glitter of a jubilee procession with the reality of war. A wounded officer wrote to Schuster on 9 May 1916, castigating 'all the people writing about war & soldiers when they haven't a notion of either. Sensible people like Yeats keep quiet, or express the feelings of non-combatants in the most touching & poignant forms imaginable, as Elgar & Binyon. How often the sad last phrases of Elgar's *For the Fallen* echo despairingly & yet somehow victoriously in my head.'

In 1924, for performance during the British Empire Exhibition at Wembley, he produced an *Empire March* and eight songs, *Pageant of Empire*, to words by Alfred Noyes. Sir Walter Parratt, Master of the King's Musick since 1893, had died the previous month and there had been rumours that the office would be allowed to lapse. In a letter to Lady Stuart of Wortley, on 16 April, he refers to this:

'I wrote to Stamfordham[1] urging that the Master of the King's Music shd. be retained—its suppression wd. have a very bad effect abroad where the effacement of the last shred of connection of the Court with the Art wd. not be understood. It is not S's dept so it was turned over to F. Ponsonby.[2] He wrote to me that it was one of the offices which it was (long ago) proposed (scheduled) to cease. I wrote again offering myself (honorary)—*anything* rather than that it shd. be publicly announced that the old office was abolished. No reply. Colebrooke[3] wrote to the Ld. Chamberlain—but as far as I can make out the three depts. simply quarrel over these things: no grit, no imagination— *no music.* No nothing except boxing, football & racing so it is. I have had no further reply & I believe the matter is to drop tacitly.'

But in May, Elgar was appointed to the vacant post, one that he graced and in the hearts of his countrymen had occupied in effect for twenty-seven years. He coveted it simply for its historical and romantic associations, not for any special feelings of loyalty. The same letter to Lady Stuart included this: 'Everything seems so hopelessly & irredeemably *vulgar* at Court.' It also refers to talk of a peerage for Elgar. 'I fear it is hopeless but it wd. please me,' he wrote; and it would have pleased him because it would have honoured music, as Tennyson's had honoured literature. He wrote to Lady Stuart, who was influential in these matters, in 1926: 'Of course I should love to have the *offer* but it is impossible for me to suggest in the remotest way that I want it: this

---

[1] Lord Stamfordham (1849–1931), the King's Private Secretary.
[2] Sir Frederick Ponsonby (1867–1935), later Lord Sysonby, Treasurer to King George V.   [3] Lord Colebrooke (1861–1939), a Lord-in-Waiting.

sort of thing I have never done and although I know well that it *is* done . . . I cannot think of it: so adieu! to all my greatness.' On 24 December 1927 he wrote to her: 'H.M. has offered me the wretched K.C.V.O.(!!!) which awful thing I must accept! Alas!'

He had been made a member of the Order of Merit in the Coronation Honours List of 1911—'the one thing which really delights him,' Alice wrote to Troyte. Curiously, King Edward, who had instituted the Order, had not conferred it upon his friend. Elgar himself was a little concerned that the Worcestershire people did not attach enough significance to the honour, for it had only been in existence nine years and had not yet acquired the almost mystical significance it holds today. He wrote to Troyte in July 1911: 'I wish you wd. write to the Worcester paper & say a little what the Order of M really is! Some . . . think it is a sort of degradation & quite unworthy of me. . . . At the Investiture Sir G. Trevelyan & I were marshalled next G.C.B. & *before* G.C.M.G. (which is Ld. Beauchamp's highest distinction!) & of course before G.C.S.I. etc. It was very nice.'

He was made K.C.V.O. in 1928, a baronet in 1931, and G.C.V.O. in 1933, years when such honours ceased to matter for him, because although they showed official recognition of his position in musical life, they did nothing to combat the neglect of his music which had by then occurred. He accepted them, no doubt, because through him they honoured English music and, perhaps, because it pleased his vanity to know that he, once an outsider, had won his right to exact this tribute from the kind of people who had resented his ascent to the head of his profession. If this can be explained as further proof of his essential insecurity, as in the case of Tennyson, it is also understandable. The professional honour which gives English musicians cause for the deepest personal pleasure and pride, the Gold Medal of the Royal Philharmonic Society, was denied him until 1925, when he was sixty-eight, and awarded to him some months after it had gone to Delius. His music had by no means frequently occurred in the Society's programmes in the previous twenty-five years.

'In Elgar', wrote Constant Lambert in *Music, Ho!* 'we get an example of a composer, in touch with both his audience and his period, expressing himself nationally in an international language.' Arthur Johnstone, thirty years before, had found 'Land of Hope and Glory' to be 'distinctively British' because it was 'beefy and breezy', which is true enough of the song though not of the tune in its orchestral dress. But is there any justification for the assumption that Elgar was a nationalist, a typically English composer, apart from the extra-musical associations of his work with typically English state occasions? It is time the whole concept of music as a national language was swept away. There is no English music, only music by Englishmen. Elgar, as Lambert realized, could and wanted to 'put himself across' to his fellow-countrymen, but there was nothing specifically English in the way that he did it, nothing that can be linked with folk-song or the Tudor composers or Purcell. To account for what is called the 'English quality' of Elgar's music can be done only by explaining it as a response to his expression of some national sub-conscious, 'the echo of the echo of a sigh', as in the Welsh tune of the *Introduction and Allegro*, the Adagio of the First Symphony and the slow movement of the Violin Concerto. The music distils a national mood by a deeply personal transmuting of emotion. All the virtues and failings of Elgar's work are traceable to the man himself, not to the fact that he was an Englishman alive in the period of England's imperial noonday. He may or may not have accepted the age in which he lived—he certainly did not rebel against it, but there are degrees of acceptance. The issue is irrelevant: the diversity of the music written in the first fourteen years of the twentieth century is sufficient in itself to explode any theories about the artist's relationship to the time in which he lives. That is why the 'Edwardianism' of Elgar's music is an outdated label which was never accurate. Elgar's world was the world of music, of Strauss's *Heldenleben*, Puccini's *La Bohème*, Schoenberg's *Gurrelieder*. The faults of taste, the descents into triteness and triviality, afflict them and others—Sibelius, for example, and Mahler—as much as they afflict Elgar; they are the faults of big men undertaking big tasks. They have nothing to do with the sun's never setting on the British Empire, even if Stanford did say to Elgar, about the D major March, 'You have translated Master Rudyard Kipling into Music . . . and said "blooming beggar" in quite his style.'

Whether this was the first association of the names Kipling and Elgar, and hence an automatic association of both with 'jingoism', it has proved a lasting one that would have been more accurate if it had been less superficial. Just as the detractors of Kipling's popular style forget the darker, mysterious side of his work, and overlook the 1897 'Recessional' about navies melting away, so the detractors of Elgar forget that what people turn to most often in Elgar's music is not the swagger and blare of the extrovert works, but the sweet, tender melancholy that is far and away the predominant characteristic of his work, one that is heightened because in his major compositions the miniature Elgar is integrated into the symphonic Elgar. He did not need to keep one style apart from the other, as Sibelius did; he was incapable of doing so—'I

L

hold nothing back'. The style was the man, which was only what H. C. Colles meant when, in *The Times* of 1 April 1939, he wrote: 'His whole output is a series of variations on one melody which was the essence of his being.' The exquisite *Chanson de Nuit* and the eloquent *Sospiri* are in the same world as the Adagio of the First Symphony. The tune of the first *Pomp and Circumstance* march is but one of a family: the opening theme of the First Symphony, the chorus 'Go forth' in *Gerontius*, the slow movements of the *Serenade*, the symphonies and the concertos, 'Nimrod', and the Angel's Farewell. The march-like opening of the First Symphony is dismissed by exhilaration akin to the quick sections of the marches, with the off-beat thumps that also highlight brilliantly effective episodes in the slow movement of the Second Symphony, in the Boar's Head and Coronation scenes of *Falstaff*, in parts of the Violin Concerto and in the finale of the Cello Concerto. Episodes which disturb some listeners, where there is incongruity between the jubilee-procession style and its context, can sometimes be traced to the relative poverty of the invention—the last bars of the *Variations*, for example, and several passages in the two oratorios. It is the fault of exuberance, of a flamboyant generosity which had no room for anaemic half measures.

He indirectly answered his critics in his first Birmingham lecture in 1905. Some people, he said, deplored vulgarity. But he deplored the commonplace much more. 'Vulgarity in the course of time may be refined. Vulgarity often goes with inventiveness, and it can take the place of initiative—in a rude and misguided way, no doubt—but after all it does something, and can be and has been refined. But the commonplace mind can never be anything but commonplace, and no amount of education, no polish of a university, can eradicate the stain from the low type of mind which is the English commonplace. English music is white and evades everything. . . . What I want to see coming into being is something that shall grow out of our own soul.'

These sentiments echoed some expressed three years earlier by one of the younger group of composers, Ralph Vaughan Williams, in an article headed 'Good Taste':[1] 'The truth is that the young Englishman is too musicianly. The "musicianly" composer . . . has found out all the mechanical means by which beautiful music is produced. . . . Many a young composer has stifled his natural impulses in the desire to be musicianly. . . . If a composer is naturally vulgar, let him be frank and write vulgar music instead of hedging himself about with an artificial

[1] Published in Vol. I, No. 2 of *The Vocalist* (May 1902).

barrier of good taste. . . . If every composer will be himself, his music will at all events be genuine.'

'English' music is not an identifiable product. It is, simply and ob-viously, music written by Englishmen out of genuine creative en-deavour or, to use Elgar's more romantic term, 'their own souls'. How the best of English composers found their own souls differs widely. Elgar and Vaughan Williams found theirs by completely varying ways, but being men of strong and original character they produced music of strong and original character, and their art has been called 'typically English'. This phrase is almost meaningless. Where is there such a person as the 'typical Englishman'? Elgar, certainly, was not one, a man so emotional that, as Compton Mackenzie has described, he trembled all over and veins and beads of sweat stood out alarmingly on his head with the excitement of listening to the 'March to the Scaffold' from Berlioz's *Fantastic Symphony*.[1]

I have used the word 'superficial' to describe the accepted response to Elgar's *nobilmente* style and to his comparison with Kipling. A more striking parallel is with Tennyson—both were countrymen always ill at ease in cities, both liable to fits of almost demented grief over the death of friends, both outsiders who had no reason to think highly of society's conduct (Tennyson's father had been excluded from his inheritance, Elgar's wife had been penalized financially for 'marrying beneath' her), both married to women who tried to protect them from the incon-veniences of the world, both needing the admiring approval of friends and colleagues, both acutely sensitive to unfavourable criticism, both pessimistic about the lasting quality of their own work, both regarded as spokesmen for the country through their art, both at their best in elegiac, wistful, intimate moods, both attacked as representative Victorian and representative Edwardian rather than as poet and musi-cian. It is perhaps significant of the personal qualities in Elgar's music that it was at its first peak of popularity when Britain's greatness was uncontested and people did not need to look below the surface, that it fell into disfavour while the Empire began to crumble, and that it won a new and more perceptive audience when Britain had ceased to be a great Power, when the Empire had disintegrated, and when people heard in the music what had always been there to hear: the funeral march of a civilization, of a spiritual and artistic way of life which was decaying.

[1] 'Dorabella' (Mrs. Dora Powell) in her *Edward Elgar: Memories of a Variation* (Second Edition, London, 1946), p. 5, says that his concert-hall neighbours became used to being elbowed or clutched by Elgar when he was excited by music and knew what it was 'to have an arm black and blue with bruises next day . . ., with practice one learnt to shift imperceptibly . . . so that the position of the grip varied.'

Elgar transcended the time in which he lived. Nervous energy and what he himself called 'stately sorrow' are the moods of the symphonies and concertos. The so-called 'complacent' tone of the music—the Trio tune of the D major March is the example usually cited—is not complacent at all. There is, as I have already suggested, a note of resignation in this melody, emphasized, as in the Larghetto of the Second Symphony, by the sepulchral scoring (horns, bassoons, clarinets in their low register). The outbursts of extrovert grandiloquence in the symphonies are always followed by withdrawn, cloistered passages of tender lyricism, the general effect, as in Mahler, emphasizing the instability of the full conception. This can be traced musically to the constant shiftings of tonality and harmony. Nowhere can this fusion of the 'laureate' and the 'mystic' Elgar—or the 'London pride' and the 'windflower' Elgar—be more profitably studied than in the pages preceding the coda of the first movement of the First Symphony and the tragic contrast in the Second Symphony's first movement between the energetic exposition and its collapse into the withdrawn, ghostly mood of the development section. It is quite possible that this elegiac side of Elgar's music has its origins in a nostalgia for childhood—'oh, the mad days'—as was the case with Mahler, and it is not surprising that movements like the poignant and fanciful trio in the second movement of the First Symphony have a strong connection with the mood of the *Wand of Youth* suites. But because Elgar was a subtler composer than Mahler, these matters are less crudely handled. There is a restraint—this, at any rate, is typically English—which perhaps half-conceals the truth, and certainly makes the music doubly effective. Elgar did not wallow; his expressions of nostalgia, excepting the Cello Concerto, have a unique, unself-pitying quality all the more remarkable because the man himself was not free from self-indulgence in the matter of 'the days that are no more'.

As for the *Pomp and Circumstance* marches themselves, for every ten people who know the much-performed Nos. 1 and 4, perhaps one or two know the full set. Their pre-eminence in their field is for the obvious reason that no one has yet approached Elgar in the sheer musical effectiveness of his ceremonial manner. Any other marches, whether by Walton, Ireland, Bliss, or Eric Coates, are but pale imitations. It is likely, too, that most of those whose lips curl at the mention of *Pomp and Circumstance* have rarely, if ever, listened to the marches as music and as a whole. If they had, they would recognize that Nos. 1 and 4 are superb in their own right, especially when played as Elgar wrote them and without overblown sentiments not implicit in the music. As for

Nos. 2, 3, and 5, they blow the 'jingoist' jibe sky-high. They are less fruity melodically than Nos. 1 and 4, totally lacking in rhetoric and pomposity. No. 2, for example, in A minor is a nervously restless piece in Elgar's symphonic manner, scored rather like a Schubertian *marche militaire* or a theatrical entr'acte. No. 3, like No. 2 also in the minor, is a subtle work, with a hint of mystery in its opening bars, and a trio section of lyrical and quite un-military charm. No. 5, written in 1930 but probably sketched much earlier, is jovial, with more than a touch of self-parodying, tongue-in-cheek humour in its final pages. The complete set, played one after the other, comprise a kind of suite, devoid of monotony except for the actual march form, consistently exciting rhythmically and scored with all Elgar's most potent command of thrilling and poetic instrumental colour.

They are great popular music. There is nothing inferior about them, and it is because he was able to transfer their 'popular' elements to his larger-scale works that Elgar remains indispensable for an expression of national sorrow or rejoicing: the death of a King, the death of a hero like Churchill or the crowning of a Queen. Not because of pomp or circumstance, but because, as Parry perceived, his essential and real message reaches the hearts of the people: that the transience of human life overwhelms all ceremony, that 'golden lads and girls all must, as chimney sweepers, come to dust'. And also because the music carries in itself the seeds of its personal and human origins, not as the celebration or commemoration of an epoch or an ideology, but as a memory of a summer-evening talk with a friend about Beethoven, the enshrinement of the soul of a woman, the remembrance of a man snatched away, as Rodewald was, in the prime of life, the fears of a man on his death-bed, apprehensive about what lies ahead—'no end of a worldly man, and now brought to book'.

10 Unfinished Trilogy

This was Elgar's position in 1901–2; he was nearing forty-five, he had had a success with the *Variations*, a failure with *The Dream of Gerontius*. He had had riotous success with two *Pomp and Circumstance* marches and the *Cockaigne* overture. At a time when choral singing in Britain was at its zenith, it was his orchestral works which had taken him to the top. *King Olaf* remained the most frequently performed of his choral music, *The Black Knight* had never established itself. As Jaeger wrote to him in 1901, it 'doesn't move much for some reason or other, chiefly no doubt because the subject is a bit gruesome & the music ends poetically pp. I have thought that if we could do something with the work for orchestra alone, we might make it better known. . . .' All of which seems to contradict the theory that Elgar was prevented from writing the orchestral music that really interested him because the taste of the time was for choral works, religious if possible. Elgar himself supported the theory when, in 1933, he told Delius that he wrote his choral works because it was 'the penalty of my environment'. This may have been true in the mid-1890s, the period of *Lux Christi* and *The Black Knight*. But by 1902 Elgar had established a new situation whereby the public acclaimed him as an orchestral composer. Yet, after beginning several instrumental projects during 1901–2, he turned aside from them to begin a large-scale oratorio. Why? The simple answer is a combination of financial and artistic necessity, with the emphasis on the latter. It helped Elgar in his pecuniary difficulties to know that a Birmingham Festival commission was available to him, but there is no merit in pretending that *The Apostles* and *The Kingdom* are potboilers, written against Elgar's better judgement in order to make ends meet. He wrote them because he wanted to. There is documentary proof to support his statement that it had long been his wish to write an oratorio on the subject of the work of Christ's Apostles, a wish prompted by a schoolmaster's casual remark in a scripture lesson.

Elgar conceived his project as a trilogy dealing with the beginnings of Christianity, Christ's call to the disciples, the years of teaching in Jerusalem, the mission to the Gentiles and, finally but never accomplished, the Church Universal. Themes for this vast work had accumulated in his sketchbooks since the 1880s though some had been used up for *Lux Christi*. Some sketches are dated 1896. It has already been seen that he was preoccupied with the idea of Judas Iscariot in the winter of 1899, and that his 'Judas theme' became the Angel of the Agony in *Gerontius*. In November 1901 he wrote the Morning Psalm section; and music that eventually found its way into *The Kingdom* was written early in 1902, notably the setting of the Lord's Prayer. To carry out his ambition he had, of course, to provide his own libretto and this he did with his customary thoroughness. Dorabella found him at work on it in December 1901, surrounded by Bibles, a book he was discovering, it is surprising to realize, almost for the first time. It was, inevitably, a scissors-and-paste job, and this is in some measure responsible for the comparative failure of the two works to grip the public. Despite the theological study which went into it, despite the novel and sympathetic approach to the character of Judas, the text lacks a focal point of issue of the kind that makes *Gerontius* compelling. It is discursive and sometimes it is inconsistent, not even making sense. Whereas the music of *Gerontius* seems to spring unbidden from the poem, much of *The Apostles* sounds very consciously 'set to music'.

Work on the music in the summer of 1902 was hindered by Elgar's old eye trouble—'My eyes are bad and I must write no more,' he wrote in May to Jaeger who had by now been told of the work. There was still some doubt whether Novello's would publish it—*Gerontius*, it must be remembered, had still not been performed in London despite its success at Düsseldorf. Littleton wrote to Elgar on 11 July: 'I have been in correspondence with Mr. Johnstone (Birmingham Festival) about *The Apostles*. He places such a high commercial value on the work that I fear there is no chance of our coming to terms. . . . I have tried hard to do my part in helping *Gerontius* and should have liked to have continued to do my best for other works.' On 3 August Elgar wrote to Jaeger from Craeg Lea: 'My eyes are better, I think, & I'm working at the Apostles—which you will not like—it's too philosophical for your *cheap publisher's side* of your mind, but just the thing for the *real* A. J. J.' He was ill again before Christmas—'I have *liver*: you know what that means!'—but on New Year's Day 1903, Alice noted that he was 'keen on his work'. Jaeger went to Malvern to hear some of it on 4 January. Dorabella had heard sketches and completed numbers, including the final Alleluias, a year before. Johnstone of the Birmingham Festival paid a visit to discuss Novello's terms for its production in October. Then on 12 January Hans Richter came and was played parts of the *Coronation Ode*[1] and *The Apostles*. Later that month, on the 21st,

[1] In preparation for a Hallé performance in Manchester.

Elgar began to let Jaeger have sections of the score for printing, although the work was by no means completed, and was again delayed by a chill on the liver—'it stops *all* work', he wrote to Littleton, '. . . I have been quite disillusioned as to the musical world for some years and so I say farewell to it without the slightest regret.' Despite this depression, he completed a first score in early February, received early proofs on the 17th and sent off the manuscript of the second scene, 'By the Wayside'—'quite new and different from anything else', said Alice, who took each parcel to the post office, as she had done for every work since they were married. The third scene, 'By the Sea of Galilee', was finished on 23 March, and by then Elgar was beginning to be anxious for more proofs, no doubt remembering the last-minute rush which had affected *Gerontius*. On 19 March he wrote to Jaeger: 'You promised me I shd. have plenty (of copies that is). You know I am not a *proper composer* & I know I ought not to try—but! well I must. Now—I prefer *revises* of course & I like to send 'em to three or four friends whose judgment I rely on (for phrasing etc. etc.)—vocalists & *sich*—that takes one copy. My wife wants one for *scoring* purposes, i.e. making the skeleton for me—that takes another & I like to have one by me to refer to, phrasing, &c. . . . don't *laugh at me for my silly ways* because I'm clever at some things but *not* at composing.' Elgar always objected to the word 'composed' on the title-pages of his scores and asked Jaeger on 20 March to make it simply 'by Edward Elgar'. (He had explained to him, on 21 June 1898, that 'this word always brings up a vision of a man scratching the back of his head with a pen—if I *do* scratch (which heaven forbid!) it's not for ideas.') 'Send along revises— anything else,' he added. 'Lumbago better, rheumatism bad, temper evil, disposition venomous, mind—vacant.'

A crisis arose at the end of May when Elgar upset Novello's engraver, Brause, by sending seventeen pages of a new chorus—'Turn you to the stronghold'—to be inserted at the end of Part I. Elgar was unrepentant and told Jaeger on 28 May: 'I have been obliged to recast on acct. of the difficulty in finding a Judas to my mind & particularly wanted these sheets as I have to travel & try vocalists—now here I am, through confounded stupidity, without any copy at all. Even if the Judas sc: cd. not be proceeded with—I suppose everybody layed him down & wept & forgot all about such things as revises. I am absolutely vexed! for once. Tell me is Messchaert singing well?'

Elgar had realized that he needed really impressive singers for the parts of Peter, who was gradually to assume a commanding rôle, and Judas. Worried by this and by further eye trouble he radically altered the design of the whole work. What we now know as *The Kingdom*, much of which was already written ('O sacrum convivium', for instance, was written at Rodewald's house in Liverpool in December 1902), was planned as Part III of *The Apostles*. In June he wrote to Littleton: 'My eyes are again in trouble—he [the doctor] forbids more work. Now I propose to the B'ham people that they produce Pts I and II of *The Apostles*—this portion is complete in itself and may well stand alone. . . . The concluding portion of the work (Pt III to round it off), much of which was written first—you can have any time later.'

A rough score of Judas's part was sent to the Dutch baritone Anton van Rooy who had been singing Wotan under Richter in *The Ring* at Covent Garden during May. Jaeger warned Elgar of the possible effects of 'foreigner's English' on the part. On returning home from the first London performance of *Gerontius*, Elgar worked at the score until 21 June when Alice's diary entry reads: 'Finished—all but the very end.' The Elgars then went to London and were presented to the King. Back at Craeg Lea, Elgar wrote on 1 July to Jaeger: 'I was bothered in town by a heap of people—principally trying to find singers *with brains*—now I have to put up with a—caste of English—I won't go into the disappointments—oh! these singers—*where* are their *brains*? . . I have some full score ready for you but will hold it for a space. . . . The only way out of the singer business was to omit "Peter"—who shines forth in Pt III & let Black[1] do Judas—It's pitiful but there are really no *good* singers beyond three & one (Bispham[2]) we can't have!' He wrote another letter on the same day in reply to a worried one from Jaeger: 'I'm not ill! & it is of no use to postpone the work as I shall *never* get English vocalists—a complete caste that is—to do my work. Pt. III was written first & most of it is ready to print—but I can find no singers.'

He was, in any case, hard on his singers in both *The Apostles* and *The Kingdom*. To a soloist who protested that he could not make himself heard over the large orchestral sound Elgar was encouraging from the rostrum, Elgar replied that it did not matter: the voice was used at that particular point 'as a vehicle to carry on the words' and the orchestra was more important.

For the rest of July he went to Rodewald's cottage at Bettws-y-Coed where he worked on the orchestration. He also wrote several long letters to Canon Charles V. Gorton whom he had met earlier in 1903 at Morecambe while adjudicating at the music festival of which Gorton was chairman. The Canon had read through the text of *The Apostles*

---

[1] Andrew Black (1859–1920). [2] David Bispham (1857–1921).

from a theological viewpoint and made several criticisms which Elgar answered. He also wrote a commentary on the text, published in the *Musical Times* of October 1903.

'Of course *we* know that the Resurrection was the climax,' Elgar wrote, 'but I was trying to look at it from the point of view of the weak man of the time. . . . The garden scene has been done too much already. . . . Thomas also was impossible on account of bringing in another principal. . . . I have endeavoured to suggest that forgiveness is for *all who repent.* To my mind *Judas'* crime & sin was *despair* (Ibsen etc. etc.); not only the betrayal which was done for a worldly purpose. In these days, when every "modern" person seems to think "suicide" is the actual way out of everything my plan, if explained, may do some good. . . . The music explains—by means of leitmotifs & general treatment—much of the "interdependence" of the words.'

In August Jaeger was examining the work in detail—the episode of the 'crude progression' has already been mentioned. He was also working on an analysis, as he had done for *Gerontius.* 'I say,' he wrote, '*do* give us a less jolly tune for Christ's "The Keys of the Kingdom", p. 102.[1] The words themselves *jingle*; *do* make the music a little more stately, dignified & monotonous (in the true sense of the word), & on p. 83 at "Ye shall lie down" you have the *notes* of "God save the King". Don't sneer at me; these things will jar on one. Simply take out the E on "lie" & there you are. . . . Your work grows on me tremendously & by leaps & bounds. It's great stuff & quite wonderfully original & beautiful. Bless you, this is your finest work so far & your greatest.'

Elgar replied: 'The "Keys" are all right, if sung intelligently—the *Keys* do not need emphasising—but the result in the next two sentences —no one but you wd. try to sing it in time, Moss. p. 83. Shan't alter it on any account—put a pause over the E.' Elgar was annoyed over the terms the Birmingham Festival were offering Jaeger for use of his analysis and told Johnstone what he thought. 'Curse the Festival,' he said to Jaeger. 'I really think the more one has to do with the practical side of music the more awful this life becomes. I am so sick of it all! Birmingham is the worst Festival programme I have ever seen, I think (talk about the 3 choirs!) Elijah! Messiah!! Legend!!! I *can't* invite any decent folk for such a week.'

Jaeger jibbed at certain points in the score, notably on p. 135 where the chorus thrice repeat the word 'cometh' in 'a band of men and officers cometh with lanterns and torches and weapons', and, two pages later, where Elgar wanted an octave leap from B to high B on the

[1] Vocal score page reference.

'Hold' of 'Hold him fast'. 'There is no objection to the repetition of cometh 3 times,' Elgar replied on 9 August, 'if done with any dramatic instinct as a good actor would do, & as a chorus, to be considered good, *must* do some day. To repeat "with lanterns" wd. be silly. It is unfortunate that all choral music shd. be affected by dull church music & by comic opera but so it is. If you could have heard van Rooy sing "Hold" you wd. not have criticised it—it is useless to try & explain to you my ideas so put "Hold him fast" [with 'Hold' on high D tied across the bar line].'

'Yah!' Jaeger replied. 'I *can* imagine an artist like van Rooy & Wüllner singing "Hold him fast" with A.1 effect. Alas, where is *your* van Rooy & Wüllner amongst English oratorio singers! If Black *can* do it as you *imagined* it, leave it for Gawd's sake. Perhaps he can be taught not to be comic. That Judas part is superb & worthy of the biggest artist living.'

By 12 August Elgar was beginning to tire. He was within a few days of completing the full score and told Jaeger, 'I want to be *quite free* for a little time—Bike touring belike—& could not undertake to do anything, *except* to revise MS pts. with the score.' Composers today should note that Elgar, with the aid of a friend, John Austin, of Worcester, worked on all the individual orchestral parts himself. He sent Jaeger various theological treatises that had helped him in his approach to his theme—by the Rev. Professor A. B. Davidson, by Franz Delitzsch, and by the Rev. F. L. Cohen—and explained the significance of certain leitmotives. On the 17th he completed the score and Jaeger wrote to him: 'The beauty of the music moves me to tears. . . . The Apostles are certainly your maturest & greatest work; the certainty of touch & style displayed throughout is wonderful. . . . But it is all so original, so individual & subjective that it will take the British Public 10 years to let it soak into its pachydermal mind; unless, of course, the story, being known by everybody, will carry the work along. . . . As for the poor critics (the dullest among them I mean) they will be bewildered I fear. . . . I believe that by the time you have completed Part III you will have given to the world the greatest oratorio since the Messiah. . . .'

Elgar was touched: 'I feel I can only say "non sum dignus". Never mind the B.P.—they must wait; so long as my intimate friends—friends I have gathered round me because of their hearts and brains—are satisfied, nay even only *interested* in my work, I have my reward. . . . The weather is awful & has upset all plans for rest & change. . . .'

He eventually got his rest by staying for a few days at Hereford with G. R. Sinclair. Schuster and Rodewald stayed with Elgar for the Three Choirs Festival there. By 15 September he was agitating for parts to correct. For the rest of the month he worked on them, becoming irritated, as he usually did, with Novello's. 'I'm sorry the parts worry you,' he wrote to Jaeger. 'I can't think *why*. Your men must be jolly slow.' He wrote to Schuster on 27 September: 'I am *dead* with fatigue correcting proofs for orchestra—*three*, yes three! copyists have become ill, insane & useless & have given up work wrestling with the complications of the score & I have to sit here (and did sit also in London) & wearily plod over their stuff.' Elgar began orchestral rehearsals with the Hallé Orchestra in Manchester on 5 October. Choir rehearsals were happier affairs than in 1900. 'I heard the chorus at Birmingham,' Elgar wrote to Canon Gorton on 23 September, '& it is fine—&, in all fear and trembling, I am not yet disappointed with my work.' Stanford attended one of the rehearsals and, according to Elgar, was 'enthusiastic over the Apostles: telling people all around (Albani etc. etc.) of its or their glory'. Albani was one of the six soloists in the first performance on 14 October. The others were Muriel Foster, John Coates, Kennerley Rumford, Andrew Black, and David Ffrangcon-Davies. There was a very different atmosphere from that which had prevailed at the first performance of *The Dream of Gerontius*, as Johnstone noted in the *Manchester Guardian* of 15 October: 'Vague hostility towards the unusual and the unknown has given way almost universally to the recognition that he is one of the great originals in the musical world of today; and he thus compels attention even in those who instinctively dislike both his particular methods and the kind of general atmosphere into which his religious art transports the listener.'

The critic of *The Daily Telegraph* called the occasion 'unique' in his experience of the Birmingham Festival. 'It has never happened that the whole musical world, not only in this country but also abroad, has gathered more or less closely around the production of an Englishman. . . . Though sturdily independent, courting nobody, he now occupies the position of a man with whom most people are determined to be pleased.'

This time there was no disaster. The critics acclaimed the work. 'Perhaps the most remarkable work of the present century', the *Telegraph* said. 'The composer is at his best in rendering the music of the heavenly choir', said Johnstone, whose notice did not commit itself as irrevocably in the work's favour as that of *Gerontius* had done; comparing the two works he wrote of *The Apostles* as 'of greater depth and significance but less perfectly finished' than *Gerontius*. Jaeger had gone to Birmingham for the final rehearsal and the first performance but had collapsed and stayed in his hotel bed. This time he received no embittered letter from Elgar, merely commiseration and the happy P.S. 'I am getting conceited now'. So the composer was evidently satisfied. Ferruccio Bonavia, however, who played in the orchestra, has written[1] that Elgar seemed 'nervous and ill at ease' during rehearsals and that while 'there was actually no obvious failing in the performance . . . the public was as far as ever from grasping all that the oratorio stood for'. The inference to be drawn is that it was a *succès d'estime*, and by 23 October Elgar was 'not very well & much worried with finance side of new work & disappointed at that side' (Alice's diary). The public's reaction to *The Apostles* was respectful but it never seized their imaginations as *Gerontius* had. After Richter's first Manchester performance in February 1904, Arthur Johnstone noted that there was 'no scene of great enthusiasm' such as had greeted *Gerontius* at the Hallé. Some thought this was because of the solemnity of the subject; Johnstone was not to be deluded, however, and added: 'The *Apostles* being unquestionably much more austere and difficult to understand than *Gerontius*, we are inclined to accept the simpler explanation that the audience did not like it so well.'

A few days after the first performance, Schuster had given Elgar a hint that Alice's idea of an Elgar Festival might very well materialize at Covent Garden—'As to your lovely scheme,' Elgar wrote to Schuster on 22 October, 'I can say nothing now save thanks: it is just like you to think of it: but plans!' Jaeger, too, was able to report good news on 30 October: Fritz Steinbach wanted to conduct *The Apostles* at the Lower Rhine Festival at Cologne at Whitsun 1904, 'crooood passages, ugly bits, awkward points & all'. Elgar was sceptical if this would occur in reality, but all elation was shattered for him a few days later by Rodewald's death. He went to Manchester to conduct in mid-November, by which time he knew that the festival would be held in March of the following year, and then, with Alice and Carice, he went to Italy in the hope of regaining his full health and of escaping the cold and damp of the English winter. Neither ambition was adequately fulfilled, and his letters from Italy are a curious mixture of high and low spirits. They spent the first ten days at Bordighera—'lovely but too cockney for me,' he told Schuster. 'I want something more Italian or *more* civilised & would prefer to be virtuous at Alassio or wildly wicked at Monte Carlo to being betwixt & between here. . . . Alice & I have been out *with a donkey* all day up in the woods & mountains—donkey's name is "Grisia"—a lovely beast. . . . Bought some figs today—did not know

[1] Op. cit., p. 84.

the name so asked for "frutti, per habilmenti d'Adam ed Eva". I got
'em. . . . Oh! that donkey. She's a love. I am going to buy her & ride
her from here to Alassio! . . . We are both riotously well & shall never
come home. We go to Alassio on Thursday.'

From Alassio a few days later he wrote to Troyte Griffith: 'The *view*
at Bordighera is the great thing, but the whole *place* is English & the
folk ½ French—also it feels like Malvern & the roads are full of English
nurserymaids & old English women & children.' To Jaeger he was even
more explicit: 'This place is jolly—real Italian & no nursemaids calling
out "Now, Master Johnny!"—like that anglicised paradise Bordighera!
pff! . . . Do come out—it seems *so easy* to come & so difficult to go
back. . . . What matters the Mediterranean being rough & grey? What
matters rain in torrents? Who cares for gales? *Tramontana!* We have
such meals! such wine! *Gosh!* . . . We are at last living a life. The
Mosquitoes are a trial & I am stung because I refused to believe in 'em
& wd. not pull down the mosquito curtains at night round my bed. . . .
I can't believe all these great Germans are doing my music: is it true?
I think it's a dream. I hope you are pleased, old boy, anyway.'

Over Christmas he was at work on the concert overture *In the South*
and concerned with plans for the Covent Garden festival. Clara Butt's
terms for *Gerontius* were said to be 'prohibitive' and Higgins had
written on 19 December to say that Muriel Foster would be in America
and unable to sing the Angel. 'I had naturally thought of Brema but I
am told on the very best authority that on the last two or three occasions on which she sang it was almost painful.' He proposed Kirkby
Lunn as a substitute, adding: 'I am fully aware of her lack of poetic
feeling . . . at the same time I cannot help thinking that no amount of
poetic feeling will compensate for a raucous voice.' The weather was
cold and by 3 January 1904, Elgar was writing to Jaeger in yet another
mood: 'This visit has been, is, artistically a complete *failure* & I can do
nothing. We have been *perished* with cold, rain & gales. Five fine days
have we had & three of those were perforce spent in the train. . . .
You must understand that when a wind *does* come—& it is apparently
always on—it is no bearable, kindly east wind of England—but a
tearing, piercing, lacerating *devil* of a wind: one step outside the door
& I am cut in two numbed & speechless: I have never regretted anything more than this horribly disappointing journey: wasting time,
money & temper.'

Jaeger was able to tell him that *The Apostles* would be performed in
Cologne on 22 May, in New York and Manchester (under Richter) in
February, and in London in March (during the festival). The Elgars had

planned to stay in Italy until the end of February but an invitation to
dine with Edward VII at Marlborough House early in February
provided a welcome excuse to return to Malvern. 'You ask why we
return,' Elgar wrote to Schuster, 'simply on account of the weather
which has been mostly *unbearable*—eleven days in the house with bitter
east winds is too much away from one's books & everything one works
with etc. etc. I have had crippling rheumatism & colds & have had the
doctor for days. . . . Next week was a convenient time to either give
up the house or take it on & the King's pleasant wish to me "clinched"
our determination, which was wavering, to fly home. . . . You see I
only want to go home to finish my work. I cannot work anywhere
else.'

No previous English composer had been accorded such a tribute as
Elgar received on 14, 15, and 16 March 1904, at the Royal Opera House,
Covent Garden. Richter, the Hallé Orchestra and Choir were the
performers. On the opening night, *The Dream of Gerontius* was per-
formed (Kirkby Lunn, John Coates, Ffrangcon-Davies), on the second
The Apostles (Agnes Nicholls, Kirkby Lunn, John Coates, Ffrangcon-
Davies, Kennerley Rumford, and Andrew Black) and on the third
evening the concert was

> Overture, *Froissart*
> Selections from *Caractacus* (Suzanne Adams, Lloyd
>   Chandos, and Charles Clark)
> *Enigma Variations*
> *In the South* (first performance; conducted by Elgar)
> *Sea Pictures* (Clara Butt)
> *Cockaigne*
> *Pomp and Circumstance* Marches Nos. 1 and 2

The theatre was filled on each evening despite the high prices. Jaeger[1]
described the festival to Dorabella, who was unable to attend: 'The new
overture is *beautiful* & new, & shows a surer touch than almost anything
else I know of E. E.'s. *The Apostles* impressed me tremendously though
nothing "came off" as the composer meant it. The acoustic defects of
the theatre were too great. . . . Elgar had a *rare* time and everything was
splendid. Ask dear little Mrs. E. She must have been in the 7th Heaven
of Happiness. *Such* swells they met, from the Queen downwards. A

---

[1] A reminder of Jaeger's comparative poverty is contained in his letter to Elgar on 24
February 1904: 'I say, *if* the C.G. people give you any tickets which you *can't* do with
remember poor "Nim". I really can't afford to pay & I *should* like to hear at least the
Overture (*In the South*). You have no poorer friend than yours ever Moss.'

great time for E. E., & some of us who have believed in him & fought for him (I had to fight hard for him at Novello's) are happy. . . .' Elgar was almost filial in his thanks 'from my heart' to Richter: 'Without you the thing could not have been done at all, and with you it was a great artistic success and your presence gave it a *dignity* which would otherwise have been wanting.'

The festival, election to the Athenaeum, friendship with his Sovereign, knighthood, acclaim at home and abroad—1904 was surely Elgar's *annus mirabilis.* 'We really have a composer who, while being recognized by musicians as a master-mind, a man of the highest ideals, and one who does not swerve one inch from his appointed path for the sake of popular favour, can yet command it sufficiently to fill Covent Garden on three nights in succession with people anxious to hear his most serious work,' said a writer in *The World.* It was less than six years since Elgar had found London still unwilling to lend an ear to his serious work and just under five since Richter had introduced the *Variations.* Even now he found a grudging attitude to his work among the London critics, and he was aware that he was looked at askance by his colleagues because busts and plaquettes of him were on sale (some showing him 'conducting his new overture *In the South*') and because he let his name be used in advertisements for pianos and pianolas. Outwardly all was sunlight and glitter: inwardly the same uncertainties, doubts, and misgivings governed his life. Something of 1898-ish petulance is contained in a letter replying to one from Jaeger about the forthcoming Cologne performance of *The Apostles*: 'I don't know *anything* about Köln—except they've asked me to go. I am quite tired of being supposed to "Bless" performances of my things which are not "coached" by me or my advice is asked when it is too late to make any change: but if I *must* go I must—only I don't want to go at all.' He and Alice went on 19 May. On the 21st the soloists failed to arrive for a rehearsal and Elgar, according to Alice's diary, showed his annoyance. He 'wd. not come up and be seen—agitation of the Steinbachs'. But the performance was 'gorgeous' (and others followed at Mainz in November and Rotterdam in December). At the end of July 1904, a month after moving into Plâs Gwyn at Hereford, Jaeger received a letter of a kind he had often had before: 'Everything is dull & goes slowly: & I am tried very much liverwise & am wofully short of money. I really think I must take some violin pupils again: only, as I have not touched it for so long, I should have to begin once more with elementary ones! Such is life & I hate, loathe & detest it.' A week later: 'It's all very well to talk to me about doing sextetts & symphonies & all the things I *want* to do, but tell me what & who is going to keep a roof over our heads. Nobody thinks of that.'

He wrote in the same vein to Lord Northampton, whose reply from Compton Wynyates on 15 August deserves quotation: 'I don't at all like what you say of yourself. Of course you know best whether you are making progress and whether you are gloomy; and you might possibly be for the moment "flat, stale and unprofitable",[1] but you say "*as ever* unprofitable" and that I have good reason to know is absolutely untrue from the artistic side. You *must* realize that you have in you a special power of bringing upon others the strongest influence for good. You have already used that power in a most remarkable degree. You have moved men's souls to the highest truths of Christianity and then you say in a fit of depression "as ever unprofitable". I can only think of you as a musical apostle, given one of God's greatest gifts.'

Already Elgar was concerned about completing the second part of *The Apostles* trilogy for Birmingham's 1906 festival, for which it was expected. Some as we know was already written and he worked on it in part of 1904. But the need for money was paramount: his new home, his social obligations, his visits to London, all these took money and time. Throughout the winter of 1904 he was low in spirits. 'I am better but jolly down,' he told Jaeger in August. At Christmas he wrote to Schuster: 'One line at this time (I *hate* it) because Alice says it's "nice". Oh! Lord. Well! I wish you everything nice and good—all, in short, everything I want and haven't got. I think that's about it. Everything here is flat, stale and distinctly unprofitable. . . . It is foggy and cold and I want to be in Italy. Oh! this dreadful life, if one could but slough it off and *end*, mark you! I don't want to live in any frightful other world —I am so sick of this.'

As I mentioned in the previous chapter, 1905 was a bad year for Elgar. The *Introduction and Allegro for Strings* was written and was a failure. The Birmingham lecture fiasco followed, and then the visit to the United States, undertaken, as he explained to Littleton, because 'my pocket gapes'. In the autumn the Three Choirs Festival, the Mediterranean cruise and the tour with the L.S.O. left little time for creative work, but in November and December 1905 he was again writing the oratorio. The whole period was punctuated by 'colds, rheumatism and liver' which occur with such regularity whenever Elgar was disturbed creatively or by trying to live two lives at once that one feels they might have stemmed from some psychological hypochondriac cause. On

---

[1] This adaptation of a line from *Hamlet* was one of Elgar's favourite quotations applied to himself.

M

New Year's Eve 1905, he wrote to Walford Davies: 'I am the same depressed (musically) being & the same very much alive (chemically & every other 'ally) mortal; keen for everything except my vocation, which I feel is not my vocation by a long tract of desert: I am working away & some of the themes are not bad.' Jaeger, who had spent a large part of 1905 in Switzerland and had been away from Novello's all year, had voiced his fears in a letter before he went to Davos in January 1905: 'I worry over your *muse*, for I fear greatly we shall get less & less out of you. This is the danger of success artistic & social! (especially social of course). I grieve over it & so do all those who most sincerely love & admire you. We know you *must live* but England *ruins* all *artists*.'[1] Elgar ignored this in his reply but he gave indirect confirmation of its accuracy the following August: 'I know nothing about Apostles pt. 2 or any analysis: if it is ever finished I imagined you might take on the analysis *if* properly recompensed: my life now is one incessant answering of letters & music is fading away.' Nevertheless a few days later he sent to Novello's his part-song *Evening Scene*, to words by Coventry Patmore. This was written in memory of R. G. H. Howson, the bank manager who conducted choirs at the Morecambe festivals—'the musical soul of the Morecambe affair', as Elgar described him. It was 'my best bit of landscape so far in that line,' he told Jaeger (24 August). 'You won't make anything of it on the P.F.—Morecambe is the place to hear it.' Jaeger found it a 'perfect gem'. It reminded him of Schubert and Goetz.

The beginnings of what was now known as *The Kingdom* went to Novello's by mid-January 1906. Novello's thoughtfully sent a set of proofs to the sick Jaeger and Elgar wrote to him on 26 January: '*Heart Friend*: I have been very evil in not writing to you but I had not the heart to do so. *Today* we hear from Mrs Jaeger that you are seeing the proofs of my new thing: I did not dare to suggest that you *should* see them & I dare not send my own sheets, so—I could not write. I am so delighted that the firm send the stuff on to you. So far it is the best thing I've done *I know*: remember it's not piano music & won't sound well on a tin kettle.'

Because of Jaeger's illness and Elgar's depression and his work against time, there are fewer letters about the genesis of *The Kingdom*. Jaeger was unfortunate enough to have one of his usual frank expressions of criticism answered, on 17 March 1906, by Alice in her most Mrs. Proudie-like mood; 'i think yr. surroundings must have depressed you

---

[1] Gustav Holst thought similarly. 'Every artist ought to pray that he may not be a "success",' he wrote to Clifford Bax.

when you wrote—It is curious that that chorus ['O ye priests'] did not fire you, it works up all who have heard it to a great pitch of excitement—& I think you might have given E. some credit for his fine literary taste & poetic feeling in his selection of words—If you cannot feel the sacerdotalism of any Church, there is the eternal priestdom of elect souls in all ages, who have stood above the lower minds & dragged them up. . . . Wait to judge of the new work, & especially to *remark* to anyone on it till you have heard E. play it—all those who have, & all those have been real musicians, think it the most original & greatest thing he has done. . . . He is better, I am thankful to say, but the strain of the work is very great for him & makes him very easily worried. . . .'

Elgar answered the next letter in the vein to which Jaeger was more accustomed: 'Your remarks about those *two* bars in the Intro. were quite right & they were *never intended* to go in—they are altered now. It is easy(!) enough to write a melody—except the last two bars: I am sure it is the difficulty of avoiding a "barn door" ending that has kept the modern school from symmetrical melody. Meyerbeer is, of course, notorious for bad endings & Mendelssohn is almost as bad—or quite as bad in another way.'

In April the Elgars paid their second visit to America where Edward conducted *Gerontius* and *The Apostles* at the Cincinnati Festival. While there he continued to orchestrate the completed parts of the oratorio, but his return to England was saddened by his father's death while he was away. He was again ill and depressed, and a doctor ordered complete change. So they went for a holiday to New Radnor where he worked hard—'I hear a lovely *tune*,' Alice wrote to Jaeger. 'He has worried so much over it so it is better not to write about it to him.' The holiday came to an abrupt end when Elgar slipped on some wet stones and twisted his knee. He was in pain and became so depressed that he wrote to Birmingham to ask if they would be prepared to accept half the work. Luckily he recovered quickly, his spirits soared and he worked at a great pace both on completing the composition and orchestrating it. On 21 July he wrote to Jaeger: 'I am just completing the final revision of my notes & sketches: the whole thing is intentionally less mystic than the A.: the *men* are alive & working & the atmosphere is meant to be more direct & simple.' Composition was finished on 23 July, and the orchestration was completed at an amazing pace: 'I scored 70 pages in the week,' he told Jaeger on 7 August. By the end of August all was finished, and he devoted himself to the Three Choirs Festival at Hereford. At the end of September he went to Manchester for orchestral rehearsals of *The Kingdom* by the Hallé, who were to play at

Birmingham, and to choir rehearsals in Birmingham. Jaeger was ordered abroad again and was desolate at missing the first performance. This, on 3 October, was conducted by Elgar, with Agnes Nicholls, Muriel Foster, John Coates, and William Higley as soloists. The hall was packed and standing-room cost a guinea, so great was the interest. Every Elgar first performance was now an Occasion, drawing every leading musician in the land to hear it. *The Kingdom* was successfully received. The first London performance was given in November. There was to be no major work for another two years. There were to be no more oratorios.

*   *   *

Why was Part III of the trilogy never completed? Some, but not much, was written, as he had told Jaeger, and it would have been called *The Last Judgement*, *The Saints*, or *The Fulfilment*. He wrote to Alfred Littleton in December 1907 that he had given up the idea 'definitely and finally'; 'I am sadly disappointed with the commercial results of the last oratorios, and for the sake of my people must not waste more time in attempting to write high "felt" music.' He wrote to Jaeger in June 1908 in a similar vein: 'I have no intention of completing my oratorio cycle or whatever it is—I am not allowed to beg a dispensation of a benevolent providence who objects to the world being saved or purified or improved by a mere musician. Of course I have the thing—the biggest of all—sketched but I cannot afford for the sake of others to waste any time on it. Alas!' Schuster and Lord Northampton pleaded with him to complete the trilogy. The latter wrote to him on 16 September 1910: 'I can quite understand that you may foresee a difficulty in getting your great work completed by next year in time for the Birmingham Festival but that does not and cannot mean that you "abandon" the wish to write the third part of the Apostles. . . . The Apostles are part of you and it is complete in you.' Finance was a constant grumble, but there must have been artistic reasons for the abandonment of the scheme. I think there can be little doubt, as he had hinted to Northampton, that he felt this vein was exhausted, and he was probably discouraged, too, by the lack of singers able to fulfil his intentions. Bonavia, in his essay on Elgar from which I have previously quoted, draws on his experience as critic and player to make a penetrating point about *The Apostles*: 'Except at the Three Choirs Festivals, we have never heard a performance of this work that could be called adequate, while some performances, even when conducted by Elgar himself, fell far short of mere adequacy. It was pitiful to see him sometimes conduct forces utterly incapable of doing justice to his music or to his direction. With the Englishman's dislike of a fuss he would say nothing, but one can well imagine what his feelings must have been and the reason why he often complained to his friends that it was useless to write music that nobody wanted.'

There were fitful efforts at resuming work on the trilogy, usually at the prompting of Henry Embleton, patron of the Leeds Choral Union, the choir that Sir Henry Coward conducted. Embleton organized an Elgar festival in Leeds in 1909 and set his heart on obtaining the third oratorio. He asked for it first in June 1914, speaking first to Lady Elgar 'in such a beautiful & delicate way like a friend who really loved E. and his work. E. had a talk when he came in & they clasped hands at parting, E. consenting. A feeling of great joy settled down on us.' Perhaps, if the war had not intervened, the mood might have lasted, but it is dubious. When a movement from *The Spirit of England* was sung in Leeds in 1916, Embleton asked again for Part III, even suggesting March 1918 for the first performance. After Lady Elgar's death in 1920, Embleton and W. H. Reed both urged completion of the trilogy as a means of taking Elgar's mind off his grief. For a time it looked as if they might have some success. In May 1921 Elgar asked Troyte Griffith if he could find him a house in Malvern. 'It is possible that I may be finishing the III part of *The Apostles* & I want to be quiet and uninterrupted *generally.* . . . What I feel now is that I am not young! and I want to complete the great work;—that I want to be near my dearest one's grave;—& that I want you not too far off.' About this time Reed records that 'after much persuasion' Elgar would take a few sheets of music from a cupboard and play them 'grunting away as he played and explaining that the motif used for the "Shofar" in *The Apostles* was going to be used again for the "Last Trump".' But the mood passed again. Nothing new was written. He looked at it again in 1926 but in June 1927 he told Embleton that there was little likelihood of its ever being written. This was the month of his seventieth birthday, and he had seen Queen's Hall half empty for the celebratory concert.

*   *   *

Much has been written elsewhere about the comparative failure of both *The Apostles* and *The Kingdom* to match the success of *The Dream of Gerontius*. There are many practical reasons. Both works, *The Apostles* in particular, are difficult and expensive to perform. For many years Novello's handicapped them by a kind of levy on every performance. They make great demands on the intelligence of performers and listeners. Much of the supreme appeal of *Gerontius* lies in its singleness of idea, its unified and complete dramatic purpose. Neither *The Apostles* nor *The Kingdom* is complete in itself. Both, too, are peculiarly composite. The number of leitmotives used is itself an indication of Elgar's preoccupation with the literary side of his work, a dangerous procedure in a work of musical art. His letters to Canon Gorton and to Jaeger reinforce this view. He was excited about his presentation of the characters of Judas, Mary Magdalene, and Peter, but he was an optimist if he thought that an audience would be as absorbed as he was, theologically and intellectually, by such abstruse matters, 'If the words are sufficiently interesting, the music will do,' he had told Jaeger: an extraordinarily fallacious doctrine for a composer to hold. Elgar's comments on Jaeger's analysis of *The Apostles* betray his preoccupation with the structure of the work:

[10 August 1903] I meant to suggest the Earthly Kingdom on p. 36. Here it is (see score also)—the germ—. I really meant to make it feel as if it *grew* out of Peter's first speech (1st bar p. 35) or rather first tune—the Apostles' first ardent feeling. You will find a weak (very) version of the theme (in small notes viola) at 185 & on p. 163 (small notes) by which you learn that the Earthly Kingdom turned out rather badly.

[14 September 1903] Your Judas is splendid—I should have liked a reference to the way a proud sinner at last confronted with the result of his sin is swayed by all sorts of feelings—prompted or suggested by the Psalm he knows so well—ending in blasphemy & despair. I don't like *plot*—it (that theme) figures more the man of action—& it staggers about at the end in a ghastly way.

A major flaw in both oratorios is that they lack that compelling, unifying, poetic impetus which makes *The Dream of Gerontius* such a powerful experience. Piety takes the place of conviction. To borrow a vulgar phrase, we can see the wheels go round in *The Apostles* and *The Kingdom*. The audience cares about Gerontius's drama because Elgar gives him life. Of the Apostles he gives only Judas much life, and he does this by giving him the same kind of semi-recitative melodic line which was successful in the earlier work. In fact Judas dominates the second part of *The Apostles* to the extent that his fate pushes the Crucifixion into the background. It was the human sinner who fascinated Elgar. He saw in Judas another Gerontius, a 'worldly man brought to book'. This was why he accepted Archbishop Whately's portrayal of Judas[1] as a zealot who overreached himself: Elgar was much better at depicting virtue than vice, as he exemplified in the Mary Magdalene

---

[1] *Lectures on the Characters of Our Lord's Apostles*, Richard Whately, Archbishop of Dublin (London, 1893).

episodes of *The Apostles*—Mary's compassionate soliloquy is exquisite, but the chorus's interjectory invocations to 'costly wine' and crowns of rosebuds suggest a naughty escapade at Malvern Girls' School. It is worth pondering that some of the most characteristic Elgarian music in *The Apostles* illustrates Judas's Iago-like 'credo': 'We shall be hereafter as though we had never been . . . our spirit shall vanish as the soft air, and our name shall be forgotten in time.' 'Judas was the clever man-of-the-world type,' Elgar wrote to Thomas Dunhill.[1] 'I have made him . . . a man with brains. Notice his first speech in "By the Wayside"; the simple people say, "He setteth the poor on high", &c. Judas can see just a little farther—the certain result of such a change, "He poureth contempt upon princes".' Elgar's conservatism evidently also favoured this interpretation. Nobody really cares about Elgar's scheme of an oratorio about the Apostles' 'Calling, their Teaching and their Mission' unless the music compels us to care. As he said to Jaeger 'It's what I feel'. These oratorios are at their best when he was 'feeling' and not when he was pasting together his leitmotives and his extracts from the Bible and the Apocrypha. It is this latter element, when secular vigour is sharply contrasted with the sensuous appeal of the lyrical passages, that causes the works to sound episodic and sermonizing. The contrast between words and music, notably in Part I of *The Apostles*, is sometimes almost comic. The composer of *Falstaff* and the symphonies lurks behind the pulpit. It is obvious where parts of the projected *Rabelais* ballet went, and there is a startling apparition of Mr. Justice Shallow's orchard between [92] and [93]. This at-odds element led another great English composer, Vaughan Williams, to write to me about *The Apostles*: 'I always feel that he was oppressed by the fact that he was writing for the Church of England and could not get rid of the bombazine and bonnets of the Anglican Sunday morning service.' My own theory is that these are two works from which Elgar himself was absent autobiographically. His masterpieces are those works into which he was able to project his own attitude to life—the *Variations*, the symphonies, the concertos. He was unable to do this with the Biblical characters, though Judas gave him some outlet. It may be said that *Gerontius* is not autobiographical, but Elgar's letters quoted in Chapter 7 reveal how closely he identified himself with a spiritual struggle and crisis that reflected his own faith. It is for these reasons, too, that I doubt, despite many encouraging pointers to the contrary in his music, whether he would have written a successful opera. Like Mahler, he was perhaps too self-centred to command the power to create dramatic characters. If he had found the

[1] Quoted in Dunhill's *Sir Edward Elgar*, p. 200.

ideal libretto, comparable with *Gerontius* in its effect on him, he might have produced a fascinating attempt, but all his best musical portraits are of himself or of his intimates as he saw them. Even when it came to Falstaff he gave us only another self-portrait.

It is inescapable that both oratorios are eclipsed by *The Dream of Gerontius*. Inspiration burns fitfully in them; in *Gerontius* it is aflame from first note to last. But hear them sympathetically performed in their right setting in Gloucester, Worcester, or Hereford, and the predominant impression can be not of their failings but of their beauties, the brilliance and colour of the orchestral writing, the superb understanding of choral sound. Whether one accepts them as a series of musical frescoes, almost pre-Raphaelite in detail, or is stirred simply by the Elgarian-ness of the music, one is likely to agree with Ernest Newman that 'time after time we feel that we are in the presence of a musical gift of the first order'. The Preludes to both works are two such times, and another is the opening chorus of *The Apostles*, followed by the great scene of the dawn, with the notes of the Shofar dominating the music, and the choosing of the Apostles. The 'At the Sepulchre' scene has a tender simplicity that never fails to touch the heart and leads into the great finale where the waves of 'alleluias' rise and fall and are woven into the texture of the music with an inevitability that is absent elsewhere, and an extra poignant touch is the reminiscence of the 'Thou art calling me' phrase from *Gerontius*. By any standards this is great music, as is the scene of Judas's death, and, in *The Kingdom*, the Whitsuntide sequence. *The Apostles* is the finer work, *The Kingdom* more even. The chorus 'O ye Priests', in *The Kingdom*, is almost as fine and stirring as 'Go forth' in *Gerontius* and is at the opposite pole from the deplorably banal afterthought 'Turn you to the stronghold' in *The Apostles* which would not have been out of place in *The Banner of St. George* and was hardly worth the trouble it gave to Novello's printer. Harsh things have also been said about the setting of the Lord's Prayer in *The Kingdom* but I think it has been maligned. However there is no doubt that the highpoint of both works is the Virgin's solo 'The sun goeth down' in *The Kingdom*, where a sweet and tranquil mellowness suffuses the music and has all the characteristics of genius. Arthur Johnstone considered some of the music in *The Apostles* to be 'greater' than that in *Gerontius*, and Samuel Langford wrote that although *The Kingdom* had not the unity of *Gerontius* 'as music it is certainly better', and went on to express the wish that Elgar would 'set himself once more to write living music to a living poem'. Both these judgements seem incomprehensible today, but one can understand how they came to be passed.

On the other hand, so distinguished and knowledgeable an Elgarian as Sir Adrian Boult regards *The Kingdom* as a finer work than *Gerontius*, and he told me that he remembered Schuster's saying to him: '*Gerontius* is the work of a raw amateur beside *The Kingdom*.' These opinions deserve respect.

These two oratorios marked the end of a tradition. Elgar tried, by a symphonic blood transfusion, to revivify the form and he succeeded only because he was Elgar and could not help pouring great music into whatever design he selected. Perhaps he cogitated the scheme too long so that, as in the similar case of Vaughan Williams's Morality *The Pilgrim's Progress*, he was able to identify himself wholly with his plan but unable, because of this intensity, to give it the objectivity of presentation which *Gerontius*, for all its seeming fluency, possesses to a notable degree. It is significant that devotees of Elgar and Vaughan Williams find in these 'problem works' so much of the essence of the composers that they can ignore the defects, whereas to the unconverted the obstacles erected by the composers themselves prove unsurmountable. The last two oratorios are the music of a great composer, but they are not consistently great music.

The Kingdom ends with what Diana McVeagh calls 'gentle, drooping chords of acceptance'. These chords are the end of Elgar's religious choral music, and it is tempting to describe the two oratorios as a swansong. But were they? Did they not show the way to other composers? Elgar gave to sacred choral music the limitless advantage of orchestral virtuosity, with the chorus playing a more subtle rôle, sometimes prominent, sometimes fragmentary, sometimes as commentators. His lesson was not lost on his contemporary juniors. Vaughan Williams, Holst, Walton, even Britten and Tippett, have consciously or unconsciously sown their seeds in the furrow which Elgar ploughed and which he abandoned when he realized that he had exhausted his capacity for inspiration by religious themes.

11 Full Orchestra

Elgar's mature orchestral output after the *Variations*, its origins, and its varying reception by the public, is best looked at as a whole. But, in returning to the year after the failure of *Gerontius* at Birmingham, it is salutary to recall that not everybody reacted to his music as recalcitrantly as the majority of that festival audience. Bernard Shaw, in his famous *Music and Letters* essay in 1920, remembered his own scepticism 'when the excitement about *Gerontius* began. . . . But when I heard the *Variations* (which had not attracted me to the concert) I sat up and said "Whew!". I knew we had got it at last.' Arnold Bax, in his teens, became an admirer on the strength of the vocal scores of *King Olaf* and *Caractacus*. 'Two years later to this admiration was added reverence, for *The Dream of Gerontius* took utter possession of what religious sense I have.'[1] Ralph Vaughan Williams also first heard the *Variations* at a concert to which some other work had attracted him. When he was in his early thirties he asked Elgar for lessons in orchestration but was told, by Alice, that Elgar did not take pupils. So he studied the scores of the *Variations* and *Gerontius*. 'The results', he wrote years later in his 'Musical Autobiography', 'are obvious in the opening pages of the finale of my *Sea Symphony*', and in another article he cited Gerontius's 'Thou art calling me' as the phrase which influenced him most, in both the *Sea* and *London Symphonies*, adding: 'I am astonished . . . to find on looking back on my own earlier works how much I cribbed from him, probably when I thought I was being most original.' Holst, too, wanted to 'victimize Elgar—bicycle to Worcester to see him a lot'. That was in 1903. The young men of English music recognized his genius from the start. Elgar was, of course, incapable of teaching composition or orchestration, and they would have been sadly disillusioned, and probably snubbed outright, if they had tried to engage him in technical discussions. Shaw's article quoted above recounts the occasion when someone tried to describe to Elgar a phrase of Wagner's by a reference to the chord of the supertonic. 'Elgar opened his eyes wide, and, with an awe which was at least very well acted, asked, "What on earth is the chord of the supertonic?" And then, after a pause, "What *is* the supertonic? I never heard of it".'

[1] Op. cit., p. 29.

Contrary man! Yet this contrariness was his very nature, and accounts for his ability, despite the embittered despair of his letters to Jaeger in the days after *Gerontius*, to turn directly to the composition of one of his cheeriest orchestral works, the overture *Cockaigne* (*In London Town*). He completed it on 24 March 1901, and it was first played on 20 June 1901, at a concert of the Philharmonic Society, who had commissioned it. Because it was published by Boosey, during the quarrel with Novello's, Jaeger had not seen it before the first performance and evidently he disliked it because on 26 June Elgar wrote to him 'Never mind about Cockaigne—I think you'll find it all right some day.' Other Germans liked it. notably Felix Weingartner who called it 'a marvellous work' and conducted several early performances in Europe. Richter soon took it up in Manchester and it was an immediate success in America. Arthur Johnstone compared it with the *Meistersinger* overture after what must have been a very fine performance by the Hallé on 24 October 1901, for Elgar wrote to Jaeger: 'Orchestra the finest I ever heard: not so big as Leeds but gorgeous. I conducted Cockayne at Rehearsal yesterday at Richter's request' and, later, 'Cockaigne was golorious last night under Richter. I don't think any of you London Johnnies know what orchestral playing is until you hear the Manchester orchestra (*in Manchester* that is, their own room). Coriolan was colossal & Brahms' No. 3 Sym. overpoweringly fine.' This, as every provincial knows, is not the thing to write to a Londoner, and his enthusiasm for Richter won him a cool response when in a letter to Canon Gorton after the Morecambe Festival of 1903—a letter published in the *Musical Times*—he made this observation: 'It is rather a shock to find Brahms's part-songs appreciated & among the daily fare of a district apparently unknown to the sleepy London Press: people who talk of the spread of music in England & the increasing love of it rarely seem to know where the growth of the art is really strong and properly fostered. Some day the Press will awake to the fact, already known abroad and to some few of us in England, that the living centre of music in Great Britain is not London, but somewhere farther North.' Honest, but tactless.

Elgar had sent the score of *Cockaigne* (which is dedicated 'to my friends the members of British orchestras') to Richter in August 1901, saying: 'Here is nothing deep or melancholy—it is intended to be honest, healthy, humorous and strong but not vulgar.' The day after the performance in Manchester, writing from Rodewald's house in Liverpool, Elgar thanked Richter for his interpretation, adding 'but it has taught me that I am not satisfied with my music and must do, or rather try to do, something better and nobler. I hope the Symphony I am trying to write will answer to these higher ideals and if I find I am more satisfied with it than my present compositions I shall hope to be allowed to dedicate it to my honoured friend Hans Richter: but I have much to do to it yet.'

Elgar's slender output in 1901 and 1902—*Cockaigne* and two *Pomp and Circumstance* marches were the bulk of it, apart from the *Coronation Ode*—is partly explained by this reference to a symphony. It was not the only project on which he was engaged. The *Rabelais* ballet has been mentioned. Sketches for a work about Falstaff were made in 1902. In 1901 he wrote a *Concert Allegro* for piano for Fanny Davies who played it at St. James's Hall, London, on 2 December of that year. Richter described it as 'like a marriage between Bach and Liszt', which is a flattering description. Schuster had introduced Elgar to Herbert Beerbohm Tree and this led to an invitation to compose incidental music for Stephen Phillips's play *Ulysses*. But this scheme foundered when Elgar, after arranging to visit Phillips at his home at Ashford, travelled there only to find that the playwright had gone out. 'I admire P. as you know,' he wrote to Schuster, 'but I do regret his manners.' In August of 1901, the Elgars went for a week's holiday to South Wales to stay in a cottage rented by Rosa Burley at the Dylan-Thomas-sounding village of Llangranog, Cardiganshire. Here, one day, as they looked across the bay they heard a choir or choral society out for the day singing as they walked over the hillside opposite. The music drifted across the water and Elgar made sketches for a 'Welsh Overture', which never materialized. But the memory of the singing found its way four years later into the *Introduction and Allegro for Strings*, and other sketches were used for *The Apostles*. Elgar, as will by now be readily appreciated, was an impulsive, responsive man, setting down uninhibitedly in his letters the reaction of the moment. But as a composer he was as cool-headed and as long-sighted as Beethoven. The strength of his music is that it is emotion recollected in tranquillity. Like Beethoven he would store up a musical idea for years until it found its right form, its right setting, and its right perspective. It has already been seen how ideas for *The Apostles* were sketched years before work began in earnest. The various 'Moods of Dan', Sinclair's bulldog, inscribed between 1897 and 1903 in Sinclair's visitors' book are in themselves proof of the long gestation of certain ideas: themes for *Gerontius* written in 1898, the opening of *In the South* in 1899, part of *Crown of India* in 1903 and of 'For the Fallen' in 1902. Themes from Powick asylum days occur in mature works. Nearly all Elgar's major works grew slowly, and nowhere is this more evident than in the case of the Second Symphony. Moreover he was an economical composer and never let good ideas go to waste if they could not be accommodated in the context for which they were first planned. Possibly this, rather than any atavistic desire to keep the *Salut d'Amour* fires burning, accounts for the continued appearance throughout his career of short pieces for orchestra. The two *Dream Children* idylls of 1902, for example. Were they perhaps discarded fragments of the 'Gordon' symphony or of some other abandoned project? It is very likely.

The first signs of an Elgar symphony date from 1898 when he considered a kind of 'Eroica' based on General Gordon. 'The thing possesses me,' he had told Jaeger, 'but I can't write it down yet.' By February 1899 he was 'making a shot at it' and in November of that year admitted to having 'written a *theme*'. Early in 1901, Alice Elgar wrote to Jaeger that 'there could be no *nobler* music than the symphony. I long for it to be finished & have to exist on scraps— Do write & hurry him, it always does *some* good.' Rodewald had also tried to hurry him by offering to relieve Elgar of financial responsibility during its composition, but Elgar would not be hurried—he knew better than to think he could hurry a symphony, and in any case he was too proud to accept money from friends. In the autumn of 1901 Jaeger was telling him how anxious Henry Wood was to conduct the symphony at the Leeds Festival but Elgar replied that 'there's not the slightest chance of my doing it, I fear', though rashly saying 'the festival shall have it, of course'. This was the beginning of the muddle and acrimony with the Leeds authorities which has already been described. From Alassio in January 1904, when there were rumours that the symphony was to be played in Essen, Elgar wrote to Jaeger: 'I wish my friends wd. not gossip about me: Ettling wrote from *Weingartner* asking for first German perfce. of sym. promising Munich Berlin etc. So I wrote to *W.* saying it wd. not be ready for him this season etc. etc. Then apparently Ettling writes off to Pitt! Bless us all!' He elucidated this a few weeks later when he said that he had had 'chiding and angry' letters because 'somebody suggested that the future Symphony might be produced at *Essen*!' He was tempted by the idea of a Weingartner first German performance in Berlin or Munich—'I suppose no introduction *cd*. be better possibly'—but he ruled out a first performance for Essen because of his long-standing promise to Richter. Just how much of a symphony was written by 1904 it is not possible to know. Dorabella saw a fat note-book labelled 'Symphony' at Craeg Lea in 1901, and was played 'scraps' of it. Her book gives no clue to the identity of the scraps, but it is reasonable to deduce from sketches dated 1904 that the symphony which Leeds wanted, even perhaps the 'Gordon' symphony, eventually became Symphony No. 2 in E flat major. As we know, it was promised to Richter, and an early version of the second subject of the finale of the Second Symphony

Ex. 6

dated about 1903-4 is marked 'Hans himself!' Parts of the slow movement of No. 2 date from May 1904, while Elgar's mind was still full of the shock of Rodewald's death six months earlier. These sketches are parallel with some for a projected second *Cockaigne* overture, in C minor, sub-titled 'City of dreadful night'.

For a while, too, in 1901 Elgar mentioned to Jaeger work on a string sextet, but this was soon lost among such remarks as 'Oh! my string Sextett—& I have to write rot & *can* do better things'. If by 'rot' he meant his music for the play *Grania and Diarmid* by W. B. Yeats and George Moore he was doing himself an injustice. This began with a request from Moore, who had heard Elgar's music at a Leeds Festival, for a horn-call to be used in the play which Frank Benson was to produce at the Gaiety, Dublin, in the autumn of 1901. Eventually Elgar wrote the horn-call, incidental music (37 bars), and a magnificent funeral march which ought to be more widely known. 'I've been awfully busy writing,' he wrote to Jaeger on 1 October 1901, '& have finished the short incidental music to that Irish play: there's a funeral march which you wd. like & it sounds big and weird—not deep in the orchl. whirlwind sense.' He thought he might use the music later for an opera, but nothing came of the idea. He hoped, too, that the march might become a best-seller and asked Novello's through Jaeger for £100 for it. It would, he said, 'arrange in every possible way & there's now room for a new dead march, I think'. Perhaps with one eye on the commercial aspect he dedicated the score to Henry Wood, and he conducted it himself in several cities, including Liverpool where, he told Jaeger on 30 December 1902, it 'made a tremendous impression. . . . *When* is it to be published?' He knew he had written something good. The march is a noble, elegiac piece, with a central trio of symphonic cast, and there is a song to a poem by Yeats, 'There are seven that pull the thread', which is as delicate and atmospheric as anything he wrote, with his familiar poetic use of the clarinet and a phrase that is another obvious clue to work progressing on sketches for the Second Symphony. When in 1903 Elgar asked Yeats's permission to publish the song, the poet agreed 'with great pleasure' and described the *Grania* music as 'wonderful in its heroic melancholy'.

Insufficient interest has been shown in the knowledge that Weingartner, Steinbach, and other German conductors of the day took up *Cockaigne* so promptly, a work that is generally regarded as thoroughly 'English' in atmosphere, especially in its evocation of brass bands and military bands marching through London streets. (Its reflection of that peculiar strain in Londoners which finds an outlet in their devotion to pearly kings and queens is not the least of its pictorial virtues.) Did they see deeper into it than did the English music critics and even, perhaps, Elgar himself? With their European background and their knowledge, if not appreciation, of Mahler's early symphonies, did they, even subconsciously, realize what is obvious today: that there is a Mahlerian contrast of banality (some would say vulgarity) and philosophy in *Cockaigne*? The particular is given a universal vision. The military band approaches and recedes, and as it does so, as the march rhythm in the bass fades, we hear not just a vivid sound-picture of London at the turn of the century but the fading of a world. The strings weave mysteries and the horn is the spirit of romance. The music exists at two levels.[1] When it came to *In the South* in 1904 they showed similar interest, though there the shadow of Richard Strauss was probably what they recognized. *In the South*, though a neglected and under-rated work, is inferior to *Cockaigne* both in quality of invention and in design. It bears all too clearly the marks of the circumstances of its composition. When the Elgar Festival of 1904 was planned there was still hope that its focal point would be a symphony. But when he himself realized this was impossible, Elgar also realized that such a unique and important occasion ought to be able to boast a new work. So from Alassio in January 1904 we find him writing to Schuster: 'I have had to write to Higgins etc. & say that the symphony is impossible—I have partly promised a concert overture for the festival, "In the South" or some better title if you can suggest one.' The score was finished when Elgar returned to Plâs Gwyn. The last pages went to Jaeger on 21 February and Richter rehearsed it in Manchester on 9 March. That evening Elgar wrote to Jaeger: 'That Overture is *good* & the Roman section absolutely *knocking over*. They [the Hallé Orchestra] read it like angels & the thing *goes* with tremendous energy & life. . . .' Later in the year he again wrote:

[1] Mahler conducted the *Variations* and *Sea Pictures* (except no. 5) in New York, 1910-11.

'I *love* it: it's alive!' He had dedicated it to Schuster, in gratitude for the materialization of the Elgar Festival. There is a letter from Elgar to Schuster's sister Adela, written after his death in 1927, in which Elgar says that he had failed to find something 'radiant, bright, and uplifting for dear Frank's memorial stone' but adding: 'I have said in music . . . what I felt long ago—in F.'s own overture *In the South* and again in the final section of the Second Symphony—both in the key he loved most I believe (E♭), warm and joyous with a grave radiating serenity'.

In the South is certainly all that Elgar intended. It was a success at its first performance, and after Richter had conducted it later in Manchester Arthur Johnstone referred to 'a kind of graphic power, arising from far-reaching play of the imagination. In thematic originality it is perhaps more strongly stamped with Elgar's originality than any other work. Its whole tone, atmosphere, and colouring are something essentially new in music. . . . The *grandioso* theme [the "Roman section"] . . . is a most extraordinary piece of musical expression of a kind scarcely ever foreshadowed by any other composer, except once or twice by Beethoven. . . .' Other critics pointed out the resemblances to Strauss's *Aus Italien* and to both composers' use of divided strings. The resemblance is too obvious for the point to be worth making; but if *In the South* is in the Straussian mould—and there is no denying that it is, though it is Strauss very much à la Elgar[1]—it is *Don Juan* that seems to be the model both in exuberance and reflectiveness. It is another example of the potent effect of landscape and historical suggestion on Elgar's musical imagination. He admitted that the idea for the work—which he ought to have called a tone-poem instead of an 'overture', misleading conductors to expect an eight-minute piece—came from the 'thoughts and sensations of one beautiful afternoon in the Vale of Andora'. On the manuscript he wrote several poetic quotations: from Tennyson's *The Daisy*:

> What hours were thine and mine
> In lands of palm and southern pine
> In lands of palm, of orange-blossom
> Of olive, aloe, and maize and vine.

From Byron's *Childe Harold*:

> . . . a land
> Which *was* the mightiest in its old command

---

[1] Elgar wrote to Jaeger on 13 August 1904, à propos Jaeger's analysis of the overture: 'I do not think I should put that about Strauss at the beginning—not necessary—S. puts music in a very low position when he suggests it must hang on some commonplace absurdity for its very life.'

And *is* the loveliest . . .
Wherein were cast . . .
. . . the men of Rome!
Thou art the garden of the world.

In the section dealing with the past glories of Rome he 'endeavoured to paint the relentless and domineering onward force of the ancient day, and to give a sound-picture of the strife and wars, the "drums and tramplings" of a later time', and again quotes Tennyson:

What Roman strength Turbia show'd
In ruin, by the mountain road.

All these 'sound-pictures' are vividly and opulently conveyed. The fault of the work, and the probable reason for its relative failure to oust some of Strauss's tone-poems from their place in at least the British orchestral repertory, is that it is too long. A work is only too long when its ideas cannot sustain the attention given to them and, despite Johnstone's perception of intense Elgarian originality, I do not believe his opinion can be upheld today. *In the South* is often padded out for no particular musical reason, though it goes without saying that the padding is scored in a virtuoso manner. Its thrilling, leaping opening—sketched in July 1899 as 'Dan triumphant (after a fight)'—is a memorable moment but it is most Elgarian in its restrained sections, where the clarinet breathes the soft air of Italy, and in the ravishing *Canto popolare* episode, where the viola has the simple and exquisite tune over an accompaniment which anticipated by five years the orchestral background of the Violin Concerto's cadenza. The viola tune is echoed by the horn: another passage, like that in *Cockaigne*, of romantic melancholy. The scoring for clarinets and harps in the coda has that evocative flavour which is uniquely Elgarian, just as his writing for strings is unique in its mellowness of sound. 'I wrote this specially for you,' he would tell the second violins of orchestras; and other players will always bless his understanding of their instruments. (A fellow-composer who asked the secret of his string-writing was told: 'Study Handel. I went to him for help ages ago.')

This understanding supremely distinguished his next major orchestral work, the *Introduction and Allegro for Strings* of 1905, although its opus number, 47, is three earlier than that of *In the South*. His 'Welsh tune', noted during that 1901 Cardigan Bay holiday, had been brought back to his mind in 1904 'by hearing, far down our own Valley of the Wye, a song similar to those so pleasantly heard on Ynys Lochtyn. The

N

singer of the Wye unknowingly reminded me of my sketch. . . . Although there may be (and I hope there is) a Welsh feeling in the one theme—to quote Shakespeare again: "All the waters in Wye cannot wash the Welsh blood out of its body"—the work is really a tribute to that sweet borderland where I have made my home.' On 28 October 1904, Jaeger wrote to Elgar suggesting that he should write a short new work for the recently formed London Symphony Orchestra. 'Why not a *brilliant* quick String Scherzo, or something for those fine strings only? a real bring down the house *torrent* of a thing such as Bach could write. . . . You might even write a *modern Fugue* for strings, or *strings & organ*! That would sell like cakes.' Elgar was abroad at the end of November 1904, visiting Mainz to hear Fritz Volbach conduct *The Apostles* and Cologne where Steinbach conducted *In the South*.[1] Then he went to Rotterdam for a performance of *The Apostles* on 2 December. Jaeger, writing from Davos in January 1905, prodded him for an orchestral work for Julius Buths—'But it must be a Uraufführung, see? First production anywhere. Now, seeing what B. has done for your fame, I think you ought to see whether you can't do something. But it must be of your *Best* entre nous, because you will be matched with Mahler whose 3rd symphony with chorus will form an important part of the Fest. most likely.' (The Lower Rhine Festival, June 1905. Mahler's Second Symphony was played.) Elgar ignored this request, but he wrote on 26 January: 'I'm doing that string thing in time for the Sym. Orch. concert. Intro: & Allegro—no *working-out* part but a devil of a fugue instead. G major & the sd. divvel in G minor with all sorts of japes & counterpoint.' The L.S.O. concert was to be on 8 March. As usual when composing Elgar protested ill-health—'I am at my wits' end to know how to do anything & have been having one liver chill after another,' he wrote to Schuster on 13 February but added 'The new Pomp and C. is a devil & the string thing most brilliant with a real tune in it however.' Schuster, most loyal and generous of all Elgar's patrons, had had a hand in promotion of the concert, which was an Elgar programme: *In the South*, the *Grania* Funeral March, *Sea Pictures* (Ada Crossley), the first performance of the third *Pomp and Circumstance* march, *Cockaigne*, the first performance of the *Introduction and Allegro*, and the *Variations*. Elgar conducted. Alice told Jaeger that 'many people think it [the *Introduction and Allegro*] the finest thing he has written, the 4t. comes in with so beautiful an effect, the peroration towards the end *is* fine. The new March is *thrilling*—the most pacific

[1] Sir Donald Tovey in his analytical note on *In the South* disclosed that Steinbach had thought the work 'patchy'.

friends were ready to fight! The critics—some of them—of course were frightened at it, but happily the audiences judge for themselves.' The *Introduction and Allegro* was repeated at a Queen's Hall concert on 19 March, but was coolly received. When Dorabella visited Plâs Gwyn in April and asked when the new work was to be played again, she was met with what she called Alice's 'stony image' look and the reply: 'Nothing has been settled yet. I think you had better not ask.' Elgar told her: 'That's good stuff. Nothing better for strings has ever been done and they don't like it.' Arthur Johnstone's untimely death in December 1904 had deprived Elgar of his most understanding and perceptive critic, but Johnstone's successor in Manchester was Ernest Newman, then at work on a book on Elgar. It is from his notice in the *Manchester Guardian* of Richter's first Hallé performance (7 December 1905) of the work that we know of a remarkable incident that tells us not only that audiences were slow to respond to the music but that Richter was quick to appreciate its qualities, although he 'treated it more staidly [than Elgar] without the lithe flexible convolutions of the melody. . . . There was a moderate amount of applause, probably intended for the orchestra. . . . Dr. Richter, however, jumped at the applause and, to everyone's astonishment, played the whole thing through again. It was more than a good many people had bargained for. . . .' Good for Dr. Richter. But the work stayed out of Hallé and other orchestras' programmes for many years. For instance, after a performance at a Philharmonic concert in 1906 it was not played in the Society's programmes until Beecham conducted it in November 1937. It was the rise in standards of orchestral playing and rehearsal achieved after the outbreak of the Second World War that enabled this masterly work to gain the position it now holds, when it is generally regarded, even by those not otherwise favourably disposed towards Elgar, as one of the three or four greatest compositions for strings. Dunhill, in his book published in 1938, acclaimed it as a masterpiece yet ended his discussion of it with the words 'It deserves to be far more widely known than it is.' Fortunately such a statement is no longer necessary. It is one of Elgar's finest creations, spacious, elusive, lyrical. The majestic opening, which as in all of Elgar's works goes straight to the point without any preliminaries, is as strong an utterance as he ever made, and is perfectly contrasted with the next, gentler, rising and falling theme (the basis of the Allegro section) over which in the manuscript Elgar wrote (from *Cymbeline*) 'Smiling with a sigh'. Then comes the 'Welsh tune', for solo viola, characterized by a falling third. Instead of a development section Elgar wrote a fugue, but it is a wayward, exciting fugue, far removed from any academic connotations, a romantic, emotional fugue which Bach would not have been ashamed to own. The weaving of the thematic material, the brilliant building-up of tension and the equally masterly relaxation of it so that the music slides gently back into the Allegro section, these are the hallmarks of a master-composer who was able to exploit every possibility of the medium he had selected. Strings had rarely sounded so sonorous, capable of such variety of expression and colour, until this work was written. It was the forerunner of many works of a similar kind and served as the model (string quartet and string orchestra) for another English masterpiece written five years later, Vaughan Williams's *Tallis Fantasia*. The subtle contrast and interplay of quartet and full strings go far beyond the concerto grosso: they opened up possibilities in the employment of string tone which have had their influence on most English music written since this superb piece was first heard.

When the anxiety of the first performance of *The Kingdom* was over, Elgar's health and morale were low. He was too sensitive a mortal to be fitted for the rôle of controversialist, and the arguments in the newspapers and journals about his Birmingham lectures depressed him and jangled his nerves. Only a week after the first performance of the oratorio Elgar wrote to Schuster: 'I don't seem to realise that I have written anything & am trying to forget all about it & myself.' He could not settle to any creative work. With Alice he went in December to Llandrindod Wells and after Christmas, despite anxiety about the financial aspect, to Capri, Naples, and Rome for most of the first two months of 1907. Canon Gorton travelled with them and they were joined by Schuster. For the first weeks Elgar was ill and worried about money. He visited Axel Munthe at Capri and was pleased in Rome to be fussed over by the Italian composers Perosi and Sgambati. Perosi showed him through the Vatican and St. Peter's. While in Rome Elgar wrote the four part-songs of op. 53 to words by Tennyson, Byron, Shelley, and Elgar himself. These were successors to the op. 45 set of *Songs from the Greek Anthology*, first sung in London in April 1904, both works being the direct result of his connection with the fine competition choirs at the Morecambe Festival. One of the songs of op. 53 was to Byron's words

> Deep in my soul that tender secret dwells,
> Lonely and lost to light for evermore,
> Save when to thine my heart responsive swells,
> Then trembles into silence as before.

This song was dedicated to Mrs. Julia Worthington, an American whom the Elgars had met in New York in 1905 and who had visited England in the following two summers. She was wealthy and unhappily married, with a villa in Italy, and was a leading American hostess—'a sort of Duchess . . . socially clever and a friend to all the distinguished people', J. B. Yeats described her in a letter to his son the poet, adding: 'She is an intimate friend of the musician Elgar.' The Elgars returned from Italy to Hereford on 26 February and four days later Elgar left for his third visit to America. Alice stayed behind. He conducted *The Apostles* and *The Kingdom* in New York and then went to conduct in Chicago, Cincinnati, and Pittsburgh. 'After our sweet & delightful time in Capri it is a hideous change to be in western America,' he wrote to Mrs. Gorton, wife of the canon. While in New York, he told Delius many years later, he refused a request to lead a meeting to pray for the failure of Richard Strauss's *Salome*! He sailed for home on 20 April. He had no big work on hand but he was writing the fourth *Pomp and Circumstance* march and he had looked out the music he had written for his brothers and sisters when he was twelve and they had performed their play 'The Wand of Youth'. He had re-scored some of it for Powick in 1879–80, but now he worked on it again. He wrote to Jaeger, who was in Germany in another attempt to regain his strength, on 28 May: 'I shall be fifty next week so they tell me, but I don't know it. I have my pipe & the bicycle & a heavenly country to ride in—so an end. I take no interest whatever in music now & just "edit" a few old boyish MSS—music is off.'

A few days later he added a P.S. to a letter from Alice to Jaeger: 'I'm busy & must not use my eyes much so I am doing trifles: poor things but mine own boyish thoughts. I wax old but not infirm. . . . The first pt. of the 4th march is good: the middle *rot* but pleasing to march to.' During this May he also composed two single and two double chants and the part-song 'How calmly the evening'. All summer his eyes gave him trouble, but the work on *The Wand of Youth* seemed to reawaken deeper impulses and by 27 June Alice was able to write in her diary that 'E.' was 'playing great beautiful tune': the opening of a symphony, not the symphony he had 'tinkered' with for eight years, but something new. It is not fanciful to deduce that this was sparked into being by the 'boyish MSS' of *The Wand of Youth*. He found he could re-charge his batteries, as it were, by re-living the days of his boyhood when he dreamed of music and thought in music. The delicate and fantastic mood of the exquisite 'Fairy Pipers' is related to the Adagio of the First Symphony; in the 'Sun Dance' and 'Serenade' the symphony's second movement stirs in the womb. He completed the first suite in September and in the same month, when Littleton visited Plâs Gwyn, he played him what Alice called his 'gorgeous new tune' and some ideas for a violin concerto for which Fritz Kreisler had asked him in 1906. He also began work on a string quartet for Brodsky. Then, as was the usual pattern with Elgar's composing, he seemed to 'dry up' and come to a halt. So he became depressed again. 'I see nothing ahead,' he wrote to 'Windflower'. He attended the festivals at Gloucester, Cardiff, and Leeds, then decided to spend the winter in Rome, not as an extravagance but because it was cheaper to rent a villa in Italy and live quietly there than to meet the obligations in England of being Sir Edward Elgar. He told Jaeger he hoped to see him while passing through London 'on my way to economize "in the South"' and from Rome he wrote to Troyte: 'One thing that gives me a little satisfaction over our exile (for it is that although "meant pleasant") is that you will be sorry we are gone.' But before he and Alice left, on 5 November, he made a kindly gesture to Jaeger, whose end was obviously not far away, racked as he was by fits of coughing and physically changed so that it distressed Elgar to see him. 'I have today', he wrote to 'my very dear Nim' on 25 October, 'asked Messrs. Novello to transfer all rights & royalties in the Analyses of Gerontius, Kingdom & Apostles to you from the last making up of the accounts. I am very much "wanted" by my poor relations, just now more than ever [his brother-in-law Will Grafton was dying] so I apologize to you for not making the transaction retrospective: this I wished to do but *cannot*. So forgive your friend & please accept the little I can do.'

In Rome they rented 38A Via Gregoriana. 'Here is my Mecca & I love it *all*' he wrote to Schuster at Christmas. 'Note the fact that I am pagan not Xtian at present & I love the pinocchi & the food & the wine! . . . Yes, I am trying to write music, but the bitterness is that it pays not at all & I must write & arrange what my soul loathes to permit me to write what *you* like & I like. So I curse the power that gave me gifts & loathe them now & ever. I told you a year ago I could see no future: now I see it & am a changed man & a *dour* creature. But not to you dear Frank, not to you. Bless you.'

What his soul loathed at this time, December 1907, must have been *A Christmas Greeting*, to Alice's words, written for Sinclair's choristers at Hereford Cathedral, and a setting of Bret Harte's *The Reveille*, a part-song for the Blackpool Musical Festival of 1908. Yet in this month he sketched the first movement of the symphony, telling Littleton that he doubted if the work would be finished, it was too noisy to work in

Rome. They were entertained by the British Ambassador at the Embassy, where the Brodsky Quartet played, and by the American composer John Alden Carpenter. Elgar had French lessons and went to the theatre with Julia Worthington. In February he had influenza, but before leaving Italy in May he went several times to the opera and visited Florence. They were in Rome during a two-day general strike after police had fired on crowds in the Piazza di Gesù who used the funeral of an Italian workman as the pretext for a Socialist demonstration. Elgar and his daughter walked to the piazza afterwards. 'Bright sun that a.m. found the streets occupied in every direction with troops, bayonets & loaded rifles,' he wrote home to his niece May Grafton. 'Bloody "war". I saw the poor human stains on the stones & the bullet marks on the walls. . . . It was wonderful to walk over that great empty square with soldiers ready for the fray all round. And all the horses of the cavalry picketed on one side.' He also visited Sgambati, 'dear man', who showed him some historic possessions given him by Liszt. He told Jaeger about them: 'The first copy of the score *Siegfried Idyll* sent by Wagner to Liszt in Rome with a little writing on the title. Also the *first* exemplar of *Faust* (Berlioz) sent by B. to Liszt! & above all (1868) the full score *Meistersinger* sent by W. to L. with words & the title "De profundis clamavi!" at the top, a date etc. below & *Richard*. How wonderful to see and touch.'

But this same letter, dated 26 April, dealt with more personal matters in a way with which poor Jaeger was only too familiar after ten years: 'I have made a sort of name by writing some big things & can only get *commissions* to write rot—ah! ha! I must *talk* to you some day about my avoiding work on big things—I have too many people *now* alas! (& the clog gets heavier every day) to allow me to think of anything I would wish to do: it is painful but it is the only reward I get . . . I cannot afford to get a *quiet* studio where I might have worked & my whole winter has been wasted for the want of a few more pounds: it seems odd that any rapscallion of a painter can find a place for his "genius" to work in when a poor devil like me who after all *has* done something shd. find himself in a hell of noise & no possible escape! I resent it bitterly but can do nothing. It is just the same now at Hereford, noise has developed in the neighbourhood—I dodged it doing the *Kingdom* at great expense by going to Wales, but I can't do it again: my lovely works do not pay the rent of a studio!'

Rome itself, he told Walford Davies,[1] had deeply interested him and he longed to return, 'but I could not reconstruct the ancient period or

[1] Letter dated 15 July 1908.

the renaissance: I could only efface the present by peopling the place with folk living from 1650 to 1800. Evelyn, Horace Walpole etc. etc. I felt a classic failure but learned much & want to learn more. Music was practically out of being . . . they asked me to conduct a concert & in fact advertised my name but I heard the orchestra & fled. . . . I am trying to work & am covering sheets of paper to no good end.' But this was not true. From the middle of June, a month after the return from Italy, he was hard at work on the symphony. 'I can't answer your letter at this moment,' he wrote to Jaeger. 'I can't say I have anything more *important* to do but it must be done & done now. Oh! such a tune.' And of course Alice agreed and wrote to their old and ailing friend two days later 'E. sends his love . . . & wants to say to you the "Sym. is A.1". It is *gorgeous*, steeped in beauty.' He worked through July, interrupting himself only with bicycle rides, bird-watching and tending his daughter Carice's rabbits. In August he went to Ostend for five days to conduct his own works and to London for a Promenade Concert of his music. The Adagio was completed on 23 August and the finale sketched on 27 and 28 August. For relaxation he went back to an interest of his teens, chemistry, and turned part of an outhouse into a laboratory which he called 'The Ark'. There he would lose himself among phials and test tubes. He enjoyed 'experiments' and blew up a water butt with one of his concoctions. He made soap and he invented a 'sulphuretted hydrogen machine' which was patented as the Elgar S. H. Apparatus. And on 25 September he finished the symphony, and collapsed with nervous exhaustion. It was dedicated, as he had always promised it would be, 'to Hans Richter, Mus. Doc. True artist and true friend'. 'You *will* like some of my latest phase,' he wrote to Schuster, 'so do I.'

The symphony was played for the first time at a Hallé concert in the Free Trade Hall, Manchester, on 3 December 1908. Jaeger was too ill so the programme-note was written by Ernest Newman, and Walford Davies also wrote a preliminary article about it. Elgar told him: 'There is no programme beyond a wide experience of human life with a great charity (love) and a *massive* hope in the future'. But he sent a pianoforte arrangement of the score to Jaeger and, a week before the first performance, received a letter which must have deeply moved him as his mind went back to *Gerontius* and the years before it:

My dear, great Edward,
    I was allowed to come down today for the first time for a month and I spent some happy quarter hours on your Adagio in the Symphony. . . . My dear friend, that is not only one of the very greatest slow movements since Beet-

hoven, but I consider it *worthy of that master*. How original, how *pure*, noble etc.
. . . It's the greatest thing you have done. . . . I detected one or two places
where the great adagio of the Choral Symphony was recalled to my memory,
nothing in the way of a reminiscence (the Satz is *quite* your own), but just the
feeling of nobility of sentiment. At [104] we are brought near Heaven.

To another friend he wrote: 'Elgar's symphony has been a perfect godsend to me, for it has made me forget for a few happy hours that I
am a doomed man.'

Jaeger's views were generally shared. This was not only Elgar's first
symphony, it was England's. Samuel Langford, writing in the *Manchester Guardian* on the day of the first performance, declared: 'That
the work is the noblest ever penned for instruments by an English
composer we are quite certain.' After the slow movement the Manchester audience burst into applause. 'Dr. Richter is not inclined to
break up a composition,' Langford wrote, 'and the fact that he encouraged the composer to come on to the platform and acknowledge the
applause . . . may be taken as a sure sign that he felt there was in this
movement something peculiarly deserving of recognition, something
supremely beautiful.' He ended his notice: 'When the music ceased we
felt that we had listened to one of the works which help music onward.'
The critic of *The Daily Telegraph* described the excitement of the evening and the effect of the music. Interestingly, he found a return to
'simpler ways and a simpler expression than he [Elgar] employed in his
later oratorios. Here we have much more the language, or rather the
idiom, of *Caractacus* and of *The Dream of Gerontius* than of *The Kingdom* and of *The Apostles*. . . . Whatever the poetic basis, whatever the
mental foundation of the symphony, the composer has maintained
from the first setting-down of the central theme to its final exposition
in the last pages of his score the sway of beauty. . . . After the extremely beautiful and poignantly expressive slow movement the composer was called on to the platform to bow several times by a crowd
that was almost beside itself with enthusiasm. Again this scene was
repeated at the close, and from none was the applause more hearty
than from the orchestral players themselves, who rose as one man and
cheered Elgar to the echo.' No English work had ever before received
such rapturous and immediate acclaim. In the audience on that historic
evening was a nineteen-year-old Manchester youth, Neville Cardus,
who many years later put into words the significance of the event:

'Those of us who were students were excited to hear at last an English composer addressing us in a spacious way, speaking a language
which was European and not provincial. No English symphony

existed then, at least not big enough to make a show of comparison with a symphony by Beethoven or Brahms and go in the programme of a concert side by side with the acknowledged masterpieces, and not be dwarfed at once into insignificance. . . . I cannot hope, at this time of day, to describe the pride taken in Elgar by young English students of that far-away epoch.'[1]

Four days later the symphony had its first London performance at Queen's Hall, with Richter conducting the London Symphony Orchestra. 'Gentlemen,' said Richter to the players, 'let us now rehearse the greatest symphony of modern times, *and not only in this country*'; and when he came to the Adagio he echoed Jaeger's words and said 'Ah! this is a *real* Adagio such as Beethoven would have written.' Jaeger attended the triumphant Queen's Hall performance. Three days previously he had written his last letter to Elgar. 'It's a great and masterly work and will place you higher among the world's masters than anything you have done. Ill as I am (& I feel so ill tonight that I want to go to the nearest Ry Station & throw myself under a Train to end my misery) I hope to go next Monday . . . .' He described the scene in Queen's Hall to Dorabella: 'I never in all my experience saw the like. The Hall was *packed* . . . . The atmosphere was electric . . . . After the first movement E. E. was called out; again, several times, after the third, and then came the great moment. After that superb Coda (Finale) the audience seemed to rise at E. when he appeared. I *never* heard such frantic applause after any novelty nor such shouting. Five times he had to appear before they were pacified. People stood up and even *on* their seats to get a view . . . .'

The great work was recognized as such from the day of its birth. In 1909 it received eighty-two performances—seventeen in London and the rest in America, Manchester, Vienna, Berlin, Bonn, Leipzig, St. Petersburg, and Sydney, among other places. In just over a year after the Manchester first performance it was played a hundred times, an amazing record especially when one remembers that there was no broadcasting to aid the spread of its fame. Here at last, in overflowing measure, was the recognition he had craved ten years before. He accepted the change with wry humour: 'The Symphony . . . is making a very wild career,' he wrote to Schuster's sister Adela on Christmas Day 1908, '& I receive heaps of letters from persons known & unknown telling me how it uplifts them: I wish it uplifted me—I have just paid rent, Land Tax, Income Tax & a variety of other things due today & there are children yapping at the door. "Christians awake!

[1] *Ten Composers* (London, 1945), p. 146.

Salute the 'yappy' morn''. I saluted it about seven o'clock, quite dark, made a fire in the Ark & mused on the future of a bad cold in my head & how far a carol could get out of the key & still be a carol: resolve me this last.' Yet on the same day he wrote to Alice Stuart-Wortley, 'That symphony is a new world, isn't it?'

The Daily Telegraph's critic, in a further article after the Manchester performance, tried to explain why the audience 'let itself go' over this particular work. He decided that its 'intense humaneness' was one reason, also its 'robustness, sincerity, power, conviction and individuality'. Those words hold good today. But perhaps the most moving personal reaction to the symphony was that of Lord Northampton, whose admiration for the personality and music of 'my most dear friend', as he always addressed Elgar in his letters, was very deep.[1] Writing after a performance in January 1910, he said: 'I hardly know what to think and certainly not what to write. That you, a mortal with whom I had just talked, had out of yourself given the world that . . . it is almost terrifying in its greatness.'

Elgar opened 1909 by conducting the symphony at Queen's Hall on New Year's Day. Alice thought he 'looked nobilmente as if he were his music'. By this date other English conductors besides Wood were making their name in the concert-hall. Landon Ronald was one who conducted the new work in 1909, and another was Thomas Beecham, who did not share the widespread adulation of Elgar's music. At this time he was touring the country with his own New Symphony Orchestra and he included the A flat symphony in his programmes. His scandalous treatment of it was noticed in Hanley by the composer Havergal Brian, who exposed what was going on in a letter to the Musical Times: 'The first movement was cut down one half: part of the "exposition" & the whole of the "development" were cut out, & some minutes were sacrificed in the succeeding movements. Those who know the symphony will be astonished to hear that the actual time occupied in its performance was only 38 minutes! [instead of approximately 55]. It was an insult to the composer. . . .' Beecham later described the work as 'neo-Gothic, the equivalent of the towers of St. Pancras Station'.

Elgar did little except conduct and play at chemistry in the first months of 1909. But in April he went, via Paris, to Italy where he and Alice stayed at Careggi, near Florence, with Julia Worthington at the Villa Silli. They visited Venice, and ideas began to stir again. As usual,

[1] Inviting Elgar to stay with him he once wrote: 'As long as we keep off politics we are not likely to fight.'

Elgar was stimulated by a place, in this case St. Mark's. It was during this visit that he wrote his biggest part-song, 'Go, Song of Mine,' to D. G. Rossetti's translation of Calvacanti (a work whose dying fall anticipates the Second Symphony), and a smaller one, 'The Angelus'. The latter was dedicated to Alice Stuart-Wortley to whom he wrote: 'I was afraid the simple words might be too papistical for you—or for your family!' It is a delightful work, but 'Go, Song of Mine' is superb, as imposing as Parry at his best. A sketchbook is headed 'Opera in Three Acts—Edward Elgar—Careggi' and another sketchbook, bought in Florence, contains a rough drawing of a stage set. About this time, too, are dated sketches which matured in *Falstaff*. But it was only at home, at Hereford, that he could work properly. On 19 August Alice wrote in her diary: 'E. possessed with his music for the Vl. Concerto'. Dorabella stayed at Plâs Gwyn that month and heard the sketches. She describes in her book an evening when, after watering the garden with the hose, they sat outside until it was dark. Then, when 'the windows were wide open and the curtains drawn back, and lovely scents came in from the garden,' Elgar played the themes of the concerto. On 3 October, he looked over his old 1903-4 symphony sketches, and his sketches written in Italy, and perhaps the remnants of the 'Gordon' symphony, and was 'quite inspired with Symphony No. 2'. But work on both projects was interrupted by the pressures of public life: the Three Choirs Festival in September, another tour as conductor of the London Symphony Orchestra in October, and an Elgar Festival organized by Embleton and the Leeds Choral Union in November. Another 'official' occasion towards the end of September was a visit to Liverpool for the three-day festival of the short-lived Music League, one of several ventures for the promotion of English music. Elgar was president and spoke at a mayoral banquet. Arnold Bax, who was one of the young composers represented, remembered him on this occasion 'in high spirits and his most genial temper . . . . At dinner he startled me by shouting down the table, "Mr. Bax! Was it you who told me the story of the two-and-ninepenny crab?" ' [1] On 24 January 1910 he conducted his three new songs with orchestra (op. 59) at the memorial concert for Jaeger, who had died in the previous May. It was early in 1910, when staying with Schuster at 'The Hut' and with the Edward Speyers at their home, Ridgehurst in Hertfordshire, that he returned to the Violin Concerto. Lady (Edgar) Speyer was a professional violinist, Leonora von Stosch, and she played parts of the work at 'The Hut'. Elgar became despondent about it, but the

[1] Op. cit., p. 31.

Speyers and Stuart-Wortleys encouraged him to persevere. 'I am not sure about that Andante,' he wrote to Mrs. Stuart-Wortley on 7 February, 'and shall put it away for a long time before I decide its fate.' He and Alice were thinking of living in London and in the same letter he tells his friend that he would find London 'too lonely'—'I think a decent obscurity in the country is all I can attain to—there is really no place for me here as I do not conduct or in fact do anything & I am made to feel in many ways I am not wanted'. But in early March, they took a flat in New Cavendish Street. There he asked his old friend Hugh Blair to hear what he had written, and one spring day in Regent Street he met the L.S.O. violinist W. H. Reed and asked him if he would go to the flat to help him with the arrangement of passage-work, bowings, and fingerings and to play over passages in different ways. Elgar's close friendship with Reed dates from these meetings. 'On my arrival in the morning', Reed wrote,[1] 'I found Sir Edward striding about with a number of loose pieces of MSS which he was arranging in different parts of the room. Some were already pinned on the backs of chairs, or fixed up on the mantelpiece ready for me to play . . . .' Reed also went to Schuster's home at Bray where much of the slow movement was sketched and re-written. 'As I saw it,' he wrote, 'in that early spring, with all the young green on the trees and the swans lazily floating by on the river, so the vision comes to me again with the music that was written there, music that depicts with such fidelity the poetry and beauty of the scene.' But still the new symphony, begun (or re-begun) in Venice, occupied some of Elgar's thoughts. From 1–10 April he was on a motoring tour of Devon, Cornwall, and Wiltshire with Schuster, visiting Tintagel on 3 April. The two place names Venice and Tintagel are written on the score of the Second Symphony. At first Tintagel, where the Stuart-Wortleys were staying, had been omitted from the itinerary. Elgar wrote to Alice Stuart-Wortley: 'I am with Frank and his sister and tomorrow commence a motor tour "round" Cornwall avoiding Tintagel, it seems, but I am not *director* or dictator or Heaven knows what wd. happen to you or to Tintagel . . . . Love, Windflower, Yours, E.' He returned to London and to a round of theatre-going—plays by Galsworthy, Shaw, Barrie, and Granville Barker—and to more work on the concerto. He was in the capital when Edward VII died on 6 May. 'These times are too cruel & gloomy,' he wrote to Schuster. 'It is awful to be here now—that dear sweet-tempered King-Man was always so "pleasant" to me. I have the Concerto well in hand & have played(?)

[1] *Music and Letters* (January 1935), pp. 30–36.

it thro' on the p.f. & it's *good*! awfully emotional! too emotional but I love it: Ist movement finished & the IIIrd well on—these *are* times for composition. I have a cold & cannot face the winds—so I did not venture to Bray today although I ventured to Cough . . . . We are dismally gay—walk like ghosts & eat like ghouls. Oh! it is terribly sad.'

At 'The Hut' on 16 June, he wrote to Mrs. Stuart-Wortley: 'I have made the end serious & grand I hope & have brought in the real inspired themes from the Ist movement. Frank approves. I did it this morning . . . the music sings of memories & hope,' But back at Plâs Gwyn a week later he wrote to her: 'I am appalled at the last movement & cannot get on—it is growing so large—too large, I fear.' He and Reed worked on it together. Reed played through the finale and Elgar became excited about the cadenza. 'We played each of the passages in every imaginable way, and the lento between [105] and [106] nearly moved him to tears as he repeated it again and yet again, dwelling on certain notes and marking them "tenuto", "espress", "animato" or "molto accel," as he realized step by step exactly what he sought to express.' On 13 July Elgar told Mrs Stuart-Wortley: 'All radiance again'. Early in July Alice had taken him to Cornwall to stay with Lady Mary Trefusis. Before they left Hereford he wrote to Schuster that he had been working too hard. 'The world has changed a little since I saw you I think—it is difficult to say how but it's either larger or smaller or something . . . . This Concerto is *full* of romantic feeling—I should have been a philanthropist if I had been a rich man—I *know* the feeling is human and right—vainglory! . . . You will like the cadenza which is on a novel plan I think—accompanied very softly by a few insts. &—it comes at the end of the last movement—it sadly thinks over the Ist movement.' The concerto had always been promised to Kreisler. In an interview the great violinist gave in November 1909, quoted in his biography,[1] he told a reporter: 'Sir Edward Elgar promised me a concerto three years ago. When he writes one it will be a labour of love rather than profit. But I can't get the first note out of him.' Now, by July 1910, he had been shown the work. 'That last movement is good stuff!' Elgar wrote to Schuster, 'Kreisler saw it on Friday & is delighted.' In the earlier letter (29 June) to Schuster, quoted above, Elgar had written: 'There are fine rows going on over the Ist performance & I am desperately annoyed at several things.' The first performance had been promised to the Philharmonic Society, but Novello's, on 24 June, sent proofs of the last movement to Robert Newman, manager of the Queen's Hall Orchestra, to show to Kreisler.

[1] Op. cit., p. 105.

Newman began to negotiate for the first performance for his own orchestra, with the support of Novello's and Kreisler. The latter, according to Sir Henry Wood,[1] also favoured a first performance with Richter in Manchester, but the Hallé Concerts Society missed their chance by saying they could not engage Kreisler until the 1910–11 season, although Richter had written to Elgar from abroad on 14 July 1910, saying: 'As conductor of the Hallé Concerts I feel obliged to ask you whether we could have the first performance of the Concerto; as *friend* I should not venture to be importunate.' When Elgar came to hear of all this, he was furious and, according to Basil Maine, became so angry when Kreisler tried to persuade him to go back on his word to the Philharmonic that he tore up Kreisler's copy of the finale. There was now no Jaeger at Novello's to smooth his path and bear his rebukes, no chance to combine business with punning.

He had finished the concerto in August. On the Sunday preceding the Three Choirs Festival at Gloucester, Schuster organized a small private party at the house Elgar had taken for the week. That evening W. H. Reed, with Elgar at the piano, played the concerto to the privileged audience, which included Julia Worthington and Alice Stuart-Wortley. 'You are not going to leave me all alone in the tuttis are you?' Elgar whispered to Reed before they began. The Gloucester Festival of 1910 was an historic week for English music: the first hearing, albeit private, of Elgar's magnificent concerto followed two days later by his conducting of *Gerontius* preceded by a new work for strings by Vaughan Williams, the *Fantasia on a Theme by Thomas Tallis*. 'Bliss was it in that dawn to be alive . . .'

The concerto had its first performance at the Philharmonic Society concert in Queen's Hall on 10 November 1910. On the evening of the 9th Schuster was Elgar's host at another of his lavish and generous parties. And on that day Elgar wrote to Richter:

'My dear Hans . . . I have feared that you may have felt a little annoyed over the first performance of the Concerto being given here, but things were not quite in my own hands regarding this, and some day I will explain. . . . It is wonderful to me to know that I have your real friendship; perhaps, no not perhaps, that I have your love. My dear friend, you have from me all the love and reverence one man can feel for another. I feel a very small person when I am in your company, you who are so great and have been intimate with the greatest. I meet now many men, and I want you to know that I look to you as my greatest and most genuine friend in the world. I revere and love

[1] Op. cit., p. 226.

you . . . . Now forgive me for sending this letter, which is about nothing, and yet is about everything, because it is about you. The man you befriended long ago (Variations), be assured this man will never forget your kindness, your nobility, and the grandeur of your life and personality. Love. Yours ever, Edward.'

But Richter was nearing the end of his career. His eyesight was failing and three months later he announced his retirement. He never conducted the concerto. The first performance nearly repeated the success of the symphony. 'The place was simply packed,' Dorabella recalled. 'Kreisler came on looking as white as a sheet . . . but he played superbly. E. E. was also, obviously, very much strung up, but all went well and the ovation at the end was tremendous. Kreisler and E. E. shook hands for quite a long time . . . . Finally they came in arm-in-arm.' It was as well that Elgar could not look into the future, for this was the last time a big work of his was to receive immediate and uninhibited public acclaim. It was dedicated to Kreisler, but the inscription on the score, already discussed in Chapter 8, provided the public with yet another Elgarian enigma: 'Aquí está encerrada el alma de . . . . .' (The quotation is from Lesage's *Gil Blas*.) Elgar translated it in a letter to Nicholas Kilburn on 5 November 1910: 'Here, or more emphatically *in here*, is enshrined or simply enclosed—buried is perhaps too definite—*the soul of*. . . . .? The final "de" leaves it indefinite as to sex or rather gender. Now guess.' Ernest Newman said in a *Sunday Times* article[1] that Elgar had told Basil Maine that the 'soul' was feminine. Elgar, whose knowledge of printer's procedure was extremely detailed, knew that three 'points' are the usual indication of an omitted passage; his use of five was obviously significant. The Violin Concerto is Elgar's most intimate and personal work; it is among the most memorable compliments ever paid to a woman, and its mood of tenderness and of wistful regret is unequivocal testimony to Elgar's feelings. On 25 October 1910 he wrote to Alice Stuart-Wortley: 'I have also been making a little progress with Symphony No. 2 and am sitting at my table weaving strange and wonderful memories into very poor music I fear. What a wonderful year it has been! With all the sad things in the great public life—the King's death downwards—the radiance in a poor, little, private man's soul has been wonderful and new and the concerto has come!'

Kreisler played the concerto in every major concert-hall of the land during a tour with the Queen's Hall Orchestra and Henry Wood, and Elgar conducted it for him in Liverpool. There is no more lamentable

[1] 21 May 1939.

indictment to be made against the gramophone recording industry
than for its failure to record Kreisler's performance of this concerto—
a recording that could have been made at any time up to about 1939.
It is tragic to read in a letter from Elgar to Lady Stuart of Wortley on
3 August 1928, this sentence: 'I am to go to Berlin to make records of
the Violin Concerto with Kreisler, but it is not quite settled.' Yet
Kreisler himself declared to his biographer that the greatest performance he ever heard was that given by Eugène Ysaÿe in Berlin in 1912.
This is supported by Vladimir Cernikoff in his book *Humour and Harmony*: 'He had a way of playing the cadenza in that very beautiful
work in such a detached manner that, for once, the expression "Music
from Heaven" seemed inadequate.'

Elgar conducted the Violin Concerto, with Ysaÿe as soloist, and the
First Symphony, in which Ysaÿe played among the first violins, in
Brussels in March 1911. Ysaÿe wanted to play the work in London
but he quarrelled with Novello's about the high performing fee which
they demanded. He did not wish to pay any fee, and had borrowed
parts for his continental performances. So the concerto dropped from
his repertoire and England never heard him play it. Once again Elgar
had good reason to detest 'the business side' of music.

After helping Ivor Atkins in an edition of Bach's *St. Matthew
Passion*, Elgar devoted the first two months of 1911 to completing the
Second Symphony. He took only a fortnight to finish and score the
first movement from his sketches. He eventually gave all the sketches
of the symphony (they are now at Broadheath) to Alice Stuart-Wortley, whose friendship with him is one of the motivations of the work.
To her he wrote on 29 January: 'I have recorded last year in the first
movement to which I put the last note in the score a moment ago and
I must tell you this: I have worked at fever heat and the thing is tremendous in energy.' To Frances Colvin, wife of Sidney Colvin, Keeper
of Prints and Drawings at the British Museum and a distinguished
littérateur and friend of R. L. Stevenson, he wrote on 1 February:
'I am too busy with the "Spirit of Delight" symphony.' He then
quoted some further lines of Shelley, from *Julian and Maddalo*, a poem
which records, like the symphony, a visit to Venice:

> I do but hide
> Under these notes, like embers, every spark
> *Of that which has consumed me*

A week later the slow movement was ready and Lady Elgar noted in
her diary: 'Very great and impressive. A. [herself] hears lament for

o

King Edward and dear Rodey in it, and all human feeling. E. wrote it all from his sketches in one week.' The third movement was done by 16 February. On that day Elgar wrote to Alice Stuart-Wortley: 'I have just put the last note to the IIIrd movement and very wild and headstrong it is with soothing pastoral strains in between and very brilliant. I bring it tomorrow and then for the great serene movement.' On the 28th Alice could write: 'E. finished his Symphony. It seems one of his very greatest works, vast in design and supremely beautiful . . . . It is really sublime . . . it resumes our human life, delight, regrets, fare-well, the saddest mood & then the strong man's triumph.' Alice posted the score to Novello's and, after his visit to Brussels, Elgar went to the United States and Canada where he was to conduct the Sheffield choir during their Coronation year tour of the New World. He had never liked America and now that his friend Professor Sanford of Yale was dead there was little to which to look forward there. To Sidney Colvin he wrote: 'I know I ought to be glad that perhaps I shall earn some money, but I would rather starve . . . . Truly parts of the world are beastly!' His every nerve was 'shattered by some angularity, vulgarity, and general horror'. From Cincinnati, 'this awful desert', he wrote to Alice Stuart-Wortley: 'It is sweet to hear of Tintagel & our own land . . . . I loathe & detest every minute of my life here! but I have lovely things to think of & shall soon be back & hope to see you. All I can do is to count the days . . . it is so raw & silly out here . . . . I am sure you are better in Tintagel—I am selfish enough to be thank-ful that you can think of me there & you will not forget Frank's car taking us to Boscastle & you will not forget the road home—how lovely it was—a year ago! . . . I long to be back & forget this worse than nightmare.' While he was away, his wife was looking at houses in London, for they had decided to live there, a decision which must have cost Elgar much heart-searching, torn as he was between his passionate love of the West Country and the demands made on his time by engagements which necessitated his presence in London, as well as his liking for the West End theatre, his clubs and the capital's nearness to Schuster at Maidenhead. While he was away, too, he worked on music for King George V's Coronation—a march and an *Offertorium*—and accepted an invitation from the London Symphony Orchestra to be its permanent conductor for the 1911–12 season now that Richter had retired.

He returned to England in May for the first performance of the Second Symphony and for the Coronation festivities. Alice Stuart-Wortley had found for them a house which Elgar and his wife both liked, 'Kelston', in Netherhall Gardens, Hampstead. It was a mansion designed by Norman Shaw, with music-room, library, billiard-room, picture gallery, servants' quarters, and acres of grounds. Elegant and palatial though it was, it was obviously very expensive. There were legal difficulties in the way of its purchase and it needed putting in order. But they decided to buy it. Today we should call its acquisition a 'status symbol', and that is what it was. For Alice it represented a victory over the attitude which had driven them from London in the first years of their marriage, a demonstration that her faith in her Edward's genius and ultimate success had been triumphantly justified, and a proclamation to all concerned that an English composer could live in style and comfort. Elgar himself had more modest tastes— Birchwood remained his idea of a home—but, as in the matter of his honours, he knew what was due to Alice, he liked the house, and there was the additional attraction—which must have weighed with him— that it had formerly belonged to a painter, Edwin Long, R.A. 'Our second-rate painters may build themselves magnificent houses . . .' he had said in 1904. Now a first-rate musician was to live in a painter's house. He must have relished this *volte-face* as a snook cocked at the English public he despised; and perhaps he remembered what he had written to Jaeger three years earlier:[1] 'What an object lesson is poor dear Madame Albani: one of the best of women. She has sung to these delightful English their own *oratorios* & sacred things for years—her husband loses all their money—she has to advertise for pupils! Now look at a battered old w—e like Melba & Co:—!!! My beloved countrymen & women wd. & will subscribe anything to help her if necessary—it makes my blood boil—where is providence? *Nothing.*'

His own need for money was still great. He knew that the Hampstead home would be a drain on his pocket. Yet he would only make money by the sweat of his brow, as it were. When Sir Edgar Speyer sent him a cheque, the result of shares speculation undertaken for Elgar, he returned it on moral grounds. He conducted the L.S.O. for nothing because their funds were in low water. Yet this is the man who is sometimes represented as the laureate of complacency and the established order. He was willing only to profit from the composition of such a work as the masque *Crown of India*, and it is apparent from a letter to Frances Colvin that he intended his stay in London only to be short: 'My labour will soon be over and then for the country lanes and the wind sighing in the reeds by Severn side again . . . .' You did not have to scratch far below the surface of Sir Edward Elgar, O.M. (as he

[1] 3 June 1908.

became on 17 June 1911) to discover Ted Elgar the Worcestershire man.

The Second Symphony was first played in Queen's Hall at the London Musical Festival on 24 May 1911. The composer conducted. It was high summer in an epoch of brilliance and wealth, London in its glory with the excitement of a Coronation less than a month away. And the work unfolded to a by no means full hall on that May night was mainly elegiac in mood and ended quietly, almost resignedly. There was no roaring ovation such as had greeted the First Symphony, no one stood on the seats to acclaim the composer-conductor. Henry Wood was at the side of the platform as Elgar walked off. 'Henry, they don't like it,' he said, 'they don't like it.'[1] To the leader, W. H. Reed, he said: 'What's the matter with them, Billy? They sit there like a lot of stuffed pigs.'[2] The comparative failure of that first performance, if failure it was, can be explained by its obvious contrast with the mood of the occasion: a fashionable audience, ready to acclaim a new king and a new reign of hope and glory and expecting Elgar to celebrate the glories of our blood and state, heard instead a restless work, full of enigmatic passages and containing a funeral elegy inspired, as they thought, by the death of the king they had mourned a year ago. Sub-consciously they were perhaps disturbed by the setting-sun finale; and if any lines of poetry were in their minds that evening besides Shelley's 'Rarely, rarely, comest thou, spirit of delight' (inscribed by Elgar on the score) then they were probably from Kipling's 'Recessional':

> Lo, all our pomps of yesterday
> Are one with Nineveh and Tyre.

It is not the sort of music to provoke, on first hearing, an ovation such as had greeted the First Symphony. But Richard Capell, then the critic of the *Daily Mail*, described the response as 'unhesitating' and spoke of 'most cordial warmth'. He told me many years later that the hall was not full because of the very high prices of admission and that there were two other composer-conducted first performances in the programme, of Walford Davies's *Parthenia* Suite and Bantock's *Dante and Beatrice*. Moreover, Elgar's view of the audience's response is contradicted by *The Daily Telegraph* report the next day which spoke of the exhilara-tion of the closing pages 'which roused the audience to much en-thusiasm'. The *Telegraph* critic unhesitatingly declared the work to be superior to the First Symphony—'there seems to be a firmer grip, not only of the symphonic form, but of the substance expressed within its

---

[1] *My Life of Music*, p. 326.   [2] *Elgar*, p. 105.

confines'. He was puzzled by 'the psychology' of the Rondo, but his most interesting comment was reserved for the Larghetto. He called its description by the programme-analyst as a 'funeral march' a 'strange misnomer. Far more is it suggestive of a deeply, poignantly-felt Lament, in its elegiac pathos and Elgarian introspection. . . . Intimate and immensely solemn, it brings up memories of the earlier Elgar more than any other of the four movements.' This wholly accurate piece of perception seems to show that Elgar's Edwardian contemporaries were not solely preoccupied, as modern caricature has it, with the panoply of regal tribute. Late in the notice the writer again speaks of a 'very warm reception', adding 'there are heights here that hitherto even Elgar himself had not touched, but we are doubtful if the greater public will realise the fact immediately.' The critics generally were divided over the work's merits and stature, the slow movement receiving most criticism. *The Times* (which said the symphony was 'received with much favour though with rather less enthusiasm than usual') surprisingly described it as 'much shorter than its predecessor', and another writer said that 'no small amount of it seems to speak of pessimism and rebellion.' When it was repeated at a London Symphony Orchestra concert on 8 June the audience was described as 'miserably small'. The symphony did not come into its own until after the First World War. One wonders how well or badly it was played in 1911–14 and suspects the worst. It should be remembered that there was still only a handful of really brilliant conductors working in England. In Elgar's music, Elgar himself could evoke a good performance if the orchestra responded to him. Otherwise the best conductor was Landon Ronald. Henry Wood rarely had enough rehearsal, Beecham would not look at the work. Richter had retired. The rest were choral conductors who would have been baffled by a score of this complexity. Thus even so Elgar-minded an orchestra as the Hallé, playing the symphony under Elgar on 23 November 1911, could only persuade Samuel Langford to this view in the *Manchester Guardian* next day: 'Elgar's original charm and his power of surprising us into wonder have diminished rather than grown as his craftsmanship and subtlety of fantastic variation have increased. In this symphony he vitalises the imagination of his hearer in listening to multitudinous transformations of a very sparse supply of melody. . . . We can hardly say that the work contains any melody in the full sense of the word. Neither can we say with confidence that it quite vanquishes the impression of coldness and hardness that will remain mixed with all our admiration of Elgar's music, despite its glowing orchestral colour.' Grudging indeed. No melody. Coldness. Hardness. What sort of performance can it have been? Three weeks beforehand Langford had also called the Violin Concerto 'short-winded in melody'. It is an interesting contemporary view. The symphony was not played again for fifteen years by the Hallé, which of all English orchestras at that time had the strongest Elgar tradition thanks to Richter, Brodsky, and the composer. It was not played at a concert of the Royal Philharmonic Society (as it became in 1912) until 1916 and not after that until 1923.

He was despondent after the first performance; not even the award of the O.M. wholly lifted his spirits. The obligations of an unofficial laureate weighed heavily on him, as Jaeger had feared. Elgar wrote to Canon Gorton on 16 July: 'I have had really no time for anything except "official" (more or less) work: now the "tumult & the shouting dies" & the net gain is little. I have my Star (which you shall see) & that is something, but troubles manifold dog me & it is *by no means* in sunshine that I walk—quite the reverse, alas!' Most of the troubles were connected with buying the Hampstead mansion, but on 27 June he had ended his agreement with Novello's. In September there was the Three Choirs at Worcester, followed by the Norwich Festival, and in October a visit to Turin to conduct some of his own works, including the concerto (soloist Zacharewitsch) at the international exhibition. The orchestra was Toscanini's, and the *Introduction and Allegro* was already in its regular repertory. Back in England there was a series of L.S.O. concerts for his debut as its permanent conductor, and on New Year's Day 1912 he and Alice moved into what they had decided to call Severn House. 'The house is divine,' he wrote three days later to Mrs. Stuart-Wortley, 'so quiet, quieter than Hereford even, where we heard trains. The heating apparatus we can't manage yet & get too hot. (I think, entre nous, it was designed for the comfort of Long's nude ladies!)'

*   *   *

The two symphonies and the Violin Concerto represent the mid-summer of Elgar's art. They have been excellently dissected and analysed in thematic detail in other books on the composer and on the sleeves of long-playing gramophone records, so it is not proposed to add further analyses here. But something may still be said about these three works, especially the symphonies, which are masterpieces of romantic music, using the modern symphony orchestra to glorious effect. Some deep puritanical strain in English criticism of the arts has often shown in a horror of the uninhibited use of colour and full-blooded emotional expression by painters, writers, and musicians. The adjectives 'gaudy' and 'vulgar' occur too frequently to allow of any other interpretation. The virtuosity of Elgar's orchestration, the acrobatic ease with which he deployed his instrumental forces, understanding to the last note the capacity of each instrument, these were regarded in his lifetime and for a time afterwards with grave suspicion. The cliché gained a hold that although the scoring was opulent in its use of tone-colour, the content of the music was empty, rhetorical, and rhapsodically uncontrolled. Because Symphony No. 1 begins with a march-tread in the basses and No. 2 is dedicated to the memory of Edward VII after having been 'designed as a loyal tribute', it was an easy step for writers in the 1920s and 1930s such as Cecil Gray and Constant Lambert to display their superficial knowledge of the works by a glib assumption that they reflected the spirit of a vulgar and complacent age. Lambert in his brilliant book *Music Ho!*[1] wrote: 'The aggressive Edwardian prosperity that lends so comfortable a background to Elgar's finales is now (1934) as strange to us as the England that produced *Greensleeves*. . . . Much of Elgar's music, through no fault of its own, has for the present generation an almost intolerable air of smugness, self-assurance and autocratic benevolence.'

Langford, living in Edwardian England, heard coldness and even austerity in that same music! In any case the Edwardians themselves regarded their own period as 'feverish'. But the predominant Elgarian mood, as was pointed out in Chapter 9, is noble, melancholy, wistful, and elegiac lyricism. It passes belief how anyone who listens attentively to the Elgar symphonies can fail to hear that, far from being smug and self-assured, they express a sense of unease and an awareness of human tragedy. Whatever they may or may not reflect of the time in which they were composed, they reflect far more of Elgar's personality. He described No. 2 as 'the passionate pilgrimage of a soul', and in both works can be heard the musical expression of the contrasts and conflicts in his make-up with which the reader will by now be familiar: exuberance followed by depression; restless gregariousness followed by loneliness and withdrawal; optimism giving way to a resigned fatalism and distrust of 'providence'; a deep nostalgia for the vanished days. No. 1 in A flat is perhaps emotionally less complex than No. 2 and its triumphant ending is one of the reasons Lambert's generation felt uneasy about it. And, of course, they equated its long opening theme with 'Land of Hope and Glory', applying political and sociological associations to what should be approached in a musical context. There again, like the trio of the first *Pomp and Circumstance* march, this tune is

[1] (Third Edition, London, 1966), p. 240.

hymn-like rather than military or martial; it is basically melancholy and it becomes heroic. To call such a long melody a 'motto-theme' is slightly ridiculous: it is more of a presence, and for Elgar it represented a moral virtue, the 'charity' mentioned in his letter to Walford Davies. This tune undergoes many transformations and vicissitudes before it emerges with banners flying fifty minutes later. Where is the 'confidence' in the first movement? Once the theme has been fully expounded the music switches violently to D minor and becomes restless and agitated. Here is a semi-military tune, obviously the villain of the piece, violent and disruptive, and with two consolatory pendant themes. The battle that rages between them is anything but complacent; the effect is of constant turbulence, of nerves on edge. When the A flat melody returns in full, after various mysterious and tentative appearances, a determined effort to crush it ends with great brass chords which have that hollow, doom-laden sound that is peculiar to Elgar. The movement ends quietly, with harps, solo violin, and clarinet contributing to the tenderness which—again it must be said—is conveyed by Elgar in music as by no one else. The second movement is also animated and nervy, with short phrases and broken rhythms for the allegro molto section and, in a central episode in B flat major, a gracefully scored, fantastic vein that belongs to the poignant world of *Dream Children* and *The Wand of Youth*. This is Elgar's nostalgia for youth, for its innocence perhaps and also for its solitude. Solo violin and woodwind repeat the main theme of this section just before the music disintegrates in broken phrases and subsides into the compassionate and heartfelt Adagio. It is the apotheosis of the withdrawn, tender side of Elgar, and to subject such emotional music to technical discussion would almost be to do it a physical injury. To borrow Vaughan Williams's words,[1] it 'has that peculiar kind of beauty which gives us, his fellow countrymen, a sense of something familiar—the intimate and personal beauty of our own fields and lanes. . . . It falls to the lot of very few composers, and to them not often, to achieve this bond of unity with their countrymen. Elgar has achieved this more often than most, and be it noted, not when he is being deliberately "popular" . . . but at those moments when he seems to have retired into the solitude of his own sanctuary.' This Adagio is certainly a sanctuary. When we reach this tune,

Ex. 7

[1] 'What Have We Learnt from Elgar?' in *Music and Letters* (January 1935), pp. 15–16.

we can agree with Jaeger that we are brought near to Heaven. The finale reverts to the restless mood of the earlier part of the symphony, from its mysterious opening to its use of a brilliant staccato theme which Elgar later transforms into one of his heart-swelling expansive tunes. It is all a preparation for the return of the A flat tune, but when it does return, in the panoply of Elgar's most glittering orchestration, it is not a rhetorical gesture nor does it have an easy passage. During this peroration note how the accompaniment tries to break up the flow of the theme with irregular crashes. The end is victory but it has not been easily achieved—'a massive hope for the future'. I hope, not assurance.

The Second Symphony is a very much more complicated structure, technically and emotionally. In places it shows signs of its long gestation; its best moments are unequalled elsewhere in Elgar's output. As every Elgarian knows, two lines by Shelley preface the score

> Rarely, rarely, comest thou,
> Spirit of Delight.

Not only is this Elgar's clue to the romantic and tragic nature of the symphony, it is a broad hint that in the rest of the poem will be found other identifications with the music and the personality of its composer: the love of the countryside, for example, and the tendency to misanthropy.

> I love all that thou lovest,
> Spirit of Delight:
> The fresh earth in new leaves dressed
> And the starry night;
> Autumn evening, and the morn
> When the golden mists are born . . .
> Everything almost
> Which is Nature's, and may be
> Untainted by man's misery.
> I love tranquil solitude
> And such society
> As is quiet, wise and good, . . .
> Thou art Love and life! Oh, come,
> Make once more my heart thy home.

The first movement is on an enormous scale, huge in its breadth and its command of orchestral resource, a supreme example of the power and originality of Elgar's symphonic style, which combines a kind of 'fragmentation' method—particles of themes are shown in new and unexpected guises—with the ability to move in large paragraphs, tele-scoping conventional development and exposition passages. The exu-berant opening, pouring forth themes in seemingly endless profusion, rarely fails to thrill the sympathetic listener with its effect as of a dam bursting. After this energy has spent itself, the group of 'second subject' themes, beginning with a long cello theme, again clearly indicates that a struggle for ascendancy between stridency and lyricism is to occur. No Mahler movement is more obviously a battleground for conflicting emotions and nervous tensions than this by Elgar—and where is the comfortable Edwardian opulence in these pounding basses, shrilling edge-of-hysteria brass, in the strange throbbing of the timpani while the cellos, in their highest registers, sing some unearthly lament for the ideal that is always out of reach? It is this passage which Elgar was describing when, after completing this movement on 29 January 1911, he wrote to Mrs. Stuart-Wortley: 'I have written the *most extraordinary* passage I have ever heard—a sort of malign influence wandering thro' the summer night in the garden'. At the height of the movement, the 'spirit of delight' phrase is hammered home with more climactic blows from the timpani supported by trombones and, after a dramatic pause, the music seems to dive back into the hurly-burly as if to escape—what is this but tragic art of deep intensity? The slow movement is unrivalled as a national elegy, yet its origins, as we now know, lay in the shock of Rodewald's death in 1903. It is personal as well as ceremonial and it contains, in the passage where the oboe sings a lament in free counter-point to the solemn tread of the funeral march, one of Elgar's most powerful strokes of imagination. Its climax, at [86], when the strings seem to be straining to express the inexpressible in grief, has a paradox-ically consolatory exaltation like the sun suddenly breaking through the clouds; and nothing is more touching than the final bars, which shuffle to a close as if overpowered by the solemnity of death. The Rondo (third) movement recaptures the exhilaration of the opening of the symphony, but its rather forced gaiety is suddenly obliterated by the enigmatic and extraordinary passage when, above a steady pulsing on E flat, the cello tune from the first movement returns—the 'malign influence in the summer night'—and the percussion, with a steady and relentless hammering, overwhelms the rest of the orchestra while the brass tear the heart out of the once-lyrical tune. The storm subsides as suddenly as it arose, but what does it mean, for some extra-musical idea must have been its inspiration? W. H. Reed is among those who have noted a kinship between the theme that gives rise to this pandemonium and one written many years later for 'The Wagon

Passes' in the *Nursery Suite*, and this leads to the deduction that there was some mental image for Elgar in the idea of wheels and hoofs, especially when it is known that he told Canon W. H. T. Gairdner that he associated this passage in the symphony with these lines from Tennyson's *Maud*:

> Dead, long dead,
>   Long dead!
> And my heart is a handful of dust
> And the wheels go over my head.
> And my bones are shaken with pain,
> For into a shallow grave they are thrust,
> Only a yard beneath the street,
> And the hoofs of the horses beat, beat
> The hoofs of the horses beat,
> Beat into my scalp and brain.

It has been said that the movement had a specific Italian origin, perhaps in the death of the demonstrator during the Italian two-day general strike while Elgar was in Rome. It seems certain that the music is intended to convey the agonized reaction of Elgar to sudden death, and it is the musical parallel to his letter to Jaeger after Rodewald's death. Some further lines from *Maud* may well have haunted Elgar:

> But up and down and to and fro
> Ever about me the dead men go.

He told orchestras when he rehearsed this section of the Rondo: 'I want you to imagine that this hammering is like that horrible throbbing in the head during some fever. It seems gradually to blot out every atom of thought in your brain and nearly drives you mad.'[1]

The last movement begins gently and with stately dignity. The rolling theme might even be called complacent—until after a very short course it is subjected to fidgety and nervous embellishment by woodwind and strings: short broken-winded sequential passages, restless and unsure. Even the *nobilmente* 'Richter' theme quoted earlier soon gives way to a fugal section—a weak passage of marking time—and more frenzy, with a top B for the trumpet piercing the texture and, as in the First Symphony, an attempt by syncopated off-beats to upset the course of the first subject when it returns. The ending is famous: a long elegiac farewell based on the 'spirit of delight' theme, radiant, tender, compassionate, full of secret regret but consolatory and hopeful. Anything but complacent. The pilgrimage is over, the passion spent.

---

[1] Bernard Shore, *Sixteen Symphonies* (London, 1949), p. 279.

I make no apology for describing these works in such language. Elgar 'felt' his music; and if one cannot 'feel' it emotionally no amount of probing into its innards will do any good. Yet, of course, both can be appreciated on a purely technical level as masterly examples of symphonic construction. The old label of 'rhapsodic' hardly stands up to analysis, for both are extremely tightly and closely organized thematic compositions. Their restlessness is accounted for by the curious tonality, which is constantly and violently switched about. In both works theme after theme is found to stem from a common source: the ingenuity, whether conscious or sub-conscious, is of a kind that only a composer of the highest, Beethovenian calibre commands. I do not mean only the more obvious transformations, such as (in the First Symphony) the scherzo theme into the adagio theme and the staccato march of the finale into a broad, truly Elgarian melody. There are literally dozens of examples in both works of a fragment of melody being expanded or transformed into a new theme which again generates another. It is a kind of fission process, and it proves that although the music sounds spontaneous, Elgar (to adapt Shaw's phrase) had paid his price in headwork to achieve his effect. What Diana McVeagh has brilliantly described as his 'mosaic method of construction' indicates the sheer power of concentrated ingenuity in the interlocking of his material and also its source in a single germinal idea. He himself told C. Sanford Terry that all the themes for a particular work came 'from the same oven' and that often it was the climax of a movement that he settled first. His modulations are nearly always inspired, and perhaps the outstanding technical feature of his work is the fluent and original use of counterpoint which binds every movement together and is the basic cause of the thematic relationships. The symphonies and the Violin Concerto are a complex interwoven pattern of contrapuntal strands, and it is the poetic use of counterpoint that accounts for some of the most memorable moments in the works. In both symphonies the orchestral scoring is of a richness and subtlety that still sound remarkable and must, from an English composer in the early 1900s, have sounded superhuman. I could fill pages with descriptions of particular passages— the end of the Adagio of the A flat symphony is paramount—but I presume that my readers will know the works and, if they do not, the music itself is its own best advocate and they should seek it out. But on this subject of Elgar's orchestration it is worth quoting the views of an orchestral player and of another composer. First, Bernard Shore, for many years principal viola of the B.B.C. Symphony Orchestra and one of England's most experienced and distinguished practitioners: 'In one respect no composer has ever matched Elgar. None other has fully exploited all the orchestral instruments and at the same time written nothing impossible. In this latter respect Strauss frequently sins, and so did Wagner. . . . Elgar was unerring '[1]

And Vaughan Williams, who was also a conductor and knew the problems of working with amateurs when 'extra' instruments were not available and either had to be omitted or written in for another instrument: 'I have found that with Wagner the extra instruments could almost always be dispensed with altogether, with a little loss of colour it is true, but with no damage to the texture. But when it came to Elgar the case was quite different. Even in the accompaniments to choral movements there was hardly anything that could be left out without leaving a "hole" in the texture.'[2]

It is invidious to decide which is the finer of the two symphonies. Much depends on the listener's mood at the time, as well, of course, as on the quality of interpretation and performance. The First Symphony contains, in the Adagio, the best single movement, and the variations between its heights and depths are less than in No. 2. But the E flat has moments when it attains the loftiest heights. It is more difficult to play and to conduct, and there are days when even a sympathetic listener can be exhausted by its quixotic moodiness. If it receives an unconvinced interpretation, one can understand why some people find it attitudin-izing music, rather self-consciously aware of its place in the history of the epic symphony, and one can sympathize with the criticism that the notes imply more than they actually convey. But when it is played and interpreted well, all doubts are swept away and it is one of the most thrilling, moving, and enduring experiences that music can provide.

The symphonies' companion-piece, the Violin Concerto, is of a more intimate nature although it is on an equally imposing scale. It is nearly as long as the symphonies, but none of these works is too long because their material justifies the length at which it is treated and sus-tains the interest in its treatment. The concerto is Elgar's most personal work, a self-communing and a declaration of secret love. Yet it is elaborate and spacious in conception and execution. No matter whose soul it enshrines, it enshrines the soul of the violin and of the composer. It depends for its perfect interpretation on a close and intuitive under-standing of the subtleties of rubato, fractional variations of tempo, infinitesimally fluctuating nuances of expression, little hesitations and catches of the breath that bestrew the soloist's part. Above all it must be played with a full and singing tone, for the writing for violin is

[1] Op. cit., p. 258.   [2] 'What Have We Learnt from Elgar?' p. 15.

almost vocal, and operatically vocal, in its curving intensity. It needs
stamina, too, and the ability to dominate a large orchestra. In short it
is a great violin concerto for great violinists. The thematic material is
copious but again is shown throughout the work to be closely related.
There are two outstanding passages, the first entry of the violin, which
remains a moving and surprising moment no matter how many times
one hears it, and the accompanied cadenza in the finale when, over an
accompaniment of strings *pizzicato tremolando* ('thrummed' was Elgar's
description) and occasionally the full orchestra, the soloist recalls themes
from the earlier movements, caresses them, lingers lovingly over them
and finally bids them a regretful farewell. The first subject of the first
movement becomes the final theme of the cadenza, its ardour changed
to wistfulness. It is a theme from the essential Elgar, a tune from his
childhood which can be heard in its earlier form in the overture to the
first *Wand of Youth* Suite. All Elgar's love and understanding of his
favourite instrument is in this concerto and especially in this cadenza
which is the most poetic cadenza in the world, for it not only displays
the instrument's technical range but enables it to show its unrivalled
capacity for emotional expression. This is sensuous music, colourful,
rich, uninhibited, for even the restraint of the Andante is soon swept
by gusts of passion. The slow movement is unequalled in Elgar's work
as an expression of passionate regret. No soloist and conductor who
does not relish the concerto for these qualities should ever approach it.
It is not music for faint hearts nor for the austere. It requires devotion,
but it must not sound devout. Elgar wrote of 'philanthropy' in connection with this concerto, and generosity above all else, notably in the
grandiose parts of the finale, is what it needs from its interpreters.

*   *   *

Installed in Hampstead, Elgar began 1912 in busy fashion, conducting
the L.S.O. in London and taking them on tour. W. H. Reed, who to
Elgar's delight was now leader of the orchestra, says that these tours
'did him a world of good, as they took him out of himself. . . . He was
on the best of terms with the orchestra and never tired of telling them
he was "one of them" . . .' While travelling by rail Elgar regaled the
impresario Percy Harrison 'and those with him in his reserved saloon
carriage with endless stories of his youth, the country people, and his
travels abroad . . . rubbing his hands together gleefully, entirely forgetting the pessimistic moods and the despondency that sometimes
overtook him'.[1] (To the end of his life he enjoyed the company of

---

[1] W. H. Reed, op. cit., pp. 107–8.

orchestral players. He understood their quirks and humour. While the orchestra were tuning up at a Queen's Hall concert to which he went with Adrian Boult in the 1920s, he said: 'Adrian, just listen to what that trumpeter is doing. Now if I'd written that, he'd say it was unplayable.') While they were in Leeds, the Festival committee asked Elgar to conduct at the 1913 festival and to compose a new work. The animosities of 1904 were forgotten. He was at work on the masque *The Crown of India*, which he soon 'cooked up' from discarded sketches. He viewed it quite frankly as a potboiler. As he told Frances Colvin: 'When I write a big serious work e.g. *Gerontius*, we have had to starve and go without fires for twelve months as a reward: this small effort allows me to buy scientific works I have yearned for and I spend my time between the Coliseum and the old bookshops. . . . I found a lovely old volume *Tracts Against Popery*—I appeased Alice by saying I bought it to prevent other people seeing it—but it wd. make a cat laugh.'

He was still physically unwell. He had ear trouble and gout. 'I have been very very dreary,' he wrote to Mrs. Stuart-Wortley in April 1912, '& have felt this terrible Titanic disaster acutely & I have been lonely. . . . Welcome home.' Another mood is described in a letter to Frances Colvin of 27 April: 'I took a walk again this p.m. & saw a flock of sheep—bless them—talking a language I have known since I was two years old—then two *excellent* anti-Socialist lectures on the heath—& last but most effective the Hampstead *prize band* playing uproarious selections also on the heath: I heard & subscribed to this mild attempt at a continental Sabbath & was very happy.' But he was homesick for Worcestershire—'I long for a sight of my own country', he told Canon Gorton. It was probably this mood that impelled him to complete the setting of Arthur O'Shaughnessy's poem *The Music Makers* on which he had been working intermittently since about 1903. (Jaeger referred to it once in a 1904 letter as 'The Dreamers'.) He had composed some of it while fishing the Wye at his favourite spot, Mordiford Bridge, and this in itself is a clue to the obsessively personal and 'secret' nature of the music. The poem, with its stress on the 'apartness' of the creative artist, appealed strongly to Elgar. In a note he wrote in July 1912 he spoke of the music as 'mainly sad' but added: 'There are moments of enthusiasm and bursts of joy occasionally approaching frenzy: moods which the creative artist suffers in creating or in contemplation of the unending influence of his creation. Yes, suffers—this is the only word I dare to use, for even the highest ecstasy of "making" is mixed with the consciousness of the sombre dignity of the eternity of the artist's responsibility.' Criticism of the music has often resolved into criticism of O'Shaughnessy's poem, but though not great verse it is no worse than many another chosen by musicians. The other major criticism of *The Music Makers* has always been of Elgar's use of quotations from his other works though why this should be reprehensible *per se* is not clear to me. To read most commentators on the work, one would think that the music was one long quotation whereas the references to previous works occupy only a small percentage (see p. 298). I think they are recalled with deeply moving effect and perfect taste. When the Nimrod theme is given to the voices it is slightly varied melodically, so that it becomes a free counterpoint to the orchestral statement of the tune. The effect is wonderful. The Enigma theme dominates the orchestral introduction, a plain indication of the autobiographical nature of the work. Elgar said: 'I have used the . . . theme because it expressed when written (in 1898) my sense of the loneliness of the artist as described in the first six lines of the ode and, to me, it still embodies that sense. At the end of the full score of the *Variations* I wrote: "Bramo assai, poco spero, nulla chieggio" (Tasso) ["I long for much, I hope for little, I ask for nothing"]. This was true in 1898 and might be written with equal truth at the end of this work in 1912.' 'The dreamers of dreams' introduces a fragment of *Gerontius*; there is a further reference to the Enigma and to the Violin Concerto at 'we dwell in our dreaming and singing a little apart'; 'wand'ring by lone sea breakers' evokes *Sea Pictures*; fragments of the symphonies are heard; at 'on one man's soul it hath broken a light that doth not depart' the Nimrod theme pays further tribute to Jaeger's encouragement. 'I do not mean to convey his was the only word or look that "wrought flame in another man's heart",' Elgar wrote, 'but I do convey that amongst all the inept writing and wrangling about music his voice was clear, ennobling, sober and sane.' It was, perhaps, again of Jaeger that Elgar was thinking when he recalled 'Novissima hora est' for 'a dreamer who slumbers and a singer who sings no more'. The choral writing is as good as any he achieved, and the second subject of the opening prelude is among the greatest tunes he wrote. The small contralto part, written for Muriel Foster, requires an intensity which she must have been well able to bring to it. 'Tinsel' and 'tawdry' have been the pejorative words applied to this cantata, but rather than finding it 'under-composed', I find it an original treatment of the poem, and one of Elgar's most endearing and unjustly under-rated works. If the words stirred personal memories, why should he not have linked them to the musical embodiment of those memories? Rather than showing a lack of inventive resource, this weaving of fragments from

The Music Room at Severn House, Hampstead

'Brinkwells', the cottage near Fittleworth, Sussex

PLATE IX   Two Elgar Homes

PLATE X

The Cello Concerto. An early sketch of the first movement with typewritten
annotations added later by Elgar

the past into the texture of what is a declaration of the artist's standpoint is, in my opinion, a most original and imaginative solution of the creator's problem of lending significance to his own 'passionate pilgrimage' in art. In the poem he found the roots of his own motivation as a composer, and it was natural, therefore, to treat it musically by showing what had grown from the roots. To the unsympathetic, the work will certainly be repellent because it so accurately reflects the subjective, self-centred, self-aware side of Elgar that is illustrated by his strange letter to Alice Stuart-Wortley (quoted in Chapter 8) about his walk on Hampstead Heath after he had finished setting the Ode. Of its importance to him as an artist one is left in no doubt by this extract from another letter to Mrs. Stuart-Wortley (29 August 1912): 'I have written out my soul in the concerto, Sym. II & the Ode & you know it . . . in these three works I have *shewn* myself.' Also, he had enshrined the souls of Nimrod, Schuster and Windflower in the Ode, as the quotations imply.

To add to its personal significance for him, he dedicated *The Music Makers* to Nicholas Kilburn who lost no time in performing it, with his Bishop Auckland Music Society, a few months after the first performance at the Birmingham Festival on 1 October 1912. Kilburn wrote to Elgar putting into words something of what he felt of music's, and especially Elgar's music's, moral force. The reply he received (written on 26 March 1913) must have startled him:

You talk mystically as becomes you & your northern atmosphere. I cannot follow you. I could have done a few years back—but the whole thing (no matter how one fights & avoids it) is merely commercial—this is forced into every fibre of me every moment. Not long ago one could occasionally shake this off & forget, but an all-foolish providence takes care that it shall not be unremembered for a moment & so—& so?? You say 'we must look up'. To what? to whom? Why? The mind bold and independent, the purpose free must not think, must not hope—yet it seems sad that the only quotation I can find to fit my life comes from the Demons' chorus! a fanciful summing up!

To what—to whom—why? The 'dreamer of dreams' was a deeply divided, unhappy man. The religious doubts evident in letters to Jaeger are here plainly stated. He could not easily settle to composing in London: there were too many distractions. Alice held court at Severn House—the Paderewskis, Siegfried Wagner, Siloti, Hamilton Harty, Chaliapin (whose first London *Boris* Elgar saw and liked): all were entertained. There were the Royal Academy dinner, the Academy Private View, the purchase of a billiard table, sitting for a portrait, news of performances of the Violin Concerto in Russia. Returning to the

P

land which had stimulated Elgar's creative faculties on previous occasions, they went in January 1913 to Naples and Capri. The trick worked, and Elgar decided that his work for Leeds should be a symphonic study of Falstaff, a project he had considered eleven years before. But before they left for home in February they heard that Julia Worthington was dying of cancer in New York. On his return to London Elgar was depressed and ill. He sketched bits of *Falstaff*, but could not concentrate. He went alone to Llandrindod Wells for a 'cure' and then to his sister's in Worcestershire. He began work in earnest in May and June, but the deaths within a few days of each other of Lord Northampton and Mrs. Worthington—'our dear dear Pippa', Alice called her—depressed him. By cruel coincidence, the news of Julia Worthington's death came on the day of a London performance of *The Music Makers*. But he finished *Falstaff* in June and July, and corrected early proofs and wrote an analytical note for *Musical Times* while on holiday at Penmaenmawr, North Wales, in August. 'Falstaff is immense,' he had written to Troyte in July, 'it lasts 20 minutes [sic!] & you will like it only it wants a gigantesque orchestra.' Other large projects were also in his mind. He wrote to Sidney Colvin on 22 July: 'Chaliapin has been here & talking over many schemes for a great part for himself "Lear"! for instance: you have seen him, I suppose—a splendid *man*—figure and mind—& the finest artist I have ever heard. But there is also a scheme for an allegorical affair on a huge scale—these two things may hold me musically for some time but I shall keep in mind the Hardy ideas [for an opera] & if my half-promises for the other two things are not wanted to be kept I will at once plunge into the Hardy work if it can be arranged.'

Elgar conducted the first performance of *Falstaff* at Leeds on 2 October 1913. It was badly placed in a long programme and was received with cold respect. Robin Legge in *The Daily Telegraph* wished that a greater conductor than Elgar had conducted, 'for much of the wondrous maze of detail in this score did not become audible at all to me'. He called it a 'masterpiece' but urged Elgar to cut the score by five or more minutes. And he noticed the music's principal defect: 'I have not yet fathomed the (to me) mystery as to why what I believe is called in theatrical language the "fat" of the music is applied to other folk and their doings, or to description, and not to the protagonist himself.' When it was played in London under Landon Ronald[1] a few weeks later, on 3 November, Legge rebuked the capital's public because there

---

[1] It is dedicated to Ronald. In the 1920s the young Barbirolli remarked to him what a wonderful work it was, to receive the reply: 'I can't make head or tail of it.'

was 'only a beggarly row of half-empty benches'. At the first Manchester performance on 27 November, the reception by the Hallé
audience was described by Langford as 'hardly enthusiastic'. It was a
bad performance and the music emerged as 'disjointed and broken'.
Elgar was missing the attentions of a master-conductor like Richter.
He sent his old friend the score on 24 November with the words 'How
I wish you were going to conduct this work!' Two and a half years
earlier, just after Richter's retirement, Elgar had sent him the score of
the Second Symphony saying 'it was meant for you to like'. It is
interesting to speculate on Richter's interpretations of the Violin Concerto, the E flat symphony, and *Falstaff*. A thousand pities that these
works came too late for him. *Falstaff* certainly came too early for it to
be a success with the 1913 public. It is a long and complex work, swift-
moving and episodic. The detail and learning in Elgar's programme-
note would daunt any audience at a first hearing. It had no chance in
the orchestral conditions of those days when very few rehearsals were
possible. For an orchestra to play *Falstaff* well, it must not only master
the notes, it must know the music thoroughly and intimately, have the
score in its head, not its head in the score.

According to Eric Fenby,[1] Elgar regarded *Falstaff* as his best work.
From the viewpoint of virtuosity, of complete command of instrumental effect and colour, this is undoubtedly true. Every point is made.
It is musicians' music. I rate it below the symphonies, the Violin Concerto, and the *Variations* because the actual quality of thematic invention shows signs of staleness. There is an air of midnight oil and of
literary knowledge about the work that is foreign to Elgar's usual spon-
taneity and expressiveness. He had loved Shakespeare since his talks
with Ned Spiers in the room above his father's shop in High Street,
Worcester, and he was something of a Shakespearean authority; it is
evident from his analysis that he had read all the leading commentaries
on the character of Falstaff and had determined to vindicate the Falstaff
of *Henry IV* rather than the buffoon of *The Merry Wives of Windsor*,
something easier to do in prose than in music. So we get a Falstaff in
C minor, almost a tragic figure who uncannily resembles Elgar himself! Elgar's Falstaff yearns nostalgically for his days in the 'Wand of
Youth' when he was page to the Duke of Norfolk; he dies not only
babbling of green fields but almost like a Gerontius with memories of
the anthems he has sung in a West Country cathedral; he is more likely
to idealize the women in the Boar's Head than pinch their bottoms.
In other words Elgar chose those aspects, as he saw them, of Falstaff

[1] *Delius As I Knew Him* (London, 1936, 2nd ed. 1966), p. 113.

which appealed to his musical style. The Falstaff theme, as apt for variation as the Enigma, lacks any suggestion of coarseness and it is hardly surprising that Tovey, in his analysis of the work, attributed a variant of it to the phrase 'blown up like a bladder with sighing and grief' when Elgar's intention was to depict 'a goodly portly man, of a cheerful look, a pleasing eye, and a most noble carriage'. Prince Hal, of course, comes out of it more simply: he has a typically Elgarian *nobilmente* theme, though I have never thought it one of the best of its kind: it is rather square and lacks the real note of nobility, and, in fact, is not marked *nobilmente*. I wonder if Elgar was ever tempted to call the work 'Henry the Fifth' as Verdi was once tempted to call *Otello* 'Iago'. For a tone-poem on this scale to succeed, the music must be so vivid that no explanation is necessary, or it must be thematically so distinguished that no explanation matters, the listener is quite happy anyway. This is where *Falstaff* several times fails—I hasten to add, once again, in my opinion. Of course when a listener has done his homework —and these days it is much easier to do so—it is obvious that all the scurrying and rustling represent the episode at Gads Hill, and the struggle for the twice-stolen booty 'got with much ease', and that one of the themes when treated in an energetic fugal manner illustrates the discomfiture of the thieves. But without that knowledge the music, I submit, is not very interesting in itself and once the knowledge is gained the passage soon palls and becomes something to be endured until the imagination is stirred again. Harmonically and contrapuntally it is magnificent and one appreciates why Tovey the analyst and professor gloated over the score at this point. I always wish Elgar's estimate to Troyte that *Falstaff* lasted twenty minutes had proved accurate, for then we should have had an unflawed masterpiece that out-Straussed Strauss, because Elgar demonstrates in the best parts of the score that he is Strauss's equal in depicting events in music and his superior in the matter of emotional expressiveness. Like *In the South*, *Falstaff* has two self-contained interludes which interrupt the main flow but paradoxically give it a binding unity. These two interludes are the finest parts of the score, indeed they are among the finest parts of Elgar, perfect examples of the miniature Elgar done with supreme taste. The first is unmistakably introduced by Falstaff (bassoon), drunk on sack, falling to sleep behind the arras. He drifts into sleep—has this state of mind ever been conveyed in music so exactly?[1]—and as he sleeps he dreams of his youth in music of the most tender nostalgic fragrance, untouched

---

[1] A similar passage in Elgar's music, which it is interesting to compare, is the link between the second and third movements of the First Symphony.

by any trace of self-indulgence. As in the Violin Concerto, a solo violin
muses on what might have been. The music henceforward is programme-
music of the highest order. The ramshackle recruits whom Falstaff
commands are recognizable without reference to any analysis, as they
slouch along, and so is the battle scene. After the battle we have another
of Elgar's masterly theme transformations which justifies the word
symphonic in the work's title. The ramshackle gait of the scarecrow
army:

Ex. 8

becomes this songful, blithe tune as they approach the orchards of the
West Country

Ex. 9

just as Elgar's heart must have lifted every time he returned from
London to Worcestershire. It is moments such as this which one
cherishes in *Falstaff*. The second interlude, Shallow's Orchard, juxta-
poses a rustic tabor and pipe tune with a sleepy melody which must
represent the peace of being in the countryside. After the interlude has
obviously ended this motive tries to continue but is brushed aside by
the violins introducing Harry's theme, now that he is King, and Falstaff
in augmentation as he sees himself at the King's right hand. The last
ten minutes of the work are magnificent. No one but Elgar could so
vividly have evoked—so that we can almost see them—the excited
crowds round the Abbey, peering on tiptoe for a sight of the King's
procession, throwing their hats in the air and cheering. (Note the little
solo for side-drum of which Elgar himself was very proud.) The King
arrives, *grandioso*, and banishes Falstaff, whose collapse is expressed in
a nonplussed, bewildered breaking-up of his theme. His death scene is
very great music. The music to which he fell asleep to dream of his
youth returns, but we can sense that this is the prelude to eternal sleep.
Themes from the past are recalled, some sharply, some hazily, as his
mind wanders. The prince's theme becomes wonderfully tender, an
idealization of their friendship. Elgar uses the clarinet for the last
moments, the King's imperious shadow falls coldly across the picture,
there is a roll of drums, and all is over. If the first part of the work was

on a similar artistic level, then *Falstaff* could be declared its creator's noblest achievement. As it is, it contains, like Strauss's *Don Quixote* to which many of the same criticisms apply, some of his greatest music. It is a work that repays the closest study of its score, which is a miracle of ingenuity and compositional skill. The nation that has produced an orchestral composer capable of writing *Falstaff* can hold its head high. Though it is rarely Shakespearean, *Falstaff* is wholly Elgarian. No wonder he asked Fenby to 'tell Delius that I grow more like Falstaff every day.'[1]

The year 1914 found Elgar at Severn House working over some of his old pieces from sketchbooks—*Carissima*, for example—and writing some of the splendid and much under-rated part-songs of op. 71, 72, and 73. On 21 January he conducted *Carissima* for a gramophone recording, its first performance and his first contact with a medium in which he took an increasing and practical interest.[2] He looked again at his sketches for a piano concerto but his heart was not in it. He was easily distracted by the operas and concerts of the London season, and, restless as ever, he went to Stratford for the Shakespeare birthday and to the Isle of Man to adjudicate at a festival. He painted heraldic shields in the billiard-room of Severn House and built a workshop above the stables. He collected prints of old Worcester to hang in his study. An odd episode is recounted in a letter to Alice Stuart-Wortley dated 3 May 1914: 'After all I did not dine at the R.A.—I went in, found they had *omitted* my O.M. & put me with a crowd of nobodies in the lowest place of all—the bottom table—I see no reason why I should *endure* insults—I can understand their being offered to me. Love & thanks for all your kind troubles: all wasted. I left at once and came here [the Athenaeum] & had a herring.' In June he conducted the Leeds Choral Union in *The Apostles* in Canterbury Cathedral; it was after this performance, as mentioned in Chapter 10, that Embleton persuaded him to think again about the third part of the trilogy of oratorios. Their holiday in July was spent in Scotland, in Ross, where they could look across to Skye and where Elgar and his daughter could take a boat out to sea to fish. 'The wild birds feed their young within 30 yards of this window—gannets, oyster-catchers and divers and a dozen others,' he wrote to Mrs. Stuart-Wortley. His wife thought it the most beautiful place they had visited except Bavaria. Six days after Alice wrote those words, Bavaria was part of enemy territory. The Elgars watched the troop trains pass through Inverness and Edinburgh as they made their way back to London. 'The spirit of the men is splendid,' he wrote on

[1] *Delius As I Knew Him*, p. 113.   [2] See Appendix IV.

6 August to Alice Stuart-Wortley, to whom he had earlier telegraphed for information about the rumours reaching Scotland in the days of no radio and slow delivery of newspapers, 'the Seaforths went first, later in the week the mounted Lovats Scouts rode through—were given a sort of tea meal here [Gairloch Hotel] by the manageress & rode off in the moonlight by the side of the loch & disappeared into the mountains. . . . I *wish* I could go to the front but they may find some menial occupation for a worthless person.' He went to the first Promenade Concert on 15 August. The audience was wildly enthusiastic about the patriotic music Henry Wood conducted. Yet in this same concert was the first performance of a new Elgar work, *Sospiri*, for strings and harp, a little masterpiece dedicated to W. H. Reed and completed the previous February. How out of place it must have sounded in an atmosphere of 'Now God be thanked who has matched us with His hour' and 'Pack up your troubles' and 'Wider still and wider'. For it is, though short, a major work of grave beauty, an epitome of Elgar's ability to express nostalgic regret. The earlier *Elegy* for strings (1909) is a formal expression of condolence compared with the wounded heart-cry of *Sospiri*. Its dedication to Reed was presumably in gratitude for his work on the concerto, and perhaps *Sospiri* was constructed from unused parts of the greater work. It breathes the same atmosphere as the slow movement and cadenza, and as it was written after the death of Julia Worthington, the personal nature of its sorrow is understandable. To that war-excited audience as yet unbaptized by fire it must have sounded out of key. If they could have looked six years ahead to the Cello Concerto, they would have recognized the note of desolate agony.

To Schuster on 25 August 1914, Elgar wrote:

Concerning the war I say nothing—the only thing that wrings my heart & soul is the thought of the horses—oh! my beloved animals—the men and women can go to hell—but my horses; I walk round & round this room cursing God for allowing dumb beasts to be tortured—let Him kill his human beings but—how CAN HE? Oh, my horses.

What manner of man was this, who had composed the death of Falstaff and the cadenza of the Violin Concerto and could consign human beings in wartime to hell?

PART III

DECLINE
1914–1934

'The bright day is done and we are for the dark'

12 War

Ernest Newman, writing in the *Musical Times* of September 1914 on 'The War and the Future of Music', remarked that in England Elgar was still 'the one figure of impressive stature'. It was nearly fifteen years since the *Variations* had first been played and the English musical scene in that time had been transformed. Yet much remained the same. Parry was still director of the Royal College of Music, Stanford still taught there and was still Professor at Cambridge, Mackenzie was still Principal of the Royal Academy of Music, Brodsky was still Principal of the Royal Manchester College of Music and still active enough as a soloist to have played the Violin Concerto in Vienna in 1913 under Franz Schalk. But Elgar's name and fame surpassed them all. He stood aloof from 'schools' of music, he had no academic position, he exerted no direct influence on the young. He had seen new names come into prominence but none challenged his supremacy. Bantock had his admirers, Josef Holbrooke enjoyed a brief spell of attention, and Delius was regarded almost as a foreign composer. Of a younger group the most successful and admired was Vaughan Williams, whose *A London Symphony*, first played in March 1914, owed something to Elgar's example. His friend Gustav Holst was known only to a restricted circle. Ethel Smyth, J. B. McEwen, Frank Bridge, Arnold Bax, Cyril Scott, York Bowen, Percy Grainger—all had work to their credit but some had yet to make their mark and others, though they did not realize it, had already made what mark was within their capacity. One thing was common to all the younger men: they could face the world of music bravely and confidently, and this they owed, as much as to anything, to the vantage-point won for them by Elgar.

When he returned to Severn House in August 1914, he joined the special constabulary in Hampstead and became a staff inspector. 'One does what one can,' he wrote to Schuster. 'It's a pity I am too old to be a soldier. I am so active. Everything is at a standstill & we have nothing left in the world—absolute financial ruin—but we are cheerful & I will die a man if not a musician.' Schuster played up to him and asked for a special constable to be posted at 'The Hut' for an indefinite period. Elgar, whose number in the force was 0015014, replied: 'State what feminine society The Hut will provide for No. 0015014. On receiving your reply the matter shall be proceeded with at once.'[1] But it was soon apparent that this was not to be a war for 'japes'. His friend and patron, Sir Edgar Speyer, was bitterly attacked in the press for his alleged pro-German sympathies and even accused of signalling to German submarines from his Norfolk home. Elgar stood by him and received a letter written on 24 October 1914, saying how much Speyer and his wife had been 'touched by your kind letter and we appreciate this friendly greeting and mark of confidence at a time when sense of fairness and proportion and logic seem to have forsaken a section of the people.' Belgium was over-run and news of supposed German atrocities horrified the British people. A patriotic poem called *Carillon* by the Belgian Emile Cammaerts stirred Elgar deeply and he provided it with a musical background. It was first performed at Queen's Hall on 7 December 1914, recited by the poet's wife, Tita Brand, who was the daughter of the first *Gerontius* Angel, Marie Brema. Early in 1915 Elgar took the L.S.O. on a provincial tour performing *Carillon* in every town, with Constance Collier and sometimes Cammaerts himself as reciter. The work caught the mood of the moment. The patriotic fervour of the words, matched by fiery and where necessary gentle music, excited audiences to white-heat and, according to Dunhill, 'created a sensation in the concert-hall the like of which London can never have witnessed either before or since'. Henry Ainley and Réjane were among those who declaimed it. So, at private gatherings, were Schuster and Lalla Vandervelde, daughter of Edward Speyer and wife of a Belgian minister. It was at one of these private performances that Alice was reminded that England still had some way to go before it could call itself musical. She found the audience 'like old county family people who knew *nothing* of music. Old Lady Lurgan said occasionally "That is pretty".' The breed is not yet extinct. *Carillon* was so closely bound to the mood of the hour that its expectation of life was obviously short, although it was revived, with new words by Laurence Binyon, in the Second World War. But nothing could revive the spirit of 1914-15. Later in the war Elgar tried but failed to repeat the success of *Carillon* with two other Cammaerts recitations, *Une Voix dans le Désert* and *Le drapeau belge*. The former was conducted by Beecham whom Alice described as 'very phantasmagoric, & not appealing to us *at all*'. He drank water and wanted to be called Thomas. It seems hardly believable.

Elgar had found pleasure in London in his friendship with Colvin and Laurence Binyon, both of the British Museum staff. His lifelong

---

[1] In 1915 Elgar resigned from the Special Constabulary and joined the Hampstead Volunteer Reserve, the First World War equivalent of the Home Guard.

passion for books, especially the esoteric, endeared them to him and him to them. As we know from his letters to Jaeger, he liked the oddities of language and inventing words. He was delighted when Troyte Griffith told him of the cobbler's word 'unsqueaken' and even more pleased when Colvin passed it on to E. V. Lucas who used it in the novel *London Lavender*. Binyon gave Elgar a copy of his poems *The Winnowing Fan* which included the now famous 'For the Fallen'. He began work on three of the poems ('The Fourth of August', 'To Women', and 'For the Fallen') in 1915, but one evening at Queen's Hall, in casual conversation with the Cambridge composer Cyril B. Rootham, he discovered that Rootham was setting 'For the Fallen' and that Novello's had agreed to publish his setting. He wrote to Binyon on 24 March: 'I cannot tell you how sad I am about your poems: I feel I cannot proceed with the set as at first proposed & which I still desire to complete: but I saw Dr. Rootham, who merely wished to thank me for my "generous attitude" etc. & said very nice things about my offer to withdraw—but his utter disappointment, not expressed but shewn unconsciously, has upset me & I must decide against completing "For the Fallen". I have battled with the feeling for nearly a week but the sight of the other man comes sadly between me & my music. . . . I am going into the country & will see if I can make the other settings acceptable without the great climax.' Typically, to Alice Stuart-Wortley, he added the comment 'After all, nobody *wants* any real music.'

Binyon was bitterly disappointed and pleaded with Elgar, but Elgar was unmoved: 'There is only one publisher for choral music in England: Dr. Rootham was in touch with Novello first—my proposal made his MS waste paper & I could not go on—that's exactly a bald statement of the case.' Sidney Colvin took the line that Elgar was being unfair to Binyon and also received the comment that 'no one wants my music'. Colvin was having none of that. 'I think you take far too censorious and jaundiced a view of your countrymen,' he replied on 13 April. 'You cannot in your heart fail to believe that there is a big minority passionately sensitive to art, to whom your work makes all the difference in their lives.' Elgar replied to this with typical asperity: 'Some of my dear friends appeal to me to work in order that the people—musical people—may have something really good (that is complimentary to me and, inferentially, to the B.P. [British Public]— something they really want—well, they do not want me & never did. If I work at all it is not for them.' He consoled himself by concocting *Polonia*, an orchestral fantasia on Polish airs, for the conductor Emil Mlynarski. The proceeds of *Carillon* and *Polonia* went to Belgian and

Polish charities, so that Elgar made nothing from the success of the former. So many friends urged him to continue with 'For the Fallen' that by July he was at work on it again, though still deeply disturbed by the thought of Rootham. In the meantime, however, Rootham's setting was published. Elgar therefore felt himself at liberty to continue with his own work and its completion was announced in *The Times* in March 1916. Rootham was offended. He no longer had any right to be, but undoubtedly salt was rubbed in the wound when Elgar detached 'For the Fallen' and 'To Women' from the complete set and allowed them to be performed separately, with Clara Butt as soloist, at Leeds on 3 May 1916. On 8 May 'For the Fallen' received the first of six consecutive performances at the Queen's Hall, when Clara Butt, in aid of the Red Cross, sang in this and in *The Dream of Gerontius* each evening.

Elgar worked hard for music in these first years of the war. In addition to conducting the L.S.O., he offered his services to the Hallé in Manchester, saying: 'I am not a rich man but what you can give to me, give me.' Visits to Manchester must have given him a foretaste of the great change that had come over the world. Richter, retired and old in Germany, had renounced his British honours. Brodsky was interned in Vienna (though he was later released and returned to Manchester). It is said that when someone asked Beecham at a Royal Philharmonic meeting where all Elgar's friends had gone, Sir Thomas replied: 'They're all interned.' It was not wholly true, but true enough. Even so it is not correct to blame the end of Elgar's fame in Germany on the war. The conductors who had liked his music were of an older generation and had retired or died. There were new suns in the sky and Buths's success with *Gerontius* was a thing of the past. But in England no cloud as yet dimmed his reputation. His love for the theatre led him in 1915 to agree to provide music for a children's play, *The Starlight Express*, adapted from a tale by Algernon Blackwood, which Lena Ashwell was to produce at the Kingsway Theatre. At first he intended only to adapt *The Wand of Youth*, but though he quoted from it he provided a new score. Some of it, notably the *Organ Grinder's Songs*, has the typical charm of light Elgar. The play had a short run, which did not surprise Elgar who thought the adaptation poor and disapproved of the scenery. Then in 1917, a black year in the war—'I cannot do any real work with the awful shadow over us'—he set four Kipling poems, *The Fringes of the Fleet*, dedicated them to Lord Beresford,[1] and suggested that they should form part of the 'show' at the London Coliseum. They

---

[1] The admiral was created an English peer on 1 January 1916.

were a success and he toured the British provincial music-halls conducting them during August, September, October, and November. They
returned to the Coliseum where the 'act' came to an abrupt end when
Kipling rather belatedly objected to his poetry being performed in this
way. 'He is perfectly stupid in his attitude,' Elgar wrote to Alice
Stuart-Wortley. 'If I do happen to write something that "goes" with
the public and by which I look like benefiting financially, some perverse fate always intervenes and stops it immediately.' In the early part
of 1917 he had at last completed the Binyon settings, which he called
The Spirit of England. 'I fear I have been a very long time,' he wrote to
Binyon on 12 April, 'but the difficulty over the one poem last year put
me off somewhat & it has taken me all this time to overtake the first
care*ful* rapture.' The first complete performance was given at the
Royal Albert Hall on 24 November 1917, with Agnes Nicholls and
Gervase Elwes as the soloists.

This was Elgar's outward and 'official' life during the war. Privately
he was deeply unhappy and frequently ill. As often as he could he
escaped to Worcestershire or to the Lake District. In Worcestershire
he stayed with his sister Pollie (Mrs. Grafton) at Stoke Prior, near
Bromsgrove, and from there in November 1914 he wrote to Alice
Stuart-Wortley: 'Yesterday [12 November] I went to Worcester &
had the joy of sitting in the old library in the cathedral amongst the
MSS I have often told you of—the view down the river across to the
hills just as the monks saw it & as I have seen it for so many years—it
seems so curious, dear, to feel that I played about among the tombs &
in the cloisters when I cd. scarcely walk & now the Dean and canons
are so polite & shew me everything new, alterations, discoveries etc.
etc. It is a sweet old place, especially, to me, the library into which so
few go. I will take you in one day.' 'I am sick of towns,' he wrote to
Schuster in 1916. He wanted to be away from London 'for a long
time'. The constant entertaining at Severn House, however acceptable
the company, was a drain on his strength. He wilted, but Alice thrived.
('So nice to be in London again after Bradford's very local atmosphere,'
she wrote in her diary after staying with the Behrens family.) News of
deaths—of Steinbach and Richter in 1916, of his Uncle Henry in 1917,
and of George Sinclair—depressed him, and so did the war news. He
kept Sinclair's last letter on the desk before him.[1] It had been obvious

---

[1] This letter, dated 5 February 1917, begins: 'My dear Edward. I want to tell you about
a wonderful viola player who played at my recital last Thursday. I never heard anyone to
approach him. . . . His name is Lionel Tertis. It would be splendid if you could write
something for him to play. . . .'

since April 1916, when Elgar was taken ill on a train and spent three days in a nursing-home, that his nerves were strained to breaking-point. He was unwell for the rest of the year, the physical cause of his depression, illness, and occasional dizziness being Menière's disease of the ear which was not diagnosed for some time. As usual, he was also worried about the state of his finances. He was confined to bed in December 1916, when Alice Stuart-Wortley's husband Charles was raised to the peerage and became Lord Stuart of Wortley. 'I am out of bed,' he wrote to her on 20 December, 'and I use the first minute to send you love & congratulations on the event—I gave you a coronet long ago—the best I had but you may have forgotten it—now you will have a real one, bless you! . . . I feel afraid of you & wonder in a vague sort of way what will be the difference? But you are still the wind-flower I think & hope. . . . Everything pleasant & promising in my life is dead—I have the happiness of my friends to console me as I had fifty years ago. I feel that life has gone back as far when I was alone & there was no one to stand between me & disaster—health or finance—now that has come back & I am more alone and the prey of circumstances than ever before.' It is sad to think that he found no consolation in such a letter as the following, written by Schuster after a wartime bereavement, when he had attended a performance of the A flat Symphony:

As long as I have *it* [Elgar's music] I can bear my losses, although I thought when I went into the hall today that I *couldn't*. I felt then as I never have but as you, I fear, sometimes do—that life was not worth the living & I would not be sorry to lose it. Then came your symphony—and in a moment I knew I was wrong. In it is *all love*—and love makes life possible. I wonder if you realise when you feel despondent & embittered what your music is to me—and therefore to countless others? You may not care to be of use to those who live after you—but surely it must be *something* to you to know you are giving happiness & hope & consolation to your fellow creatures? Bless you for it anyway.

Elgar's letters to Alice Stuart-Wortley in the spring and summer of 1917 reveal the extent of his spiritual bleakness and his growing nostalgia for Worcestershire and an irrecoverable and perhaps imaginary past. Deprived by bad weather of a visit with his wife to Harrogate he wrote: 'I was dreaming of woods & fields . . . or a journey to Fountains or some lovely remembrance of long ago idylls, and now deep snow! Well, I have put it all in my music, & also much more that has never happened.' Alice Stuart-Wortley had been visiting his old haunts and he wrote: 'So you have been to B[roadheath]. I fear you did not find the cottage [his birthplace]—it is nearer the clump of scotch firs—I can smell them now—in the hot sun. Oh! how cruel that I was not there—

Elgar in the 1920s
With W. H. Reed

With Bernard Shaw

PLATE XI

PLATE XII

Elgar conducting massed choirs in Parry's *Jerusalem* at the opening of the British Empire Exhibition, Wembley, April 1924

there, nothing between that infancy & *now* and I *want* to see it. The
flowers are lovely—I knew you wd. like the heath. I could have shewn
you such lovely lanes.' Later: 'I am glad you "feel" Stoke [Prior].
That is a place where I see & *hear* (yes!) you. A. has not been there
since *1888* & does not care to go & no one of my friends has ever been
but you. No one has seen my fields & my "common" and my trees,
only the Windflower, and I found her namesakes growing there—
aborigines I'm sure—real pure sweet forest folk. Bless you.' In Chatham
in September 1917, on tour with *The Fringes of the Fleet*, he wrote to
her again: 'Alice & I are here—no performance last night. Terrible gun-
firing, raid etc. etc. . . . I am not well and the place is so noisy & I do not
sleep. The guns are the quietest things here. I long for the country &
Stoke. I think all the time of it—and you. I have been thinking also so
much of our lost festivals—no more music. . . . Everything good &
nice & clean & fresh & sweet is far away—never to return.'

Alice Elgar realized that his need to recapture the peace and solitude
of Birchwood was paramount. She and Carice found an oak-beamed
cottage, Brinkwells, near Fittleworth in Sussex, which answered the
need. 'It's *divine*,' Elgar wrote to Schuster, 'simple thatched cottage . . .
with wonderful view.' There was a studio in the garden in which he
could work and, best of all, there were woods in which he could walk
for hours. The cottage was small and isolated, on a hill overlooking the
Arun and the South Downs. Like Gladstone, he found delight in
chopping wood, and he learned to make hoops for barrels. Back in
London early in 1918 he was again ill. He went to the theatre, and
Lalla Vandervelde introduced him to Bernard Shaw—no doubt the
occasion of the outburst to Roger Fry[1]—but his old throat trouble was
now seriously aggravating him. In March a septic tonsil was removed,
an operation which caused him pain and discomfort. Both before and
after the operation he turned for relaxation to books and wrote to
Troyte Griffith in Malvern who shared his passion for reading. Passages from these letters give us some idea of Elgar's voracious and wide-
ranging literary appetite: 'I have always avoided Lafcadio Hearn but
have read his Lectures on Literature with the greatest joy. . . . Now I
have the Life and Letters which also interest me hugely. As to the
many Japanese books by Hearn I cannot stand 'em: I feel like E. V.
Lucas about Tagore. He says that some people admire the poems but
adds, "Me, they, for the most part, stump". I think the contempt conveyed by this purposely contorted sentence is really juicy. . . . Colvin's
Life of Keats is of course new and first class. Morley's Reminiscences,

[1] See p. 136.

Q

or whatever they are, first vol. good, second vol. too Indiany and dull. "Some Hawarden Letters" are interesting as shewing the hopeless mutual-admiration of the Gladstone party: some of the letters are really beneath contempt; Balfour-Browne has pubd. a book of Rems. also; not much good; slipshod sort of arrgt. . . .' 'I have read "South Wind" and enjoyed it; he N. Douglas is really clever and I regret that he doesn't write more carefully, the book is so slipshod and with talent like his so much more might be done. Get his book about "Calabria" and say what you think. . . .'

After convalescing for a few days in April at Schuster's, Elgar went for most of the rest of 1918 to Brinkwells. There he rapidly regained strength. He enjoyed the isolation and the peaceful routine which he described in a letter to Lady Stuart of Wortley written on 12 May 1918: 'I rise about *seven* work till 8-15—then dress, breakfast—pipe (I smoke again all day!) work till 12-30 lunch (pipe)—rest an hour— work till tea (pipe)—then work till 7-30—change, dinner at 8. Bed at 10—every day practically goes thus. . . . We go lovely walks . . . the woods are full of flowers, wonderful. . . . We will order the pony for you & I shall be at the station of course . . . the only thing to remember is that it is difficult to alter the pony arrgts. for conveyance as he—it—is in request. I am looking forward to your coming with acute joy: it really is lovely here—food good & plentiful—*much beer!*—but *do not mention it.*' A few days later he wrote again: 'The woods are still carpeted with bluebells but the heavy rain of three days ago tried them severely and they look rather faded: I have been down the wood & told them you are coming & asked them to remain for your loved visit. . . . You need bring very little of anything but if quite convenient some dry biscuits *might* be a joy as the stock in these villages . . . has run out for days: but the thing is to bring yourself & rest: there will be a full moon & all lovely & nightingales.' He was glad to hear the Allied advances had freed Percy Hull, who from 1896 (when he was eighteen) had been assistant to George Sinclair at Hereford until 1914 when he was interned while on a walking tour. 'You have had a dreadful time with those appalling Yahoos the Prussians,' Elgar wrote to him, 'and it is a mercy you have been allowed to leave their unsavoury clutches. . . . We shall welcome you home again with enthusiasm and I trust the post of organist in your own cathedral will be yours. I was only too glad to do what I could to further your claims, which I believe are generally recognised, but I do not pretend to understand the corkscrew minds of one at least of the people at Hereford.' A month later (1 July) he wrote to Schuster: 'High summer! and divine warmth which I know you enjoy with me. . . . I am better but not fit for the world & don't seem to want it—I get a few fish & read & *smoke* (praise be!) but there are only about six people I want to see & you are one—number one I mean, the rest follow. . . .'

In fact he was at work again. Elgar's creative spells followed a pattern. They were usually preceded by a period of acute depression. The *Variations* and *Gerontius* followed one such period; the bleak and despondent 1907 was followed by a burst of activity which produced two symphonies and a concerto; now, five years after *Falstaff* during which time he had written nothing of any substance and had withdrawn into solitude, the fires blazed up in him for the last time. While in the nursing-home for his operation he began to make sketches for the chamber music he had long wanted to write. On returning home he began a string quartet and a sonata, and then began a piano quintet too. At Brinkwells, Reed was a frequent visitor during the summer, and Elgar got him to play through the works as they proceeded. Alice was overjoyed. 'E. writing wonderful new music, different from anything else of his,' she wrote in her diary. 'A. calls it wood magic. So elusive and delicate.' The sonata was completed first and dedicated to Marie Joshua, an old friend of the Elgars. She died four days after he had inscribed her name on the score and he inserted a reminiscence of the slow movement before the coda of the finale in tribute to her memory. The work also contains other personal allusions. Alice Stuart of Wortley had broken her leg while at Tintagel in the late summer of 1918 and Elgar sent her some sketches of the sonata with this letter (11 September): 'The first movement is bold & vigorous, then a fantastic, curious movement with a very expressive middle section: a melody for the violin—they say it is as good as or better than anything I have done in the expressive way: this I wrote just after your telegram about the accident came & I send you the pencil notes as first made at that sad moment. . . . The last movement is very broad & *soothing* like the last movement of the IInd symphony. I have been sketching other things which are full of old times.' These 'other things' were the quartet and quintet on which work progressed in the intervals of woodcutting and bonfires. Alice's diary is especially valuable in regard to the quintet: 'Wonderful weird beginning—same atmosphere as "Owls"[1]—evidently reminiscence of sinister trees & impression of Flexham Park . . .'

---

[1] 'Owls' to words by Elgar, is No. 4 of the op. 53 part-songs written in Italy in 1907. Describing it to Jaeger (26 April 1908), Elgar wrote: 'It is only a fantasy & means nothing. It is in a wood at night evidently & the recurring "Nothing" is only an *owlish* sound.'

'Sad "dispossessed" trees & their dance & unstilled regret for their evil fate—or rather curse—wh. brought it on . . .' 'The sinister trees & their strange dance in it—then a wail for their sin—wonderful.' Flexham Park was near Fittleworth. A group of withered trees there was connected by the inhabitants with a fraternity of Spanish monks who had once lived there. While participating in some form of black magic they were, according to local legend, struck by lightning and turned into trees. This was the sort of lore that excited Elgar, who was in any case fascinated by trees, as we know from *Caractacus* and his exultant phrase to Jaeger, 'The trees are singing my music—or have I sung theirs?' W. H. Reed described the 'haunted' trees: 'with gnarled and twisted branches, bare of bark or leaves—a ghastly sight in the evening, when the branches seem to be beckoning and holding up gaunt arms in derision. . . . Their influence is also apparent in the Sonata (second movement) and the finale of the Quartet, in which there is a striking ponticello effect.'[1]

Sussex in its autumn uncertainty held Elgar in thrall, just as Worcestershire did. 'Here we have had much bad weather,' he wrote to Colvin, 'but the sunrises have been wonderful & quite made up for a lot of rain & gales: I have never seen anything so wonderful as the sun climbing over our view in golden mist. I see now where Turner found such sights as Norham Castle, etc.' That was written on 26 September. The following day Alice's diary refers to 'wonderful new music, real wood sounds & other lament wh. shd. be in a war symphony'. This new music, I feel sure, was the start of the Cello Concerto. A few days later the Elgars returned to Severn House which had been burgled in their absence. That night he composed the *moderato* theme of the first movement of the concerto, writing on the sketch: 'Very full, sweet and sonorous'. Alice and he attended Parry's funeral in St. Paul's Cathedral. On 15 October, Reed and Elgar played the Sonata to Schuster, Muriel Foster, the Colvins, Landon Ronald, and others. Writing for the piano had made him look again at his Piano Concerto and he showed it to Irene Scharrer, promising her the first performance. The war was obviously drawing to an end and Colvin and Binyon tried to interest him in setting an ode about peace which Binyon had written. Elgar's letter to Binyon on 5 November 1918 is of prime importance in a consideration of the mood in which he began work on the Cello Concerto: 'I think your poem beautiful exceedingly—but I do not feel drawn to write peace music somehow—I thought long

[1] Article on Elgar's chamber music in Cobbett's *Cyclopaedic Survey of Chamber Music*, (Second Edition, London, 1963).

months ago that I could feel that way & if anything could draw me your poem would, but the whole atmosphere is too full of complexities for me to feel music to it: not the atmosphere of the poem but of the time I mean. The last two divisions VI and VII are splendid altho' I regret the appeal to the Heavenly Spirit which is cruelly obtuse to the individual sorrow & sacrifice—a cruelty I resent bitterly & disappointedly.'

Later Elgar reconsidered the ode and wanted to set it, but he never did. He returned to Brinkwells on Armistice Day and showed Reed the early sketches of the Cello Concerto. He and Alice were both rather forlorn figures at this time. The burglary had upset them; it was becoming obvious that Severn House was much too expensive to run and would have to be sold or Brinkwells would have to be given up. Alice had not been well after a minor operation. 'My poor dear Alice is better now,' he wrote to Colvin on 21 November. '. . . I have commenced music again & hope to proceed: the axe however claims me & I make huge fires in the wood, meanly delighting in the fact that I can burn more than anyone I know—a frame of mind I am ashamed of in the cold hours.' The parallel with Millais must inescapably be drawn, the Millais of 'Autumn Leaves' and his saying about bonfires: 'Nothing brings back sweeter memories of the days that are gone; it is the incense offered by departing summer to the sky.' The Elgars' summer had departed. At the end of the year they returned to Hampstead for a run-through of parts of the Quartet and Quintet but the prospect did not please Elgar. 'It means another interruption,' he told Schuster, '& the future is *dark* as A. poor dear is not well & of course is bored to death here while I am in the seventh heaven of delight: so we may only return here to clear up—we shall see. But it seems that if I have to live again at Hampstead composition is "off"—not the house or the place but *London*—telephone etc. all day and night drives me mad.'

The first performance of the Sonata was given by Reed and Anthony Bernard at a meeting on 13 March 1919 of the British Music Society, yet another organization to promote British music. It had been formed in June 1918 by Arthur Eaglefield Hull, and E. J. Dent and Bernard Shaw were prominent participants. The first public performance was on 21 March, by Reed and Landon Ronald, at the Aeolian Hall. Elgar had not liked the music at the morning rehearsal and was with difficulty persuaded to attend the concert. The critics' response was cautious and reserved. But before this there had been private performances of the Quintet, one of which Shaw had attended. He wrote to Elgar afterwards (8 March 1919), and it was after this that their acquaintance turned into firm friendship. 'The Quintet knocked me over at once,' he wrote. 'I said to myself, with the old critic's habit of making phrases for publication, that this was the finest thing of its kind since *Coriolan*. I don't know why I associated the two; but I did: there was the same quality—the same vein. Of course you went your own way presently. There are some piano embroideries on a pedal point that didn't sound like a piano or anything else in the world, but quite beautiful, and I have my doubts whether any regular shop pianist will produce them: they require a touch which is peculiar to yourself, and which struck me the first time I ever heard you larking about with a piano.'[1]

Shaw also entered a 'solemn protest' about the fugue: 'You cannot begin a movement in such a magical way as you have begun the Quintet and then suddenly relapse into the expected.' There is a considerably mollified reminder in this letter of the Corno di Bassetto whose writings in the 1880s and 1890s Elgar had enjoyed and remembered: the astuteness in spotting the weakness of the fugal section and the unconventional, though not entirely unpianistic, writing for the pianoforte. At any rate this work and the Quartet were warmly received when they were first played in public at a Wigmore Hall concert (in which the Sonata was included) on 21 May 1919, given by William Murdoch (piano) with the British String Quartet (Albert Sammons, W. H. Reed, Raymond Jeremy, and Felix Salmond). Elgar had invited Salmond to give the first performance of the Cello Concerto and asked him down to Brinkwells that summer to work with him. 'I am frantically busy writing,' he wrote to Colvin on 26 June, '& have nearly completed a Concerto for Violoncello—a real large work & I think *good* & alive. It is impossible to say when it will appear or be heard—probably next winter. Would Frances & you allow me to put on the title page To Sidney and Frances Colvin? Your friendship is such a real & precious thing that I should like to leave some record of it; I cannot say the music is worthy of you both (or either!) but our three names wd. be in print together even if the music is dull & of the kind which perisheth.' On 23 July he wrote to Alice Stuart: 'I am arranging the next bit of the violoncello concerto for piano & writing it out fair—which I detest.' On 3 August he told her that Salmond and he had 'polished' the concerto and he added: 'I want to finish or rather

---

[1] Writing to Lady Stuart of Wortley about the Sonata, Elgar said (1 October 1918): 'I have *struggled* hard to make my piano passages fit other fingers—& I wanted help in this direction.'

commence the piano concerto which *must* be windflowerish so I hope
you will come but somehow I know you will not.'

The first performance of the Cello Concerto was at Queen's Hall on
26 October. Elgar was to conduct it. The rest of the concert—Scriabin's
Poème de l'Extase and Borodin's Second Symphony—was conducted
by Albert Coates. The events at the rehearsal were a permanent disgrace to British music. Coates was at that time fervently championing
Scriabin's cause, and he continued rehearsing for an hour after the time
when it had been agreed that Elgar should take over the rostrum. The
greatest English composer of his age was kept waiting as he had been
thirty years before when he was unknown. If he had not put Salmond's
reputation first, Elgar might have withdrawn from the concert. Members of the orchestra, which included a nineteen-year-old cellist, John
Barbirolli, would not have blamed him if he had walked out. The performance was a disaster and the audience's response politely cordial.
Alfred Kalisch, who had heard all the major Elgar first performances,
wrote in the *Musical Times* of December 1919 '. . . an important new
work by our foremost living composer . . . did not suffice to fill the
hall to overflowing, and . . . was obviously under-rehearsed'. *The
Daily Telegraph* dismissed the occasion in a few lines, complaining of
'a lack of exaltation' and lack of surprise. A 'godsend to players on the
violoncello' was the best the writer could muster. Ernest Newman
fixed the blame where it belonged, writing that the orchestra 'made a
lamentable public exhibition of itself'.

It is, of course, understandable that the public should have been
puzzled by the contrast between the pre-war Elgar of the symphonies
and Violin Concerto and the end-of-war Elgar of the three chamber
works and the Cello Concerto. Autumn had indeed followed high
summer. The colours were browner, the days were shorter and the
composer himself was tired and growing old. The works have their
virtues, they are all moving, but it seems to me that they show un-
mistakable signs of the decline of Elgar's creative gift in a lack of im-
mediacy in the material and its treatment. This deficiency is not transformed into a virtue in itself, except in the Concerto. The Sonata for
violin and pianoforte is almost casual in its leisurely treatment of
lyrical but not strikingly effective tunes. The central Romance has a
Southern flavour, recalling as do all three chamber works, the Elgar of
his youthful days. Perhaps that is why Alice Elgar had a close affection
for the Quartet. It is the most consistent in mood. Its hesitant, autumnal
(the word is inescapable) opening is a typically Elgarian tune, promising much. But the movement soon deteriorates into sequential

development; attempts to re-energize the music sink into lassitude. The slow movement, marked *Piacevole, poco andante*, has this beautiful and intimate theme:

Ex. 10

p dolce
2nd Violin

It is fresh and 'smiling with a sigh'. But, until the memorable coda, there is much in the movement to justify belief that the quotation from *Chanson de matin* was not an unconscious reminiscence. The finale is the finest movement, with vivid themes best suited to the medium and a toughness of fibre that refutes the charge of excess of sentiment invited by the remainder of the work. The Piano Quintet is the most ambitious of the chamber music, unlike the Quartet in character, being impulsive and exuberant. Again in only three movements, it is of large design, with an air of magniloquence that almost recalls the music of ten years before. Its mysterious and romantic opening is arresting, foretelling richness to come. The Adagio is the finest movement—Elgar thought the whole work was one of his best —expansive, ripe, and eloquent of the deep disturbances that were shaking the composer. The marvellous tune for the viola and sudden and dramatic use of pizzicato are Elgar at his best. The Quintet has a tinge of bitterness, even steeliness, for all its romanticism, which gives it strength. The piano is treated as one among equals except at moments of climax, when it has a quasi-concerto rôle. Elgar used cyclic form as a unifying factor. The work's weakness, as Shaw realized, was in the fugue, which has none of the unconventional brilliance of its forerunner in the *Introduction and Allegro*, but the finale, impetuous and magniloquent, is finely organized. None of these three works has yet established itself in the repertory, and on the whole I cannot feel that, except in the case of the Quintet, any severe injustice has been done. Many better sonatas and quartets by English composers are equally and more unforgivably neglected. Because Elgar's are by Elgar, they are to be cherished by his devotees and occasionally revived, but for all their moments of splendour, they are not first-rank Elgar, let alone first-rank music.

The Cello Concerto, however, like the Quintet, is first-rank, and is generally rated among his masterpieces. This is not to say that it is without its problems. Of all Elgar's orchestral works it is the most elusive and withdrawn, the most subdued in its orchestral dress. The rhetorical flourish for the soloist with which it opens—a moment akin to the opening of the *Introduction and Allegro*—soon subsides into a long, deceptively simple tune which needs as skilful a judgement of its tempo as does the opening of Brahms's Fourth Symphony if it is not to sound merely weary instead of numbed with despair. This is overpoweringly the music of wood smoke and autumn bonfires, of the evening of life; sadness and disillusion are dominant and the music comes perilously close to what Jaeger would have called a 'whine' of self-pity. As in the symphonies, this emotional element is conveyed by shifts of tonality and in addition by a certain harmonic austerity. The scherzo's brightness of mood sounds forced ('the heart dances, but not for joy'): there is an air of unreality and fantasy about the cello's tessitura, the use of pizzicato, and the woodwind scoring. In the very lovely adagio there is no attempt to disguise the melancholy: a short, sustained, songful lamentation, the music of a broken heart. And although the finale rattles the skeleton of the old, swaggering, rumbustious Elgar, the high spirits are short-lived. Chromatic string harmonies make the tragedy unequivocal. Following Dvořák's pattern, Elgar recalls a theme from the slow movement, and the music assumes a nihilist note that is unequalled in intensity elsewhere in his output, surpassing even the note of agony and ruin in *Gerontius*. The opening recitative returns, plunges to the depths and the work ends in almost indecent haste as if too much has been revealed. It is sometimes said that this Concerto is Elgar's war requiem but the phrase, accurate in some respects, needs clarification. He was an egocentric artist, and the requiem here is not so much for the dead in Flanders fields as for the destruction of a way of life. With an artist's vision, he saw that 1918 was the end of a civilization. Here, rather than in the finale of the Second Symphony, is the elegy for an age. The slaughter of war, whether of men or horses, had grieved Elgar, but this requiem is not a cosmic utterance on behalf of mankind, it is wholly personal, the musical expression of his bitterness about the providence that was 'against great art' and the Heavenly Spirit that was 'cruelly obtuse' to individual sorrow and sacrifice. There is no 'massive hope for the future' in this music, only the voice of an ageing, embittered man, a valediction to an era and to the powers of music that he knew were dying within him. For the paradox is that whereas this Cello Concerto bears the marks of a faltering inspiration, this very uncertainty of invention is used to advantage to create a marvellous impression of a relaxed and epigrammatic change of style. With his superb technical resource and, once again, perfect understanding of the instrument, Elgar created one of the great cello works of the world, surpassed only by Dvořák's for its exploitation of the instrument's capacity for expressive melody and surpassing it in exploration of its more bizarre and playful characteristics. The orchestra used is the same size as that employed for the Violin Concerto but it is scaled down to allow the cello always to dominate the score. To all intents and purposes this concerto was Elgar's last word. It was a word of resignation, but it was also a farewell to beauty in music of poignant pathos. Of *Gerontius* he had said: 'This is the best of me.' He could equally well now have said: 'This is the last of me.'

The cry of anguish that rends the finale of the Concerto might almost have been a moment of vision. Only Mahler, with the hammer-blows of destiny in his Sixth Symphony, has foretold so accurately in music his own immediate fate. After the first performance Elgar went to conduct his own works with Mengelberg's Concertgebouw Orchestra in Amsterdam. Thence he went to Brussels where Lalla Vandervelde's husband had arranged that he should be honoured in gratitude for *Carillon*. He was shown the battlefields and the new buildings— 'shoddy ugly & degraded', he described the latter to Troyte. 'The suburbs of, say, Wigan are noble compared to these atrocities. The Belgians swagger & do nothing but eat & drink—have forgotten the war. . . .' He returned in mid-November to find that Alice was ordered by her doctor to stay indoors. She had been ill, he told Binyon, since 2 November, but it was not considered serious. He left her in Hampstead while he went north to conduct Kilburn's choir. After Christmas they decided to sell Severn House, and now Elgar was irritated by prospective buyers who came to look it over. 'Every ring of the bell plunged poor Elgar into melancholy,' Reed recorded,[1] 'and if he heard the ring followed by the shuffling of strange feet . . . he ran out of the house incontinently by a side-door that had been used by the previous tenant [Edwin Long] as an entrance and exit for his models.' They hoped they might be able to buy, instead of rent, Brinkwells. He was looking over his sketches for the third oratorio but he had no real work on hand. He might have been expected to contribute to the ceremony for the unveiling of the Cenotaph in Whitehall but he took no part. 'I fear (private) the Cenotaph affair will not include me,' he told Alice Stuart of Wortley in January 1920. 'The *present* proposals are vulgar & commonplace to the *last degree*. I really cannot appear in it!' The same letter refers to Alice having 'a fresh cold & is a notably poor thing—it is very wearing'. 'My poor dear A. does not rid of the tiresome cough,'

[1] *Elgar*, p. 129.

he told Colvin on 5 February when he wrote to express his delight at
being elected to the select membership of the Literary Society (probably on the strength of his remarkable and erudite long letter on the
'Quadruple Alliance' of Horace Walpole, Gray, West, and Ashton
published in *The Times Literary Supplement* of 4 September 1919).
Other honours came at this time: membership of the Accademia in
Florence and of the French Académie des Beaux-Arts; he was elected
to the Council of the Royal College of Music. These were compensa-
tions for Alice in her disappointment over Severn House. But she
received the greatest pleasure on 16 March, when a thirty-year-old
conductor hardly known in London, Adrian Boult, conducted a magnificent performance at Queen's Hall of the Second Symphony, revealing
for the first time the work's true stature. She went a week later to hear
the three chamber works. Elgar had begun, after thirty years, to keep
a diary and that night he wrote: 'Thoughts of the 30 (weary fighting)
years of her help and devotion.' He, too, must have noticed, like Reed,'
that she was getting 'mysteriously smaller and more fragile. She seemed
to be fading away before one's very eyes.' On 25 March she took to
her bed. Her last visitor was Muriel Foster. On 6 April, Elgar wrote to
Schuster, 'I tried to be frivolous yesterday but I am heartbroken: our
poor little dear one is inarticulate and can understand nothing. It is too
awful. Pity *us* more than her even.' In the evening of 7 April Alice
Elgar died. She was seventy-one.

Elgar was stunned. Landon Ronald went to stay with him; Schuster
and Carice made the arrangements for the funeral at St. Wulstan's,
Little Malvern, and asked Reed's string quartet to play the slow movement of the Quartet at the service. Elgar stayed for the rest of the month
in Worcestershire, at Little Malvern and at Stoke Prior. In letters to
Schuster he poured out his woe:

[12 April] . . . We can see the little grave in the distance & nothing cd. be
sweeter & lovelier, only birds singing & all *remote* peace brought closely to us. I
cannot thank you for the quartet—it was exactly right & just what she wd.
have loved . . . the boys played like angels. . . . The place she chose long years
ago is too sweet—the blossoms are white all round it & the illimitable plain. . . .
[17 April] I am doing my best here. . . . Juno seems to know that something is
wrong & never leaves me—such wonderful things are dogs. Here [Stoke Prior]
my dear A. never came so I can bear the sight of the roads & fields. . . . After 37
years my poor old sister may have to turn out—everything being sold—&
although the 70 acres or so of land has been let with anr. farm for more than
200 years the new rich refuse to sell the house & paddock separately—after 200
years! . . . So I am in a sad house. The same fate is due on May 1 for my poor

old *eldest* sister—stone deaf etc. her little house has been bought 'over their heads' & she is turned out—nowhere to go! So you see I am unhappy. You write to me of my music, etc. like the good fellow you are. . . . Don't talk to me of achievement. I drank spider juice for my mother's sake, went thro' penurious times to buy my dear wife a car for her old age—1 failed of course. . . . But Juno's nose presses against me & says a walk is near.

He returned to Severn House at the beginning of May, and wrote to Walford Davies: 'All I have done was owing to her and I am at present a sad and broken man—just stunned. . . . I cry out "Leave me with my dead"—and creatures have to come in and count over her pretty valueless little rings and the most private things to see what they are worth—it drives me to distraction, and I am no fit company for human beings.' After his death, among his papers was found a sheet of notepaper on which he had written the date of Alice's death and these lines by Swinburne:

> Let us go hence, my songs; she will not hear,
> Let us go hence together without fear;
> Keep silence now, for singing-time is over,
> And over all old things and all things dear.

His friend Ernest Newman, to whom he had dedicated the Piano Quintet, commented on Elgar's bereavement in a letter to his wife Vera on 7 April 1920.[1] 'I am sad today over the death of Lady Elgar,' he wrote. 'I am very fond of Edward, and I know that, whatever people may say, to a man of his fine and sensitive nature, the severance of a long tie like this must inevitably mean much bitterness and suffering, much dwelling in the past and self-reproach. We always seem heavy debtors to the dead: we feel they have not had their chance and that life has given us an unfair advantage over them. . . .'

[1] Vera Newman, *Ernest Newman: A Memoir* (London, 1963), p. 18.

13 Submission

The last fourteen years of Elgar's life are a long and slow diminuendo. Towards the end, the old energy tried to reassert itself but it was too late: by then, not only the mind but the body was tired. He did not retreat from the world and shut himself away after Alice's death, but her departure from the scene hastened the process of creative decline which can be detected from *Falstaff* onwards. When he returned to 'cold and empty' Severn House he found interest and amusement in his microscopes and in games of billiards with his old friend and benefactor, Hugh Blair, whom he had never deserted in the hard times which had come upon him. Elgar's life from now onwards could almost take as its motto the passage from *Antony and Cleopatra*: ' "The music, ho!" "Let it alone; let's to billiards".' There was no one to encourage him to work, to rule the barlines, to post the manuscript to the publishers, to remind him by her devotion of her faith in his music. Yet the decline of interest in his work which was to add its discouraging force to the other pressures upon him had not in 1920 gathered momentum. The reverse was true. Shaw's article in the first issue of *Music and Letters* had given him a rare accolade: 'Elgar is carrying on Beethoven's business. . . . Elgar alone is for Westminster Abbey.' In the same number a critic and composer of the younger generation, Philip Heseltine (Peter Warlock), praised the symphonies and called for more performances. Boult's performance of No. 2 had been a major event, and Elgar himself was due to conduct it at Cardiff in the South Wales Festival organized by Lord Howard de Walden and Cyril Jenkins, a pupil of Stanford and composer of some choral works which Elgar thought 'very good'. He decided to keep the engagement, as he had also kept one to conduct *The Apostles* at Newcastle upon Tyne. Fortunately the *Manchester Guardian* sent Langford to Cardiff, so that we have a contemporary view of the occasion by one who had signally failed to respond to the symphony in 1911.[1] Now things were changed: 'Small as the audience was, the composer could not have had a more enthusiastic or more cordial reception. His recent bereavement gave also an additional note of solemnity, and the appropriateness could not but be felt with the beauty of each passing movement. . . . In the

[1] See Chapter 11.

experimental performances before the war the thing would not rise, and though the players laboured with it the result remained heavy and comparatively lifeless. How different today. The music really seems to inhabit the air. . . . Harshness there was none. We learn afresh, from such a work, to prize our emotions of beauty. The composer has not set himself to be austere, but the lines of beauty are so clearly conceived that the music shines, the sun glistening on its wings as it passes with a touch so light that the intensity of our delight is as quick as tears.'

The First Symphony was included in a London concert in June 1920, given by the New York Philharmonic Orchestra conducted by Walter Damrosch. Elgar did not attend, but Damrosch wrote to tell him that the applause was so tumultuous that he had lifted the score from the desk and pointed to it 'to show to whom the real tribute was due'. Yet these plaudits had a hollow sound for Elgar. He was looking for a purchaser for Severn House; the landlord of Brinkwells had changed his mind and decided not to sell the cottage to him; Alice's estate was being settled, with Schuster's ready help as a trustee. 'C[arice]. & I have now a comfortable two hundred a year! and anything I can make—but that cannot be much now; my race is run,' he wrote to Schuster on 2 July. But to Alice Stuart of Wortley he confided (18 July): 'Frank gives a rosy picture of our finances as he had to sign some papers being a trustee but (as I told him) he knows *nothing* of the affairs (money left dear A. for life) outside the one trust he is in: I fear he is unwittingly making out things much better than they are. My friends always remind me of the gillie who said to Dr. Johnson (when he was nearly dead riding over the moors) by way of encouraging & amusing him "Oh! such pretty goats!" That's about all they say.' This same letter, from Brinkwells, gives a frank self-portrait of Elgar at this time: ill and lonely. 'I have had *three* more slight attacks [of dizziness] & do not like the outlook at all: I take no notice of the conditions only I have to lie down for a day or two. . . . Music I loathe—I did get out some paper, but it's all dead. . . . The old life is over & everything seems blotted out. . . . It seems odd that Stoke [his sister Pollie's farm at Stoke Prior] was advertised last Saturday week (the sale)—the *same* day Birchwood Lodge (our old Worcester cottage) advertised & *sold*—I wanted it, & then in *Country Life same day*!! all the Wye fishing where I used to lie & fish & write & dream & where you & I walked once. Does it not seem strange that the *three* only havens of rest, to which in my busy life I have always fled for comfort & rest, should all be sold in the same week? Strange such a clean sweep of my old life. . . . I am "numb", I could not have borne the many memories but they have cut down the woods [near Brinkwells] so much & made a road etc. which alters the look of the place but of course dear A. *made* it & it is full of remembrances—too too sad for words. One odd thing I must tell you: in the shelter which Mark [a handyman] built for her & which I do not allow anyone to use, touch or look at, a wren has built a nest just where A's head used to touch the roof-twigs. Muriel [Foster] always called her the Little Wren so it seems pitifully curious. Now, my dear W. do not think we are gloomy—far from it; but everything in life has changed—I, to all intents and purposes, am an invalid—you see the stronger I get (& I am fairly well) the worse my ear is—if I am low in health & unable to get about, my ear is less troublesome; so there it is—in a vicious circle.'

He went for a short visit to his old friends the Speyers at Ridgehurst but things were changed there too. 'I cannot say that I appreciate the influx of *Germans*,' he told Alice Stuart. 'The —s (now Americans) came over & Frank, also some extraordinary females, friends of the youth whom F. introduces as his *nephew*—are we all mad! After this, *what*? Then at Ridgehurst we had a German lady & her daughter who sang to the Germans in Brussels!!! . . . About Stoke—I asked a millionaire friend—I descended so low—& begged he wd. save it: he sympathised & sent an agent who reported it wd. only *pay four per cent* —so my friend cd not entertain it!!! That is the end: the public have all my best work for nothing & I have not one single friend who cares— except you! My whole past is wiped out & I am quite alone. . . . I am glad you played the Cello Concerto—I have forgotten it . . . there is absolutely nothing left in the world for me. . . . It is useless to pretend to a real friend—Int he midst of it all I am not really depressed—only I see the inevitable. . . . I hear nothing of anyone & do not write at all— in fact I have "gone out"—& like it.'

W. H. Reed gave him companionship and Elgar wrote many letters to Troyte whom he had asked to design a headstone for Alice's grave: 'I fear the arms must be on a lozenge; Boutell says "A Lozenge takes the place of a shield to bear the arms of Ladies, *with the sole exception of the Sovereign*". That seems conclusive. . . . Could the motto "Fortiter et fide" go in: it suited dear A. so well.' When Schuster first visited the grave in 1923 and wrote his approval of the stone, on which the inscription begins 'Pray for the soul of Lady Elgar . . .', Elgar replied (23 September): 'I know quite well that it is incorrect to put *Lady*—it should be Dame but in these days polluted by all sorts of awful women now *Dames* I would not let myself put the desecrated word. My God! Clara B. and Melba in the same world, either this or the next, with Alice!!'

He went to Worcester in September for the first post-war Three

Choirs Festival, staying quietly in the house in the Cathedral precincts where his Uncle Henry had lived for many years until his death in 1917. This saddened him and he shunned social gatherings. He conducted *Gerontius*, 'For the Fallen' *The Music Makers*, and the *Introduction and Allegro*. Not only was his mind full of his nearest loss: Parry and Sinclair were commemorated, too, and the war dead. 'A glorious week', he called it to Schuster, and afterwards to Alice Stuart he wrote: 'I like to think of the Worcester days & you & the flowers & the fruit & the warm sun & my cathedral & the music: but it *is* lonely.' To the Colvins he confided his memories of a happy past at Brinkwells—'a past gone, shattered. I am . . . a sad, sad man & not fit for company. I could not see you two dears—Kreisler came & I went out to see him but no more, & I felt that I was no longer "in" the world, or rather that the old artistic "striving" world exists for me no more; so my one short attempt at life was a failure. . . . Inscrutable nature goes on just the same—young larks, six, in a nest on the lawn, & many other birds; nightingales sing; but I miss the littlest gentlest presence & I cannot go on.'

Christmas in 1920 was especially trying—'this horrible season of Christmas—I always loathed it,' he wrote to Frances Colvin on 30 December. He had stayed at Kempsey and had taken his relatives to lunch at an hotel at Stratford upon Avon that he used to know. What he found disgusted him, he told Lady Colvin—'under new management, *U.S.A.* I believe. A three weeks carnival at Christmas, a *Jazz Band specially engaged*—dances every night—the whole place "booked-up" with an abandoned set of filthy wretches! I have known S-on-A since 1869 and wish it cd. have been spared—we did not honour Shakespeare in this way in those sweet old years. Think of a Jazz Band.' Describing the same events to Alice Stuart he added: 'There goes another (I think the last) of my peaceful poetic old haunts.'

But if he would not go to the world, the world went to him. He was host to several musicians and composers, among them the brilliant young violinist Jascha Heifetz, for whom he polished up a very early violin study 'for strengthening the third finger'. He now saw more of Ernest Newman, whom he and his daughter very much liked but who had been *persona non grata* with Alice from about 1905 because of his criticisms of the oratorios. He went to conduct in Amsterdam and Brussels (where he was made a member of the Belgian Ordre de la Couronne by King Albert) and he spoke at a London banquet for Landon Ronald. He was introduced by Robert Nichols to Siegfried Sassoon and to Arnold Bennett who was later to describe him as 'a disgruntled old man'. In January 1921 he sustained the 'ghastly shock' of

Gervase Elwes's tragic death when he accidentally fell beneath a train at
Boston, Massachusetts. As he told Percy Hull, 'apart from the acute
sorrow at losing so good & great a gentleman & so great an artist, we
must both feel that his loss is a severe thing for the festival . . . my
personal loss is greater than I can bear to think upon but this is nothing
—or I must call it so—compared to the general artistic loss—a gap
impossible to fill—in the musical world'. This was the time when he felt
he might complete the trilogy, but he never went beyond playing over
his old sketches. On the first anniversary of Alice's death he wrote to
Frances Colvin, 'Yes, it is a year ago; I have tried everything but with
no result save that I can do no more and, for the first time in my life, I
am "running away"!' 'I have tried to take up the old life,' he wrote
to Colvin from Brinkwells in July, 'but it will not do and so there's an
end. I feel like these woods—all aglow—a spark wd. start a flame—but
no human spark comes.' And a month later, in another letter to Colvin,
he said: 'There is no work left for me to do: my active creative period
began under the most tender care and it ended with that care. All my
friends, dear though they may be, seem rough, violent, and in most
cases *coarse* in comparison—no more.' He joined gleefully with Troyte
in deriding an article Troyte had sent him in which Hope Bagenal
wrote about the effect of church acoustics on choral music: 'I shewed
the art: to Hull & we both laughed at the notion of the brass being
more "harsh"—the effect of the large nave, especially Worc: & Glouc:
cathedrals is to enhance the "round" tone; if the writer had heard
Beethoven's *Engedi* he wd. perhaps have learnt something.' He wrote
another learned letter to the *Times Literary Supplement* about references
to Shakespeare in Scott's novels. He was delighted by Norman Allin's
singing of Judas at a run-through of *The Apostles* in preparation for the
1921 Hereford Festival. Such artistry compensated for an opinion he
had expressed a month earlier in a letter to William Starmer, conductor and organist at Tunbridge Wells: 'I am not a song writer . . .
my best songs are not sung for the reason that they require *"breath"*—
the modern singers seem to emulate young terriers and prefer a staccato
falsetto bark which is not pleasing to me—so I think you may safely
avoid my productions.' He took a delight in the success of Percy Hull's
first Three Choirs Festival as Hereford conductor. He had recommended Holst's *Hymn of Jesus* to him and hoped the choice was
financially justified—'we all detest the Box Office but we all have to
bow down to it even if we cannot worship it'. He was always warmed
to life by friendship and devotion, and these he received from Hull. He
was warmed, too, by his growing closeness to Shaw who had heard

R

Falstaff for the first time and had written to him enthusiastically: 'Talk of *Till Eulenspiegel* or *Don Quixote*! This ought to be played three times to their once. Composing operas is mere piffle to a man who can do *that*.' 'I don't think we should have "liked" Aristophanes personally,' Elgar wrote to Colvin on 13 December 1921, 'or Voltaire (perhaps) but I cannot do without their works. G. B. S.'s politics are to me appalling but he is the kindest-hearted, gentlest man I have met outside the charmed circle which includes you.' He orchestrated Bach's Fugue in C minor, telling Eugène Goossens that he depended on 'people like John Sebastian' for inspiration now that his wife was dead and he could not be original. He finished the score in May 1921, telling Lady Stuart: 'I think it is *brilliant*—a word I wanted in connection with Bach, who, in arrangements, is made "pretty" etc. etc.' During August he left Brinkwells for the last time and in September prepared to leave Severn House and 'go forth into the world alone as I did forty-three years ago—only I am disillusioned and old'. He took a flat in St. James's Place and also became a member of Brooks's, which he liked because it was 'real XVIII century & full of memories of Fox etc. etc'. On 15 October he wrote one of his last letters from Severn House to Alice Stuart, who had been instrumental in finding it for him. 'I could not help feeling until about really I think a few weeks ago that my dear A. wd. be sure to come back & take charge of things. I cannot explain but I never touched anything without feeling—I cannot say *thinking*, one doesn't think—that I was responsible to her for every movement. Now I feel the desolation & hopelessness of it all & curiously, feel more satisfied—not happy but *calmer* over the situation. It must be. With all my artistic stupidity I have always been in other peoples' troubles the strong man—but I failed for myself & no one did anything to help. Selah! The end of Severn House was more *radiant* than the beginning.' To Troyte Griffith he wrote, 'Now I know & submit.'

*   *   *

'I submit.' Was this an echo of the letter to Jaeger after the failure of *Gerontius*? In this case, however, the reaction was not an original piece of music like *Cockaigne*. Five days after he wrote to Troyte, his transcription of the Bach fugue was conducted at Queen's Hall by Eugène Goossens. ('The conductor sat a little heavily on it—no champagne,' he told Alice Stuart.) Its free-ranging and romantic approach caused some controversy. Neo-classicism was in the air; a purer, more authentic approach to Bach was gaining ground. It was a significant pointer. Goossens was one of two composers whom Elgar recommended in

December 1920 to Herbert Brewer in response to Brewer's request for advice about young British composers who might provide new works for the 1922 Gloucester Festival. The other recommendation was Arthur Bliss,[1] whose early string quartet Elgar and Alice had heard and liked in 1916. 'It would be a first-class thing for the festivals to get in real new blood and away from the heavy dullness of the—well, you know,' he wrote to Brewer. 'Whatever they do has some vitality and grip. . . . These young men will . . . do away with the remnant of the notion that everything must be a sort of Ch. of E. propaganda.' Brewer hoped for a new work from Elgar, too, but was disappointed. 'I only regret the appearance of my own name so often,' was his comment on the inclusion of *The Apostles*, *The Kingdom*, and 'For the Fallen'. 'I cannot yet see my way to writing. The upset in my life has been too great.' All that Brewer got from him was the full transcription of the Bach C minor *Fantasy and Fugue* (the *Fantasy* being added to the already completed *Fugue*). The young men he helped were grateful. Bliss wrote to him of 'the fine and rare encouragement your presence is' and Bax dedicated a string quartet to him, but he never went to hear it. How interested he really was in their music is problematical. He did not, as Vaughan Williams did when he attained a similar pre-eminence in English music, attend almost every first performance of a new English work. The truth is that, like Delius, he was not very interested in the work of his contemporaries and juniors. He helped people he liked as men rather than as musicians, as in the case of Bantock, or because he thought they had had a raw deal, like Holbrooke. In 1898 he had been a generous champion of Coleridge-Taylor, but by January 1900 he was writing to Jaeger: 'I think you are right about C. Taylor—I was cruelly disillusioned by the overture to Hiawatha which I think really only "rot" . . . his later work is insincere & cannot do any real good.' The only really enthusiastic compliments he ever paid to other English composers were to Edward German and, in his last months, to Delius.

But by giving a helping-hand to the new generation he seemed to be emerging from his numbed state of grief. He was able to tell Schuster in January 1922 that he had been to hear Thibaud and Cortot play his Sonata, had taken Edith Evans out to dinner, and had 'brought the house down' with his remark at a social gathering that 'It seems if you scratch the Russian Ballet you get the Tartar emetic.' Like many others, he was irritated by the balletomanes. In January 1922, his daughter Carice was married to Samuel Blake, and he spent more of his time in his clubs, where he entertained the theatre folk—Squire Bancroft.

[1] The works concerned in 1922 were Bliss's *Colour Symphony* and Goossens's *Silence*.

Seymour Hicks, Granville Barker—whose company he found so agreeable, particularly that of Norman Forbes, brother of Sir Johnston Forbes-Robertson. He went to Leeds in March to conduct *The Apostles*, where, as he recounted ruefully to Lady Stuart, 'my friend . . . was too busy looking after five young soldiers to pay any attention to me! It does seem rather odd & shews what adulation is worth that the composer & conductor should be left *alone* to find his way on foot thro' dark streets!! What an odd world it is. I rather like the complete isolation, but it seems odd.' He hankered after the country. He would often go to visit his ailing sister and brother in Worcestershire, and he was always glad to unburden himself to Troyte. He invoked his aid in an unsuccessful attempt to prevent Worcester buying his portrait by Philip Burne-Jones which now hangs in the Guildhall there. 'Weak-kneed' he called it. 'Phil is a good creature but is feeble & makes me stand like himself.' And the same letter contains comments on the Playfair production of *The Beggar's Opera* that have a tang of the Elgar-Jaeger correspondence: 'The Beggar's Opera is amusing & awfully improper—a jingle of songs & one great proof—if an added one is needed—that the English are entirely unmusical—this burlesque is about as far as their intelligence can go & its amazing long run is unthinkable in any other country.'

This sentence is characteristically Elgarian, as many other letters I have quoted will have shown. But perhaps its sour mood was engendered by personal disappointment because the public were beginning to ignore his great works. When the Leeds Choral Union sang *The Apostles* at Queen's Hall in June 1922 the audience was so small that Shaw wrote to the *Daily News* to apologize to Elgar 'for London society, and for all the other recreants to English culture' and to posterity 'for living in a country where the capacity and tastes of schoolboys and sporting coster-mongers are the measure of metropolitan culture'. Although a June afternoon is not the most sensible day on which to perform an oratorio, it was just about this time that a strong reaction against Elgar's music began to be obvious. The mood of the twenties was not the nobility and depth of an Elgar; it was either brittle or experimental, or looked back to an earlier age. Stravinsky, Milhaud, Honegger, Lord Berners, and Walton's *Façade*: these were one side of the musical twenties; Vaughan Williams's *Shepherds of the Delectable Mountains* and *Pastoral Symphony* were another; the songs of Warlock were a third. These composers were producing new music: Elgar was silent. More hurtful to him than the change of public mood was the change he detected among his friends. A few days after the

London performance, the Leeds choir sang *The Apostles* in Canterbury Cathedral—a memorable occasion—and Elgar received one letter after the Queen's Hall performance and one (from Alice Stuart) after Canterbury. To Lady Stuart he wrote on 14 June: 'I have *seen* no one, *no one* has written or taken the slightest notice & I have read nothing & seen no papers: truly I *am* a lonely person if I liked to think so—but my "friends"!!! where, oh, where! are they? Silence profound. I was talking to Claude [Phillips] last week & he said "Don't be a Timon". I am not—but do these horrible frauds expect me to continually "attend" them when they happen to want me?' In the same vein he had written to her in 1923: 'My barren honours are dust. Not a single friend has shewn any sign of life, except your house, for years. . . . I only feel with the D. of Wellington that I only hope that they do not think I am (or rather *was*) such a d—d fool as to believe them.'

The year 1923 brought from him only some slight incidental music to Binyon's play *Arthur* for Lilian Baylis's Old Vic production. It was in 1923 that he said to Compton Mackenzie, who had just founded the magazine *The Gramophone*, that he supposed all the young critics of the paper would be sneering at him. 'Not that I care,' he added, 'I take no more interest in music. . . . The secret of happiness for an artist when he grows old is to have a passion that can take the place of his art. I have discovered the joy that diatoms can give me. This miraculous world of beauty under the ocean revealed by the microscope is beyond music.' [1] He defended himself from the indifference of those who were not in sympathy with his music by taking the offensive—'I take no interest in music', or, as he said to Vaughan Williams at the Three Choirs Festival in 1923 after a rehearsal of the Cello Concerto, 'I am surprised that you come to hear this vulgar music.'

The end of Elgar's composing career is mainly explained by Alice's death, but there is more to it than that. After the first grief, such a loss might have inspired him to some further great effort, but his flame had gone out. It had begun to flicker in 1912, when the move to London and the participation in social life sapped his strength. The war continued the process, although Brinkwells gave him a respite before it was too late, so that the final masterpiece, the Cello Concerto, was born. But the combination of Alice's death with the emergence of a post-war world that he hated was enough to extinguish the creative life of such a highly strung man. It is perhaps difficult today to realize the change that 1918 wrought in England, but Elgar realized it in every fibre of his being and he wanted no part of it. He was appalled and repelled by the

---

[1] *The Gramophone* (June 1957), p. 1.

rise of Socialism. Already lonely without his wife, he grew lonelier and more aloof. 'I have . . . settled into servile slipperdom very easily,' he wrote to Colvin from Kempsey on 27 May 1923, 'and wonder why I ever worked. What fools we were to have tried to do anything decent —I regret everything good I have ever done.' To strangers this attitude took an unfortunate form. At a small party at Schuster's, at which Adrian Boult was present, a young contralto was among the guests. Schuster opened a bookcase and took out an album of Elgar songs, calling across the room 'Edward, you must come and meet Miss —. She's going to sing *After* for us.' Elgar heaved himself off a settee, went over to the singer and said 'Good evening, Miss —. You've spoiled my evening for me,' and turned his back. One's condemnation of such boorish conduct is tempered by compassion that so great a composer could have become so disenchanted with his own art.

He thawed only to those who shared his memories of his heyday. Thus to Alice Stuart after the 1923 Worcester Festival, he was able to say: 'I am so delighted you were there & liked the dear old things—they sounded well in the cathedral but I cannot see the future—Where are the new soloists? . . . *The Kingdom, Gerontius* & 'For the Fallen' are not bad; I think I deserve my *peerage* now when these are compared with the new works!!!' He remained the outsider. If the young men like Bax and Bliss liked to salute him as their leader, that was very kind of them, but he did not seek to be a figurehead and he played no active part in any post-war scheme for the propagation of English music. He believed an artist had his personal view to state and that was all there was to it. He played his part in healing the wounds of war: he renewed his friendship with Kreisler and he extended a welcome to Richard Strauss when Strauss visited England in 1922. But he excused himself from a reception for Sibelius and in later years did not attend receptions for Schoenberg and Ravel. He had had enough of London; in April 1923 he took a summer lease of Napleton Grange at Kempsey, five miles from Worcester towards Tewkesbury, so that his sister, who had been ill, could stay with him there. On his visits to London he spent most of his time at the theatre, although he rarely enjoyed the plays. 'I have been to 12 theatres since I returned,' he told Lady Stuart, 'I am so desperately lonely & turn in to see anything.' A play by Conrad he described to her as 'the most amateurish, childish, drivelling imbecile futile rubbish you ever saw'. He also said he could not 'stand' Galsworthy, though later he admired the Forsyte novels. He was determined, he wrote, not to be old-fashioned, adding: 'I am only old-fashioned in loving you.' In the autumn of 1923, perhaps remembering that a change of scenery used to stir him to new endeavour, he went on a cruise to South America and travelled 1,000 miles up the Amazon. But nothing came out of the journey except, according to Reed, that he was impressed by the importance of the opera house in South American towns. On his return he wrote his music for the Wembley Exhibition which opened on 23 April. He wrote his *Empire March* at Perryfield, Bromsgrove, in January 1924. Sending a sketch of the opening to Lady Stuart he added, 'It should rouse people up—I *could* rouse Brazilians but not English.' The rehearsals, he told Lady Stuart, tried his patience, 'overwhelmed with etiquette & red tape . . . the K. insists on Land of Hope & there were some ludicrous suggestions of which I will tell you —if we ever meet. But everything seems so hopelessly & irredeemably *vulgar* at Court. . . . I was standing alone (criticising) in the middle of the enormous stadium. . . . 17,000 men, hammering, loudspeakers, amplifiers, four aeroplanes circling over etc. etc.—all mechanical & horrible—no soul & no romance & no imagination. Here had been played the great football match[1]—even the turf, which is good, was not their [sic] as turf but for football—but at my feet I saw a group of real *daisies*. Something wet rolled down my cheek—& I am not ashamed of it: I had recovered my equanimity when the aides came to learn my views—Damn everything except the daisy—I was back in something sane, wholesome & *gentlemanly* but only for two minutes.'

His pessimistic outlook extended, of course, to the world of music: he prophesied (as Beecham and Harty also did) that there would be no orchestral concerts because 'broadcasting is killing all the concert rooms'. Most surprising of all, the same letter contains a distasteful piece of gossip about his most loyal friend, Schuster: 'This afternoon he was sitting in the back of a smart car . . . driving with an *odd looking*—I hate to say it—"*bit of fluff*"!! in flamboyant *pink* on the front seat. All laughing loudly; they did not see' me & I was glad for I shd. have been thoroughly ashamed.' Since Elgar must have known that similar conclusions were drawn, however wrongly, about his own friendships with women, it is strange that he was not more charitable to a man who had helped him so much. But even at Schuster's home he had found evidence of change: nothing was the same. He disapproved of some members of Frank's household. 'You cd. not say the one word to F. as usual,' he wrote to Alice Stuart after a visit to 'The Hut' in October 1922. 'I tried to write but the effect has been that all idea of composition is "choked off" so we will forget my little delusion about taking up music again: that is over.' A year later, after another visit to Schuster's

[1] The first Wembley Cup Final.

he wrote to her: 'I cd. not enjoy it: — and — were there but—poor dear old Frank.' He grew further away from even his oldest friends when in 1924 he in effect retired to the life of a country gentleman in Worcester. He took to race-going; he surrounded himself with dogs; he became passionate about cars. 'I am in the throes—& have decided on the newest Lea Francis—I think,' he wrote to Percy Hull in the autumn of 1924. 'We all went to Coventry & wallowed in cars. I bought an *Austin 7* a fortnight ago for my sister who loves it.' He was reconciled to the continual snapping of links with the past. In 1924 Kilburn died and Stanford. Sir Walter Parratt, too, and late in the year Fauré. 'His chamber music never had a chance here in the old Joachim days,' he wrote to Schuster. 'I may be wrong but I feel that it was "held up" to our loss. . . . As far as I can resent anything—which is not far—I resented such neglect.' Schuster tried to persuade Elgar to support a Fauré memorial concert. 'I suppose he only wants a pound for a ticket!' he wrote to Alice Stuart. 'I am tired of the world which never notices my existence except to ask for a pound.' Nevertheless, he tried to persuade Brewer to perform Fauré's *Requiem* at the 1925 Gloucester Festival, but this exquisite work was still considered too risky at the box-office. (He had himself sought Lady Stuart's influence in 1923 for a knighthood for Brewer: 'I fear he has not the goodwill of the R.C.M. —quite unnecessary but those sort of people pull only their own strings & not being content to do that cut other people's.' Brewer was knighted three years later.) A few weeks earlier Puccini had died. 'I thought the notices [obituaries] of Puccini dreadfully inadequate,' he told Schuster, having characteristically prefaced this with 'I fear you will have nothing more from "my pen"—but if that's all to look forward to you will not miss much. Music is dying fast in this country.' Yet on 15 June 1925, he was telling Alice Stuart: 'I *am* doing the piano concerto but do not tell anyone as I may switch off at any moment—as is usual.' Family illnesses and deaths also beset him. 'I am here in the midst of invalids, operations, deaths & nursing homes for my relatives,' he wrote to Schuster on 4 November 1925, 'This has been going on for a year & I do not trouble my friends with letters in consequence—there is really nothing to say apart from macabre festivities.' Some weeks later, just before Christmas 1925, he himself went into a nursing-home for three weeks for an operation, his last entreaty to his daughter Carice being to 'be sure the cows in the field don't get into the garden'. At this period of his life he spent hours travelling round Worcestershire with W. H. Reed, revisiting old haunts and pointing out to his companion places he loved. Reed, in *Elgar As I Knew Him*, remarks that Elgar 'seemed to know every inch' of his native county and Herefordshire and the Severn and Wye. 'He never tired of talking of them, exploring and re-exploring them.' This close knowledge of places he liked extended beyond the West Country. In a letter to Lady Stuart he mentions a Lake District journey which Percy Anderson and Frank Schuster had made together, adding: 'They must have driven over the bridge and under the castle which they never saw and also they went thro' Gosforth and never saw the cross. Oh! these motorists.' His knowledge of architecture, history, and folklore was characteristic of the agile mind of the truly self-educated man—all his life he read, absorbed and retained knowledge.

His presence as a resident of Worcestershire naturally made itself felt at this period at the Three Choirs Festivals. His music had always had a principal place in the programmes, but now his eminence, his age, and his powers as his own interpreter conferred a special accolade on the concerts. It is forgotten that he was not a 'Three Choirs' composer in the fullest sense. None of his major works had a first performance there (those that did were *Froissart*, *Lux Christi*, the second *Wand of Youth* suite, the suite from *Crown of India* and 'Go, Song of Mine'). The three biggest choral works had held a regular place, but it is surprising to discover that the *Variations* were not played there between 1903 and 1926, the Violin Concerto between 1911 and 1927, the First Symphony between 1910 and 1925 and the Second between 1913 and 1927, *Cockaigne* between 1909 and 1927, and *In the South* between 1904 and 1930. Under his baton and with his devoted Billy Reed leading the orchestra, Elgar's music at the Three Choirs between 1920 and 1933 was performed with unchallengeable authority. Langford, in the *Manchester Guardian* in September 1924, summed it up: 'The very walls [of Worcester] cry out to us from the same romantic past that has bred his music. His music, heard within them, is redolent of England in the complete sense which in other places may fail it.' Not that everything always went well. Elgar had to feel that the performance was 'alive' or he lost interest, and, so deep was the wound from *Gerontius*, he could not tolerate a lack of interest among the performers. Percy Young, in his biography,[1] quotes the recollection of a member of the Worcester chorus at rehearsals in July 1927 for the Hereford festival. The Gloucester and Hereford contingents had had only a few days in which to re-learn *The Music Makers* and this very soon became obvious. Elgar was furious, threw down his baton, said 'You don't appear to know anything about the work. That will be all', and walked out. Bernard Shore recalls [2] a rehearsal of *Falstaff* when the side-drummer

[1] *Elgar, O.M.*, p. 259.   [2] Op. cit., p. 262.

came in late at the moment of Falstaff's death. He made the same error in the performance. 'We were horrified to see a spasm of anger on Elgar's face. He stopped conducting and made no attempt to control things again.' Perhaps the most celebrated similar occasion was at a Three Choirs performance of *The Kingdom* in 1924 which Sir Adrian Boult has vividly described:[1] 'It was at once apparent that the choir were perhaps resting too much on last year's laurels. . . . Bad intonation was evident near the start, and I felt that Sir Edward was losing interest, as he began to drive the performance, getting faster and faster as if the one thing he wanted was to get out of the Cathedral and forget about music. We endured this for nearly an hour when we came to the wonderful scena "The sun goeth down", which was written for that great soprano, Agnes Nicholls. She had, if I remember rightly, practically retired at that time, but returned at short notice to take over the part which she had made her own many years before. I shall never forget the intense concentration with which she began that gentle opening phrase, and the way the orchestra seemed instantly to spring to life and, immediately after, the disgruntled composer's interest quickened, and from that moment the performance returned to the extraordinary beauty of the year before.'

How much this kind of singing must have meant to the old composer can be gauged from an extract from a letter to Schuster written a month after that performance: 'There is not a single voice coming on in the solo world & young people have given up choral work & the distressingly *thin* physique of the modern boys & girls who *do* try to sing makes their voices so frail & metallic that the general tone is miserable.'

Elgar's conducting has been described by Sir John Barbirolli, who played in the orchestra under him in London and at the Three Choirs, as 'not great by the highest professional standards' but 'it was extraordinary how he could make you feel exactly what he wanted if you were in sympathy with him.'[2] Sir Adrian supports this view: 'His nervous, electric beat unfailingly added a tension and a lustre which produced a tone quality one came to recognise as highly personal. . . . Musicians who heard Elgar conduct are getting fewer in number, but I think they will all agree that if they could make a list of the finest performances they had ever heard of Elgar's works, nearly, if not all of them would turn out to have been conducted by Elgar himself.' Bernard Shore is more detailed: 'It was his face and certain expressive gestures of his left hand that would sometimes lighten up a page.'[3]

---

[1] *Elgar Centenary Sketches* (London, 1957), pp. 9-10.
[2] *A Personal Note*, in LP recording of *Gerontius*, E.M.I. 1965.   [3] Op. cit., p. 261.

Elgar re-lived his music as he conducted it and, says Mr. Shore, 'in-variably clouded' the climax of the first movement of the Second Symphony at one bar after [42]. 'The silent break . . . never came off to perfection. . . . His eye would fail to hold us and his usually clear beat became fluffy.' One important point is also made by Mr. Shore: 'Jog-trot, humdrum conducting is the death of this emotional, highly-strung music. . . . Elgar's own tempos were always fluctuating.' This last statement was confirmed to me by Sir Adrian, who said that he noted Elgar's own treatment of certain passages in his works and would discover, when he went to another Elgar-conducted performance a year later, that the treatment of the same passages was varied. It supports Elgar's own preference, expressed to Jaeger, for elasticity in perfor-mances of his music. It is imperative that this should be realized for, although Elgar was the first great composer to record most of his own music for the gramophone, it would be a mistake for any conductor rigidly to follow Elgar's interpretations as definitive.[1] The recordings are fascinating and historic, but had he made them again a year or two later, they might have differed considerably. It is music of changing moods, acutely responsive to atmosphere and occasion. 'I *feel* & don't invent.' That is the key.

Although he told Schuster that 'my influence at the 3 choirs is nil', it became the focal point of his year. Wearing the robes of one or other of his doctorates or court dress with orders, he was a magnificent and striking figure except to those who found his delight in dressing up merely a pompous affectation. He made several small musical contri-butions to the festivals' atmosphere, arranging two Bach chorales for brass so that they could be performed from the tower of Worcester Cathedral, writing a civic fanfare, orchestrating accompaniments to motets by S. S. Wesley, Battishill, and Purcell. He even took issue in the local paper in 1926 with a canon of Worcester who appeared to be objecting to a proposal to perform parts of *Parsifal* at the Three Choirs because Wagner was a sensualist. This was too much for Elgar, who quoted John Donne to the canon and added: 'If the Canon really believes that such emotions in early life debar a man from taking part in the services of the church in riper years he should at once resign his canonry and any other spiritual offices he is paid to hold.' Sad to report, there was no *Parsifal*, except the Prelude, at Worcester in 1926.

---

[1] His published orchestral scores contain detailed markings of tempi, bowing, phrasing, and nuances of expression. In vocal music, he told McNaught of Novello's in 1908, 'I overdo this sort of thing (necessary in orchestral stuff) as I put down all my feelings as I write and then haven't the heart to take 'em out.'

14 Finale

In 1927 Elgar was seventy. The anniversary coincided with one of the lowest points that his reputation among the arbiters of fashion had reached. A birthday concert at Queen's Hall was given to a hall no more than half full. 'I have had some satisfaction & even pleasure in my life,' he wrote to Charles Volkert who had been head of Schott's London branch when Elgar was in London in the 1880s, 'but have no pleasant memories connected with music.' It is a terrifying and tiresome statement, for surely even that year he must have had pleasure from a concert in Manchester on 20 January when, to salute him in his seventieth year, Adolph Brodsky, then seventy-five, had returned to the Hallé platform to play the Violin Concerto? Elgar conducted. *Froissart, In the South, Sea Pictures*, and the *Variations* were also in the programme. Memories of Richter's heyday in Manchester and of his own triumphs there, the presence of Brodsky symbolizing the interest of a European generation in his work: was there nothing pleasant in the occasion? On 26 June Schuster, himself now seventy-five, performed his last generous act of homage to his friend, arranging performances of the three chamber works at 'The Hut' (by then re-named the 'Long White Cloud') by Sammons, Murdoch, Reed, and others. As it had always been, Schuster's home was a focal point for artistic people of all generations and outlooks. Among the audience on that Sunday were Siegfried Sassoon, Arnold Bennett, William Walton, and Sacheverell and Osbert Sitwell. Elgar described the day to Lady Stuart of Wortley, who had not been present: 'You were sadly missed last Sunday at The Hut—or rather at the new place as the Hut atmosphere has gone never to return. Dear old Frank was radiant &, as usual, a perfect host. . . . I *hope* I behaved as becomes an old visitor. . . . I *wish* you could have heard the things which seem to me to be of my best & the Quintet is not of this world; but you know more of this than I do.' Sir Osbert Sitwell has written, in *Laughter in the Next Room*,[1] an ironic and unsympathetic account of the occasion, omitting to mention that it was a seventieth birthday concert and admitting that he found Elgar's music 'in spite of its genius . . . obnoxious, so full of English humour and the spirit of compulsory games,' whatever that may mean.

[1] (London, 1949).

I seem to recall [he wrote] that we saw from the edge of the river, on a smooth green lawn opposite, above an embankment, and through an hallucinatory mist born of the rain that had now ceased, the plump wraith of Sir Edward Elgar, who with his grey moustache, grey hair, grey top hat and frock coat looked every inch a personification of Colonel Bogey, walking with Frank Schuster. . . . In the main the audience was drawn from the composer's passionately devout but to me anonymous partisans. . . . It is true that these surviving early adherents of Elgar's genius seemed to be endowed with an unusual longevity, but even allowing for this, it was plain, looking round, that in the ordinary course of nature their lives must be drawing to an end. One could almost hear, through the music, the whirr of the wings of the Angel of Death. he hovered very surely in the air that day, among the floccose herds of goodtime Edwardian ghosts, with trousers thus beautifully pressed and suits of the best material . . . or decked and loaded with fur and feather. . . . The glossy motors waited outside to carry them home, like the vans drawn up to take the fine beasts away from an agricultural show. Some of the motors were large and glassy as a hearse.

This evocative passage is a prototype for the superficial view of Elgar. He did look like a retired general, he was something of a dandy. But Sitwell and others like him saw only what they wanted to see—the military bearing. They did not notice the troubled and withdrawn eyes. They heard only what they wanted to hear, the pomp and circumstance; they did not listen to the note of resignation, nor realize that Elgar ten years earlier had seen the hearses drawn up. No doubt Sitwell was oppressed by the atmosphere, for even W. H. Reed refers slightingly in *Elgar As I Knew Him* to feminine 'Elgar worshippers'. He was accurate in one respect. Death was claiming Elgar's friends. Lord Stuart of Wortley had died on 24 April 1926, two days before Elgar conducted the L.S.O. in the *Variations* and the First Symphony. 'It was a great ordeal,' he told Alice Stuart, '& I missed something too great to express—I looked at the familiar seats & my eyes filled.' Colvin died in 1927 and Schuster on 26 December of that year, Herbert Brewer in 1928. 'Only his most intimate friends could realize how easily that sensitive soul was lacerated,' Elgar said of Schuster in a letter to Adela Schuster on 24 January 1928. Schuster might well have said the same of him. Even after death this loyal friend's devotion was proclaimed. He left Elgar £7,000 because he had saved England from the reproach of having produced no composer 'worthy to rank with the great masters'. The loss of his friend and confidant was a heavy blow to Elgar. 'He was always the most loving, strongest and wisest friend man ever had,' he wrote to Adela Schuster on 8 January, 'I seem dazed—to have lost a limb, to have grown older, suddenly.' To Alice

Stuart he was able to speak his whole mind: 'It is a dispensation of whoever controls us that in remembering childish holidays we recollect always the *fine* days—the bad ones do not come back so easily; in the passing of friends it is somewhat the same: the radiant happy & sunny Frank I have before me as I write & the small temporary little irritations which worried me at the time are gone & forgotten for ever.' The death of his brother Frank in 1928, after years of illness, was another distressing blow.

Elgar had left Kempsey in the autumn of 1927, rented another house (Battenhall) for a few months, and then moved from Worcester to Stratford-upon-Avon where he rented Tiddington House. Here he could indulge his old love of Shakespeare by visits to Bridges Adams' company at the memorial theatre. He spoke of writing incidental music; not Shakespeare but a playwright named Bertram P. Matthews was the recipient of music for his play *Beau Brummel*, produced by Gerald Lawrence at Birmingham in November 1928. Elgar conducted on the first night; he still fulfilled many engagements to conduct his own works,[1] but his life was now centred on his dogs—on his 1929 Christmas card he quoted Whitman's 'I think I could turn and live with animals. . . . They do not make me sick discussing their duty to God.' His sentimentality over dogs had been growing since Alice's death. She had not liked dogs and used Elgar's and her frequent absences from home as an excuse for not keeping one. But he loved them, and in the fourteen years after Alice's death he made up for the deprivations of the previous thirty. The death of his sister's Juno had upset him and when in 1923 his daughter's dog had been killed by a car he wrote to Lady Stuart: 'I cannot keep back my tears & am not ashamed.' When his spaniel Marco was ill in 1925 he abandoned his London engagements, telling Lady Stuart: 'He is now the only thing left in the world to me— and he's ill & looking for me everywhere ' Elgar was not well at this time—'it is my *ear* which has failed (& is painful) after threatening for years,' he told Lady Stuart in May 1929. But at the end of the year he made a spirited attack in letters to the press on a Labour M.P.'s proposed Musical Copyright Bill, which would have forbidden a composer to charge more than twopence for the perpetual right of public performance of a work—'the most serious blow ever aimed at the unfortunate art of English music', he called it. Ironically a year later he was trying to sell his original full scores and told Lady Stuart: 'Last year . . . the copyright of *The Dream* had to be renewed in U.S.A. &

---

[1] But he cancelled an engagement at Bristol in 1928 because the orchestra was to be reduced in numbers.

it was seriously questioned if it was worth while to pay the fee—two dollars. I said "I suppose Gerontius is merely waste paper", & the official answer was "yes"—but I risked the two dollars which [neither] I nor my heirs will ever see again. Such things are really humorous.'

His ally in opposition to the Copyright Bill was Bernard Shaw with whom he had an understanding, mutually respectful relationship. One letter from Shaw, dated 4 April 1928, refers to Schuster's bequest to Elgar which was subject to death duty of £700: 'Schuster really deserves to be buried in the Abbey, though he overlooked ME. I grudge Churchill [then Chancellor of the Exchequer] his share. Why don't they make us duty-free instead of giving us O.M.s and the like long after we have conferred them on ourselves?' Elgar opened a Shaw exhibition at the 1929 Malvern Festival, when Shaw publicly stated that Elgar was a greater man than he. This was the year of *The Apple Cart*, for which Barry Jackson, the festival director, had entertained hopes of an overture by Elgar, 'but,' Shaw wrote to Elgar, 'on obtaining from Boult a rough estimate of the cost of an Elgar orchestra, and letting his imagination play on the composer's fee, he went mournfully to his accountants. . . . My own view was that six bars of yours would extinguish (or upset) the A.C. and turn the Shaw festival into an Elgar one; but that it would be a jolly good thing so. . . .' Shaw returned the compliment by becoming a regular attender of the Three Choirs Festivals where, at Worcester in 1929, Sir Neville Cardus remembers seeing him listening to the First Symphony, 'moved to his foundations'. In 1930 Elgar acceded to requests for a test piece for the National Brass Band Championship and wrote the *Severn Suite*, much of it derived (as was all the later music) from old sketchbooks. He dedicated it to Shaw who said it would 'ensure my immortality when all my plays are dead and damned and forgotten. . . . The Salvation Army bands and Besses o' the Barn should be taught by you how to score.' Shaw went to the brass band competition at the Crystal Palace on 27 September, hearing the suite eight times. 'If there is a new edition of the score I think it would be well to drop the old Italian indications and use the language of the bandsmen,' he wrote to the composer. 'For instance. Remember that a minuet is a dance and not a bloody hymn; or steady up for artillery attack; or NOW—like Hell. I think that would help some of the modest beginners. . . . The scoring is, as usual, infallible. You should have heard the curiously pleasant oboe quality of the muted flugels picking up after the cornets. The held note of the soprano cornet *in excelsis* was enormous. These chaps have iron lips. . . . Nobody would have guessed from looking at the score and thinking of the thing as a toccata for brass band how beautiful and serious the work is as abstract music.' The work has never established itself in the brass band repertoire nor has the orchestral version, first played at Worcester in 1932, been often heard. Its early origins show through too plainly.

Elgar had not attended the Crystal Palace with Shaw because of an attack of sciatica: a warning sign of his fatal illness. He had been in pain while conducting at the Hereford Festival but, Reed says, 'made his usual witty and pleasant remarks *sotto voce* as he was being helped on and off the platform.' He was living in Worcester again by now, having bought a house called Marl Bank on Rainbow Hill. It was large with a large garden, but Elgar told Adela Schuster that it was 'a very little house'. He had, he said, to reduce all possible outlay 'owing to the extraordinary state of music in this country.' He was 'retiring . . . the rest is silence.' In fact he was more productive at this period than he had been for years. At the end of 1929, as Master of the King's Musick, he had written a short 'carol' to mark King George V's recovery from a severe illness. Then came the *Severn Suite* and a fifth *Pomp and Circumstance* march, the completion of one sketched many years earlier and now dedicated to Percy Hull. He wrote a song and dedicated it to Joan Elwes, a soprano whose voice had caught his fancy. He sketched an oboe work for Léon Goossens. He began another suite, the result also of looking over the sketches of his youth and his days at Powick. This was a much more successful effort than the *Severn Suite*, probably because it looked back nostalgically yet with piquant humour to the days of *The Wand of Youth*. Called the *Nursery Suite*, Elgar dedicated it to the two little Royal princesses, Elizabeth and Margaret Rose, daughters of the Duke and Duchess of York (later King George VI and Queen Elizabeth). It was the birth of Princess Margaret in August 1930 which had given him the impetus to start work on the music, and this re-visiting of old sketches by the practised hand resulted in a masterpiece with all the freshness and wistful charm of *The Wand of Youth*. It is a moving testament of old age, fresh as spring in the opening Aubade, and hitting off with uncanny musical accuracy the difference between a serious and a sad doll, the latter with a recognizable echo of *Gerontius*. The famous fifth movement, 'The Wagon Passes' is a vignette immediately vivid and attractive, but with a slightly sinister reminder of the Rondo of the Second Symphony and the 'hooves that beat into the brain'. Finally, in 'Dreaming (Envoy)' he recaptures the atmosphere of the Adagio of the First Symphony. Dr. Percy

PLATE XIII

Elgar with his brother Frank at the Gloucester Festival, 1922

PLATE XIV

With Marco

Young finds this movement 'tedious'. I find it hauntingly pathetic as, for the last time, the old composer calls upon his favourite instrument, the violin, to interrupt the dreaming with cadenzas. It is not sentimental to imagine that he was seeing himself again as the young fiddler giving recitals in Malvern and Worcester.

The first performance was unusual, and probably unique. The Suite was played privately, in the presence of the Duke and Duchess, at the Kingsway Hall, London, on 4 June 1931, and was then recorded by H.M.V. The Royal visitors asked for an encore of 'The Wagon Passes'. The work had an immediate success after its first public performance at the Promenade Concerts in August, but the year generally was clouded by a return of the enmities of a quarter of a century earlier. This arose from an article on modern English music contributed by Edward J. Dent, professor of music at Cambridge University since 1926, to Adler's *Handbuch der Musikgeschichte* (Second Edition, 1930), in which Dent referred to Elgar's music as 'for English ears . . . too emotional and not quite free from vulgarity. His orchestral works . . . are animated in colour but pompous in style and of a too deliberate nobility of expression.' The chamber music was dismissed as 'dry and academic'. This last remark is all the more surprising when one discovers that on 30 April 1919 Dent had written to Elgar in these terms: 'I hope I may write a line to say how deeply I was impressed with your quartet and quintet on Saturday afternoon. They are both intensely characteristic of yourself, especially in the slow movements. . . . I rejoice that you have taken to chamber music. . . . I hope you will go on writing more. . . .' Even more complacently damning was the assertion in the article that Elgar 'possessed little of the literary culture of Parry and Stanford'. As far as his compositions are concerned, that might have been to his advantage; but, in fact, as has been amply demonstrated, Elgar was probably one of the most widely read men of his time, with a brilliantly retentive memory. The literary allusions and quotations in his Birmingham lectures would do credit to a professor of English literature. Dent's article displayed an intellectual arrogance which might have been lessened had he not taken it upon himself to speak 'for English ears' instead of for E. J. Dent's ears when, of course, such opinions would have been irreproachable, although a handbook is a dangerous place in which to give permanence to such deeply felt prejudices. Dent devoted 16 lines to Elgar, 66 to Parry and 41 to Stanford. The controversy that he provoked raged in the musical journals, where some of Elgar's defenders (as is usual on these occasions) showed themselves in no better a light than those they were attacking. A letter signed by

s

eighteen people[1] was sent to editors in England and Germany protesting against Dent's 'unjust and inadequate treatment' of Elgar. It would, perhaps, have been better had they taken the view that the article, which would probably have reached only a very select minority, would be better ignored. But no doubt it was only the tip of the iceberg. Someone else dredged up another contribution by Dent to an Italian periodical in 1925 in which he linked Elgar not very accurately with Liszt (as he did in the later article) and added that Elgar was 'repugnant to many English musicians by reason precisely of that chevalieresque rhetoric which badly covers up his intrinsic vulgarity'. In England, Dent said, 'the best musicians have a real horror of Liszt'—and, by implication, of Elgar. It was an intolerably narrow and smug attitude. Dr. Percy Young, writing from personal experience, ascribed the episode to 'the Stanford cult which was practised and preached in Cambridge at that time, and of the fashion of withholding approval from all living English composers who failed in showing a knowledge of the 16th century and, second, a desire to embellish folk song. There was an obligation on the part of Cambridge music students then to avoid all mention of Elgar. The name appeared to suggest something slightly indecent. . . .'[2] This was no exaggeration. Anybody who has experienced the later manifestation of this supercilious attitude, even on the fringe, will know that Elgar's name provoked an automatic curl of the lip from those who failed to resist the influences of the Stanford-Dent-Allen brigade. A hint of this approach, in lesser, more rationalized form, was noticeable in the music criticism of *The Times* after the Second World War, as Bernard Shaw perceived when he wrote in 1949: 'The critics are getting tired of his music. There is a very marked reaction in *The Times*.' An atavistic puritanism in some English musical criticism has never been able to reconcile the Elgar of *Gerontius* with the Elgar of *Salut d'Amour*. Much ink and space have been devoted to regrets that a man of his ability could stoop to salon music. No apology was necessary. The light music has been beneficial in its influence on its *genre*, as the work of Eric Coates testifies. It is beautifully scored and always melodically distinctive. The only pity is that it never earned the composer performing fees proportionate to the harmless pleasure it has given to thousands.

For Elgar, at seventy-four, this unhappy Dent affair meant that life

---

[1] The signatories were: Emile Cammaerts, John Goss, Harvey Grace, Beatrice Harrison, Hamilton Harty, Leslie Heward, John Ireland, Augustus John, Robert Lorenz, E. J. Moeran, André Mangeot, Philip Page, Landon Ronald, Albert Sammons, Bernard Shaw, Richard Terry, William Walton, and Peter Warlock.   [2] *Elgar O.M.*, p. 235.

had come full circle. He was back in Worcester, a baronet now and a local celebrity as he had been fifty years before. The names of Parry, Stanford, and Mackenzie clashed with his in the columns of the London musical press. No wonder that when his boyhood friend Hubert Leicester wrote a book called *Forgotten Worcester* and asked him to write a preface, he took the opportunity to hit back at the resurgence of the old academic snobbery which had beset his years of struggle: 'From among the crudities which one of the many—why are there so many? —unbrilliant university men has used in reference to myself, the following comes to mind. I am said to have "left the humdrum atmosphere of Worcester for"—etc. I object to this. I deny that any atmosphere could be exactly humdrum while Hubert Leicester and myself were of it and in it; it might well have been disagreeable, but that is another matter. . . .' The gibe was unworthy of him, but one may sympathize with him for making it. And just to complete the illusion of a nightmare returned, the national economic crisis was hitting his pocket. 'I must give up my little car and many other small comforts,' he wrote to Adela Schuster. 'Most of the serious musicians are in the same plight.'

Since 1927 he had gained great pleasure from his gramophone and kept trying to persuade Lady Stuart of Wortley also to buy one. 'I have just been playing over your symphony [No. 2],' he wrote, '& most of it sounds divine'. His letters to her for the next six years mention the gramophone as his 'one joy' and he speaks of his particular pleasure in records of the Brahms symphonies and of Wagner's *Siegfried Idyll*. He retreated further into the past, revisiting Birchwood with Billy Reed. Together they played sonatas by Rubinstein, concertos by Spohr, and a suite by Ries—all works he had played as a youth and which led him into spoken reminiscence of 'the old days'. As throughout his life, he hated the winter and each year longed for the coming of spring and the return of warmth, never failing to gather the first wild windflowers to send to 'Windflower' or sending her news of his doings, adding, at Christmas 1929, that his card 'brings my love or rather a remembrance of it since 1897—thirty-two years accumulation.' He still enjoyed motoring round the Worcester lanes and going to the races—Neville Cardus found him elated in the Hereford Club after a performance of *Gerontius* because he had backed the winner of the St. Leger—he still enjoyed going to the theatre; he still liked meeting his fellow-composers at the Three Choirs. He was by now on amiable terms with Ralph Vaughan Williams, realizing that V. W., despite his connections with the anti-Elgarians, was not a man for cliques but a man who could share friendships without sharing opinions. He admired Vaughan Williams's *Sancta Civitas*, telling the composer that the work had completed his own trilogy for him, and he introduced him to the poetry of Skelton, saying 'One day I must make an oratorio out of Elinor Rumming.' He never did, but Vaughan Williams wrote the *Five Tudor Portraits*. Yet, for all this gregariousness and outward jollity, he was on the defensive. He tried to deter Basil Maine from writing a book about him by saying 'The interest in my music is too slight and evanescent to be worth such concentration as you propose to devote to it.' Yet after conducting the Second Symphony in London in the autumn of 1931 he wrote to Lady Stuart: 'The Sym: scarcely sounded 20 years old —oh, that awful first performance.' 1932, the year of his seventy-fifth birthday, was a great year for interest in his work. He conducted it in many towns, some of the occasions being sentimental journeys—that, for example, to Hanley when he conducted *King Olaf* in the hall where he had conducted its first performance in 1896. He had recorded *Falstaff* in November 1931 and took delight in playing it to any visitor to Marl Bank. After the second interlude he told Basil Maine 'That's what I call music', and, to John Barbirolli, after the exuberant little solo for side-drum he said 'Well, that's a good bit, anyway.' Reed remembered the joy that 'suffused his face' when he conducted this passage. He attended the first performance at Sadler's Wells of Ninette de Valois's ballet of the *Nursery Suite*. Constant Lambert conducted and remarked that when Elgar came on to the stage to acknowledge the applause it was as if one of the great masters from the past had materialized into the modern age. At the Three Choirs at Worcester he conducted *Gerontius*, 'For the Fallen', the *Severn Suite*, *The Music Makers*, and the First Symphony, and it was about this time that he went to conduct Alan Kirby's Croydon choir in *The Apostles*. He became, Kirby wrote,[1] 'more and more lost in the music. A slow smile came over his face, and he almost stopped conducting; his spirit seemed to have taken wings. . . . When Elgar left the rostrum it was obvious that he was greatly moved.' Yet the quirkiness remained, to flash out in certain company. After a concert at Queen's Hall in 1930 at which Toscanini had conducted the *Variations*, Bax and Harriet Cohen found Elgar at the Savoy Grill 'characteristically surrounded by actors, Norman Forbes and Allan Aynesworth amongst them. Harriet, of whom Elgar was really very fond, rushed up to him and began vivaciously and charmingly to congratulate him upon . . . the evening's wonderful music. With—as I thought—rather ridiculous affectation

[1] *Centenary Sketches*, p. 26.

and ungraciousness, the old composer turned to his actor friends and spreading out his hands in mock-mystification, exclaimed "What on earth *are* these people talking about?" '[1]

But he can perhaps be forgiven, for he had known Toscanini's interpretation for twenty-five years, just as he had known Steinbach's and Nikisch's. Foreign views of his music were no novelty to him, and he was irritated by the attitude of some English critics who, while denying him wholehearted approval, seemed at the same time determined to keep him exclusively English property and warned intruders to 'keep off the grass'. Musicians like Bax and Malcolm Sargent were thrilled to their foundations by Toscanini's conducting of the *Variations*, but critics—even Ernest Newman—complained of its lack of an 'English' quality. Well as the English violinist Albert Sammons played the concerto—and he played it unforgettably well—there was room for other interpretations, but no foreign violinist was allowed to feel that he had succeeded in the work which was created by the Austrian, Kreisler. And when Pablo Casals, the Spaniard, revealed the true qualities of the Cello Concerto, which languished in semi-obscurity for several years, he too was accused of playing it *too* beautifully, *too* intimately, with too much care for phrasing and not enough 'austerity' and 'gruffness'. Well might Elgar ruefully have remembered his 1905 lecture: 'English music is white, it evades everything.' Elgar liked Toscanini's, Menuhin's, and Casals's interpretations of his music: all he wanted, he told Neville Cardus, was that it should sound stylish, well written, and colourful; he did not compose 'in sackcloth'. Indeed, he had been excited and astonished by the fifteen-year-old Yehudi Menuhin's playing and understanding of the Violin Concerto and his heart warmed to this 'wonderful boy', as he described him to Shaw. When H.M.V. arranged for Menuhin to play the work to Elgar, with Ivor Newton accompanying, in a London hotel room, Elgar listened to a few bars, said he had no qualms about the performance and went to the races. Together they made an historic recording of the concerto on 14 and 15 July 1932, performed it together at the Royal Albert Hall a month later, and gave the first Paris performance at an Enesco concert on 31 May 1933. Elgar went to France and back by aeroplane, his first flight. He was thrilled. The man who had welcomed the bicycle and the motor-car also welcomed the aeroplane. To Adela Schuster, who was perturbed about this adventure, he wrote: 'The risk, according to the insurance people, is at the same rate as railway travelling which

[1] Arnold Bax, *Farewell, My Youth*, p. 32. Bax dates this episode in 1933 but Forbes died in September 1932.

shows that the commercial people are not afraid. . . . It is wonderful to avoid changes, oily-smelling boats & the hundred other troubles of the channel crossing.' Yet to Shaw he struck a deeper note: 'I wd. love to have a reassuring word from you & Charlotte before my final departure—I somehow feel I shall not return.' Perhaps he did not care. After the concert, at the insistence of Fred Gaisberg of the Gramophone Company, he went to Grez-sur-Loing to see the paralysed Delius, taking him records of Sibelius and Wolf. The two great English composers, both with barely a year of life left to them, liked one another, rather, one suspects, to their surprise. They were survivors of an alien culture. Both had written in 1899 orchestral works (the *Variations* and *Paris*) which showed that English music had come of age. Little though they had in common, except a romantic nostalgia very differently expressed, they had both owed their first fame to German acclaim. And now, in the spring of 1933, Elgar was writing to Adela Schuster: 'I am in a maze regarding events in Germany—what are they doing? In this morning's paper it is said that the great conductor Bruno Walter &, stranger still, Einstein, are ostracised: are we all mad? The Jews have always been my best & kindest friends—the pain of these news is unbearable & I do not know what it really means.'

'Your friendship . . . has given me a new zest in life,' Elgar wrote to Menuhin. He had been moved, too, by the B.B.C.'s Elgar Festival in December 1932. 'The orchestra gave him everything it had,' Bernard Shore wrote.[1] '. . . It was something like the attachment felt by passionately loyal subjects to a monarch.' At the end of the festival it was announced that the B.B.C. had commissioned a third symphony (for £1,000). This had been engineered by Shaw, who had written to Elgar at the beginning of the year 'Why don't you make the B.B.C. order a new symphony? It can afford it.' Shaw himself took the matter further, with the help of Sir Landon Ronald, and Elgar was 'overwhelmed' by his friend's 'lofty idea'. Yet, ironically, after the long years of virtual silence, he was also at work on another major scheme, an opera. Over the years he had toyed with several ideas for operatic subjects. In 1913 Binyon had brought Thomas Hardy and Elgar together as potential collaborators. Hardy had written on 28 July of that year saying that the first consideration was 'whether it should be a production in the grand style based on "The Dynasts" or a romantic or tragic Wessex opera based on one of my best-known stories. . . . I have thought "A Pair of Blue Eyes" would be good for music, as it would furnish all the voices and has a distinct and central heroine, with a wild

[1] Op. cit., p. 261.

background of cliffs and sea.' The war put paid to the idea, and Elgar later complained to Walford Davies that he had always wanted 'something heroic and noble' but had only been offered 'blood and lust' as libretti. Now his friendship with Barry Jackson of the Malvern Festival had induced him to think over a plan he had formulated years before for turning Ben Jonson's *The Devil is an Ass* into an opera. 'My difficulty in trying to "plan" it years ago,' he wrote to Jackson in September 1932, 'was the end—the actual wind-up—this you may be able to "see"—I don't know if clubs were "raided" at the time of B. J.—but that wd. make a tremendous scrambling finale—last ensemble.' Jackson agreed to act as librettist and by the beginning of 1933 Elgar had started writing the music, though writing is perhaps too strong a word. As can be seen from Dr. Young's detailed account of the sketches,[1] most of the music is a tentative re-working of old sketches from as far back as 1879 and the 'Shed Books', with bits of discarded material from the oratorios, *Crown of India* and works that came to naught. He told Jackson that the work would be on 'a grandiose scale'. He devised a better title—*The Spanish Lady*—and sent for Reed to play the sketches to him, excitedly interrupting the music with descriptions of the stage action and making drawings of the settings. Then he would switch to the symphony, which was in scrappy sketch-form, and, getting tired, would take the dogs for a walk. Was he happy, feeling that he was at work, or did he know that it was all a charade, that his inspiration was fitful, if not wholly extinct? He continued to dwell much on the past, constantly talking about his youth and telling the romantic story of his own career. Part of this *recherche du temps perdu* may have been the actual business of having work in progress, a reminder of the days at Craeg Lea and Birchwood. We can never know. In any case the activity was to be short-lived. Just before the visit to Paris he had had another bout of sciatica. He recovered and conducted his last recordings, of the youthful *Serenade for Strings* and the *Elegy*, on 29 August 1933. But at the Hereford Festival in September Reed found him 'more than usually tired' between his cathedral appearances. He conducted *Gerontius* and *The Kingdom* and Lionel Tertis's transcription of the Cello Concerto for viola, to which he gave his blessing.

In October he was taken to the South Bank nursing-home, Worcester, for an operation. The 'sciatica' was found to be a malignant tumour, pressing on the sciatic nerve. There was no hope for him. He suffered bouts of intense pain, followed by remissions when it was possible to hope for recovery. But always the pain returned. His

[1] *Elgar O.M.*, pp. 363–73.

thoughts turned to his oldest friends: to Hubert Leicester, to whom he wrote 'We have had some good times', and to Florence Norbury. To her he said: 'I lie here hour after hour, thinking of our beloved Teme—surely the most beautiful river that ever was and it belongs to you too—I love it more than any other—some day we will have a day together there—on it? by it? You shall choose the place—I shall come & see you as soon as possible but it will be sad to return in winter—it would have been nicer to get better in spring.'

He expressed a wish that he should be buried at the confluence of Severn and Teme, without religious ceremony. He had for many years avoided going to church and while dying he refused to see a priest. Shaw told Hesketh Pearson that, in their talks together, Elgar avoided the subject of religion 'with a deliberate reticence which convinced me that he was a nineteenth century unbeliever, though he wouldn't have admitted it and wouldn't have liked to be told so.' In the intervals of consciousness his mind was full of his unfinished symphony. He wrote four bars on a piece of music paper and handed them to Reed, 'fighting back the tears which were choking him as he said: "Billy, this is the end".'[1] To Ernest Newman, over Christmas 1933, he sent some quotations from the Adagio, writing in the margin: 'I send you my stately sorrow; naturally what follows brings hope.'[2] He asked Reed to promise that no one should ever attempt to complete, or 'tinker with', the symphony. He must have realized that the sketches as they existed could give no inkling whether his flame was burning again. They are bare bones, and no one can ever know whether he could have given them life in the refining processes of creation. His friends did their best to ease and brighten his last days. Shaw sent him *Too True to be Good* and a letter telling him to 'trust to your mighty Life Force and damn the doctors'. Thanking him, Elgar could not respond to the mood—'I am still in the depths of pain. . . . I am low in mind.' Gaisberg arranged that Harriet Cohen and the Stratton Quartet should record the chamber music, and he went down to Worcester with the records and a new gramophone. The dying man played them again and again. 'Such was his growing weakness,' Reed wrote, 'that he could not refrain from weeping whenever the slow movement [of the Quintet] was reached.'[3]

In November he had collapsed, and, while unconscious, had been given the Last Rites. But he rallied and after Christmas returned to Marl Bank. He grew weaker, but he made one final contact with his

[1] Op. cit., pp. 146–7. [2] *The Listener*, 11 March 1954, p. 422.
[3] Op. cit., p. 145.

own music. Gaisberg arranged a recording of extracts from *Caractacus*, conducted by Lawrance Collingwood, and with the co-operation of the G.P.O., a microphone connected Elgar's bedroom with the recording studio in London. In the morning of 22 January Elgar was half-conscious but he rallied in the afternoon. At 4 p.m. he made a little speech to the orchestra, listened to the first recording session for the *Triumphal March*, and made some criticisms which were clearly heard in the studio. When recording of the second part of the March began he said to Gaisberg: 'I say, Fred, isn't that a gorgeous melody? Who could have written such a beautiful melody?'[1] At the end he specially asked for the *Woodland Interlude* to be played and repeated twice, that music inspired by the Worcestershire countryside around Birchwood, the music he had heard the trees singing. Early in February he asked for Ernest Newman to come to see him. Newman described the meeting in the *Sunday Times* many years later:

He had altered tragically since I had seen him a little while before; and he obviously knew his end was near . . . he spoke despondently of his fear that his music would not live after him. . . . Then, after a brief silence, he made a single short remark about himself which I have never disclosed to anyone and have no intention of ever disclosing, for it would lend itself too easily to the crudest of misinterpretations. . . . It explains a good deal in him that has always been obscure or puzzling to us; it has a particular bearing, I am convinced, on that passion of his for public mystification of which the most remarkable outward expressions were his two 'enigmas'—that of the *Variations* and that of the Soul' enshrined in the violin concerto.[2]

His final days were dreadful indeed, but at the end the pain left him and he died at 7.45 a.m. on 23 February 1934, aged seventy-six years and eight months. He was buried three days later, at Alice's side, at Little Malvern.[3] There was no music and no mourning. He is commemorated in Worcester Cathedral by a window on the subject of *The Dream of Gerontius*. Beneath it is a tablet bearing the words of the Priest at Gerontius's death-bed: 'Proficiscere anima Christiana de hoc mundo.'

[1] *Music on Record*, by Fred Gaisberg (London, 1946), pp. 249–51.
[2] *Sunday Times*, 6 November 1955. In a letter to Dr. Gerald Abraham, quoted in *The Listener* of 23 July 1959, Newman said: 'Elgar's distressing remark consisted of only five words, but the scope they would give to a "reading" of him is infinite, so I am determined to keep them to myself: they are too tragic for the ear of the mob.'
[3] In Elgar's last days, Father Gibb, S.J., was admitted to his room. He told Mrs Blake afterwards that her father had reaffirmed his adherence to the Roman Catholic faith. This meant that Elgar's wish for a riverside grave could not be fulfilled.

15 Coda

Anybody who spends some time among the great collection of letters to Elgar preserved at Worcester will come away with an overwhelming impression of the respect and affection with which he was surrounded and which he and his music inspired. Yet throughout his life, as we have seen, he remained lonely and unsure. When he was old and full of honours, a young couple with Worcester connections spent an evening with him. He was brimming with humour and good stories. He played them records of his music, striding about the room humming. When they had gone, he asked his niece: 'Do you think they *really* loved my music?' Many, like A. H. Fox Strangways, knew him only as a man with an 'endless curiosity about everyday things and his power of finding fun in chance people and ordinary incidents'. They would never have suspected the dark side of his soul that was bared to Jaeger and Lord Northampton. The intellectuals who despised his patriotism and emotion and found his liking for the racing fraternity an incomprehensible aberration could never have realized the sensitivity that the mask of worldliness concealed. Langford said of Mahler's music: 'With his lighter hand he draws us to and with his heavier thrusts us from him.' These words could equally be applied to Elgar's personality. It seems almost perverse of him to have maintained in the face of all the devotion and admiration he received that music meant nothing to him, that he regretted every good thing he had ever done, that his influence on everything and everybody was 'evil', that it was better to enjoy a 'jape' than to enjoy *The Apostles*. It can be explained only by the sense of inferiority and hurt and humiliation that he carried with him from the struggles of his youth. He resented to his last breath that he had reached his fifth decade before he achieved the recognition he felt was his due and could concentrate on the works he wanted to write instead of on teaching and playing. Sending to Lady Stuart in 1929 a cutting of an article he had written in a Malvern paper in 1887, he added: 'I feel that I really was something apart from the ordinary country violin teacher even then.' He resented the class of society which had dominated the Worcester social scene in his youth, and this resentment took the form of a strange mixture of dislike and respect in his attitude to them in later life. The indelible stain of an inferiority complex is to be found in his constant expectation that he would be slighted, his music disliked, and his intentions misunderstood. Not all the adulation of an era, not all the devotion and homage of great men and musicians, could wash it away. Somewhere in his past something or somebody wounded him so deeply, so irreparably, that he never fully recovered. Though he revealed so much about himself in his letters, he buried the secret of this wound in his heart. It showed itself only in the anguish and solitude of certain passages in his music.

Although he desired popular appreciation, he also regarded himself as a 'dweller apart'. The lack of professionalism in English music-making annoyed him. His Birmingham lectures reveal him as a progressive in his time, conscious of the narrowness of outlook in English musical life, of its deficiencies and of the possibilities of improvement. He who is supposed to be a 'typical Edwardian', accepting the *status quo*, saw clearly the sham of much English artistic life. He despised the standards of acting and production in the theatre of the early 1900s; he knew from bitter experience the shortcomings of performers; he held a poor opinion of public taste. As he grew older, he became disillusioned because the more things changed, the more they remained the same or, in his view, became worse. He hated the vulgarity of the 1920s and 1930s. When he saw the new Memorial Theatre at Stratford-upon-Avon he withdrew his support in protest against its ugliness. When Ramsay MacDonald was elected to the Athenaeum he sent in his resignation. Though for Alice's sake and his own sense of enjoyment and material fulfilment he had been prepared to live the life of a *grand seigneur* in Hampstead, he soon fled from it, and though he kept one foot in the door in his later years he did so in the rôle of country-gentleman-about-town. He never satisfactorily resolved the conflict within him between the desire for worldly success and acclaim and the equally strong desire for the withdrawn, solitary life of the artist. His own veering from 'japes' and gregariousness to sudden black despair were the outward signs of the conflict; the inner signs are writ large across the music, especially the Second Symphony. There is, through his whole life, a discontent with circumstances; certainly he experienced penuriousness but never real poverty. Though he ought to have been treated better by publishers, he was always able to live in comfort, indulging his fancies and hobbies, keeping a manservant, living in fine houses. Many another struggling composer must have envied him and his domestic peace in Malvern and Hereford. It is perhaps impossible for anyone to be sure about his religious views, but enough documentary evidence has been quoted in this book for it safely to be deduced that his opinions were unorthodox and unconventional, and that he had no thought of, or wish for, an after-life. It is no coincidence that, after *The Kingdom*, he wrote no sacred works with the exception of short motets for special occasions, and that the trilogy remained unfinished. Providence, or the Heavenly Spirit, or God, whatever he called the deity, was 'against' art. If he had wanted a suitable subject for an opera, he could have done no better than resort to his beloved Shakespeare's *King Richard II*, the monarch who willed his own deposition, the ambitious man who was at heart the poet who longed for 'a little, little grave'.

*   *   *

After Elgar's death, Fox Strangways, editor of *Music and Letters*, wrote:[1] 'More than one who was present at the six B.B.C. concerts of British music in January [1934] was struck by the way in which Elgar's A flat symphony stood out head and shoulders above all the rest. . . . As we listened, it suddenly came across us: this is mastery.'

His mastery, the success with which he achieved his musical purpose, is unchallengeable. 'It is within his limitations that the master finds himself,' Goethe said; and Elgar knew his limitations, worked within them, and created a distinctive and distinguished personal idiom. His influence on other English composers can easily be traced but he remains what he always was: an unexpected, unheralded phenomenon. It required a musician who had settled in Britain as Jaeger had done to point out that the English belief in Elgar's insularity and lack of appeal to the Continent was partly a 'group delusion'. 'There are far more Elgar performances on the Continent than the English think,' wrote Hans Keller,[2] who then stimulatingly argued that 'the conservative Elgar's manner is still a little too new for the broad Continental public. . . . The stunning effect of the Schoenbergian revolution has made itself felt, and the Continent is far too busy assimilating the changes thus wrought in its own musical tradition to appreciate the full significance of Elgar's conservative progressiveness.'

His truest qualities remain unique and inimitable. 'Music is in the air all around you, you just take as much of it as you want,' he said in 1904, and in his work—'peculiarly composite', as Langford wrote in 1924— we hear the music that was all around Elgar: Franck, Brahms, Schumann,

---

[1] *Music and Letters* (April 1934), p. 109.
[2] *Music and Musicians* (June 1957), p. 17.

Dvořák, Wagner, Delibes. He took what he wanted, and changed it by his own personality and technique into something rich and strange. He had a poet's perception of the fleeting moment: the wagon passing, the excitement of a Coronation crowd, the veil that comes over the eyes as the vanished past is recalled. He believed in inspiration ('Music is written on the skies') and saw himself as the vessel into which music was poured from he knew not where. More prosaically, he called himself an 'incubator'. Oscar Wilde's son Vyvyan Holland, whom the Elgars befriended at Plâs Gwyn in 1909, remembered walking with him along the banks of the Wye while Elgar, humming to himself, jotted down themes on small sheets of music paper. 'He once told me that he had musical day-dreams in the same way that other people had day-dreams of heroism and adventure, and that he could express almost any thought that came into his head in terms of music.'[1] Like the romantic poets and artists of the mid-nineteenth century he was acutely responsive to landscape and to travel. The place names inscribed on his scores all had a special significance for him—Venice and Tintagel in the Second Symphony, Alassio in *In the South*, 'Birchwood—in summer' in *Gerontius* and 'In Longdon Marsh' in *The Apostles*, Judge's Walk ('my spiritual home for many years', he told Alice Stuart-Wortley) in *The Music Makers*. Trees were part of the inspiration of the chamber music and of *Gerontius*: 'the summer wind among the lofty pines'. On a postcard showing the Via Appia Antica he wrote the first three bars of the First Symphony, adding: 'Here it was!' And at the very last, when music was dead within his dying body, his thoughts were of the Teme, 'Severn's wild sweet daughter, a wayward child', as Francis Brett Young described it. Always, through his life and music, there runs this motif of the river—'I am at heart the child on Severn side' . . . 'What the reeds were saying' . . . 'Like something you hear down by the river'. By some alchemy he put this into his music, a fresh wistful quality, whenever his thoughts went back to his youth, to the land of lost content, alone by the river.

'A man's attitude to life' was how he described the broken-hearted Cello Concerto. This directly personal appeal is the secret of his music. The technical expertise is but the means by which he speaks to the hearts of large numbers of his fellow-beings. What his message is will vary with each listener—perhaps he did not fully comprehend it himself. In *Gerontius*, the symphonies, *The Music Makers*, most of all in the Violin Concerto, are a human soul's hopes and regrets, disappointments and beliefs, universally shared experiences, strengths and weaknesses,

[1] Vyvyan Holland, *Time Remembered* (London, 1966), p. 20.

faults and foibles. That he was a great master of the art and fabric of music, a genius of the orchestra, is only an aspect of the final portrait of Elgar as one of those rare beings who make men dream dreams and see visions.

APPENDIX I
Chronological List of Works

c. 1867 Music for Elgar children's play *The Wand of Youth* (see **1907**).

c. 1870 *Fugue in G minor* for organ (unfinished).

1872 Song, *The Language of Flowers* (Percival). Dedication: To my sister Lucy on her birthday. Unpublished.
Chantant, pianoforte solo.

1874 Anthem, arranged for strings with original introduction. Performed at All Saints Church, Worcester, 1874.

1877 Five well-known pieces arranged as studies for the violin. 1. *Larghetto*, Mozart; 2. *Cavatina*, Raff; 3. *Romance*, de Bériot; 4. *Romance*, Vieuxtemps; 5. *Gigue*, Ries. Publisher: Schott, 1877.
Study for strengthening the third finger. (Re-copied 1920 and dedicated to Jascha Heifetz).

1878 *Arrangements:*
Adeste fideles arr. for orchestra.
Beethoven, *Violin Sonata* op. 23, finale, arr. for wind quintet.
Corelli, *Concerto*, arr. for wind quintet.
Handel, Overture *Ariodante*, arr. for small orchestra.
Weber, *Oberon*, 'O 'tis a glorious sight', arr. 'for Mr. F. J. Pedley'.
Chamber music:
Fantasia for violin and pianoforte (unfinished).
String Quartet in D minor (unfinished).
String Quartet in B flat (unfinished).
String Trio in C (unfinished).
Trio for 2 violins and pianoforte (unfinished).
Promenades for wind quintet (2 flutes, oboe, clarinet, bassoon): 1. Moderato e molto maestoso; 2. Moderato ('Madame Tussaud's'); 3. Presto; 4. Andante; 5. Allegro molto; 6. Allegro maestoso ('Hell and Tommy').
Allegro for oboe, violin, viola, and violoncello (unfinished).
Romance, for violin and pianoforte. Opus 1. First performance: Worcester, 20 October 1885. Dedication: Oswin Grainger. Publisher: Schott, 1885.
Orchestral:
Menuetto (scherzo) (re-copied 1930).
Symphony in G minor after Mozart (part of first movement exists).
Introductory Overture for Christy Minstrels. First performance: Worcester, 12 June 1878, cond. by E. E.

Vocal:

Salve Regina. First performance: St. George's Church, Worcester, 6 June 1880.

Domine Salvam fac. First performance: St. George's, Worcester, 29 June 1879.

Tantum Ergo. First performance: St. George's Church, Worcester, 29 June 1879.

Easter anthem, *Brother, For Thee He Died.*

Hymn Tune in G major.

Hymn Tune in F major. Published as Drake's Broughton in *Westminster Hymnal,* 1898 and 1912. Also used in *Nursery Suite,* Aubade, **1931.**

Song, *If She Love Me* (Temple Bar Rondeau).

1879 *Chamber Music:*

Two Polonaises for violin and pianoforte (unfinished). Dedication: For J. K. with esteem.

Harmony Music for wind quintet. 1. Allegro molto; 2. Allegro non tanto (dedication: W. B. Leicester); 3. Allegro (unfinished); 4. Allegro molto (The Farmyard); 5. Allegro moderato (The Mission), Minuet, Andante (Noah's Ark), Allegro; 6. Allegro molto, andante arioso.

Intermezzos for wind quintet. 1. Allegro molto; 2. Adagio; 3. Allegretto (Nancy); 4. Andante con moto; 5. Allegretto.

Menuetto—allegretto for wind quintet.

Gavotte (The Alphonsa) for wind quintet.

*Sarabande—*Largo for wind quintet (re-copied for *The Spanish Lady*).

Gigue—allegro for wind quintet.

Andante con variazioni ('Evesham andante') for wind quintet. Dedication: H. A. L. (Hubert Leicester).

Adagio cantabile for wind quintet.

Orchestral:

Minuet—grazioso. Performed at Worcester 22 January 1879. MS. lost or destroyed.

Music written for Worcester City and County Pauper Lunatic Asylum, Powick, and scored for piccolo, flute, clarinet, 2 cornets, euphonium, 2 violins, viola, cello, bass, and pianoforte:

Five Quadrilles, La Brunette. Dedication: Geo. Jenkins (asylum clerk).

Five Quadrilles or Caledonians, Die Junge Kokette. Dedication: Miss J. Holloway (pianist and organist).

Five Quadrilles, L'Assommoir (No. 5 also occurs as sixth movement of *Wand of Youth Suite No. 2*).

Organ:

Adagio Solenne. Re-scored for small orchestra as *Cantique,* op. 3

(1912). First performance: London, Royal Albert Hall, 15 December 1912. Dedication: Hugh Blair. Publisher: Novello, 1913.

1880 *Arrangements (c. 1880):*

Mozart, *Violin Sonata in F* (K.547), Allegro, arr. as Gloria for St. George's, Worcester.

Beethoven, Themes from *Symphonies Nos. 5, 7, and 9,* arr. as Credo by 'Bernhard Pappenheim' (E. E.) for St. George's, Worcester.

Schumann, *Scherzo,* from *Overture, Scherzo and Finale,* op. 52, arr. for pianoforte solo.

Orchestral: (Music for Powick).

Polka (Maud).

Five Quadrilles, Paris. 1. Chatelet; 2. L'Hippodrome; 3. Alcazar d'Eté (Champs Elysées); 4. La! Suzanne!; 5. Café des Ambassadeurs: La femme d'emballeur. Dedication: Miss J. Holloway.

Five Lancers (The Valentine).

Vocal:

O Salutaris hostia (four-part chorus). Publisher: Cary, 1888.

Credo in E minor.

1881 *Chamber music:*

Fantasia on Irish Airs for violin and pianoforte (unfinished).

Fugue in F sharp minor (unfinished—incorporated into *The Spanish Lady*).

Harmony Music for wind quintet (see **1879**) No. 7, Allegro; scherzo —allegro giusto.

Orchestral:

Polka (Nelly) for Powick band.

1882 *Orchestral:*

Air de Ballet—Pastorale ⎫ Performed: Worcester, 14 March 1882
March—Pas Redoublé ⎬ (March was incorporated into *The Spanish*
 ⎭ *Lady* and into *Suite in D*—see below).

Air de Ballet. Performed: Worcester, August 1882. MS. lost.

Polka (La Blonde) for Powick band.

Rosemary for pianoforte solo (composed at Settle, Yorks., September 1882). Originally entitled *Danse Pensée.* Scored for small orchestra; published 1915 by Elkin.

Suite in D for small orchestra. 1. Mazurka; 2. Intermezzo—Sérénade Mauresque; 3. Fantasia gavotte; 4. March—pas redoublé. No. 2 was first performed at Birmingham, 13 December 1883, cond. by W. C. Stockley, and No. 4 at Worcester, 14 March 1882. Suite first performed complete at Birmingham, 1 March 1888, cond. by W. C. Stockley, Nos. 1 and 3 may not have been written until 1883 or 1884. Suite revised **1899** as *Three Characteristic Pieces,* op. 10. 1. Mazurka; 2. Sérénade Mauresque; 3. Contrasts: The Gavotte A.D. 1700 and 1900. Dedication: Lady Mary Lygon. Publisher: Novello, 1899.

T

Vocal:

O Salutaris hostia, bass solo. (Incomplete but edited by Dr. Percy Young.)

Four Litanies for the Blessed Virgin Mary (*a capella choir*). Dedication: Fr. T. Knight, S.J. Publisher: Cary, 1888.

1883   *Arrangement:*

Wagner, *Tannhäuser*, Act II, Entry of the Minstrels, arr. for pianoforte.

Chamber music:

Une Idylle, op. 4, No. 1, for violin and pianoforte. Dedication: E. E., Inverness. Publisher: Ashdown, 1910, and by Beare in 1885.

Pastourelle, op. 4, No. 2, for violin and pianoforte. Dedication: Miss Hilda Fitton, Malvern. Publisher: Swan, 1906; Novello,1912.

Virelai, op. 4, No. 3, for violin and pianoforte. Dedication: Frank W. Webb. Publisher: Swan, 1906; Novello, 1912.

Fugue in D minor, for oboe and violin.

Orchestral:

Polka (*Helcia*) for Powick band.

1884   *Orchestral:*

Polka (*Blumine*) for Powick band.

Sevillana, op. 7. First performance: Worcester Philharmonic Society, cond. by Dr. W. Done, 1 May 1884. First London performance, Crystal Palace, cond. by August Manns, 12 May 1884. Dedication: W. C. Stockley. Publisher: Tuckwood, 1884. Revised version of 1889 published by Ascherberg, 1895.

Vocal:

A Soldier's Song (C. Flavell Hayward). First performance: Worcester Glee Club (Crown Hotel, Broad Street), 17 March 1884. Dedication: F. G. P., Worcester (F. G. Pedley). Published: *Magazine of Music*, 1890. Re-named *A War Song* and re-published by Boosey, 1903, and sung at Royal Albert Hall, 1 October 1903.

1885   *Arrangements:*

Maud Valerie White, *Absent and Present*. Cello obbligato. C. H. Dolby, *Out on the Rocks*. Cello obbligato. C. W. Buck, *Melody*. Pianoforte accompaniment.

Chamber music:

Gavotte for violin and pianoforte. Dedication: Dr. C. W. Buck. Publisher: Schott, 1886.

Orchestral:

Overture, *The Lakes*. MS. lost.

Scottish Overture. MS. lost.

Vocal:

Song, *Through the Long Days* (John Hay). Composed at Settle, August, 1885. Dedication: Rev. E. Vine Hall. First performance: London, St. James's Hall, 25 February 1897. Publisher: Stanley

Lucas Weber, 1887; Ascherberg, 1890; in *Seven Lieder of Edward Elgar*, Ascherberg, 1907, op. 16, No. 2.

1886 *Chamber music:*

Trio for violin, violoncello, and pianoforte. Fragment only of first movement. Re-copied 21 September 1920.

Vocal:

Song, *Is she not passing fair?* (Charles, Duc d'Orléans, tr. L. S. Costello). Publisher: Boosey, 1908.

1887 *Chamber music:*

String Quartet, op. 8. MS. destroyed.

Sonata for violin and pianoforte, op. 9. MS. destroyed.

Vocal:

Ave, Verum Corpus (Jesu, Word of God Incarnate), op. 2 No. 1. Dedication: In mcm. W. H. Publisher: Novello, 1902.

Ave Maria (Jesu, Lord of Life and Glory), op. 2, No. 2. Dedication: Mrs. H. A. Leicester. Publisher: Novello, 1907.

Ave Maris Stella (Jesu, Meek and Lowly), op. 2, No. 3. Dedication: Rev. Canon Dolman, O.S.B., Hereford. Publisher: Novello, 1907.

1888 *Chamber music:*

String Quartet in D (unfinished: 3rd movement, Intermezzo, used as No. 3 of *Eleven Vesper Voluntaries*, see **1889**.)

Allegretto on G E D G E for violin and pianoforte. Dedication: The Misses Gedge, Malvern. Publisher: Schott, 1889.

Orchestral:

Three Pieces for String Orchestra. MS. lost, but probably revised as the *Serenade in E minor*. 1. Spring Song, allegro; 2. Elegy, adagio; 3. Finale, presto. First performance: Worcestershire Musical Union, 7 May 1888. See **1892**.

Salut d'Amour (*Liebesgruss*), op. 12 (written as pianoforte solo and orchestrated). First performance: London, Crystal Palace, cond. by August Manns, 11 November 1889. Dedication: à Carice.[1] Publisher: Schott, 1889.

Vocal:

Ecce sacerdos magnus for chorus and organ. First performance: St. George's Church, Worcester, 9 October 1888. Dedication: Hubert Leicester. Publisher: Cary, 1888.

Song, *As I Laye a-thinking* (Richard Barham, 'Thomas Ingoldsby'). Publisher: Beare, 1888.

Song, *The Wind at Dawn* (C. Alice Roberts). Dedication: Dr. Ludwig Wüllner. Publisher: *Magazine of Music*, 1888; Boosey, 1907 (with dedication added).

1889 *Chamber music:*

Liebesahnung for violin and pianoforte. Dedication: Alice. (Intended as companion piece for *Liebesgruss*.)

[1] Carice in this case is Elgar's wife, not his daughter.

Mot d'Amour for violin and pianoforte, op. 13, No. 1. Publisher: Orsborn and Tuckwood; Ascherberg, 1890.

Bizarrerie for violin and pianoforte, op. 13, No. 2. Publisher: Orsborn and Tuckwood; Ascherberg, 1890.

Organ:

Eleven Vesper Voluntaries for organ, op. 14. (No. 3 is from unfinished string quartet of 1888.) Dedication: Mrs. W. A. Raikes. Publisher: Orsborn and Tuckwood, 1891; Ascherberg, 1891.

Vocal:

Song, *Queen Mary's Song* (Tennyson). Dedication: J. H. Meredith (honorary member, Worcester Amateur Instrumental Society). Publisher: Orsborn and Tuckwood, 1889; Ascherberg, 1892. Republished in *Seven Lieder of Edward Elgar*, Ascherberg, 1907.

1890   *Orchestral:*

Violin Concerto, destroyed during 1890.

Concert Overture, *Froissart*, op. 19. (Written at 51 Avonmore Road, West Kensington, between 6 April and a date in July.) First performance: Worcester Festival, Public Hall, 9 September 1890, conducted by E. E. Publisher: Novello, 1901.

Vocal:

Part-Song (S.A.T.B.) *O happy eyes* (C. A. Elgar), op. 18, No. 1. Publisher: Novello, 1896.

Part-Song (S.A.T.B.), *Love* (Arthur Maquarie), op. 18, No. 2. Dedication: C. A. E. Publisher: Novello, 1907 (after revision, 1907).

Part-Song (S.A.T.B.), *My Love dwelt in a Northern Land* (Andrew Lang). First performance: Tenbury Musical Society, 13 November 1890. Dedication: Rev. J. Hampton, M.A., Warden of St. Michael's College, Tenbury. Published: Novello, 1890.

Folk-Song arrangement, *Clapham Town End*, for voice and pianoforte.

1891   *Chamber music:*

La Capricieuse for violin and pianoforte, op. 17. Dedication: Fred Ward (a Worcester pupil of Elgar). Publisher: Breitkopf and Härtel, 1893.

Vocal:

Part-song (S.A.T.B.), *Spanish Serenade* (*Stars of the Summer Night*), op. 23. Orchestral accompaniment added June 1892. First performance: Herefordshire Philharmonic Society, 7 April 1893. Publisher: Novello, 1892.

1892   *Chamber music:*

Very Melodious Exercises in the First Position for solo violin, op. 22. Dedication: May Grafton (Elgar's niece). Publisher: Chanot, 1892; Laudy, 1927.

Etudes Caractéristiques pour violon seul, op. 24. Dedication: Adolphe Pollitzer. Publisher: Chanot, 1892. (No. 4 is known to have been written on 30 April 1882, and it may be assumed that all the rest were earlier than 1892.)

Orchestral:

Serenade in E minor for string orchestra, op. 20. 1. Allegro piacevole; 2. Larghetto; 3. Allegretto. First performance: Larghetto only, Hereford, 7 April 1893, and in London, St. Andrew's Hall, 19 June 1894. First performance of complete work, Antwerp, 23 July 1896; in England, New Brighton, 16 July 1899; in London, Bechstein Hall, 5 March 1905, cond. by E. E. Dedication: W. H. Whinfield. Publisher: Breitkopf and Härtel, 1893. (See also **1888**, *Three Pieces for Strings.*)

Choral and vocal:

The Black Knight, cantata for chorus and orchestra, op. 25. (Poem by Uhland, tr. H. W. Longfellow.) First performance: Worcester Festival Choral Society, cond. by E. E., 18 April 1893. Dedication: Hugh Blair, M.A., Mus.B. Publisher: Novello, 1893.

Song, *A spear, a sword.*

Song, *Millwheel Songs I and II.*

Song, *Like to the Damask Rose* (Simon Wastell). First performance: London, St. James's Hall, 25 February 1897. Publisher: Tuckwood, Ascherberg, 1893. Re-published in *Seven Lieder of Edward Elgar*, Ascherberg, 1907.

Song, *The Poet's Life* (Ellen Burroughs). Composed in 1892. Published in *Seven Lieder of Edward Elgar*, Ascherberg, 1907.

Song, *A Song of Autumn* (Adam Lindsay Gordon). Dedication: Miss Marshall. Publisher: Orsborn and Tuckwood; Ascherberg, 1892. Re-published in *Seven Lieder of Edward Elgar*, Ascherberg, 1907.

Song, *Shepherd's Song* (Barry Pain), op. 16, No. 1. Publisher: Tuckwood, 1895; Ascherberg, 1896. Re-published in *Seven Lieder of Edward Elgar*, Ascherberg, 1907.

1894 *Arrangement:*

Wagner, *Parsifal*, Good Friday Music, arr. for small orchestra for Worcester High School, 13 June 1894.

Orchestral:

Sursum Corda for strings, brass, and organ, op. 11. First performance: Worcester Cathedral, 9 April 1894. Dedication: H. D. Acland. Publisher: Schott, 1901.

Vocal:

Part-songs (S.S.A. with 2 violins and pianoforte), *The Snow* and *Fly, Singing Bird* (C. A. Elgar), op. 26, Nos. 1 and 2. Dedication: Mrs. E. B. Fitton, Malvern. Publisher: Novello, 1895. Orchestration added December 1903; first performance of this version, London, Queen's Hall, 12 March 1904.

Song, *The Wave.*

Song, *Muleteer's Song.*

Song, *Rondel* (Longfellow, from *Froissart*), op. 16, No. 3. First performance: London, St. James's Hall, 7 December 1897. Publisher: Ascherberg, 1896. Re-published in *Seven Lieder of Edward Elgar*, Ascherberg, 1907.

1895   *Sonata in G* for organ, op. 28. First performance: Worcester Cathedral, 8 July 1895, Hugh Blair. Dedication: C. Swinnerton Heap, Mus.D. Publisher: Breitkopf and Härtel, 1896.

Choral and vocal:

From the Bavarian Highlands. Six choral songs with pianoforte (1895) or orchestral (1896) accompaniment, op. 27. (Bavarian folksongs adapted by C. A. Elgar.) 1. The Dance; 2. False Love. 3. Lullaby; 4. Aspiration; 5. On the Alm; 6. The Marksmen; First performance: Worcester Festival Choral Society cond. by E. E., 21 April 1896. Orchestral version of Nos. 1, 3, and 6 first performed in London, Crystal Palace, 23 October 1897, cond. by August Manns. Dedication: Mr. and Mrs. Henry Slingsby Bethell, Garmisch, Bavaria. Publisher: J. Williams, 1896; orchestral versions, (*Three Bavarian Dances*) Novello, 1907.

Song, *After* (P. B. Marston), for voice and pianoforte, op. 31, No. 1. First performance: London, St. James's Hall, 2 March 1900. Publisher: Boosey, 1900.

Song, *A Song of Flight* (C. Rossetti), for voice and pianoforte, op. 31, No. 2. First performance and Publisher as for *After*.

1896   *Choral and vocal:*

Oratorio, *The Light of Life* (*Lux Christi*), for soprano, contralto, tenor, and bass soloists, chorus, and orchestra, op. 29. (Libretto written and arranged by the Rev. E. Capel-Cure.) First performance: Worcester Festival, 10 September 1896, Anna Williams, Jessie King, Edward Lloyd, Watkin Mills, cond. by E. E. Dedication: C. Swinnerton Heap, Mus.D. Publisher: Novello, 1896.

Scenes from the Saga of King Olaf, cantata for soprano, tenor, and bass soloists, chorus, and orchestra, op. 30. (Libretto by Longfellow and H. A. Acworth.) Work was begun 15 July 1894, completed August 1896. First performance: North Staffordshire Music Festival, Hanley, 30 October 1896, Medora Henson, Edward Lloyd, Ffrangcon Davies, cond. by E. E.; first performance in London, Crystal Palace, 3 April 1897, cond. by August Manns. Publisher: Novello, 1896.

Extract available in separate form, Part-song (S.A.T.B.) *As torrents in summer.*

1897   *Instrumental and orchestral:*

Minuet for pianoforte or for small orchestra, op. 21. First performance: New Brighton, 16 July 1899, cond. by Granville Bantock (orchestral version). Dedication: Paul Kilburn. Publisher: *The*

Dome and J. Williams, 1897 (pianoforte); J. Williams, 1899 (orchestra).

Chanson de Nuit for violin and pianoforte and for orchestra, op. 15, No. 1. First performance (orch.): London, Queen's Hall, 14 September 1901. Dedication: F. Ehrke, M.D. (violinist in Worcestershire Philharmonic). Publisher: Novello, 1897 (vn. & pfte.), 1899 (orch.).

Chanson de Matin for violin and pianoforte and for orchestra, op. 15, No. 2. First performance (orch.): London, Queen's Hall, 14 September 1901. Publisher: Novello, 1899 (vn. & pfte.), 1900 orch.). I consider that these two works were almost certainly composed in 1889 or 1890.

Imperial March for orchestra, op. 32. First performance: London, Crystal Palace, 19 April 1897, cond. by August Manns. Publisher: Novello, 1897.

Choral and vocal:

The Banner of St. George, ballad for chorus and orchestra, op. 33 (Shapcott Wensley). First performance: London, St. Cuthbert's Hall Choral Society, 18 May 1897. A version of this work had been performed in London on 14 March 1895, and it may have been written still earlier. Publisher: Novello, 1897.

Te Deum and Benedictus for chorus and organ, op. 34. First performance: Hereford Festival, 12 September 1897. Dedication: G. R. Sinclair. Publisher: Novello, 1897.

Part-song, *Grete Malverne on a Rock*. Private Christmas Card, 1897. Published in 1909 as the carol *Lo, Christ the Lord is born*.

Song, *Rondel: The Little Eyes that Never Knew Light* (Swinburne). First performance: Worcester Musical Union, 26 April 1897, Gertrude Walker, acc. by E. E.

Song, *Love Alone Will Stay (Lute Song)* (C. A. Elgar), for voice and pianoforte. Written 30 May 1897. Publisher: *The Dome*, 1898. Revised, orchestrated, and incorporated into *Sea Pictures*, op. 37, No. 2, 1899 as *In Haven (Capri)*. See **1899**.

1898 *Arrangement:*

The Holly and The Ivy for chorus and orchestra, for Worcestershire Philharmonic Society, 9 January 1899.

Orchestral:

Festival March in C. First performance: London, Crystal Palace, 14 October 1898, cond. by August Manns. Fragment only remains.

Variations on an Original Theme (Enigma) for orchestra, op. 36. Theme (Enigma) (andante); Var. 1. C. A. E. (andante); 2. H. D. S.-P. (allegro); 3. R. B. T. (allegretto); 4. W. M. B. (allegro di molto); 5. R. P. A. (moderato); 6. Ysobel (andantino); 7. Troyte (presto); 8. W. N. (allegretto); 9. Nimrod (adagio); 10. Intermezzo, Dorabella (allegretto); 11. G. R. S. (allegro di molto); 12. B. G. N.

(andante); 13. Romanza (moderato); 14. Finale, E. D. U. (allegro). First performance: London, St. James's Hall, 19 June 1899, cond. by Dr. Hans Richter. Dedication: To my friends pictured within. Publisher: Novello, 1899.

Choral and vocal:

Caractacus, cantata for soprano, tenor, baritone and bass soloists, chorus, and orchestra, op. 35 (H. A. Acworth). First performance: Leeds Festival, 5 October 1898, Medora Henson, Edward Lloyd, Andrew Black, John Browning, cond. by E. E. Dedication: H.M. Queen Victoria. Publisher: Novello, 1898.

Extract available separately, part-song S.A.T.B., *The Sword Song*. *O Salutaris hostia*, in Tozer's *Benediction Manual*, No. 47. Publisher: Cary, 1898.

1899–
1900 *Orchestral:*

Sérénade Lyrique for small orchestra. First performance: London, St. James's Hall, 27 November 1900. Dedication: Composed for Ivan Caryll's Orchestra. Publisher: Chappell, 1899.

Choral and vocal:

❧ *The Dream of Gerontius* (Cardinal Newman) for mezzo-soprano, tenor, and bass soloists, chorus, and orchestra, op. 38. Sketches dated 1898, composed 1899–1900 (vocal score finished 6 June 1900, orchestration finished 3 August 1900). First performance: Birmingham Festival, 3 October 1900, Marie Brema, Edward Lloyd, Plunket Greene, cond. by Dr. Hans Richter. First London performance: Westminster Cathedral, 6 June 1903, cond. by E. E. with Muriel Foster, Ludwig Wüllner, and David Ffrangçon-Davies. Dedication: A.M.D.G. (Ad Majorem Dei Gloriam). Publisher: Novello, 1900.

Part-song (S.A.T.B.), *To Her Beneath Whose Steadfast Star* (F. W. H. Myers). Composed 7 February 1899. First performance: Windsor Castle, 24 May 1899, as one of a group of songs dedicated to Queen Victoria in the manner of *The Triumphes of Oriana*. Publisher: Macmillan, 1899.

Song, *Dry Those Fair, Those Crystal Eyes* (Henry King). First performance: London, Royal Albert Hall, 21 June 1899. Publisher: Souvenir of Charing Cross Hospital Bazaar, 1899.

Song, *Pipes of Pan* (Adrian Ross). First performance: London, Queen's Hall, 12 May 1900. Publisher: Boosey, 1900.

Song-cycle, *Sea-Pictures*, for contralto or mezzo-soprano and orchestra, op. 37. 1. Sea-Slumber Song (Roden Noel); 2. In Haven (Capri) (C. A. Elgar); 3. Sabbath Morning at Sea (E. B. Browning); 4. Where Corals Lie (Richard Garnett); 5. The Swimmer (Adam Lindsay Gordon). Composed July 1899 at Birchwood, with exception of No. 2 (see **1897**, *Love Alone Will Stay*). First performance:

Norwich Festival, 5 October 1899, Clara Butt, cond. by E. E. Publisher: Boosey, 1900.

1901 *Instrumental:*

May Song for pianoforte. Publisher: W. H. Broome, 1901; Morrice Music Publishing Co.,1901; orchestral version, Elkin, 1928.

Concert Allegro for pianoforte, op. 46. First performance: London, St. James's Hall, 2 December 1901, by Fanny Davies. Dedication: For Fanny Davies, MS. rediscovered in 1968 and published by Novello, 1973 (edited by John Ogdon and Diana McVeagh).

Dramatic:

Incidental Music for *Grania and Diarmid* (W. B. Yeats and George Moore) op. 42. 1. Incidental music; 2. Funeral March; 3. Song, *There are seven that pull the thread.* First performance; Dublin, Gaiety Theatre, October 1901. *Funeral March* performed London, Queen's Hall, 18 January 1902 cond. by Sir Henry J. Wood. Dedication: Henry J. Wood. Publisher: Novello, 1902.

Orchestral:

Military Marches, *Pomp and Circumstance*, op. 39, No. 1 in D major and No. 2 in A minor. First performance: Liverpool Orchestral Society, cond. by A. E. Rodewald, 19 October 1901; first London performance: Queen's Hall, 21 October 1901, cond. by Henry J. Wood. Dedication: No. 1—A. E. Rodewald and the members of the Liverpool Orchestral Society: No. 2—Granville Bantock. Publisher: Boosey, 1902. See also *Land of Hope and Glory*, **1902**. For March No. 3 see **1904**; No. 4, **1907**; No. 5, **1930**.

Concert Overture, *Cockaigne (In London Town)*, op. 40. First performance: London, Queen's Hall, Philharmonic Society, 20 June 1901, cond. by E. E. Dedication: To my friends the members of British orchestras. Publisher: Boosey, 1901.

Orchestration of *Emmaus*, by H. A. Brewer. Publisher: Novello, 1901.

Vocal:

Song, *Come, gentle night* (Clifton Bingham). Publisher: Boosey, 1901.

Song, *Always and Everywhere* (Krasinski, tr. F. E. Fortey). Publisher: Boosey, 1901.

Songs, *In The Dawn* and *Speak, Music* (A. C. Benson), op. 41, Nos. 1 and 2. First performance: London, Queen's Hall, 26 October 1901. Dedication, No. 2: Mrs. E. Speyer, Ridgehurst. Publisher: Boosey, 1901.

1902 *Arrangement:*

God Save the King for soprano solo, chorus, and orchestra. Publisher: Novello, 1902.

Orchestral:

Dream Children, two pieces for small orchestra (or for pianoforte), op. 43, after Charles Lamb. First performance: London, Queen's Hall, 4 September 1902. Publisher: J. Williams, 1902; Schott, 1913.

Choral and vocal:

Coronation Ode (A. C. Benson), for soprano, contralto, tenor, and bass soloists, chorus, and orchestra, op. 44. 1. *Crown the King with Life*, soloists and chorus; 2. *Daughter of Ancient Kings*, for chorus; 3. *Britain, Ask of Thyself*, bass and men's chorus; 4. *Hark upon the hallowed air*, soprano and tenor soloists; 5. *Only let the heart be pure*, S.A.T.B. soloists; 6. *Peace, gentle peace*, S.A.T.B. soloists and chorus unaccompanied; 7. Finale, *Land of Hope and Glory*,[1] contralto solo, chorus, and orchestra. First performance: Sheffield Festival, 2 October 1902, Agnes Nicholls, Muriel Foster, John Coates, Ffrangcon Davies, cond. by E. E. First London performance: 26 October 1902. Dedication: H.M. King Edward VII. Publisher: Boosey, 1902.

Separate arrangement from the *Ode*—Song, *Land of Hope and Glory*. First performance: London, June 1902, Clara Butt (contralto).

Hymn, O *Mightiest of the Mighty*. First performance: Westminster Abbey, Coronation of Edward VII, 9 August 1902. Dedication: H.R.H. The Prince of Wales. Publisher: Novello, 1902.

Part-song (S.A.T.B.), *Weary Wind of the West* (T. E. Brown). Composed November 1902. First performance: Morecambe Festival, 2 May 1903. Dedication: Composed for Morecambe Musical Festival. Publisher: Novello, 1903.

Song, *Speak, my heart* (A. C. Benson). Publisher: Boosey, 1903.

Five Part-songs from the Greek Anthology (T.T.B.B.), op. 45. Completed on 11 November 1902. 1. Yea, cast me from heights (Anon., tr. Alma Strettell); 2. Whether I find thee (Anon., tr. Andrew Lang); 3. After many a dusty mile (Anon., tr. Edmund Gosse); 4. It's oh to be a wild wind (Anon., tr. W. M. Hardinge); 5. Feasting I watch (Marcus Argentarius, tr. Richard Garnett). First performance: London, Royal Albert Hall, 25 April 1904. Dedication: Sir Walter Parratt. Publisher: Novello, 1903.

1903 *Instrumental:*

Skizze, pianoforte solo. Dedication: Prof. Julius Buths, Düsseldorf. Publisher: *Musik-Beilag zur Neuen Musik-Zeitung*, Stuttgart—Leipzig XXIV Jahrgang.

Offertoire (andante religioso) for violin and pianoforte. Dedication: Serge Derval, Antwerp. Publisher: Boosey, 1903.

✝ *Choral and vocal:*

The Apostles, an oratorio for soprano, contralto, tenor, and three bass soloists, chorus, and orchestra, op. 49. (Libretto compiled by Elgar from the Bible.) First performance: Birmingham Festival,

[1] Adaptation of trio section of *Pomp and Circumstance March No. 1 in D major*.

14 October 1903, Albani, Muriel Foster, John Coates, Kennerley Rumford, Andrew Black, Ffrangcon Davies, cond. by E. E. Dedication: A. M. D. G. Publisher: Novello, 1903.

Orchestral:

Concert Overture, *In the South* (*Alassio*), op. 50. Composition begun 1903, finished 21 February 1904. First performance: London, Elgar Festival, Royal Opera House, Covent Garden, 16 March 1904, The Hallé Orchestra, cond. by E. E. Dedication: To my friend Leo F. Schuster. Publisher: Novello, 1904.

Extract available separately: *In Moonlight* (*Canto popolare*) for small orchestra, and various instrumental combinations.

1904 *Orchestral:*

Introduction and Allegro for String Quartet and String Orchestra, op. 47. First sketches, 1901, completed February 1905. First performance: London, Queen's Hall, 8 March 1905, London Symphony Orchestra, cond. by E. E. (Solo quartet, A. W Payne, W. H. Eaynes, A. Hobday, B. P. Parker.) Dedication: Professor S. S. Sanford, Yale University, U.S.A. Publisher: Novello, 1905.

Military March, *Pomp and Circumstance*, op. 39, No. 3 in C minor, completed November 1904. First performance: London, Queen's Hall, 8 March 1905, cond. by E. E. Dedication: Ivor Atkins. Publisher: Boosey, 1905. (See also **1901, 1907,** and **1930.**)

1905 *Instrumental:*

In Smyrna, pianoforte solo. Publisher: Daily Mail, Queen's Christmas Carol Book, 1905.

Vocal:

Part-song (S.A.T.B.), *Evening Scene* (Coventry Patmore). Composed 25 August 1905. First performance: Morecambe Festival, 12 May 1906. Dedication: In memoriam, R. G. H. Howson. Publisher: Novello, 1906.

1906 *Piece for Organ.* 'For Dot's nuns.' (His sister was in a convent.)

Choral and Vocal:

The Kingdom, an oratorio for soprano, contralto, tenor, and bass soloists, chorus, and orchestra, op. 51. (Libretto compiled by Elgar from the Bible.) Composed between 1901 and August 1906. First performance: Birmingham Festival, 3 October 1906, Agnes Nicholls, Muriel Foster, John Coates, William Higley, cond. by E. E. Dedication: A. M. D. G. Publisher: Novello, 1906.

1907 *Arrangement:*

Victor Berard, *Berceuse—Petite Reine*, arr. for violin and pianoforte. Publisher: Ashdown, 1907. (Probably arranged *c.* 1880).

Chamber music:

Andantino for violin, mandoline, and guitar. Unfinished. Sketched 15 June 1907 in Capri for a barber's shop where Elgar found the customers making music while they waited.

Orchestral:

The Wand of Youth, Suite No. 1 for orchestra, op. 1A. Final revision of music Elgar wrote for a children's play (see **1867**) which he had revised at various earlier dates. 1. Overture; 2. Serenade; 3. Minuet; 4. Sun Dance; 5. Fairy Pipers; 6. Slumber Scene; 7. Fairies and Giants. First performance: London, Queen's Hall, 14 December 1907, cond. by Sir Henry J. Wood. Dedication: C. Lee Williams. Publisher: Novello, 1907.

Military March, *Pomp and Circumstance*, op. 39, No. 4 in G major. (Completed 7 June 1907.) First performance: London, Queen's Hall, 24 August 1907, cond. by E. E. Dedication: G. R. Sinclair. Publisher: Boosey, 1907. (See also **1901**, **1904**, and **1930**.)

Vocal:

Two Single Chants for *Venite* in D and G. Publisher: New Cathedral Psalter, and Novello, 1909.

Two Double Chants in D for Psalms 68 and 75. Publisher: Novello, 1909.

A Christmas Greeting (C. A. Elgar), carol for two sopranos, male chorus *ad lib.*, two violins, and pianoforte, op. 52. First performance: Hereford Cathedral, 1 January 1908. Dedication: Dr. G. R. Sinclair and the choristers of Hereford Cathedral. Publisher: Novello, 1907.

Part-song (S.A.T.B.), *How calmly the evening* (T. Lynch). Publisher: Novello, 1907, in *Musical Times*.

Four Part-Songs (S.A.T.B.), op. 53. Composed in Rome in February 1907. 1. There is sweet music (Tennyson), dedication: Canon Gorton; 2. Deep in my soul (Byron), dedication: Julia H. Worthington; 3. O Wild West Wind (Shelley), dedication: W. G. McNaught; 4. Owls (E. E.), dedication: Pietro d'Alba (Peter Rabbit).[1] Publisher: Novello, 1908.

The Reveille (T.T.B.B.), op. 54 (Bret Harte). Composed in Rome, 1907. First performance: Blackpool Music Festival, 17 October 1908. Dedication: Henry C. Embleton. Publisher: Novello, 1908.

1908 *Orchestral:*

The Wand of Youth, Suite No. 2 for orchestra. op. 1B (see **1907**). 1. March; 2. The Little Bells; 3. Moths and Butterflies; 4. Fountain Dance; 5. The Tame Bear; 6. The Wild Bears. First performance: Worcester Festival, 9 September 1908, cond. by E. E. Dedication: Hubert A. Leicester. Publisher: Novello, 1908.

Symphony No. 1 in A flat major, op. 55. Composed between June 1907 and September 1908. First performance: Manchester, Free Trade Hall, 3 December 1908, The Hallé Orchestra, cond. by Dr. Hans Richter; first London performance: Queen's Hall, 7 December 1908, L.S.O., cond., by Richter. Dedication: Hans

---

[1] A white rabbit belonging to his daughter Carice.

Richter Mus. Doc., true artist and true friend. Publisher: Novello, 1908.

Vocal:

Song, *Pleading* (A. L. Salmon), op. 48. Orchestration added November 1908. Dedication: Lady Maud Warrender. Publisher: Novello, 1908.

Song for S.A.T.B., *Marching Song* (Capt. de Courcy Stretton). First performance: London, Royal Albert Hall, Empire Day Concert, 24 May 1908. Publisher: Novello, 1908. (See also **1914**, *Follow the Colours.*)

1909 *Orchestral:*

Elegy for string orchestra, op. 58. First performance: London, The Mansion House, 13 July 1909, at memorial concert of Worshipful Company of Musicians. Dedication: In memoriam late Junior Warden of Musicians' Company, Rev. R. H. Hadden, M.A. Publisher: Novello, 1910.

Vocal:

Part-song (S.A.T.B.), *Angelus (Tuscany)*, op. 56. (Words from Tuscan dialect.) First performance: London, Royal Albert Hall, 8 December 1910. Dedication: Mrs. Charles Stuart-Wortley. Publisher: Novello, 1909.

Chorus (S.S.A.A.T.B.), *Go, Song of Mine*, op. 57 (Calvacanti, tr. D. G. Rossetti). Composed at Careggi in May 1909. First performance: Hereford Festival, 9 September 1909, cond. by G. R. Sinclair. Dedication: Alfred H. Littleton. Publisher: Novello, 1909.

Carol (S.A.T.B.), *Lo! Christ the Lord is Born* (Shapcott Wensley). Composed in 1897. Publisher: Novello, 1909. (See **1897.**)

Song, *The Kingsway* (C. A. Elgar). Composed 25–27 December 1909. First performance: London, Alexandra Palace, 15 January 1910. Publisher: Boosey, 1910.

Song, *A Child Asleep* (E. B. Browning). Dedication: Anthony Goetz (son of Muriel Foster). Publisher: Novello, 1910.

Elegy (S.A.T.B.). *They are at rest* (Cardinal Newman). First performance: Royal Mausoleum, on anniversary of Queen Victoria's death, 22 January 1910. Publisher: Novello, 1910.

Song-cycle with orchestra, op. 59, Nos. 3, 5, and 6. (1, 2, and 4 never composed) (words by Gilbert Parker). Composed December 1909–January 1910. 3. Oh, soft was the song; 5. Was it some golden star?; 6. Twilight. First performance: London, Queen's Hall, 24 January 1910, Jaeger Memorial Concert. Muriel Foster (mezzo-soprano) and orchestra cond. by E. E. Publisher: Novello, 1910.

Song with pianoforte or orchestra, *The Torch*, op. 60, No. 1. (Eastern European folk-song paraphrased by 'Pietro d'Alba' and E. E.) Composed 23 December 1909, orchestrated 26 July 1912.

First performance: Hereford Festival, 11 September 1912. Dedication: Yvonne. Publisher: Novello, 1910. (See also **1910**.)

1910 *Orchestral:*

Concerto in B minor for violin and orchestra, op. 61. Composed between April 1909 and August 1910. First performance: London, Queen's Hall, Philharmonic Society concert, 10 November 1910, Fritz Kreisler and orchestra cond. by E. E. Dedication: Fritz Kreisler. On the score is inscribed a quotation in Spanish: 'Aquí está encerrada el alma de . . . . . (1910).' Publisher: Novello, 1910.

Romance for bassoon and orchestra, op. 62. First performance: Herefordshire Orchestral Society, 16 February 1911. Edwin F. James (bassoon), cond. by E. E. Dedication: Edwin F. James. Publisher: Novello, 1910.

Vocal:

Song with pianoforte or orchestra, *The River*, op. 60, No. 2. (Eastern European folk-song paraphrased by 'Pietro d'Alba' and E. E.) Composed 18 February 1910, orchestrated July 1912. First performance: Hereford Festival, 11 September 1912. Publisher: Novello, 1910. (See also **1909**.)

1911 *Arrangements:*

J. S. Bach, *St. Matthew Passion*. Two chorales, arr. for three trumpets, four horns, three trombones, tuba. First performance: Worcester Cathedral (from the tower), Three Choirs Festival, 14 September 1911.

J. S. Bach, *St. Matthew Passion*. Performing edition, with Ivor Atkins. Publisher: Novello, 1911.

Orchestral:

Symphony No. 2 in E flat major, op. 63. Composed between 1903 and February 1911. First performance: London Music Festival, Queen's Hall, 24 May 1911, Queen's Hall Orchestra, cond. by E. E. Dedication: to the memory of His Late Majesty King Edward VII. Publisher: Novello, 1911.

Coronation March, op. 65. Parts of *Rabelais* ballet (**1902**) incorporated. First performance: Westminster Abbey, Coronation of King George V, 22 June 1911. Publisher: Novello, 1911.

Vocal:

O hearken thou, offertory for chorus and orchestra, op. 64 (*Intende voci orationis meae*). First performance: Westminster Abbey, Coronation of King George V, 22 June 1911. Publisher: Novello, 1911.

1912 *Dramatic:*

Masque, *The Crown of India* (Henry Hamilton), for contralto and bass soloists, chorus, and orchestra, op. 66. Sketches from 1902 to 1912 used in composition. 1. (*a*) Introduction, (*b*) Sacred Measure; 2. Dance of Nautch Girls; 3. Hail, Immortal Ind; 4. March of Mogul Emperors; 5. Entrance of John Company; 6. Rule of

England; 7. Interlude; 8. Warriors' Dance; 9. Cities of India; 10. Crown of India March; 11. Crowning of Delhi; 12. Ave Imperator. First performance: London Coliseum, 11 March 1912. Marion Bealey, Harry Dearth, cond. by E. E. *Suite* from *Crown of India* first performed Hereford Festival, 11 September 1912, L.S.O., cond. by E. E. Publisher: Enoch, 1912.

Choral and vocal:

Ode, *The Music Makers* (O'Shaughnessy), for contralto or mezzo-soprano, chorus, and orchestra, op. 69. Work in progress from 1902, completed 21 August 1912. First performance: Birmingham Festival, 1 October 1912, Muriel Foster, cond. by E. E. Dedication: My friend Nicholas Kilburn. Publisher: Novello, 1912. (See p. 298).

Anthem (S.A.T.B.), *Great is the Lord* (Psalm 48), op. 67. Composed between August 1910 and March 1912. First performance: Westminster Abbey, 16 July 1912. Dedication: Very Rev. J. Armitage Robinson, D.D., Dean of Wells. Publisher: Novello, 1912.

1913 *Orchestral:*

Carissima, for small orchestra. First performance: Gramophone Co. recording at Hayes, Middlesex, cond. by E. E., 21 January 1914. First public performance: London, Royal Albert Hall, 15 February 1914, cond. by Landon Ronald. Dedication: Winifred Stephens (sister of Muriel Foster). Publisher: Elkin, 1914.

Symphony Study, *Falstaff*, in C minor, with two interludes, op. 68. Early sketches dated 1902, completed July 1913. First performance: Leeds Festival, 1 October 1913, cond. by E. E. Dedication: Landon Ronald. Publisher: Novello, 1913.

1914 *Orchestral:*

Sospiri for strings, harp and organ, op. 70. First performance: London, Queen's Hall, 15 August 1914, cond. by Sir Henry J. Wood. Dedication: W. H. Reed. Publisher: Breitkopf and Härtel, 1914.

Carillon, op. 75, recitation with orchestra (E. Cammaerts). Composed November 1914. First performance: London, Queen's Hall, 7 December 1914, Tita Brand (speaker), cond. by E. E. Publisher: Elkin, 1914.

Vocal:

Harvest anthem (S.A.T.B.), *Fear not, O Land* (Joel ii, vv. 21–24, 26). Publisher: Novello, 1914.

Anthem, *Give Unto the Lord* (Psalm 29), for S.A.T.B., organ, and orchestra, op. 74. First performance: London, St Paul's Cathedral, Festival of the Sons of Clergy, 30 April 1914. Dedication: Sir George Martin, M.V.O., Mus.D. Publisher: Novello, 1914.

Part-song (S.A.T.B.), *The Birthright* (G. A. Stocks). Publisher: Novello, 1914.

Follow the Colours, adapted for solo and optional male chorus from

Marching Song (see **1908**). First performance: London, Royal Albert Hall, 10 October 1914. Publisher: Novello, 1914.

Song, *Arabian Serenade* (Margery Lawrence). Publisher: Boosey, 1914.

Song, *Chariots of the Lord* (John Brownlie). First performance: London, Royal Albert Hall, 28 June 1914. Publisher: Boosey, 1914.

Two choral songs (S.A.T.B.), op. 71, No. 1, *The Shower* (Henry Vaughan), dedication: Miss Frances Smart, Malvern; No. 2, *The Fountain* (Henry Vaughan), dedication: W. Mann Dyson, Worcester. No. 1 composed at Mill Hill, No. 2 at Totteridge. Publisher: Novello, 1914.

Choral song (S.A.T.B.), *Death on the Hills*, op. 72 (Maikov, tr. Rosa Newmarch). Composed January 1914. Dedication: Lady Colvin. Publisher: Novello, 1914.

Two choral songs (S.A.T.B.), op. 73. No. 1, *Love's Tempest* (Maikov, tr. Rosa Newmarch), dedication: C. Sanford Terry. No. 2, *Serenade* (Maikov, tr. Rosa Newmarch), dedication: Percy C. Hull. Composed January 1914. Publisher: Novello, 1914.

1915 *Dramatic:*

Incidental Music for *The Starlight Express*, op. 78 (play by Violet Pearn based on *The Prisoner in Fairyland* by Algernon Blackwood). 1. To the Children (Organ-Grinder's 1st Song); 2. Come Little Winds and Wind Dance; 3. Curfew Song (Orion); 4. The Laugher's Song; 5. The Blue-Eyes Fairy (Organ-Grinder's 2nd Song); 6. Tears and Laughter; Sunrise Song; 7. My Old Tunes (Organ-Grinder's 3rd Song); 8. Hearts must be soft-shiny dressed (duet); 9. Finale. First performance: London, Kingsway Theatre, 29 December 1915, Clytie Hine (soprano), Charles Mott (bass), cond. by Julius Harrison. Publisher: Nos. 1, 5, and 7, Elkin, 1916.

Orchestral:

Symphonic Prelude *Polonia*, op. 76. First performance: London, Queen's Hall, Polish Victims' Relief Fund Concert, 6 July 1915, cond. by E. E. Dedication: I. J. Paderewski. Publisher: Elkin, 1915.

Une Voix dans le Désert, op. 77, recitation with orchestra, included song, *Quand nos bourgeons se rouvriront*, for solo soprano (E. Cammaerts). First performance: London, Shaftesbury Theatre, 29 January 1916, Carlo Liten (reciter), Olga Lynn (soprano), cond. by E. E. (Later performances by Beecham). Publisher: Elkin, 1915.

Choral and vocal:

The Spirit of England, op. 80—see **1916**.

1916 *Choral and vocal:*

The Spirit of England (Laurence Binyon) for soprano and contralto or tenor soloists, chorus, and orchestra, op. 80. Nos. 2 and 3 com-

posed 1915, performed separately 1916; No. 1 completed 1917.
1. The Fourth of August. First performance: Birmingham, 4 October 1917, Rosina Buckman (soprano), cond. by Appleby Matthews; 2. To Women. First performance: Leeds Choral Union, 3 May 1916, John Booth (tenor), cond. by E. E.; 3. For the Fallen, First performance: Leeds Choral Union, 3 May 1916, Agnes Nicholls (soprano), cond. by E. E. First London performances of 2 and 3, Queen's Hall, 8 May 1916, Clara Butt. First performance of complete work: London, Royal Albert Hall, 24 November 1917, Agnes Nicholls (soprano), Gervase Elwes (tenor), cond. by E. E. Dedication: To the memory of our glorious men, with a special thought for the Worcesters. Publisher: Novello, 1917.
Song, *Fight for Right* (William Morris). Dedication: Members of the Fight for Right Movement. Publisher: Elkin, 1916.

1917 *Dramatic:*
The Sanguine Fan, Ballet (based on a Fan by Charles Conder), op. 81. First performance: London, Chelsea Palace Theatre, 20 March 1917, as part of revue *Chelsea on Tiptoe*. Ballet arranged by Mrs. Christopher Lowther, conducted by E. E.
Extract, *Echo's Dance*, for pianoforte, published by Elkin, 1917.
Orchestral:
Le drapeau belge, op. 79, recitation with orchestra (E. Cammaerts). First performance: London, Queen's Hall, 14 April 1917, Carlo Liten (reciter), cond. by Hamilton Harty. Publisher: Elkin, 1917.
Vocal:
The Fringes of the Fleet (R. Kipling), four songs for four baritones.
1. The Lowestoft Boat; 2. Fate's Discourtesy; 3. Submarines; 4. The Sweepers. First performance: London Coliseum, 11 June 1917, Charles Mott, Harry Barratt, Frederick Henry, Frederick Stewart, cond. by E. E. Dedication: Admiral Lord Beresford. Publisher: Enoch, 1917.
Inside the Bar (Gilbert Parker), song for four baritones. Added to *Fringes of the Fleet* and first performed London Coliseum, 25 June 1917, by above singers. Dedication: The 4 Singers. Publisher: Enoch, 1917.

1918 *Chamber music:*
Sonata in E minor for violin and pianoforte, op. 82. First public performance: London, Aeolian Hall, 21 March 1919, W. H. Reed (violin) and Landon Ronald (pianoforte).[1] Dedication: Marie Joshua. Publisher: Novello, 1918.
String Quartet in E minor, op. 83. First public performance: London, Wigmore Hall, 21 May 1919, Albert Sammons, W. H. Reed,

---

[1] First performance was by Reed and Elgar on 15 October 1918, at Severn House. It was played on 13 March 1919, by Reed and Anthony Bernard at a British Music Society Meeting.

U

Raymond Jeremy, Felix Salmond. Dedication: The Brodsky Quartet, Publisher: Novello, 1918.

Song, *Big Steamers* (Kipling). Publisher: *Teachers' World*, 19 June 1918.

1919 *Chamber music:*

Quintet in *A minor* for strings and pianoforte, op. 84. Composed between summer 1918 and spring 1919. First public performance: London, Wigmore Hall, 21 May 1919, Albert Sammons, W. H. Reed, Raymond Jeremy, Felix Salmond, William Murdoch (pianoforte).[1] Dedication: Ernest Newman. Publisher: Novello, 1919.

Orchestral:

Concerto in *E minor* for violoncello and orchestra, op. 85. First performance: London, Queen's Hall, 26 October 1919, Felix Salmond, and L.S.O., cond. by E. E. Dedication: Sidney and Frances Colvin. Publisher: Novello, 1919.

Arrangement of above as *Viola Concerto* by Lionel Tertis. First performance: London, Queen's Hall, 21 March 1930. Lionel Tertis (viola), B.B.C. Symphony Orchestra, conducted by E. E.

1921 *Transcription:*

J. S. Bach, *Fugue in C minor* [Elgar op. 86]. Completed 24 April 1921. First performance: London, Queen's Hall, 27 October 1921, cond. by Eugène Goossens. Publisher: Novello, 1921. (See also **1922**.)

1922 *Transcription:*

J. S. Bach, *Fantasy in C minor*. First performance: Gloucester Festival, 7 September 1922, L.S.O., cond. by E. E. Publisher: Novello, 1922. (See also **1921**.)

Parry, *Jerusalem*, orchestration added. First performance: Leeds Festival, 1922.

1923 *Transcription:*

Handel, *Overture in D minor* (Chandos Anthem II), transcr. for orchestra. First performance: Worcester Festival, 2 September 1923, L.S.O., cond. by E. E. Publisher: Novello, 1923.

Batitishill, Motet, *O Lord, look down from heaven*, orchestral accompaniment. First performance: Worcester Festival, 6 September 1923.

S. S. Wesley, Motet, *Let us lift up our hearts*, orchestral accompaniment. First performance: Worcester Festival, 6 September 1923.

Dramatic:

Incidental music to *Arthur* (Laurence Binyon). First performance: London, Old Vic, 12 March 1923, cond. by Charles Corri. Unpublished.

Instrumental:

Memorial Chimes for a Carillon. First performance: Opening of Loughborough War Memorial Carillon, 22 July 1923. Unpublished.

[1] The Quartet and Quintet were first performed privately at Schuster's London house 22 Old Queen Street, on 22 April 1919.

Vocal:

Part-song (T.T.B.B.), *The Wanderer* (Anon. adapted from *Wit and Drollery*, 1661). Publisher: Novello, 1923.

Part-song (T.T.B.B.), *Zut, zut, zut* (Richard Marden). Publisher: Novello, 1923.

1924 *Chamber music:*

March for violin, violoncello, and pianoforte. For the Grafton family. Unpublished. (It is a sketch for the *Empire March.*)

Orchestral:

Empire March. First performance: Wembley, British Empire Exhibition, 21 July 1924, cond. by Henry Jaxon. Publisher: Enoch 1924.[1]

Vocal:

Pageant of Empire (Alfred Noyes), Eight songs for solo or S.A.T.B. 1. Shakespeare's Kingdom; 2. The Islands; 3. The Blue Mountains; 4. The Heart of Canada; 5. Sailing Westward; 6. Merchant Adventurers; 7. The Immortal Legions; 8. A Song of Union. Nos. 5, 7, and 8 arr. for S.A.T.B. First performance: Wembley Exhibition, 21 July 1924. Publisher: Enoch, 1924.

1925 *Vocal:*

Part-song (T.T.B.B.), *The Herald* (Alexander Smith). Publisher: Novello, 1925.

Part-song (S.A.T.B.), *The Prince of Sleep* (Walter de la Mare). Publisher: Elkin, 1925.

1927 *Instrumental:*

Civic Fanfare. Written for mayoral procession, opening of Hereford Festival, 4 September 1927. Dedication: Percy C. Hull. Unpublished.

1928 *Dramatic:*

Incidental music to *Beau Brummel* (B.P. Matthews). First performance: Birmingham, Theatre Royal, 5 November 1928, cond. by E. E. Unpublished, with exception of *Minuet*, Elkin, 1929.

Vocal:

Carol (S.A.T.B.), *I sing the birth* (B. Jonson). Dedication: Rev. Harcourt B. S. Fowler, Elmley Castle, Worcs. Publisher: Novello, 1928.

1929 *Arrangement:*

Purcell, Motet, *Jehova, quam multi sunt hostes mei*, accompaniment for orchestra. First performance: Worcester, 10 September 1929.

Vocal:

Carol (S.A.T.B.), *Good Morrow* (George Gascoigne). 'A simple carol for His Majesty's happy recovery.' First performance: Windsor, St. George's Chapel, 9 December 1929. Publisher: Novello, 1929.

[1] This march was not played at the opening ceremony on 23 April because of 'difficulties in the way of the Brigade Bands co-operating etc etc' (Elgar to Lady Stuart, 16 April 1924).

1930 *Orchestral:*

Severn Suite, op. 87, for brass band. Sketches of 1879 and 1903 were used in this work. 1. Introduction (Worcester Castle); 2. Toccata (Tournament); 3. Fugue (Cathedral); 4. Minuet (Commandery). First performance: Crystal Palace Brass Band Festival, 27 September 1930. Dedication: G. Bernard Shaw. Publisher: R. Smith, 1930. (See also **1932** and **1933**.) Fugue composed 1923.

Military March, *Pomp and Circumstance*, op. 39, No. 5 in C major. First performance: London, Queen's Hall, 20 September 1930, cond. by Sir Henry J. Wood. Dedication: Percy C. Hull. Publisher: Boosey, 1930. (See also **1901**, **1904**, and **1907**.)

Vocal:

Song, *It isnae me* (Sally Holmes). First performance: Dumfries, October 1930. Joan Elwes (soprano). Dedication: Joan Elwes. Publisher: Keith Prowse, 1931.

1931 *Orchestral:*

Nursery Suite. 1. Aubade (uses Hymn Tune in F of 1878); 2. The Serious Doll; 3. Busy-ness; 4. The Sad Doll; 5. The Wagon Passes; 6. The Merry Doll; 7. Dreaming—Envoy. First performance: London, Kingsway Hall, H.M.V. recording session, 4 June 1931, L.S.O., cond. by E. E.; first public performance: Queen's Hall Promenade Concert, 20 August 1931, cond. by E. E.; as a ballet arr. Ninette de Valois, Old Vic, 21 March 1932, cond. by Constant Lambert. Dedication: Their Royal Highnesses the Duchess of York, and the Princesses Elizabeth and Margaret Rose. Publisher: Keith Prowse, 1931.

Vocal:

Unison Song, *The Rapid Stream* (Charles Mackay). Publisher: Keith Prowse, 1931.

Unison Song, *When Swallows Fly* (Charles Mackay). Publisher: Keith Prowse, 1931.

1932 *Instrumental:*

Sonatina for pianoforte. Dedication: May Grafton. Publisher: Keith Prowse, 1932.

Adieu for pianoforte (also transcribed for violin by Josef Szigeti). Publisher: Keith Prowse, 1932.

Serenade for pianoforte. Dedication: John Austin, friend and editor for many years. Publisher: Keith Prowse, 1932.

(These works were almost certainly written many years earlier.)

Orchestral:

Severn Suite, op. 87. Arranged for orchestra. First performance: London, H.M.V. Abbey Road Studios, recording session 23 June 1932, L.S.O., cond. by E. E. First public performance: Worcester Festival, 7 September 1932, cond. by E. E. Publisher: Keith Prowse, 1932. (See also **1930** and **1933**.)

Vocal:

Ode for chorus, *So many true princesses who have gone* (Masefield). First performance: London, Marlborough House, 9 June 1932, at unveiling of memorial to Queen Alexandra.

1933 *Transcription:*

Chopin, *Funeral March from Sonata in B flat minor.* First performance: London, Queen's Hall, 25 February 1934, Royal Philharmonic Society memorial concert to Elgar. Publisher: Keith Prowse, 1933.

Instrumental:

Organ Sonata No. 2, op. 87A (arr. by Ivor Atkins of *Severn Suite*). First performance: London, Organ Music Society, 1933. Publisher: Keith Prowse, 1933.

Orchestral:

Mina[1] for small orchestra. First performance: H.M.V. recording, 8 February 1934. Publisher: Keith Prowse, 1934.

Vocal:

Unison Song, *The Woodland Stream* (Charles Mackay). First performance: Worcester Schools Music Festival, 18 May 1933. Dedication: Stephen S. Moore, Worcester. Publisher: Keith Prowse, 1933.

PROJECTED WORKS

The following are works which Elgar, in his maturity, contemplated writing. Some of the sketches remain in the British Museum; others he used in other works. His plans for a Hardy opera and *King Lear* are not included because no sketches exist.

1901 'Welsh Overture' (sketch used in *Introduction and Allegro,* **1905**)

1902–3 *Rabelais,* a ballet.

1903 Concert overture, *Cockaigne No. 2.*

Fantasia for Strings. Dedication: Hans (Richter).

1906 Oratorio: *The Last Judgement* (third part of trilogy).

1908 *In Memoriam* (2 June 1908), 'In memory of a seer.' (This may have been a work planned to commemorate Jaeger, whose death was by then inevitable.)

1909 *Tuscan Fantastico* in A flat.

Scherzo for pianoforte and orchestra.

Opera in Three Acts.

Choral Suite, some to words by W. S. Landor. Planned as 1. Introduction; 2. In a Vineyard; 3. Angelus; 4. Dance; 5. Vintage; 6. Envoi. No. 3 was completed and published as op. 56, No. 1.

1913 Scena, *Callicles* (Matthew Arnold). For Muriel Foster.

[1] Mina was Elgar's cairn terrier.

1917   *Ozymandias* (Shelley).
1930   *Soliloquy* for oboe, for Léon Goossens. (Orchestrated 1967 by Gordon
           Jacob. First performance: B.B.C. Television, 11 June 1967, Léon
           Goossens, conducted by Neils Gron).
1932–3 Concerto for pianoforte and orchestra, op. 90. Sketches worked on in
           1909, 1914, 1917, 1925, and 1932.
           Tarantella (Belloc) for baritone and orchestra.
           Opera in two Acts, *The Spanish Lady*, op. 89. (Libretto by Sir Barry
           Jackson from Ben Jonson's *The Devil is an Ass*.) Sketches incorporate
           material dating from 1878. For details see *Elgar O.M.* by Dr. Percy
           Young (London, 1955), pp. 360–75. Two songs, *Modest and Fair* and
           Still to be Neat, edited by Percy Young, were published by Elkin in
           1955, and a suite for strings, edited by Dr. Young, in 1956.
           Symphony No. 3, op. 88. Fragmentary sketches in British Museum.
           The sketches were reproduced in W. H. Reed's *Elgar As I Knew Him*.

APPENDIX II

Quotations in 'The Music Makers', Op. 69

Following is a list of Elgar's self-quotations and quotations in *The Music Makers*.
The page numbers refer to the vocal score:

PAGE

3–4.   Prelude: 'Enigma' theme from *Variations*, op. 36.
5.   At 'dreams': theme from *The Dream of Gerontius*, op. 38.
6.   At 'sea breakers': theme from *Sea Pictures*, op. 37.
       At 'desolate streams': 'Enigma' theme.
8.   At 'for ever it seems': 'Enigma' theme.
11.   At 'empire's glory': *Rule, Britannia* and *La Marseillaise*.
42.   At 'on one man's soul': 'Nimrod' theme from *Variations*.
44.   At 'and his look': theme from finale of Symphony No. 2, op. 63.
65.   At 'the glorious futures we see': 'Enigma' theme.
66–67. At 'in our dreaming and our singing a little apart': theme from Violin
       Concerto, op. 61.
69.   At 'out of the infinite morning': main theme of Symphony No. 1, op.
       55.
84–85. At 'a singer who sings no more': 'Novissima hora est' from *Gerontius*.

APPENDIX III
Select Bibliography

A. WRITINGS BY ELGAR

Preface to *The Singing of the Future*, by David Ffrangcon Davies, London, 1904.
Lectures delivered to Birmingham University, 1905–6.
Falstaff: analytical note, London, 1913.
My Friends Pictured Within (Enigma Variations), London, 1923.
Notation, London, 1920.
Foreword to *Forgotten Worcester* by H. A. Leicester, Worcester, 1930.
Programme Notes for Worcestershire Philharmonic Society, 1898–1904.
'The Quadruple Alliance', letter in *Times Literary Supplement*, 4 September 1919.
'Scott and Shakespeare', letter in *Times Literary Supplement*, 21 July 1921.
'A Visit to Delius', *The Daily Telegraph*, 1 July 1933.

B. BOOKS AND ARTICLES ABOUT ELGAR AND HIS TIME

Anderson, W. R. *Introduction to the Music of Elgar*, London, 1949.
Barber, Cecil. 'Enigma Variations—The Original Finale', *Music and Letters*, April 1935.
Bax, Sir Arnold. *Farewell, My Youth*, London, 1943.
Bennett, Joseph. *King Olaf, Analytical Note*, London, 1896.
Bonavia, Ferruccio. 'Elgar' in *Lives of the Great Composers*, Vol. 3, London, 1935.
  Elgar' in *The Music Masters*, Vol. 3—The Romantic Composers, London, 1952.
  'Edward Elgar' in *The Symphony* (ed. Ralph Hill), London, 1949.
Buckley, R. J. *Sir Edward Elgar*, London, 1905.
Byard, Herbert. 'Edward Elgar' in *The Concerto* (ed. Ralph Hill), London 1952.
Cardus, Sir Neville. 'Elgar' in *A Composers' Eleven*, London, 1958. (Originally in *Ten Composers*, London, 1945.)
Colles, H. C. Analytical notes of First Symphony, Quintet, and Violoncello Concerto in *Musical Times* of, respectively, December 1908, November 1919, February 1920.
  Articles on Elgar in *Grove's Dictionary of Music and Musicians*, 3rd and 5th editions, London, 1927 and 1954.
Cox, David. 'Edward Elgar' in *The Symphony*, Vol. 2 (ed. Robert Simpson). London, 1967.
Cumberland, Gerald. 'Elgar' in *Set Down in Malice*, London, 1919.
Dann, Mary G. 'Elgar's Use of the Sequence', *Music and Letters*, July 1938.

Dunhill, Thomas F. *Sir Edward Elgar*, London, 1938.

Fox Strangways, A. H. 'Elgar' in *Music and Letters*, April 1934.

Gaisberg, Fred. *Music on Record*, London, 1946.

Goossens, Eugène. *Overture and Beginners*, London, 1951.

Gorton, Canon. *Interpretation of the Librettos of the Oratorios:* 1. The Dream of
     Gerontius; 2. The Apostles; 3. The Kingdom. London, 1907.

Gray, Cecil. 'Edward Elgar' in *A Survey of Contemporary Music*, Oxford, 1924.

Greene, H. Plunket. *Charles Villiers Stanford*, London, 1935.

Grew, Sydney. 'Sir Edward Elgar, O.M.' in *Our Favourite Musicians*, London,
     1924.

Howes, Frank. 'Edward Elgar' in *The Heritage of Music*, Vol. III, Oxford, 1951.
     'The Two Elgars' in *Music and Letters*, January 1935.
     The English Musical Renaissance, London, 1966.

Jackson, Sir Barry. 'Elgar's "Spanish Lady" ', *Music and Letters*, January 1943.

Jaeger, A. J. *Analytical notes* of *The Dream of Gerontius, The Apostles, In the
     South* and *The Kingdom*, London, 1900, 1903, 1904, and 1906 respectively.

Johnstone, Arthur. *Musical Criticisms*, Manchester, 1905.

Keeton, A. E. 'Elgar's Music for "The Starlight Express" ' in *Music and Letters*,
     January 1945.

Lambert, Constant. *Music, Ho!* London, 1934.

Langford, Samuel. *Musical Criticisms* (ed. N. Cardus), London, 1929.

McVeagh, Diana M. *Edward Elgar: His Life and Music*, London, 1955.
     'Elgar's Birthplace' in *Musical Times*, June 1957.

Maine, Basil. *Elgar: His Life and Works*, Vols. I and II, London, 1933.

Mason, Daniel Gregory. *Contemporary Composers*, New York, 1918.

Moore, Jerrold N. *An Elgar Discography*, London, 1963. (A detailed and valuable
     list of Elgar recordings, including notes on all those made by Elgar him-
     self, with dates of recording sessions, etc.)

Music and Letters. Elgar Memorial Issue, January 1935.

Musical Times. Elgar Memorial Issue, April 1934. (Contains list of articles on
     Elgar published in *Musical Times* in his lifetime.)

     Elgar Centenary Number, June 1957. (Contains contributions by Vaughan
     Williams, John Ireland, Julius Harrison, Sir Arthur Bliss, Herbert Howells,
     Gordon Jacob, Edmund Rubbra, Patrick Hadley, Sir Jack Westrup, Sir
     Steuart Wilson, H. W. Sumsion, Eric Blom, Frank Howes, Sir George
     Dyson, Sir Thomas Armstrong, Sir Ernest Bullock, W. Greenhouse Allt,
     Edric Cundell, R. J. F. Howgill, Maurice Johnstone, Eric Warr.)

Newman, Ernest. *Elgar*, London, 1905.
     'Edward Elgar', No. 2 in *The New School of British Music* in *The Speaker*,
     22 December 1901.
     'Elgar and his Enigma' in *Sunday Times* 15, 23, 30 April, 7 May 1939.
     'Elgar and his "Stately Sorrow" ' in *The Listener*, 11 March 1954.
     Analytical notes of Violin Concerto, Second Symphony, and Spirit of
     England in *Musical Times* of, respectively, October 1910, May 1911, and
     May 1916.

Porte, John F. *Elgar*, London, 1921.

Powell, Richard C. 'Elgar's "Enigma"' in *Music and Letters*, July 1934. (See reply by Fox Strangways in January 1935.)

Powell, Mrs. Richard C. ('Dorabella'). *Edward Elgar: Memories of a Variation* London, 1937, 2nd ed. 1947.

Reed, W. H. *Elgar As I Knew Him*, London, 1936.

  Elgar, London, 1939.

  'Elgar' in *Cobbett's Cyclopaedic Survey of Chamber Music*, London, 1929, 2nd ed. 1963.

  'Elgar's Violin Concerto' in *Music and Letters*, January, 1935.

  'Elgar's Third Symphony' in *The Listener*, 28 August 1935.

Shaw, G. Bernard. 'Sir Edward Elgar' in *Music and Letters*, January 1920.

Sheldon, A. J. *Edward Elgar*, London, 1932.

Shera, F. H. *Elgar: Instrumental Works*, London, 1931.

Shore, Bernard. 'Elgar's Second Symphony' in *Sixteen Symphonies*, London, 1949.

Speyer, Edward. *My Life and Friends*, London, 1937.

Stockley, W. C. *Fifty Years of Music in Birmingham, 1850–1900*. Birmingham, 1913.

Strand Magazine. 'Dr. Elgar': an interview by Rupert de Cordova, May 1904.

Thompson, Herbert. *Analytical Note on Caractacus*, London, 1898.

Tovey, Sir Donald F. Analytical notes of Elgar's Symphony No. 2, Falstaff, Enigma Variations, Cockaigne, In the South, Introduction and Allegro, Violin Concerto, Violoncello Concerto in *Essays in Musical Analysis*, Vols. II, III, IV, and VI, London, 1935–9, also in *Some English Symphonists*, London, 1941.

  'Elgar, Master of Music' in *Music and Letters*, January 1935.

Various Authors. *Edward Elgar: Centenary Sketches* (contributions by Sir John Barbirolli, Carice Elgar Blake, Sir Adrian Boult, H. A. Chambers, Bernard Herrmann, Alan J. Kirby, Yehudi Menuhin, Dora M. Powell, Stanford Robinson, David Willcocks, Percy M. Young), London, 1957.

Vaughan Williams, Ralph. 'What Have We Learnt from Elgar?' in *Music and Letters*, January 1935.

Vaughan Williams, Ursula. *R.V.W. a Biography of Ralph Vaughan Williams*, London, 1964.

Watkins Shaw, A. *The Three Choirs Festival*, Worcester, 1954.

Wood, Sir Henry J. *My Life of Music*, London, 1938.

Young, Percy M. *Elgar, O. M.* London, 1955.

  Letters of Edward Elgar and other writings (ed.) London, 1956.

  Letters to Nimrod from Edward Elgar (ed.), London, 1965.

  A Future for English Music: and other lectures by Edward Elgar (the Birmingham lectures) (ed.), London, 1968.

APPENDIX IV

Recordings conducted by Elgar

Here is a list of gramophone records conducted by Elgar, who was the first
great composer to take advantage of the opportunity presented by the invention
of the gramophone for preserving his interpretations of his music. The dates
and facts are taken from Jerrold N. Moore's invaluable *An Elgar Discography*,
to which readers are recommended for fuller and fascinating detail. The list is
in chronological order of recording sessions, of which the dates, where known,
are given. All recordings were made for the Gramophone Company and
appeared under the H.M.V. label.

1914 21 January:

Carissima (D 176). The orchestra in pre-electric recordings until 1921
is described as 'Symphony Orchestra'.

1915 ? January:

Pomp and Circumstance Marches Nos. 1 and 4 (D 179); *Salut d'Amour*
(D 180); *Bavarian Dances* Nos. 2 and 3 (D 175–6).

29 January:

Carillon (Henry Ainley, reciter) (D 177).

1916 19 February:

The Starlight Express, Agnes Nicholls (soprano), Charles Mott (baritone): To the Children and The Blue-Eyes Fairy (D 455), Curfew
Song and My Old Tunes (D 456), Tears and Laughter, Sunrise Song
and Come, Little Winds, Wind Dance (D 457), Hearts must be soft-
shiny dressed and The Laugher's Song (D 458).

13 and 16 December:

Violin Concerto (severely cut), Marie Hall (violin). (D 79–80).

1917 4 July:

Fringes of the Fleet, Charles Mott, Frederick Henry, Frederick Stewart,
Harry Barratt (baritones). 'Fate's Discourtesy' and 'The Lowestoft
Boat' (D 453), 'Submarines' and 'The Sweepers' (D 454).

1919 22 May:

Polonia (cut) (D 493); *Chanson de Nuit* (D 180); *Wand of Youth Suite
No. 1:* 'Overture', 'Sun Dance', 'Serenade', 'Little Bells' (D 48), 'Fairy
Pipers', 'Moths and Butterflies', 'March', 'Fairies and Giants' (D 468).

22 December:

Violoncello Concerto, Beatrice Harrison (cello) (D 541 and D 545).

1920 24 February:

Selection, *The Sanguine Fan* (D 596).

Enigma Variations, 'Nimrod' and 'Dorabella' (D 582).

302

? November:
Enigma Variations (R. B. T., W. M. B., and R. P. A.) (D 578); re-recording of Adagio, *Violoncello Concerto* (D 545).

1921 May:
Enigma Variations (Theme, C. A. E. and H. D. S.-P.) (D 578); (G. R. S., B. G. N., and E. D. U.) (D 602); (E. D. U. conclusion) (D 596).
December:
Fugue in C minor (Bach–Elgar) (D 614); *King Olaf*: A Little Bird in the Air (D 614); *In the South*, Part I (D 785). Royal Albert Hall Orchestra.

1922 January:
In the South, Parts II, III, and IV (D 785–6). R.A.H. Orchestra.
November:
Sea Pictures, Leila Megane (contralto). 'Sea-Slumber Song', 'In Haven', 'Where Corals Lie' (D 674), 'Sabbath Morning at Sea', 'The Swimmer' (D 675).

1923 October:
Overture in D minor (Handel–Elgar), *Fantasia in C minor* (Bach–Elgar) (D 838). R.A.H. Orchestra.

1924 March:
Symphony No. 2 in E flat (D 1012–17). R.A.H. Orchestra.

1925 April:
The Light of Life (Lux Christi): Meditation (D 1017). R.A.H. Orchestra.
All the above were acoustical recordings. The remainder are electrical.

1926 27 April:
Overture, *Cockaigne* (D 1110–11); *Pomp and Circumstance* marches Nos. 1 and 2 (D 1102); *Chanson de Nuit* (D 1236). R.A.H. Orchestra. Recorded in Queen's Hall. *Chanson de Nuit* re-issued on HLM 7005.
28 and 30 April:
Enigma Variations (D 1154–7); *Meditation (Light of Life)* (D 1157). R.A.H. Orchestra. Recorded in Queen's Hall. The *Variations* re-issued on WRC SH 162. Also on RLS 708.

1927 26 February:
The Dream of Gerontius (recorded at a performance in the Royal Albert Hall), Margaret Balfour (contralto), Steuart Wilson (tenor), Herbert Heyner (bass), Royal Choral Society, R.A.H. Orchestra. 'Praise to the Holiest' and 'And now the threshold' (D 1242), 'Go, in the name of angels and archangels', and 'Come back, O Lord' (D 1243). Some extracts unpublished and now destroyed.
1 April:
Symphony No. 2 in E flat (D 1230–5). *Chanson de Matin* (D 1236). London Symphony Orchestra. Recorded in Queen's Hall. Symphony re-issued on WRC SH 163 (also on RLS 708), *Chanson* on HLM 7005.

July:
Pomp and Circumstance, marches Nos. 3 and 4 (D 1301); *Bavarian Dances*, Nos. 1 and 2 (D 1367), L.S.O. in Queen's Hall.

4 September:
Civic Fanfare (first performance, recorded at opening service of Three Choirs Festival, Hereford Cathedral, L.S.O.). *The Spirit of the Lord is upon me* from *The Apostles*, recorded at same time but not issued.

6 September:
The Dream of Gerontius (recorded at Three Choirs Festival, Hereford Cathedral, Margaret Balfour (contralto), Tudor Davies (tenor), Horace Stevens (bass), Sir Herbert Brewer (organ), L.S.O., Festival Chorus). 'So pray for me, O Jesu, help' (D 1350), 'Jesu! By that shudd'ring dread' and 'Take me away' (D 1348). Other extracts not issued.

8 September:
The Music Makers (recorded at Three Choirs Festival, Hereford Cathedral, Olga Haley (contralto), Festival Chorus, L.S.O., Sir H. Brewer (organ)). 'We are the music makers', 'A breath of our inspiration' (D 1349), 'For we afar in the dim ages' (D 1347). Other extracts not issued. The above Hereford recordings re-issued on RLS 708. Also on WRC SH 175.

1928 3 February:
Land of Hope and Glory, God Save the King, O God Our Help in Ages Past (Croft), Margaret Balfour (contralto), L.S.O., Philharmonic Choir (C 1467). Recorded in Queen's Hall.
The Banner of St. George: 'It Comes from the Misty Ages': not issued.

23 March and 13 June:
Violoncello Concerto (Beatrice Harrison, New Symphony Orchestra) (D 1507–9). Re-issued on RLS 708. Also on WRC SH 175.

November (some re-takes made March 1929):
Wand of Youth, Suite No. 1, 'Overture', 'Serenade', 'Minuet', 'Sun Dance' (D 1636), 'Fairy Pipers', 'Slumber Scene' (D 1637), 'Fairies and Giants' (D 1638).
Wand of Youth, Suite No. 2, 'March', 'Little Bells', 'Moths and Butterflies' (D 1649), 'Fountain Dance', 'The Tame Bear', 'The Wild Bears' (D 1650).
Minuet (Beau Brummel) (D 1638). L.S.O.
Contrasts: The Gavotte (not issued).

1929 7 and 8 November:
Sérénade Lyrique and *Rosemary* (D 1778).
May Song (D 1949).
Salut d'Amour and *Carissima* (E 547).
Falstaff: Two Interludes and *Minuet*, op. 21 (D 1863).
Mazurka (Japanese Victor JF 38 only).
New Symphony Orchestra, recorded in Small Queen's Hall. *Salut d'Amour* and *Mazurka* re-issued on HLM 7005.

1930 September:
Suite, Crown of India, Introduction and Dance of the Nautch Girls,

Minuet, Warriors' Dance (D 1899), March of the Mogul Emperors (D 1900).

Pomp and Circumstance march No. 5 (D 1900). Re-issued on HLM 7005.

In the South (DB 1665–7). L.S.O.

20, 21, and 22 November:

Symphony No. 1 in A flat (D 1944–9). L.S.O. in Kingsway Hall. Re-issued on WRC SH 139, also on RLS 708.

1931 4 June:

Nursery Suite, 'Aubade', 'The Serious Doll', 'Busy-ness' (DB 1998), 'The Sad Doll', 'The Wagon Passes', 'The Merry Doll', 'Dreaming, Envoy' (DD 1999). L.S.O. (W. H. Reed, violin; Gordon Walker, flute).

11 and 12 November:

Falstaff (DB 1621–4). L.S.O., in Abbey Road Studio (DB 1622 re-recorded 4 February 1932). Violin solo played by W. H. Reed. Re-issued on WRC SH 162, also on RLS 708.

1932 4 February:

Bavarian Dance No. 3 (DB 1667). L.S.O. Re-issued on HLM 7005.

23 June:

Severn Suite (orchestral version), Introduction and Toccata (DB 1908), Fugue and Minuet (DB 1909), Minuet, Part II and Coda (DB 1910). L.S.O.

14 and 15 July:

Violin Concerto (Yehudi Menuhin, L.S.O.) (DB 1751–6). Re-issued on LP (mono) ALP 1456 and on RLS 708.

October:

Pomp and Circumstance marches Nos. 1 and 2 (DB 1801). B.B.C. Symphony Orchestra, Berkeley Mason (organ). Re-issued on HLM 7005.

1933 21 February:

Overture, Froissart (DB 1938–9).

Contrasts: The Gavotte (DB 1910). London Philharmonic Orchestra.

11 April:

Overture, Cockaigne (DB 1935–6). Re-issued on LP (mono) ALP 1464.

Pomp and Circumstance march No. 4 (DB 1936). Re-issued on HLM 7005.

Prelude, The Kingdom (DB 1934). B.B.C. Symphony Orchestra. Re-issued on WRC SH 139.

29 August:

Serenade for Strings (DB 2132–3). Re-issued on LP (mono) ALP 1464.

Elegy for Strings (DB 1939). L.P.O.

Because of their historical interest, the details are included here of the recording Elgar supervised from his death-bed:

1934 22 January:

Caractacus. Triumphal March (DB 2142); Woodland Interlude (DB 2147). L.S.O., conducted by Lawrance Collingwood.

CLASSIFIED INDEX OF WORKS

Arrangements and Transcriptions of Music by other Composers

Chamber Music

Choral Works (cantatas, oratorios, etc.)

Church Music (including early unpublished items)

Dramatic Works
(ballet, incidental music, masque, recitations, etc.)

Orchestral

Organ

Part Songs, etc.

Pianoforte Solos

Solo Songs and Song-Cycles

Unpublished and Unfinished Works
(including Juvenilia, excluding Church Music)

GENERAL INDEX